SOCIAL PROBLEMS AND THE CITY:
GEOGRAPHICAL PERSPECTIVES

SOCIAL PROBLEMS AND THE CITY

Geographical Perspectives

Edited by
DAVID T. HERBERT
and
DAVID M. SMITH

OXFORD UNIVERSITY PRESS
1979

Oxford University Press, Walton Street, Oxford OX2 6DP

OXFORD LONDON GLASGOW
NEW YORK TORONTO MELBOURNE WELLINGTON
KUALA LUMPUR SINGAPORE JAKARTA HONG KONG TOKYO
DELHI BOMBAY CALCUTTA MADRAS KARACHI
NAIROBI DAR ES SALAAM CAPE TOWN

Published in the United States
by Oxford University Press, New York

© *Oxford University Press 1979*

British Library Cataloguing in Publication Data
Social Problems and the city.
    1. Social problems   2. Cities and towns–Great
Britain   3. Great Britain–Social conditions
I. Herbert, David T   II. Smith, David Marshall
365'.042'0941   HN385.5   78–41144

ISBN 0-19-874079-4
ISBN 0-19-874080-8 Pbk

typesetting by Hope Services, Abingdon
and printed in Great Britain by
Richard Clay (The Chaucer Press) Ltd
Bungay, Suffolk.

for all our families

LIST OF CONTRIBUTORS

Fred W. Boal	Queen's University, Belfast
David S. Byrne	Northern Ireland Polytechnic
John Eyles	Queen Mary College, University of London
John A. Giggs	University of Nottingham
Chris Hamnett	Open University
David T. Herbert	University College of Swansea
Philip N. Jones	University of Hull
Roger Lee	Queen Mary College, University of London
Russell Murray	Queen's University, Belfast
Ray E. Pahl	University of Kent
Steven Pinch	University of Southampton
Brian T. Robson	University of Manchester
David M. Smith	Queen Mary College, University of London
Bill Williamson	University of Durham

PREFACE

The social problems of the city are a matter of great current concern. Quite suddenly, it seems, 'inner-city deprivation' has replaced the so-called regional problem as the major geographical manifestation of inequality in contemporary Britain. The analysis and possible solution of urban social problems poses searching challenges to social scientists—including the geographer.

This collection of papers attempts to convey something of geographical approaches to the examination of social problems in cities. The empirical frame of reference is largely the modern British city, but quite a lot of what is said will have a wider relevance. Our aim is not to convince the sceptic (geographer or otherwise) of the efficacy of a geographical approach—far less to argue that the geographer has somehow grasped the essence of issues that have eluded lesser mortals. The intent is much more modest—to exemplify geographical analysis as currently adopted, with its weaknesses revealed as well as its strengths, and allow the reader to judge the overall merits of the case. There is ample material to provoke a few awkward questions about our disciplinary perspective, questions that are easily overlooked in unduly defensive displays of spatial chauvinism.

It is hard to find much common ground in contemporary geography, the more so on such a controversial issue as the origin and solution of social problems. Hence the variety of individual perspectives in this book. Even the editors themselves do not see eye to eye on every matter. But we do share the strong opinion that to understand the problems that we confront requires a broad multi-disciplinary approach in which the geographer has an essential part to play. It is the opportunities and limitations of this single-disciplinary perspective that we seek to reveal.

In planning the book, our objectives were to discuss the origins of social problems in the city, to provide examples of ways in which these problems have been studied by geographers, and to help form some overall assessment of the geographer's role. Our contributors were selected not only for their individual eminence in their own field, but also because it was anticipated that they would be representative of the variety of empirical interests, ideological stances, and methodologies found among what we like to think of as the 'community of scholars' working on urban problems from a spatial perspective. It has never been our intention to convey some false solidarity or common front.

The book is divided into three main parts. Part One offers some quite divergent perspectives on the general question of the nature and origin of social problems in cities. Part Two provides a series of case studies of specific problems, themselves the outcome of a rather brutal process of selectivity in which we have tried to match individual authors with topics on which their expertise is already well established. Finally, in Part Three, we address the related issues of the merits or otherwise of area-based policies for the solution of problems and explanations in which the nature of areas figures prominently, in the geographical tradition.

As editors, we are grateful to our contributors for providing what we consider to be quite stimulating papers, to a demanding schedule. Andrew Schuller of Oxford University Press has done much to help turn our original plans into reality. To the numerous patient typists, dedicated cartographers, deprived wives, neglected children, and other assorted aids and intimates who have to bear the brunt of this kind of endeavour, we also extend our thanks. Finally, we are very grateful to Peter Goodyear for reading the proofs and compiling the index.

DAVID HERBERT
DAVID SMITH

CONTENTS

x   Contents

1

INTRODUCTION:
GEOGRAPHICAL PERSPECTIVES
AND URBAN PROBLEMS

David T. Herbert

The evolution of western societies has been closely associated with the process of urbanization. The city has become a microcosm of the social formation, acting as agent for both stability and change. Whilst western societies have been in the vanguard of modern urbanization, increasingly the rise of large cities and the development of urban systems is also coming to characterize the 'non-western' societies, including socialist countries and the so-called Third World.

Whilst large-scale urbanization has clearly become a universal phenomenon, its general desirability remains a matter for conjecture. There are advantages and disadvantages and how these are balanced depends very much on value judgements —once the facts have been established. Many states have sought to limit urban growth, with measures which range from land-use zoning and migration controls to the destruction of shanty towns. The massive forced depopulation of cities by the Cambodian government in the mid-1970s provides an extreme example of anti-urban measures, though special circumstances did surround that event. Wherever cities have emerged, they have tended to become identified with the problems which seem inevitably to accompany them. Many of these problems are results of rapid growth, excessive density, and sheer size: the urban fabric is simply unable to cope with the demands placed upon it and the capacity to manage the metropolis is strained to its limits and perhaps beyond. There are other problems, the nature of which is less well understood, but which have none the less been closely related to the scale of urbanization over long periods of time. For well over a century official records have documented the close links between urban growth and increases in crime, particularly crimes of violence. High incidence rates of mental illness and suicide seem to correspond similarly with the growth of the city. Within the urban system it is the inner city in particular which has a long and almost universal association with the various manifestations of life in squalid 'slums', now commonly referred to as multiple deprivation.

Some of these apparent associations do not really stand up to close scrutiny; these are problems both *of* and *in* the city (see Herbert and Johnston, 1976). The fact remains, however, that they are largely accepted and have become part of the public image of the city. Amongst the motivations of people moving to suburbs and of businesses which relocate are fears and doubts arising from the image the inner city possesses. The suburb becomes the refuge or haven which many find a necessity in order to tolerate life in a major city. For those with the means to make such a choice, the inner city becomes a separate part of a sharply compartmentalized urban world. Others might escape, voluntarily or otherwise, from substandard inner areas only to find that peripheral housing projects possess their own range of disadvantages. At the same time, however, there is continuing evidence that the city as a whole retains a strong, almost magnetic attraction, as rural-to-urban migration persists on a major scale in many countries. It is, in fact, the inner city that offers to selected groups—the young, the ambitious, the romantic—the range of excitements and facilities they cannot resist, which, to them, makes the city what it is.

Geographical Perspectives

The city represents a complex of social, economic, and political forces mediated by local culture and history. That other disciplines have a role to play in understanding urban problems is beyond dispute: what however is to be said for a geographical approach? The main message which we seek to convey in this book is that the contemporary geographical approach is characterized by a broadening view and by an ethos more capable of integration with a general social-science perspective than has been the case in the past. Urban geography as a field of study has moved a considerable way in the last two decades. At the beginning of this period it was still principally based upon morphological views of urban structure, with some increasing interest in the economic functions of towns but with very little awareness of the social qualities of urban life and organization. This reflected the contemporary paradigms which serviced geography as a whole (Wrigley, 1965), just as the changes since the later 1950s have reflected changing philosophical bases in the discipline (Herbert and Johnston, 1978). For several of the most recent and on-going changes, urban geography was to provide a testing ground and source of innovations. The 'spatial analysis' paradigm and trends such as increased quantification found early application in urban studies; central-place theory and its testing being perhaps the best single example. Shifts to a nomothetic approach and the adoption of model-building were in many ways the antitheses of the earlier practice of urban morphologists, with their emphasis on uniqueness and description.

The spatial-analysis paradigm has always posed problems for human geographers. For some it was the mere difficulty of technical procedure (Taylor, 1976). For others, more tellingly, it was the danger of an increasing abstraction from reality and the apparent stereotyped, even sterile nature of much quantitative analysis. Reactions to these sources of disillusionment have themselves now generated alternative approaches.

One alternative was the move towards behaviouralism, which found parallels elsewhere in the social sciences. Phenomenology, already a significant growth area in the psychological and sociological sciences, had an appeal for some geographers. By these approaches, individuals were given a new primacy in geographical analysis, particularly in their roles as decision-makers. The themes of spatial imagery and cognitive mapping were systematically—if not yet fully—developed as further expressions of the subjectivist approach.

If behaviouralism provided one new and still evolving perspective, more fundamental protests against existing geographical methodology and practice provided another. The so-called radical critique, which began to exert itself in the social sciences as a whole, found expression as 'radical geography' (Peet, 1977). The thrust of this critique was largely structuralist, with the writings of Karl Marx attaining a major influence. Radical geography did not seek to modify but to replace existing approaches: 'The existing geography showed us what not to do and the establishment geographers showed us what kind of people we should not be' (Peet, 1977, p. 250). One effect of this critique has been to re-focus attention upon some central but neglected issues in urban analysis. These include the need to understand the nature of the society within which cities are placed, the organization of production and its associated distributive mechanisms, the socio-political processes and the significance of key decision-making roles in the general class structure of society. The contemporary concern for 'relevance', broader than the platform of radical geography *per se*, has emphasized the need to maintain contact with reality and to contribute more directly to the comprehension of urban problems. Increasingly, academics feel impelled to justify their existence in practical terms but have also found considerable satisfaction from extending their researches into more applied contexts.

It is in response to these several stimuli that the methodology of 'mainstream' urban geography has broadened and diversified. On the one hand there has been a quickening of academic change and a widening of intellectual horizons, on the other an intensification of urban problems and a greater awareness of them. It is possible to identify a range of fronts along which research in urban geography is now advancing and to recognize within them a number of 'levels' of analysis. Some of these 'levels' are already well developed, others are as yet scarcely exposed to the empirical tradition of geographical study. We shall seek to argue that all have a role in the future form of our perspective.

Figure 1.1 provides a schematic representation in which these various levels of analysis are identified, elaborated, and related to urban problems. One broad division which can be made initially is between the structural levels concerned with the antecedents of urban problems and the local-environment level at which studies are concerned with the problems themselves and their spatial outcomes in the form of patterns, processes, and relationships. The empirical research record of geographers shows a considerable imbalance between these two divisions. Whereas the activities of urban geographers up to the 1970s, and a good deal of them since, have been restricted to analyses at the local-environmental scale, more recent years have been characterized by a growing interest in the antecedents of urban problems. Some comments may be made on each of the identified levels of analysis.

The Political-Economy Approach

This first level has produced little research which could be labelled 'geographical'. It can be argued that this fact in itself is unimportant. At a level at which the ideologies, values, and traditions of a society and its economic bases are the focus of attention, disciplinary boundaries have least meaning and validity. There are broad questions on the nature of society and its prevailing mode of production which are fundamentally multi-disciplinary (or perhaps 'a-disciplinary') in their very nature. At this level, within the social sciences as a whole, the main thrust has been to expose the basic structure of the established social formation. Peet's (1977) review of the emergence of radical geography in the United States documents this stance and its desideratum of a holistic social science. The iconoclastic attitude towards society also becomes an iconoclastic attitude towards human geography as a separate discipline. The essence of this new social science, as conceived by radical geographers and others, is that it would be *structuralist,* in the sense of revealing underlying forces hidden by surface manifestations of problems. It would be *critical,* in the sense that it would seek perpetually to question, refine and replace existing concepts and theories. And it would be *applied,* in the sense that it would contribute to the creation of a new kind of society in which the forces making for urban problems would be constrained or eliminated.

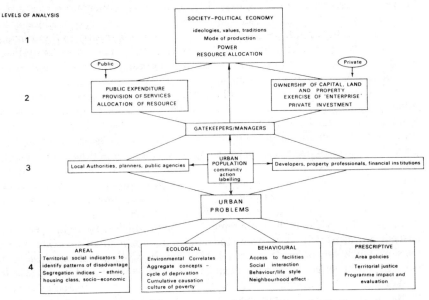

Figure 1.1 Geographical perspectives and urban problems: levels of analysis.

Some elements of this political-economy approach are clearly exemplified by Roger Lee in his essay on the economic bases of social problems (Chapter 4). Lee argues that an 'urban problems' approach (like a spatial approach) artificially constrains subsequent analysis unless it is concerned in essence with the fundamental problem of social reproduction. Three alternative perspectives on the economy—market, welfare, and 'mode of production'—are identified and Lee argues that it is vital to recognize the concept of society being adopted by any one approach and to question its relevance to reality. This essay identifies some of the alternative forms of society and economy and traces their effects upon the urban system. It also exemplifies the scale and dimensionality of analysis at this level. As more geographers acquire the rather exacting mental discipline of a political-economy, structuralist, or historical-materialist approach, it is likely to figure much more prominently in the analysis of urban problems with a spatial dimension.

Resource Allocation and Provision

At the second level of analysis we are concerned with the ways in which the economy or social formation begins the process of allocating power and resources. It is the distribution of power amongst various groups in society which determines their ability to influence resource allocation: this distribution reflects the 'class' structure of a given society. In Figure 1.1 the public and private sectors are identified separately. This is the level at which central government allocates its public expenditure and, reciprocally, generates its tax income. Public expenditure is a major component of governmental activity at this level. As the global sum rises and falls, major repercussions are felt throughout the system. Within the global sum, various government departments compete for budget allocations in debates which are often only heard and resolved within the Cabinet (Crossman, 1977). How these budgets are balanced depends upon the conflict of social and economic forces at any particular time and upon the strengths and weaknesses of individual Ministers in the bargaining process. Once determined, the expenditure begins to produce spatial effects such as the slowing down of a road-building programme, added incentives for industrial location in a particular region, and the refurbishment of some inner-city environments. It also has the effect of producing 'externalities' with their impact on real incomes, as interpreted, for example, by Harvey (1973).

Outside the direct sphere of government the generation of funds and resources is largely a function of financial institutions, large companies, and the class structure of society. External forces are powerful, as money flows are set in motion by world financial markets and investment decisions made from an international view of profit potential and political stability. Within a state the government may seek to control money flows and the social formation may affect investment decisions. Again, the effects filter downwards through the system and have pronounced spatial outcomes. In one city a large-scale office development may be promoted, in another the local labour force in a factory may be reduced; generally, the amount of money available for house building or purchase may be increased or decreased.

There is very little empirical evidence on the ways in which resources are allocated in the urban system and on their distributive effects. Harvey's (1973) evocative 'hidden mechanisms' have yet to be fully exposed. Partly because of the scarcity of data and the problems of disentangling the allocative procedures, examples of work by geographers are rare. There are several discussions on the nature of the problem (Harvey, 1973; Smith, 1977) but few detailed analyses. Webster and Steward (1975) have offered a closely argued discussion of the distributional impacts of local-government policy and the general notion of territorial justice (Davies, 1968) is closely related to questions raised at this level of analysis. Steven Pinch (1976), in his doctoral research on Greater London, examined the record of social provision by individual metropolitan boroughs. On the one side of his equation he measured social need or conditions with a composite index; on the other, he attempted to assess social provision and consider the extent of mismatch and its underlying reasons. In Chapter 11 of this book Steven Pinch develops this theme.

The Urban Managers

At the third level of analysis, researchers have concentrated upon the roles of key decision-makers in the urban context. The terms 'gatekeeper' or 'urban manager' can best be reserved for those individuals who hold power at an intermediary position in the allocation system and whose decisions directly affect the urban enironment. Whatever the form of the political or economic system within which they operate, these are the specific agents who ultimately control and allocate resources made available at the local level. In Chapter 3 Ray Pahl argues for recognition of the primacy of what he terms the managerialist viewpoint: 'Someone has to invent rules and apply them; no matter what the macro-structure, the socio-political process of intra and inter-organizational conflict will prevail.'

Urban geographers have already begun to accumulate a useful research literature on urban managers and gatekeepers and it is a field in which research potential is high. There are, as Figure 1.1 suggests, key gatekeepers in both public and private sectors. Studies of public-sector managers (Gray, 1976) have examined ways in which local-authority housing managers operate allocative procedures for council-house tenancies. The emergence of 'problem estates' is a complex process, but one which is not unrelated to the way in which allocations are made. Other studies have concentrated upon managers in the private sector of housing, such as Boddy's (1976) analysis of building-society mortgage allocations and Palm's (1976) investigations of the ways in which real-estate agents structure residential space and represent the urban environment to vendors. The behavioural perspective offers useful concepts at this level of analysis, which is essentially concerned with the decision-making of key individuals and their socio-economic and spatial outcomes.

The decision-makers, both nationally and locally, are not divorced from the communities they are intended to serve. Mechanisms such as the electoral system and community action groups offer means by which the population at large can make their wishes known and their objectives felt. These possibilities are indicated in Figure 1.1; how effectively they are used will vary with societal contexts, issues, quality and power of leaders, and a host of other variables.

Local Environment

It is at this fourth level of analysis that the majority of urban geographical research has taken place. However, there still remains much potential as the amount of recent activity indicates. Figure 1.1 seeks broadly to identify some of the main compartments within which this activity has focused. It suggests, in general, that we are concerned with the socio-spatial outcomes of structural processes. These include patterns of distribution, their tendency to concentrate in specific areas or 'territories', broad environmental contexts, urban behaviour with its associated spatial imagery, and both area policies and territorial justice as prescriptive elements of the socio-spatial planning process.

The development of territorial social indicators has strong links both with traditional analyses of patterns and with more recent methodologies for residential differentiation (Johnston, 1971; Herbert, 1972). Social indicators, however, and related concepts of 'well-being' or 'quality of life' have broader social-science derivations and have proved a useful vehicle for interdisciplinary research. David

Smith's Chapter 2 discusses the role of these approaches and exemplifies ways in which both subjective and objective indicators can be developed. Various students of social malaise (Boal, Doherty, and Pringle, 1978) and deprivation (Edwards, 1975; Herbert, 1975) have attempted to construct and justify sets of composite indicators and have employed these to identify spatial concentrations of urban problems. In other urban studies identification of 'pattern' has been the starting-point from which investigative research proceeds.

Having identified patterns, urban geographers have sought explanation or, at least, correlation in what might be termed the ecological mode of analysis. Small-area statistics from national censuses, in particular, made possible a plethora of quantitative analyses of association. There are well-known limitations to such studies, but they continue to offer guidelines for developing research and are in themselves capable of constructive interpretation. Contributions in this book by John Giggs (Chapter 6) on health and David Herbert (Chapter 7) on crime, provide examples in which ecological analyses have been widely used. Much ecological analysis now tends to be repetitive and restricted in its scope for new insights, but this kind of aggregate study continues to underpin conceptual frameworks which have been used to help comprehend the incidence of poverty and deprivation. The set of relevant theories has been discussed in recent Community Development Project reports (1975) whilst Rutter and Madge (1976) have made a detailed investigation of the concept of cycles of disadvantage.

Behaviouralism forms another element at this level of analysis and recent research activity in this mode reflects intensified interest by many urban geographers. How people actually behave in urban environments, as consumers with preferences to satisfy and with constraints which limit their activities, is a social process well worth closer attention. In some ways, behavioural geography has been eclipsed by other reactions against the positivist tradition. Many younger geographers have found the perspectives of political economy and resource allocation more attractive avenues for their research endeavours than a behavioural approach which focuses upon individualism, subjectivity, and somewhat unrealistic choice mechanisms. A coherent 'theory' for behavioural geography has yet to emerge. Nevertheless there are many useful concepts and research procedures and work on gatekeepers as decision-makers, for example, is in the behavioural mode. Similarly, the still developing study of cognitive mapping (Boyle and Robinson, 1979), analyses in urban geography of social interaction (Irving, 1978) and electoral voting patterns (Taylor and Johnston, 1978), and the renewed interest in environment and behaviour (Michelson, 1970) all offer the possibility of new insights.

In the final component of Figure 1.1—prescription—we can identify the contributions of urban geographers both as advocates and analysts of area-based policies and as exponents of a territorial-justice perspective. This prescriptive mode, which for many may be the most important criterion by which to judge the value of geographical approaches, is evident at several points in this book. It is implicit in Roger Lee's (Chapter 4) early support of the welfare economy as the basis for societal reorganization (see also Smith, 1977), it receives empirical attention in Steven Pinch's (Chapter 11) study of territorial justice in London and in Part Three of the book, John Eyles (Chapter 12) and Chris Hamnett

(Chapter 13) debate the relative merits of area policies and area-based explanations.

Conclusion

Figure 1.1 has been used to identify a series of broad, inter-connected fronts along which geographers are pursuing analyses relevant to social problems in the city. It is not of course argued that urban geographers have any exclusive presence on any of these fronts. Urban studies demand multi-disciplinary attention and geographers, never unwilling to look outside their subject for ideas, models and theories, now more than ever need to retain that flexibility. There is good reason to believe that the increased breadth of vision which now typifies much urban geographical research has allowed it to enter levels of analysis not previously countenanced by its practitioners. Again, geography, with its early interest in land-use inventories and close contact with the planning profession, has always possessed a strong applied quality. The increased political awareness of recent years and real concern with urban problems have provided new thrusts for this applied tradition, in a variety of directions.

References

Boal, F. W., Doherty, P., and Pringle, D. G. 1978 *Social Problems in the Belfast Urban Area: an Exploratory Analysis*, Queen Mary College, Occasional Papers in Geography No. 12, London.

Boddy, M. 1976 'The structure of mortgage finance: building societies and the British social formation', *Transactions, Institute of British Geographer*, N.S. 1, 58–71.

Boyle, M., and Robinson, M. E. 1970 'Cognitive mapping and logical understanding', in Herbert, D. T., and Johnston, R. J. (eds.), *Geography and the Urban Environment*, Vol. 2, Wiley, London, 59–82.

Community Development Project, 1975 *Coventry and Hillfields: Prosperity and the Persistence of Inequality*, C.D.P. Final Reports, Coventry.

Crossman, R. 1977 *Diaries of a Cabinet Minister*, Vol. 3, Hamilton & Jonathan Cape, London.

Davies, B. P. 1968 *Social Needs and Resources in Local Services*, Michael Joseph, London.

Edwards, J. 1975 'Social indicators, urban deprivation and positive discrimination', *Journal of Social Policy*, 4. 275–87.

Gray, F. 1976 'Selection and Allocation in Council Housing', *Transactions, Institute of British Geographers*, N.S. 1. 34–46.

Harvey, D. 1973 *Social Justice and the City*, Edward Arnold, London.

Herbert, D. T. 1972 *Urban Geography: A Social Perspective*, David & Charles, Newton Abbot.

—— 1975 'Urban deprivation: definition, measurement and spatial qualities', *Geographical Journal*, 141. 362–72.

—— and Johnston, R. J. (eds.) 1976 *Social Areas in Cities*, Vol. 1, Wiley, London.

—— and Johnston, R. J. 1978 'Geography and the urban environment' in *Geography and the Urban Environment*, Vol. 1, Wiley, London, 1–33.

Irving, H. W. 1978 'Space and environment in inter-personal relations', in

Herbert, D. T., and Johnston, R. J. (eds.), *Geography and the Urban Environment*, Vol. 1, Wiley, London, 249–84.
Johnston, R. J. 1971 *Urban Residential Patterns*, Bell, London.
Michelson, W. A. 1970 *Man and His Urban Environment*, Adison-Wesley, Toronto.
Palm, R. I. 1976 'The role of real estate agents as information mediators in two American cities', *Geografiska Annaler*, 58B. 28–41.
Peet, R. 1977 'The development of radical geography in the United States', *Progress in Human Geography*, 1. 240–63.
Pinch, S. P. 1976 'The Geography of Local Authority Housing, Health and Welfare Resource Allocation in London, 1965–73', Unpublished doctoral thesis, University of London.
Rutter, M., and Madge, N. 1976 *Cycles of Disadvantage*, Heinemann, London.
Smith, D. M. 1977 *Human Geography: a Welfare Approach*, Edward Arnold, London.
Taylor, P. J. 1976 'An interpretation of the quantification debate in British geography', *Transactions, Institute of British Geographers*, N.S. 1. 129–42.
— and Johnston, R. J. 1978 *Geography of Elections*, Penguin, Harmondsworth.
Webster, B., and Stewart, J. 1975 'The area analysis of resources', *Policy and Politics*, 3. 5–16.
Wrigley, E. A. 1965 'Changes in the philosophy of geography', in Chorley, R. J., and Haggett, P. (eds.), *Frontiers in Geographical Teaching*, Methuen, London, 3–20.

PART ONE

THE BACKGROUND

We begin at the broadest possible level, with some background discussion of the nature and origins of social problems in urban areas. The three chapters that follow, taken in sequence, reflect something of the changing perspectives of recent years, from the conventional concern with geographical patterns, through consideration of the management of resource allocation, and on to the contemporary political-economy approach. These discussions raise basic questions concerning how our perception of 'urban problems' is formed as well as considering the identification of problems and the manner in which they arise. Such general issues are easily lost in the detail of case studies, so it seems wise to raise them at the outset. They should, of course, help to elucidate specific cases, as we shall see in Part Two.

Chapter 2 explores the empirical identification of the spatial incidence of social problems. David Smith takes as given that certain conditions constitute social problems in the advanced capitalist industrial world—a common position in geography which is open to some of Roger Lee's critical observations in Chapter 4. He then goes on to explain how territorial social indicators facilitate the definition of 'problem areas' in cities. London provides a case study within which some assumptions as to the degree of regularity and overlap in the spatial occurrence of social problems are examined briefly. The general thrust of this chapter reflects the tradition of pattern identification in geographical research, and leads logically to some of the cases in Part Two. But it also looks beyond them, to anticipate Part Three by sounding a few warning notes concerning the 'area-based' interpretations and policies that the type of ecological analysis favoured by geographers is inclined to promote.

In Chapter 3 the emphasis shifts to interpretation. Ray Pahl argues for a holistic view of the process of resource allocation, from which differential life chances arise. He finds some guidance in the Marxian thinking that underpins much contemporary urban analysis, and which is reflected in Chapter 4. But he sees the role of the agents who actually control and allocate resources as transcending the specific economic and political system or mode of production. Pahl identifies a process of competitive bargaining among those who manage the system as the critical determinant of who gets what when, and thus of its local outcomes sometimes manifest as social problems. Whether the prevailing mode of production is capitalist or socialist, its organizations are essentially frameworks for bargaining. Inequality will thus be an outcome of who has power where, as well as of more obvious features of economic geography such as where the goods in most demand are produced. Pahl's argument reflects the recent interest in decision-making behaviour, giving primacy to the actions of critical individual participants in resource management.

Chapter 4 takes a deliberately provocative line. In the spirit of modern structuralist or Marxist analysis, Roger Lee seeks to persuade us that our concern for 'problems' is in some fundamental sense misguided. It arises from particular conceptions of the economy and society that divert attention from the structural origin of the conditions that we tend to view as problems. A 'market' conception of the economy as a production system predisposes us to find 'problems' where the supposedly natural equalizing tendencies of market forces in the general equilibrium model of neo-classical theory have somehow become frustrated. Thus local problems of poverty, unemployment, and so on arise from imperfections in factor mobility, which public policy then attempts to correct. An alternative conception of the economy as a rationally managed 'welfare' system detects problems when the outcomes in the form of human need and want satisfaction fails to conform to some notion of distributive justice. As these departures from the ideal are identified, the system is modified to adjust the outcomes. To Lee, both these conceptions of the economy fail to recognize the underlying imperative of social reproduction. This is the basic function of the economy, not production or welfare generation. The historical-materialist concept of the mode of production enables us to see more clearly how economic activity is organized around the process of social reproduction, which includes the reproduction of the labour force and the means of production and also of the social relations of production (the prevailing 'social order'). The implication is that 'problems' arise when social reproduction is frustrated, retarded, or prevented. Social problems are conditions that are dysfunctional in this respect. Our focus should be on the entire economic and social formation, for it is only in this context that problems can be identified and understood. Thus Lee cannot accept the autonomous role of the individual manager implicit in Pahl's analysis, stressing that individual behaviour must be viewed within the general process of social reproduction. Nor can he accept the autonomous role of geographical space, the diversionary nature of which is analogous to that of the focus on *a priori* problems. Something of how this kind of approach can be applied to a specific problem is shown in the discussion of education in Part Two, though we will also find the broad political-economy perspective in various forms elsewhere in our case studies.

2

THE IDENTIFICATION OF PROBLEMS IN CITIES:
APPLICATIONS OF SOCIAL INDICATORS

David M. Smith

This chapter is concerned with the identification of social problems in cities. It addresses some of the conceptual and practical difficulties involved in the development of social indicators at the intra-urban level, making a distinction between the so-called subjective approach and one that relies on 'hard' numerical data. Illustrations are used to explore the particular problem of the identification of 'target areas' for remedial programmes directed towards specific conditions of social concern. The working premiss is that a useful analytical and social purpose is served by the empirical recognition of 'urban' problems as manifest in geographical space—a matter to which we shall return at the end of the chapter.

Before proceeding, a word is required about the kind of conditions to be investigated. Social problems are clearly both culturally and historically specific. Like the city itself, they reflect the prevailing values, ideology, and structure of the existing social formation. At the most general level they will reflect the nature of the urban environment at the particular stage of development achieved, and the way in which the people (or those who rule) perceive conditions of life within them. More specifically they will relate to the level of development of the economy, its capacity to support social services, the degree of cohesion or conflict within the population, the prevalence of forces making for behaviour that might be considered deviant or threatening to the existing social order, the strength of social control, and so on. In so far as any city has a unique history and cultural milieu, it will present a unique set of social and economic conditions within which 'problems' might be identified. What are social problems in London might not be judged as such in Lima or Leningrad, and vice versa.

In this discussion we shall reflect prevailing conceptions of social problems in what may be termed the advanced capitalist world. The kind of conditions included—health, housing quality, education, economic status, employment, crime, and so on—are those generally stressed in western Europe and North America, though they are clearly of more general interest. In embracing something of the current concern with environmental satisfaction, quality of life and personal happiness, we shall also be taking a culturally specific stand, rooted in the individualistic social philosophy of the advanced capitalist world in which the status of the individual is considered to be of paramount importance (in rhetoric if not always in practice). We accept this as a framework within which to discuss the matters at hand—which is not necessarily to embrace such a philosophy.

Social Indicators in Urban Areas.

Any attempt to establish the extent of social problems involves 'counting heads', in one form or another. People afflicted by conditions deemed to constitute a problem must be identified by some characteristic, preferably one that can un-ambiguously be associated with the condition of concern. For spatial ecological analysis the individual observations must be aggregated on a suitable territorial basis. Among other things, this means overcoming the familiar geographical problem of unsuitable areal units of observation. For causal analysis and policy prescription, further complementary data will generally be required—on economic, social, environmental, and institutional factors likely to have a bearing on the particular problem under review.

Until fairly recently the collection of data on social problem conditions proceeded in a highly unsystematic manner. Statistics on the incidence of crime, delinquency, illness, various forms of 'social deviance', and so on, were generated largely as a by-product of the administrative procedures of institutions charged with some responsibility for regulating or curing the problem, e.g. the police force and hospitals. Compared with the way in which national economic accounts are kept, the recording of the social state of nations was unsophisticated in the extreme. Mounting concern at this situation, coupled with shifting societal pre-occupations in the direction of more 'social' (as opposed to 'economic') aspects of life, came to a head in the latter part of the 1960s in the 'social indicators movement'. This has subsequently focused an unprecedented volume of academic and official attention on the problem of accurately monitoring various aspects of social life and the way in which it is changing. The work of pioneers in America, such as Gross (1966) and Bauer (1966), spawned a vast body of literature— enough to fill a book-length annotated bibliography by the early 1970s (Wilcox *et al.*, 1972). A journal, *Social Indicators Research*, was started in 1974. Government interest is shown by publication of the series *Social Indicators* (U.S. Office of Management and Budget) and *Social Trends* (H.M.S.O.). International concern is exemplified by the social indicators project of O.E.C.D. (1976) and the on-going work of the U.N. Research Institute for Social Development in Geneva.

The early recruits in the social indicators movement were predominantly economists, political scientists, psychologists, and (less frequently) sociologists. The emphasis was very much on national-aggregate conditions. Regional statistics were rarely considered and the need for small-area (e.g. intra-city) social indicators was almost completely ignored. More recently, however, a spatial perspective has emerged, prompted by the recognition of an important geographical dimension to national social 'performance'—e.g. national figures look bad (or good) because of conditions in particular places. Geographers have now been drawn into social-indicators research (Smith, 1973, 1974, 1977; Knox, 1975), with the result that there is more stress on the territorial disaggregation of national populations.

As numerical measures of social conditions, social indicators can take a variety of forms, each with a different role. They can convey the present state of affairs, with respect to the incidence of a particular condition or problem. They can combine data on a multiplicity of conditions into composite indicators. They can comprise statements of the desired situation, as sets of targets for plans.

They can express 'need', as the gap between the present and desired state. They can also indicate the effectiveness of programmes designed to close the gap, as social production functions—e.g. number of lives saved by a particular health-care innovation per unit of expenditure. To date, it is descriptive research in social indicators that has shown the most progress, for the fairly obvious reason that this is much easier than establishing need and the cause-and-effect relationships implicit in the derivation of cost-effectiveness measures. We shall confine our attention in what follows to this descriptive role, though there will be some policy implications.

Two alternative yet complimentary approaches or schools of thought may be identified within the social-indicators movement. The distinction between them is especially important at the city scale. The first is concerned with the development of *subjective* social indicators, based on the direct monitoring of human life experience. The second relies on less direct measurement, often employing aggregate data compiled on a territorial basis. This latter approach lends itself more readily to work of a geographical nature, but some of the opportunities and limitations of the subjective approach deserve brief mention.

Subjective Social Indicators

The subjective approach takes as its implicit point of departure the proposition that it is how individuals feel that matters most. Objective conditions such as housing quality, level of pay, security on the streets, and services available affect people's level of life satisfaction or happiness. Different people, in different classes and inhabiting different places, can react differently to the same objective conditions. This effect is assumed to be measurable, both with respect to the existing situation and to the impact of some change that might result from public policy or private action.

This approach can be viewed as an updated attempt on the part of social psychologists to solve the problem of measuring individual 'utility', which bedevilled welfare economics until theory became so abstract as not to require any empirical reference. The subjective approach to social indicators relies largely on attitudinal survey instruments, designed to find out how people view their own life quality and its contributory 'domains', e.g. employment, neighbourhood quality and social services. Respondents may also be asked to compare their existing situation with some past or anticipated future state, so as to reveal whether life at present seems better or worse that at some other point in time. This type of work tends to be the province of major survey research institutions such as the Institute for Social Research at the University of Michigan (Andrews and Withey, 1974), the Research Group for Comparative Sociology at the University of Helsinki (Allardt, 1973) and, formerly, at the Social Science Research Council in Britain (Abrams, 1973). This general line of inquiry is reviewed in more detail in Campbell (1976) and Gordon (1977) and in a broader context by Knox and MacLaren (1978).

The subjective approach can be concerned with individual perception of well-being with respect to such obvious conditions as income, housing quality, and health which figure prominently in the more 'objective' approach to social

indicators (see below). But it tends towards a more personal and perhaps existen-
tial view of life. As an example, Table 2.1 lists a large number of words and
phrases that evoke something of the quality of life as perceived by a sample of
American college students (Dalkey and Rourke, 1973; Environmental Protection
Agency, 1973). The students were asked to list items that they regarded as most
important to their personal sense of well-being or satisfaction with life. Similar
items were then grouped together, as in the table, and weighted by the participants by what is known as the Delphi technique for arriving at group value

Table 2.1
*Components of the quality of life and their relative importance,
as determined by Dalkey and Rourke*

Component	Relative Importance
1. Love, caring, affection, communication, interpersonal understanding; friendship, companionship; honesty, sincerity, truthfulness; tolerance, acceptance of others; faith, religious awareness.	15·0
2. Self-respect, self-acceptance, self-satisfaction; self-confidence, egoism; security; stability, familiarity, sense of permanence; self-knowledge, self-awareness, growth.	11·5
3. Peace of mind, emotional stability, lack of conflict; fear, anxiety; suffering, pain; humiliation, belittlement; escape, fantasy.	10·0
4. Sex, sexual satisfaction, sexual pleasure.	9·5
5. Challenge, stimulation; competition, competitiveness; ambition; opportunity, social mobility, luck; educational, intellectually stimulating	8·0
6. Social acceptance, popularity; needed, feeling of being wanted; loneliness, impersonality; flattering, positive feedback, reinforcement.	8·0
7. Achievement, accomplishment, job satisfaction; success; failure, defeat, losing; money, acquisitiveness, material greed; status, reputation, recognition, prestige.	7·0
8. Individuality; conformity; spontaneity, impulsive, uninhibited; freedom.	6·0
9. Involvement, participation; concern, altruism, consideration.	6·0
10. Comfort, economic well-being, relaxation, leisure; good health.	6·0
11. Novelty, change, newness, variety, surprise; boredom; humorous, amusing, witty.	5·0
12. Dominance, superiority; dependence, impotence, helplessness; aggression, violence, hostility; power, control, independence.	3·5
13. Privacy.	2·0

Note: The 'relative importance' of each component reflects the collective opinion
of the people involved in the survey, using two independent weighting schemes.
Source: Environmental Protection Agency (1973, I−51).

judgements. The results emphasize highly individualistic, personal, and emotional aspects of life. They are culturally and historically specific, reflecting the views of a relatively privileged and articulate group of people in a rich society. They are the views of people not concerned about where the next meal will come from or with arbitary arrest, persecution, or elimination. Such conceptions of well-being will clearly vary with who people are, what their previous life experience has been, and with the nature of their expectations. It will also vary with *where* they are.

How place or neighbourhood of residence might affect subjective conceptions of well-being or feelings of life satisfaction is a matter of obvious geographical interest. Some limited research along these lines has been undertaken in recent years. For example, Robert Marans and his colleagues at the Survey Research Center, University of Michigan, have been investigating how people in Detroit evaluate their residential area. The finding—that the thing people appear to like best about living in their particular neighbourhood is the people around them—stresses the importance of interpersonal relationships in a country (and world) increasingly accustomed to seeking an engineering or bricks-and-mortar solution to community social problems. Neighbourhood satisfaction varies geographically: in the Detroit Metropolitan Area satisfaction levels are highest outside the city, in Wayne County suburbia—which is much as would be expected on the basis of a positive association with socio-economic status. It is not easy, of course, to separate the satisfaction derived specifically from neighbourhood of residence from other contributors to individual well-being—one of the many practical difficulties facing this type of research.

An interesting illustration of the relationship between perception of social problems, socio-economic status, and place of residence is provided by a survey conducted for the City of Fresno, California. The city was divided into six 'neighbourhood areas', differentiated with respect to living standards. Area 1, known as West Fresno, has 70 per cent of its population black and a further 20 per cent Mexican Americans: it is the lowest area on socio-economics status. Areas 2 and 3 come next on the socio-economic scale. Areas 4 and 6 have the highest status, followed by Area 5. The low-status areas comprise the southern half of the city, the others the north. A survey of about 2,500 residents was taken, to identify 'potential problems' as people view them (City of Fresno, 1973). Eighty-three such problems were specified, and placed in rank order in accordance with how serious the survey respondents in aggregate saw them. The twelve most serious are listed in Table 2.2. This shows the ranking of each problem, by the survey respondents living in each of the six areas. There is a high degree of agreement on the first two problems—cost of health care and drug addiction. This reflects distinctive features of contemporary American society, in which market forces have the rather perverse effect of making narcotics more readily available than medical care in many poor communities. But after this, quite considerable differences in rankings emerge, as between people in the north and south. The third problem—flooding—is mainly a concern of the more affluent north; it reflects specific physical conditions and the fact that suburban development in America often proceeds with disregard for such vagaries of nature as the tendency of flood plains to experience flooding periodically. The difference in subsequent rankings reflects the greater concern with job provision, neighbourhood cleanliness, access to health services, and so on in the poorer Areas 1, 2, and 3. The different views on pollution are revealing; this is very much a 'middle-class' issue, of little interest to the poor people whose major concerns are related to the pressures of day-to-day existence. What constitutes a social problem in a city depends, then, on who you are and where you live, at least to some extent.

Table 2.2
Ranking of twelve leading problems in Fresno, California, 1973

| Overall Ranking | Description | Neighbourhood Areas | | | | | |
| | | South | | | North | | |
		1	2	3	4	5	6
1	Health services cost too much	1	1	1	1	1	1
2	Too much misuse of drugs	2	2	4	2	2	2
3	Too much flooding when it rains	21	7	17	3	3	3
4	Too many people get welfare who should not get it	29	6	3	5	4	4
5	Not enough jobs	3	5	2	15	6	15
6	Jails do not do enough to rehabilitate criminals	4	19	13	7	8	9
7	Not enough safety from crime in parks	30	10	23	6	7	22
8	Not enough of the education money is spent on basic education	7	11	14	11	17	10
9	Not enough clean up of roadside litter, trash, old cars, lots etc.	24	12	29	8	10	6
10	Most places to live cost too much to buy or rent	11	3	7	9	14	19
11	Too hard to get emergency health treatment	14	4	5	17	16	18
12	Too much air pollution	55	24	35	4	9	5

Source: City of Fresno, 1973, p. 19.
Note: the rankings refer to a full list of eighty-three problems.

A variety of survey techniques may be applied to the empirical identification of individual satisfaction levels. The Fresno study used an open response to elicit the problems as people see them. A more structured survey can present a pre-determined list, at the risk of perhaps imposing the values of the researcher on the respondent at least as a constraint on choice. Ladder scales and semantic differentials can be used to simplify scoring. In a particularly interesting British study Knox and MacLaran, (1978) have generated rankings on eleven 'life domains' for neighbourhoods of different types in Dundee, and have explored the relationship between peoples' perceptions and the 'objective' conditions in which they live. There is scope for further research of this kind, setting house-holds surveys within a broader spatial context.

The subjective approach presents both practical and conceptual problems, however, as a possible avenue for geographical research. On the practical side is the expense involved in conducting large-scale surveys with a sample great enough to provide reliable estimates of variations among neighbourhoods. There is also the difficulty of designing and using effective survey instruments. On the conceptual side is the extreme difficulty of establishing anything at all of substance about how groups of people differ with respect to their quality of life, subjectively perceived. It may be possible to say that people in one area believe that their city services (for example) are generally 'good' while in another area they are judged 'poor'. But these will be relative evaluations rooted in the life experience of the people concerned, not measures on some uniform areally comparable scale. What seems good to the people of one area may be considered poor by people in another. At the simplest possible level, it is extraordinarily difficult to think of a satisfactory rule for deciding which of two people is better off in the sense of feeling that he has the better deal in life, except that one is deemed better off if both agree that this is so. Ultimately this subjectivist approach confronts the well-known problem of inter-personal utility comparison, on which neo-classical welfare economics has already foundered. While providing much grist to the academic mill, subjective social indicators may yet prove to be an unrewarding *cul-de-sac* in so far as policy is concerned.

The only practical way out of the ethical dilemma implicit in this individualistic utilitarian approach is to resort to some independent arbiter. Our two imaginary people, unable to agree on who is better off, would soon have to abandon subjective feelings as a basis for comparison. They might abide by the decision of some independent expert who 'knows best' what the good life is all about. But, more likely, they would themselves look to objective conditions—how much they earn, the kind of house they have, their material possessions, access to services and so on. They might still wish to weight all these things differently, in their personal quality-of-life equation (or utility function). But at least there is the possibility here of some tangible yardstick. This is, in fact, how the identification of social problems in cities generally proceeds, especially research in the ecological tradition. It is to this approach that we now turn.

'Problem Areas' in Cities

The ecological approach to the identification of social problems in cities is, on the face of it, extremely simple. Data are compiled on the incidence of a particular condition, and then mapped as sets of individual observations or as aggregates for territorial subdivisions. Cause-and-effect relationships may be sought via ecological correlation or, for example, by relating the frequency of incidents to distance from the city centre. Such an approach has its antecedents in the work of the Chicago school of urban sociology (Faris and Dunham, 1939; Shaw and McKay, 1942).

The difficulties and shortcomings of this approach are now well known, and will be underlined in some later chapters of this book. Briefly, the so-called hard numerical data on the incidence of social problems is often incomplete, because all such incidents are not necessarily known and reported, and in any event the ecological approach offers a dubious basis for explanatory analysis. The agencies involved in compiling the data may themselves be responsibile for certain aspects of control, which gives them a vested interest in the trends that might be revealed;

crime is a case in point, where statistics can take on a special political and ideological significance, in addition to some difficulties in the normative interpretation of the data (Smith, 1974). Ecological association, distance-decay effects and so on seldom penetrate to the root cause of social problems; they can indeed divert attention from the structural origins of social deprivation, by focusing on the resemblance between geographical patterns revealed with such misleading clarity in cartographic analysis. These and other problems raise serious questions about the validity of conventional geographical approaches, especially when directed towards policy recommendations—a matter which we shall take up again later in this book.

Returning to our original concern with the descriptive role of social indicators, two types of research can be identified—both of which are subject to at least some of the criticisms just raised. In the first type, attention is confined to one specific problem: crime, delinquency, health, education, and so on. This is the context of most of the individual case studies in Part Two. Nothing further will be said of this approach here, except that it traces its origin to the Chicago school referred to above, with its stress on individual 'social pathologies'. The second type of research emphasizes the multi-dimensional nature of social deprivation. It is based on the proposition that the incidence of different social problems will tend to coincide, with respect both to individual people and to population aggregates defined on a territorial basis. There is a causal implication here, namely that the incidence of one problem carries with it a predisposition to others. Different conditions are thus seen as mutually reinforcing. The current concern with what is usually referred to as multiple deprivation in Britain exemplifies this view.

The multiple-deprivation approach has less obvious antecedents in the development of social analysis in cities than does the focus on individual pathologies. Social-area analysis is broader in scope, concerned as it is with the totality of the social ecology of cities, not simply with the poor or those beset with social problems. In fact, social-area analysis has, over the years, revealed very little of substance either about the incidence of social problems in cities or about their origin. The factorial-ecology version of social-area analysis soon degenerated into a sterile form of speculative empiricism quite devoid of relevance to social problems, as content became subservient to technique. The normative approach implicit in multiple-deprivation studies is more closely related to the social-indicators movement outside geography, though there was some early geographical involvement in the U.S.A. (Smith and Gray, 1972; Dickinson, Gray, and Smith, 1972; Bederman, 1974). What distinguishes this research from the factorial-ecology approach is the choice of conditions included in the data base: whereas the factor-analytical studies were generally confined to the most easily accessible data (usually the census) in the haste to get onto the computer, the social indicators or quality-of-life studies generally embraced a much wider range of life experiences. The guiding concept varies: Amos (1970) labels it 'social malaise' in the Liverpool study, Maloney (1973) uses the equally evocative term 'social vulnerability', while Boal et al. (1978) adopt simply 'social problems'. But all seek implicitly to identify areas of the city in which social conditions fall to a level that might be regarded as a problem requiring public attention.

Two important problems arise in any attempt to derive composite territorial social indicators (Smith, 1973, 1977; Knox and MacLaran, 1978). These are the choice of conditions to be included and their relative weights. The range of

Table 2.3
Alternative criteria of human well-being

1. *U.N. components of level of living*
   Health, including demographic conditions
   Food and nutrition
   Education, including literacy and skills
   Conditions of work
   Employment situation
   Aggregate consumption and savings
   Transportation
   Housing, including household facilities
   Clothing
   Recreation and entertainment
   Social security
   Human freedom

2. *Composition of Drewnowkski's level-of-living index*
   Nutrition
   Clothing
   Shelter
   Health
   Education
   Leisure
   Security
   Social environment
   Physical environment

3. *O.E.C.D. areas of social concern*
   Health
   Individual development through learning
   Employment and the quality of working life
   Time and leisure
   Personal economic situation
   Physical environment
   The social environment
   Personal safety and the administration of justice
   Social opportunity and participation
   Accessibility

4. *Criteria of social well-being in the United States*
   Income, wealth, and employment
   The living environment
   Health
   Education
   Social order
   Social belonging
   Recreation and leisure

Sources: UNO (1954); Drewnowski (1974); O.E.C.D. (1976); Smith (1973).

variables used in different studies reflects the diverse concepts adopted (explicitly or otherwise) as well as the vagaries of local data sources and availability. It is frequently noted that there is no general theory to provide a 'correct' set of conditions along with their relative importance, analogous to the national economic accounts in which prices supposedly reflect consumer preferences as to different goods and services offered in the market-place. There is, however, a fairly broad consensus as to the meaning of human well-being, at least in the advanced industrial world. Table 2.3 lists the criteria proposed by four different authorities; the degree of overlap among them is considerable. The identification of 'problem areas' in cities might sensibly be guided by such criteria. Each of them requires specific variables, of course—a matter discussed at length in Smith (1973), Drewnowksi (1974), OECD (1976) and in the voluminous recent literature on social indicators generally. Ignorance of large sections of this literature has limited descriptive research on social problems in British cities, particularly in the field of geography where the factor-ecological tradition has been a more important influence. The prevailing approach is still for individual researchers or city agencies to proceed in virtual isolation from one another, and from the mainstream of the social indicators movement, so that systematic comparisons of results are seldom possible. A major exception is the nation-wide study done at the Department of the Environment (Holtermann, 1975).

We shall now proceed to a specific case study, in which some of the issues raised by the 'hard-data' social indicators approach to the identification of social problems in cities may be more clearly revealed, along with some of the objective conditions to which these problems are related.

A Case Study: Greater London

The localized incidence of poverty, deprivation, or social problems in London has been recognized for a long time. Karl Marx, in Volume I of *Capital*, identified inner-London slum 'colonies'—areas that remain, more than a hundred years on, 'stuck in the same vicious circle despite extensive intervention by both local and central government' (Holland, 1976, 47). Charles Booth's *Life and Labour of the People of London* provided detailed maps of poverty, which was found to be well above average along both banks of the Thames and in the City of London (Shepherd, Westaway, and Lee, 1974, 24–5). Today, 'multiple deprivation' in inner London could be described as the single most important social problem in Britain, at least in so far as public and media concern is any guide. A number of attempts have already been made to identify 'problem areas', in connection with policy directed towards improving housing and education in deprived districts by a process of positive discrimination (see Knox, 1975, 14–19) and other area-based programmes to which further reference is made in the chapter by Eyles later in this book.

We shall look briefly at social conditions in the metropolis at two different geographical scales: by Greater London Boroughs and at a more local level within the Borough of Tower Hamlets.

For the broader description, we draw on data compiled by Imber (1976), in a general study of English personal social service authorities. From a wide range of

Table 2.4
Indicators of need for personal social services

Variable (percentages)	National average	G.L.C. average	Borough of Harrow	Borough of Islington	Average correlation (r) with others
Households with more than one person/room	6·6	8·2	3·8	15·1	·561
Households in privately rented furnished property	5·2	10·1	4·7	19·2	·319
Households lacking at least one basic amenity	18·4	23·4	7·1	48·9	·516
Pensioners living alone	24·7	25·4	19·1	33·5	·489
Persons out of employment	4·9	4·6	3·4	6·0	·559
Unskilled workers in the economically active population	7·3	6·8	3·2	10·6	·421
Married women working with children under five	31·3	40·1	28·5	51·4	·204
Lone parent families with children	9·4	11·3	7·0	17·0	·485
Married couples with four or more children	4·2	3·9	2·9	4·7	·419
Households in council rented accommodation	29·1	25·7	11·0	28·7	·176

Source: Imber (1976)
Note: all variables are expressed as percentages of the appropriate population. Data from *1971 Census of Population*.

census data, ten variables were chosen as indicative of 'need' for personal social services (Table 2.4). The conditions included cover various aspects of housing, along with groups of people who can be expected to exhibit special needs by virtue of family circumstances. Taken together, these conditions represent a fairly broad conception of need—perhaps even of deprivation—within the constraints of census data, though they are clearly more selective than the lists in Table 2.3. The summary measures and the figures for the least needy borough (Harrow) and the most needy (Islington) show something of the range of conditions within Greater London. For most variables there is a moderately high positive correlation with the other conditions.

A composite indicator of need or social deprivation can be derived in various ways (Smith, 1975, Chapter 5). The most suitable in the present context is the summation of standard scores (i.e. the original data on each variable transformed into standard deviates). This has the advantage over the common alternative of summing rankings, that it preserves the interval nature of the data. In the summation, each variable has the implicit weighting of unity. Unequal weights can be assigned on the basis of evidence as to the relative degree of seriousness of the conditions involved, but any such weightings are bound to be value judgements (as of course, is equal weighting), in the absence of any general theory to justify such a procedure. The popular practice of using areal factor scores as a composite social indicator (in which the individual variables are weighted according to their loadings on the factor concerned) has much intuitive appeal, but is no less arbitrary than any other method based on the purely empirical associations among the data. Leaving weighting decisions to the computer by no means renders them value-free.

The pattern revealed by summing standard scores in a composite indicator is illustrated in Figure 2.1. A clear picture of geographical regularity emerges: social deprivation or need falls away from the inner city to suburbia, in a close approximation to the concentric rings beloved of the Chicago school and its followers. Most of the ten individual variables conform to this pattern fairly closely. Given the rather limited conception of social deprivation that can be made operational from the data used, which is confined to conditions measured in the census, it can be questioned whether other conditions such as crime, health, and educational attainment, will follow the same pattern—a matter which cannot be resolved completely by resort to other published data. However, the pattern in Figure 2.1 does closely resemble that of inter-borough variations in conditions reflecting need for services for old people, identified by Pinch in a later chapter of this book: the correlation between rankings of boroughs on these two different sets of standard score summations is ·936 (Spearman's coefficient). All this adds to the impression of neatness, order and predictability in the spatial incidence of social problems, in so far as the data used are an adequate representation.

When we turn to a more spatially disaggregated level, this impression looks somewhat simplistic, however. The national analysis of 'urban deprivation' undertaken at the Department of the Environment by Holtermann (1975) has called into question the common assumptions as to the degree of spatial concentration of social problems and the extent to which different conditions coincide. Analysis at the level of the census enumeration district (ED) shows areas with some form of deprivation to be more scattered geographically than was hitherto supposed. This is true of London as for other major cities (D.O.E., 1976). To quote the simple geographical observation of Holtermann (1975, p. 42): 'the pattern of spatial association between different kinds of deprivation may vary significantly from place to place, being the outcome of a complex combination of many forces, some of which can operate anywhere while some are specific to particular places.' If this is so, then any cause-and-effect model from which effective policy might be derived must incorporate these two types of forces. To focus on purely local conditions, or even 'urban' conditions generally, risks missing the forces operating at a less clearly visible but possibly more significant level.

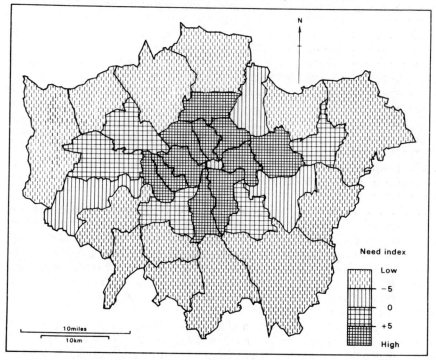

Figure 2.1 Level of social deprivation or need for personal social services, by Greater London boroughs.
Source: Data in DHSS Statistical and Research Report Series (see Imber, 1976).

To look at this spatial incidence of social problems at the more local level, we turn briefly to the London Borough of Tower Hamlets. Tower Hamlets is in London's East End and is among the most 'needy' local authorities in the country according to the data compiled by Imber (1976). As part of a broader study being undertaken at Queen Mary College, University of London, an attempt has been made to identify the level of deprivation in each of about 400 enumeration districts. Eight variables have been selected from census data (Table 2.5), the first four measuring actual deprivation while the others identify potentially vulnerable population groups. The differences between this list and that in Table 2.4 reflect judgements as to the most sensitive indicators within this one Borough, given its distinctive conditions. Again, reservations must be made as to to the adequacy of census data; ideally a wider range of conditions is required.

Table 2.5
Selected indicators of social deprivation
for the London borough of Tower Hamlets

Variables (percentages)	Greater London average	Tower Hamlets average
Households with more than 1·5 persons per room	1·2	4·8
Households lacking basic amenities (hot water, bath, W.C.)	26·0	32·7
Economically active males unemployed but seeking work or sick	4·7	8·2
Households without a car	54·7	74·2
Economically active and retired males in socio-economic group 11 (unskilled)	7·4	18·1
Population aged 0−14	20·6	22·4
Population of pensionable age	16·7	28·6
Population of new Commonwealth origin	8·1	9·5

Source of data: 1971 Census of Population.

The first point that can be made concerns the degree of association among the variables. Contrary to what might have been expected, the intercorrelation is generally low. Of the twenty-eight coefficients in the correlation matrix, only one greatly exceeds ·5; this is r = ·70 between overcrowding (more than 1·5 persons per room) and population of new Commonwealth origin. Ten of the coefficients are less than ·1. This indicates the diversity of social and demographic conditions at this local scale, given the general low level of performance in the Borough as a whole.

The spatial pattern of deprivation can be identified by a composite indicator calculated in the same way as for Figure 2.1. The variables are as listed in Table 2.5. The results are mapped in Figure 2.2. While there is a clear tendency for the most deprived EDs to be concentrated in the western part of the Borough, the predominant impression is one of scatter rather than of order and regularity.

To illustrate the extent of overlap among different conditions, the first four variables (the more direct measures of deprivation) may be considered. The ten worst EDs on each condition have beem mapped in Figure 2.3. In none of the 400 or so EDs do all four conditions coincide, and only two of the EDs fall into the worst ten on three of the conditions. Only six overlaps on two conditions are observed. Furthermore, the map shows that the deprived EDs are quite scattered, though there is some tendency towards clustering in Spitalfields in the western extremity of the Borough. It is at this local level that the unique features of particular places upset the spatial regularity that can be found at higher levels of

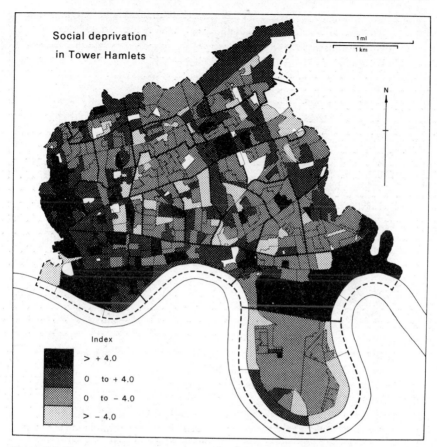

Figure 2.2 The pattern of social deprivation in the London Borough of Tower Hamlets. *Source*: Data in 1971 Census of Population. Map by courtesy of Kevin Woods (Department of Geography, Queen Mary College, University of London).

territorial aggregation. This is part of the culturally and historically specific nature of the incidence of social problems, to which reference was made at the start of this chapter, and which is underlined by the comments of Holtermann quoted above. For example, slum clearance and the rehousing of people in modern council flats has eliminated the problem of insanitary dwellings in most of Tower Hamlets, but the people may still be unemployed, without a car, or living in overcrowded conditions. The extent of these problems within individual EDs may reflect the distinctive social (or racial) make-up of the population, as well as the external forces that bring factory closures or determine low wage levels.

Some indication of the actual conditions prevailing in the most deprived parts of Tower Hamlets is given in Table 2.6. Here we show the situation in the two EDs identified in Figure 2.3 as being in the worst ten on three of the four conditions illustrated. Data for England and Wales put these local conditions in

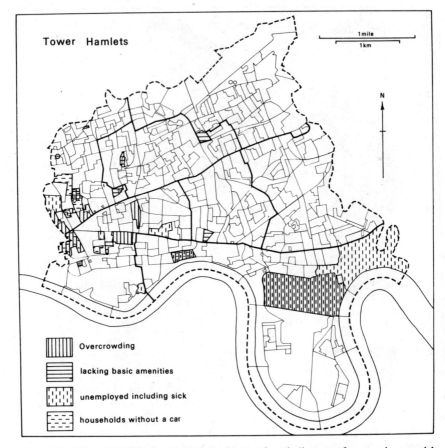

Figure 2.3 The ten worst enumeration districts on four indicators of economic or social deprivation, in the Borough of Tower Hamlets.
Source: Data in 1971 Census of Population.

perspective. With the exception of unemployment in the Spitalfields ED, the Tower Hamlets figures are very much worse than the national averages. Indeed, they are hard to reconcile with the image of the humane, careing society supposedly fostered by Britain's Christian tradition, liberal values, and welfare state. If they do nothing else, small-area data of this kind bring us (almost) face to face with the reality that we still live in an unequal society in which the worst-off suffer extreme economic and social hardship when compared with the lot of the average citizen, not to mention the better-off sections of the community. Quite apart from the policy implications, such facts deserve a prominent place in the purely academic or educational literature of urban social geography. To overlook or omit them in favour of the bland generalizations of urban morphology or factorial ecology is far more 'partial' and 'ideological' than the explicit treatments of social ills still decried by some geographers as 'political'.

Table 2.6
*Conditions in two enumeration districts
within the London Borough of Tower Hamlets*

Variable (percentages)	England and Wales average	Tower Hamlets:	
		Spitalfields ED A57	Shadwell ED A51
Households with more than 1·5 persons per room	1·5	32·1	53·7
Households lacking basic amenities	19·1	96·2	61·1
Economically active males unemployed but seeking work or sick	5·0	3·2	25·5
Households without a car	47·3	95·0	98·1

Source of data: 1971 Census of Population; ED figures by courtesy of the Department of the Environment.

Conclusion

The empirical identification of 'problem areas' in cities is a deceptively simple exercise. Undertaking this type of descriptive research is encouraged by the cartographic tradition in geography, by the ready availability of numerical data (not always accurate or useful), and by the positivist leanings of contemporary urban analysis and policy studies. The deficiencies of area-based approaches are considered fully in Part Three of this book. However, certain general points are worth making at this stage.

The evidence summarized in the latter part of this chapter suggests that the deprived population of British cities is less spatially concentrated than is generally supposed. As Townsend (1976, pp. 18–19) emphasizes, this raises important questions as to both the efficiency and the justice of policies confined to what appear to be the most deprived *areas*, as many of the needy will be found outside them. There is also evidence that different problems do not coincide (in a spatial sense) to the extent perhaps implied by such monolithic concepts as 'multiple' or 'urban' deprivation. The implication is that policies for the elimination of social problems are somehow missing the target, being guided to an ineffectual level by the modes of analysis employed and the concepts on which they rest. Solutions might better be sought at both the more individual level of the actual people experiencing deprivation and the broader features of economic and social structure, than in policies of positive discrimination and in spending on a local-area basis.

But against this is the reality that the deprived do live in geographical space as well as in an economic system and class structure. *Where* resources are allocated is clearly relevant to the individual. This cannot be ignored in public policy, however much poverty and other social problems may be identified as an out-come of the prevailing social formation and its economic structure. The important thing is to get location, space, and distance in a broader perspective.

The main lesson from recent experience with the use of social indicators in urban-problem identification is of a more basic scientific nature, however. It concerns the validity of the measurement of social and economic conditions, on which we base conclusions as to degree of spatial concentration, overlap, and possible cause-and-effect relationships. We are still a long way from being able to translate the life experience of people into the type of numerical data required by the positivist social science and by the managerial-rationality approach to policy. For example, can we really claim that, on their own, such census variables as access to basic amenities adequately measure housing quality, when this makes no distinction between a tower-block flat and a stockbroker-belt mansion? And what really comprises good health, environmental quality, social security, and so on? There is still much basic thinking and research to be done before such concepts can be measured in a manner truly relevant to human satisfaction and societal 'performance', never mind such broader notions as 'multiple social deprivation'. Meanwhile, the inhabitants of the Spitalfields and Shadwells of Britain's cities continue to endure miserable conditions, the remedy to which requires giving more substance to political rhetoric as well as more effective social science.

Acknowledgement

The London case draws on work by Kevin Woods, research fellow in community health, and Fiona Rees, research assistant, in the Geography Department, Queen Mary College, University of London.

References

Abramš, M. 1973 'Subjective Social Indicators', *Social Trends*, 4, H.M.S.O., London, 35–50.

Allardt, E. 1973 *About Dimensions of Welfare: An Exploratory Analysis of a Comparative Scandinavian Survey*, Research Group for Comparative Sociology, University of Helsinki.

Amos, F. C. 1970 *Social Malaise in Liverpool: Interim Report on Social Problems and their Distribution*, The City Planning Office, Liverpool.

Andrews, F. M., and Withey, S. B. 1974 'Developing Measures of Perceived Life Quality: Results from Several National Surveys', *Social Indicators Research*, 1. 1–26.

Bauer, R. A. (ed.) 1966 *Social Indicators*, M.I.T. Press, Cambridge, Mass.

Bederman, S. H. 1974 'The Stratification of "Quality of Life" in the Black Community of Atlanta, Georgia', *Southeastern Geographer*, 14. 26–37.

Boal, F. W., Doherty, P., and Pringle, D. G. 1978 *Social Problems in the Belfast Urban Areas: An Exploratory Analysis*, Occasional Papers 12, Dept of Geography Queen Mary College, London.

Campbell, A. 1976 'Subjective Measures of Well-Being', *American Psychologist*, 31. 117–24.

City of Fresno 1973 *1973 Citizen Survey: Problem Ranking/Rating*, Fresno Community Analysis Division, Fresno, Calif.

Dalkey, N. C., and Rourke, D. L. 1973 'The Delphi Procedure and Rating Quality of Life Factors', *The Quality of Life Concept*, Environmental Protection Agency, Washington, D.C., ii. 209–21.

Dickinson, J. C., Gray, R. J., and Smith, D. M. 1972 'The "Quality of Life" in Gainesville, Florida: An Application of Territorial Social Indicators', *Southeastern Geographer*, 12. 121–32.

D.O.E. 1976 Census Indicators of Urban Deprivation: Greater London. Working Note 11, E.C.U.R. Division, Department of the Environment, London (mimeo).

Drewnowski, J. 1974 *On Measuring and Planning the Quality of Life*, Mouton, The Hague.

Environmental Protection Agency 1973 *The Quality of Life Concept: A Potential New Tool for Decision-Makers*, Office of Research and Monitoring, Environmental Studies Division, Washington, D.C.

Faris, E. L. R., and Dunham, H. W. 1939 *Mental Disorders in Urban Areas*, University of Chicago Press, Chicago.

Gordon, I. 1977 'Subjective Social Indicators and Urban Political Analysis: Or, What Do We Need to Know About Who's Happy?', *Policy and Politics*, 5. 93–111.

Gross, B. M. 1966 *The State of the Nation: Social Systems Accounting*, Tavistock Publications, London.

Holland, S. 1976 *Capital Versus the Regions*, Macmillan, London.

Holtermann, S. 1975 'Areas of Urban Deprivation in Great Britain: An Analysis of 1971 Census Data', *Social Trends*, 16, H.M.S.O., London, 33–47.

Imber, V. 1976 *A Classification of the English Personal Services Authorities*, Statistical and Research Report Series, 16, Dept. of Health and Social Security: H.M.S.O., London.

Knox, P. L. 1975 *Social Well-being: A Spatial Perspective*, Oxford University Press, Oxford.

—— and MacLaran, A. 1978 'Values and Perceptions in Descriptive Approaches to Urban Social Geography', D. T. Herbert and R. J. Johnston (eds.), *Geography and the Urban Environment*, Vol. 1, John Wiley, London, 197–247.

Maloney, J. C. 1973 *Social Vulnerability in Indianapolis*. Community Service Council, City of Indianapolis, Ind.

O.E.C.D. 1976 *Measuring Social Well-Being*, Organization for Economic Co-operation and Development, Paris.

Shaw, C. R., and McKay, H. D. 1942 *Juvenile Delinquency and Urban Areas*, University of Chicago Press, Chicago.

Shepherd, J. W., Lee, T. R., and Westaway, E. J. 1974 *A Social Atlas of London*, Clarendon Press, Oxford.

Smith, D. M. 1973 *The Geography of Social Well-being in the United States: An Introduction to Territorial Social Indicators*, McGraw-Hill, New York.

——1974 *Crime Rates as Territorial Social Indicators: The Case of the United States*, Occasional Papers, 1, Dept. of Geography, Queen Mary College, London.

—— 1975 *Patterns in Human Geography: An Introduction to Numerical Methods*, David & Charles, Newton Abbot; Penguin, Harmondsworth, 1977.

—— 1977 *Human Geography: A Welfare Approach*, Edward Arnold, London.

—— and Gray, R. J. 1972 *Social Indicators for Tampa, Florida*, Urban Studies Bureau, University of Florida, Gainesville (mimeo).

Townsend, P. 1976 *The Difficulties of Policies based on the Concept of Area Deprivation*, Barnett Shine Foundation Lecture, Dept. of Economics, Queen Mary College, London.

UNO 1954 *Report on International Definition and Measurement of Standards of*

Living: Report by Committee of Experts, United Nations Organization, New York.
Wilcox, L. D. *et al.* 1972 *Social Indicators and Social Monitoring: An Annotated Bibliography,* Elsevier, Amsterdam.

3

SOCIO-POLITICAL FACTORS
IN RESOURCE ALLOCATION

R. E. Pahl

Introduction

Resources comprise people, objects, services, qualities, or positions which are socially defined as desirable. They may be desirable in themselves, such as beauty, strength, or easy access to medical facilities, or they may be desirable as means to obtain other more desirable ends, such as power over the opposite sex or feelings of health and well-being. Some resources may seem freely available to all, such as air or water, but down a mine or in a desert this need not be the case. Resources are desired partly because they are scarce and anything can become scarce. Struggle for these scarce resources generates conflict (Collins, 1975; Lenski, 1966).

The distribution of scarce resources is socially controlled: it can be argued that even beauty is determined and controlled by those who influence fashion. Since most physical attributes are valued somewhere in the world, it ought to be possible for a man or woman to move to a context where his or her physical attributes are most highly valued. Evidently this is a far-fetched example and some resources appear to be biologically limited. However, anyone with an eye for the opposite sex would agree that different packaging can sometimes move someone considerably up market. This is more clearly the case with other personal attributes such as intelligence or charm which are at least partially determined by the surrounding social environment. If a random selection of children are called the 'A' stream and are treated as high flyers in a school they will become more 'intelligent' than an equally randomly selected group labelled the 'B' stream.

More generally we do not think of people or their personal attributes when we think of resources. Rather we have in mind material objects, services, and facilities. In market societies large quantities of convertible currency can generally command large quantities of the resources that those societies can produce. But wealth is only one way to secure resources and it cannot always be converted into other dimensions such as power and prestige. Arabs backed with their oil wealth can certainly buy most material objects in British society. They may also acquire considerable prestige in certain circles and also have political influence. However, the more general response to a rapidly rising economic class is for the class that is being superceded to withhold status or prestige. Only in completely closed or in completely open societies do economic and social class lines coalesce (Weber, 1968).

We are thus dealing with three analytically distinct ways of controlling resources—political power, economic wealth, and social prestige (Weber, 1968,

Vol. I). Those who follow one strand of Marxian thinking would argue that in the last instance economic relations determine social and political relationships (Mandel, 1975; Poulantzas, 1975). Those, like myself, who see these connections to be important but not necessarily overwhelming, take a more pragmatic stance and are willing to be convinced by empirical evidence (Miller, A. S., 1976; Winkler, 1978). The relationship between the political ('the state') and the economic (industrial and financial capital) is open to discussion and debate and different types of Marxists have different types of views about the importance of the State and the theoretical concepts that are most appropriate to handle it (Pickvance, 1977). However, one view that is common to Marxists and non-Marxists alike is that all societies, with the possible exception of certain hunting and gathering societies, must concentrate power (Lenski, 1966). Inequality is an inevitable concomitant of material progress. Of course this inequality may be more or less acceptable: an exactly similar pattern of distribution of resources in terms of outcomes may on the one hand be a tyranny maintained by force and terror yet, on the other hand, the same unequal distribution of rewards may be accepted by a free and democratic society as a desirable and necessary basis for material development (Moore, 1967).

Unequal societies are the only kind of societies about which we know much at all. The concentration and redeployment of a surplus is part of a necessary process of social development. In the beginning muscle power was undoubtedly important: the Big Man became the Head Man (Sahlins, 1963). Once surplus became conserved as capital those who controlled that became the *de facto* Head Men. These new men of power in New York, Geneva, Moscow, and Peking control the investment decisions which in turn determine the material well-being of given populations. Yet those who control capital allocations cannot work in isolation to proceed with the process of capital accumulation. On the one hand they are simply part of a world economic system of competitive states and this system imposes its own logic on what is possible within states (Pahl, 1977b). On the other hand internal cohesion and social stability has to be maintained and the power of those who generate the surplus limits accumulation and demands more redistribution. The position of a given state in the world competitive system to a very large degree determines the relations between socio-economic elements within that state. Structures of inequality cannot be upheld unilaterally without considerable difficulty, as the example of the Republic of South Africa illustrates.

The theme of this chapter is to show how the process of resource allocation has certain common elements no matter what the scale of organization or the specific mode of production with which we are concerned. However, before we do this, it is worth pausing to consider what an odd task the editors have set me. For geographers to be concerned with what is, after all, one of the most fundamental questions in politics and sociology is a little surprising. In a sense I am being asked to say all I know about politics and sociology. A discussion of resource allocation inevitably involves the discussion of power, privilege, and distributive systems. I could just as well have been given the title 'the comparative political economy of distributive systems' or 'decision making in complex organizations'. I find it interesting that geographers are concerned with non-geographical questions but the fact that they pose such issues in terms of 'factors' reflects the lack of a coherent framework of analysis. It is significant that in recent years geographers have been less concerned with the distributions *per se* but more with the structured inequalities such distributions reveal or the processes which sustain them. How a specific system or society produces a distribution is seen to be a more relevant, if less geographical, question.

That geographers should at this late stage become concerned with structured inequality is perhaps what is surprising. The territorial division of labour produces inevitable inequalities. Societies on the ground develop unevenly. Towns, cities, and regions rise and fall in their prosperity over time. Within cities there are inevitable inequalities of access which are inherent in the nature of concentration. Not everyone can live close to all the services and facilities they require or sufficiently far from all the dis-benefits they abhor. People age, their needs change, and places wear out and their functions alter. Inequalities of stability may be matched with inequalities of change. Yet the inequality of physical access is not as significant as the inequality of social access: the poor seem always to be with us and their deprivations may even be compounded. Yet in absolute terms the poor are less poor than they were: the very poorest in Liverpool, Lyons, or Leipzig are probably much better off now than at any time in history. More and more people absolutely and proportionately live longer and healthier lives in the advanced societies than at any time in history. The very success of the advanced societies in extending the average expectation of life has led in turn to the creation of the 'social' problem of old age. The very success in reducing inequality has also been associated with a growth of concern about the topic amongst geographers.

The unprecedented and enormous wealth-generating machine which emerged out of the rationality of the Enlightenment carried with it an introspective questioning and analytical doubting (Polanyi, 1957). The spirit of entrepreneurial capitalism had, as its corollary, the spirit of doubt and dissent. Marx's radical critique of capitalism was itself produced by capitalism and the new order. The might of industrial capitalism created its own antithesis with a workforce able to elect its own political leaders and withhold its own labour. The power of organized labour has slowly grasped its potential: whilst some may have urged a more rapid and radical attack on the basic levers of the socio-economic system, the workers of western social democracies were probably right to resist (Lindberg *et al.*, 1975, chs. 8 and 9). Too early a reaction would have provoked a crude display of civil or military force. The gradual education of their masters means that force of arms is no longer accepted as a legitimate way of resolving industrial or employment disputes: instead we have arbitration, conciliation, the formal legal processes, and a dampening and distracting mass media (Lindberg *et al.*, 1975, part III). But it would be an insult to workers' intelligence to assume that they are so easily bemused. Only arrogant media men themselves would imagine that they can so easily manipulate their audiences. There may be proletarian confusions, fallacies, and prejudices—as the Alf Garnett figures caricature—but these are as much produced in reaction to the mass media as a product of them. However, current interest in Gramsci's ideas about hegemonic power reflect some Marxist intellectuals' belief in large-scale manipulation (Boggs, 1976; Glasgow Media Group, 1977).

The very interesting thing about this new and unprecedented development of industrial capitalism was the parallel development of doubting, questioning, and the search for a more humane and egalitarian order (Plamenatz, 1975). Forces for the concentration of resources developed in harness with forces for the dispersal of these resources. Marx, Weber, and Durkheim were all in their different ways concerned with the practical problems created by the development of industrial capitalism and all hoped to provide certain keys to unlock some of the secret parts of a better form of social organization (Giddens, 1971). Geographers came late on the scene, being influenced by a different intellectual tradition and being kept apart from social scientists by their links with geology, cartography, hydrology, and other physical sciences. The inter-war economic geographers such as Rudmose Brown or Dudley Stamp listed heaps of 'factors' which were said to influence the distribution of commodities and their flows between localities. Climate and location were 'geographical' factors; non-geographical factors like colonial policies had to be taken into account but were as much 'given' as the climate. Building up a better understanding of the interrelationships of these factors was said to provide a better geographical understanding. Inevitably this produced a conservative bias: things were as they were for apparently 'good' reasons. Everything could be explained in an apparently satisfactory way. Differences between places were the very heart of geography so that, in a curious way, attempts to reduce differences somehow undermined the importance of the subject. In the same way that ecological differences were given, once discovered, so, by association, were social and economic differences. I am not referring to a crude environmentalism, although that evidently existed. I am referring to a whole style of descriptive geography, which students had to learn if they were to develop as geographers. They could indulge in debates about 'possibilism' as a kind of luxury after the basic elements of the subject had been learnt. The basic problematic of the subject did not include normative or evaluative questions about the nature of these distributions, unless these offended ecological criteria. Bad systems of cultivation leading to soil erosion were a geographical problem: bad systems of human exploitation leading to greater inequality and social misery were simply part of the context in which geographers worked. The founding fathers of geography were explorers and cataloguers. This all helped to create a massive taken-for-granted world, to doubt which would be to doubt geography.

So geographers notice that certain localities or certain populations get more of the 'goodies' of that particular society than would be the case if the system of distribution followed either some principle of distributive justice or the principle of chance (Miller, D., 1976). Models of distributive justice certainly provide a target to aim for even if in practice actual distributions of resources fall far short of the ideal.

There is, of course, the standard functional argument for explaining gross variations in life chances. Those who visit either capitalist or state-socialist societies can generally be shown show-places where domestic life is good and the money economy provides some material satisfaction if not happiness. When we think of these 'good', 'efficient', 'highly subsidized', 'islands of labour aristocracy', depending on what we consider to be the more appropriate way of describing them, it is not hard to see what processes lie behind the prosperity.

Almost certainly such new towns or suburbs will be based on a productive activity which is highly significant for the society at that particular time. The surplus generated by the workers is likely to be substantial: the work they do is likely to be highly skilled and may also be dangerous or secret but it will certainly be of considerable importance to the leading elements in the society. I am not referring now to those areas where one finds the palaces and villas of industrialists, film stars, and commissars. I am referring to the 'ordinary' workers' housing which the government propaganda machine makes much of. If attention is directed to these show-places the mysteries of resource allocation become more transparent. High wages produce good services and consumer goods, key workers can claim the best state provision. This hypothesis can be tested quite easily: take any country, do a simple analysis of its industrial structure, and pick out industries with high growth rates and high output per head. They will almost certainly be technologically advanced and capital-intensive. Now look at where the workers in these industries live and inspect the school provision, health services, and leisure facilities available to these workers. Choose some indicator for these facilities and compare it with similar indicators for an area where the workers are employed in declining, low-skilled industries. This is a simple functional hypothesis which will account for the privilege of key workers in China, Cuba, Yugoslavia, Britain, Sweden, or wherever you choose.

Now consider certain other social categories within the advanced societies. I am referring to the people who are now described as 'the new poor'.

First, there are those who are unable to work: the elderly (especially those living alone); the sick and disabled; and people whose other commitments make regular, paid work an impossibility (e.g. single parent families). Secondly, there are those whose opportunities for regular, well paid work are most at risk, including those left with skills no longer required or who lack any basic skills; new entrants to the work force, especially school leavers without any qualifications; and those who for one reason or another may be unfairly discriminated against. (D.O.E. 1977, p. 81)

Notice that those categories which are low in access to resources are put in that position largely because of their position in labour markets. The processes that influence these markets operate overwhelmingly at a national or international level and are less likely to be open to local control or influence. Yet it is at the local level that the symptoms of poverty and deprivation appear and it is at the local level that previous attempts both to solve the problem and to focus the research have been located. This is what I would call 'the fallacy of misplaced geographical concreteness'.

It is true, nevertheless, that deprivations are perceived at a local level and if we want to make a contrast with the rich, well-provided 'show-places', it is not difficult to find physical areas in all societies where poor access to resources is physically evident. Typically, such contexts are in remote rural areas or in the inner parts of cities. All societies, whether capitalist, state socialist or anything else have these deprived areas and increasingly the State determines the nature and scale of resources which are allocated (Lindberg et al., 1975, part I).

State Allocation of Public Expenditure

In Britain the state is playing an increasing role in allocating resources. Housing, education, health, the social services, and so on consume enormous resources: the ratio of public expenditure to gross domestic product in Britain is now about 60 per cent. What determines the level of expenditure in one area as opposed to another? Evidently it is extremely difficult to be certain how the various policy decisions are taken and what factors and arguments weigh with those concerned. This is shown most clearly in a consideration of the White Paper *Public Expenditure to 1979–80* (Cmnd. 6393, 1976). One analysis of the White Paper discussing Government aid to industry rightly notes:

The difficulty in interpreting and assessing such policy decisions is precisely that *they* conflate the social, economic and political considerations which have shaped them. Each tends to merge into the other, and it is in fact almost impossible to attribute what proportion of the expenditure might be attributed to the various strands of policy thinking . . . It is never clear in what policy context the decisions were taken, and what competing claims for resources were taken into account. (Klein *et al.*, 1976, 24)

In the words of a Principal Finance Officer in Central Government, 'Ministers are always in a dilemma. The public policy of their party requires restraint in spending but their political future depends on spending.' (Heclo and Wildavsky, 1974, p. 129) The consequence of this, Klein *et al.* point out in their analysis of the Public Expenditure White Paper, is a whole series of competing, if not conflicting policies. Redistribution in one field is offset by inegalitarian, if not punitive, measures in another. Attempts to reduce public expenditure by cutting down in capital expenditure may be traded off against increased current expenditure on wages and salaries: more and perhaps better paid employees attempt to operate a service with less back up facilities. The pressure for even further expenditure is thus increased.

   All organizations develop a tendency towards maintenance and expansion for its own sake (Michels, 1949; Weber, 1968, III, ch. 11). So long as individual and collective success is defined in terms of bigger, better and more, so people will advance their careers in organizations by developing their own area of operation and creating more opportunities for others (Crozier, 1964; Downs, 1967). Even if individuals are given jobs to axe or to reduce particular services or facilities, it is always understood that successful experience of expansion is an appropriate qualification for the job.

   These processes appear to be universal and, indeed, may be more likely in state socialist societies where the power of the centralised bureaucracy is open to fewer checks and constraints than in more aggressive market societies (Bahro, 1977; Djilas, 1957; Hegedus, 1976; Wiles, 1962). There is also a functionalist argument about the role of the state in maintaining the existing system of concentration and dispersal of surplus value which is inherently irrefutable and tautological. Such an argument applied to the capitalist economic system would claim that continued accumulation of capital and measures to avoid the tendency of the rate of profit to decline as 'necessary' for the 'survival' of the system. Failure to continue accumulating and raising levels of profit would lead the system to collapse, or rather to change into a different system. Such a functional logic appears able to subsume a very wide range of practices, policies, and distributional outcomes in different industrial societies under a single theoretical umbrella. Whilst this may indeed be possible at some high level of abstraction, it helps little to explain *specific* instances of resource distribution, it being of the nature of such functional arguments to claim that if a given practice takes place it must be necessary since if it were not, it would not take place (Pahl, 1977a; Pickvance, 1977).

All states are constrained by external economic and political forces; all states develop bureaucratic structures to allocate resources and facilities necessary for social reproduction and all organizations have their internal logic of displacement of goals (Collins, 1975; ch. 6; Selznick, 1949; Thompson, 1967). Increasingly market allocations are taken over by various forms of social accounting in spheres such as education, housing, health, environmental services, and the social services. Those who administer these systems of allocations we may term the managers and generally they have considerable discretion either in determining the rules or in administering the rules determined elsewhere (Lewis, 1975; Pahl, 1977c). Complexity creates confusion and ignorance: those at the top of complex systems of social organizations are forced to defer to the knowledge and local experience of those beneath them (Crozier, 1964). Power from below is an inevitable and inherent element in modern organizations (Winkler in Abell, 1978). In Winkler's words some decisions float at the top but many more sink. Those who deal with the sinking decisions are the managers and those working for managers face to face with recipients are the gatekeepers. These latter also have discretion in the application of rules or in the time they take to implement them. Hence, seen from the position of the applicant, client, or recipient of urban services and facilities the gatekeeper is the source of power. Yet more strenuously organized protest against local-level controllers, allocators, and gatekeepers leads them to retreat for support to a further level where power 'really' lies. This tendency for decisions to be pushed or to float to different levels in organizations under various types of pressure provides one of the biggest challenges to empirical research. These basic processes which are inherent in all large organizations underlie resource allocation as all other aspects of organizational decision-making.

Local territorial variations in outcomes

Geographers are increasingly recognizing the importance of social and political processes as determinants of local outcomes. Different places offer different life chances and these differences are important. It may be helpful to list some of the most obvious of these local determinants for Britain:

Political

(i) The political history of the area—the degree of single party rule; the level of conflict over particular issues and its effect on councillors and officers; the pattern of responsiveness to local interest groups.
(ii) The organization of the local parties—the relationship between older or longer-established elements and younger or more newly arrived elements.

(iii) The organization of the professional officers—the importance of chief officers' cabals; the degree of corporate or area management; the degree of inter-departmental rivalry or cooperation.
(iv) The degree of overlap between economic interests and party membership.
(v) The existence of alternative putative power bases in the local area—e.g. large landowners, owners of businesses or large-scale employers (who may be public or private); groups of organized labour; tenants' or ratepayers' associations.
(vi) The pattern of relationships with central government—bargaining over the Rate Support Grant (RSG) (see below).

Socio-Economic

(i) The determination of the needs element in the RSG
A formula has been designed to reflect variations between authorities in their spending needs so that 'the cost for each local authority of providing a standard level of service should be a standard amount per head'. (Cmnd. 4741, 1971, para. 4: 18) The factors included in the 1974/5 regression equation for the determining the needs formula were: education units, personal social-service units, decline in population, acreage if in excess of 1·5 and not greater than 3·0 acres per head, acreage if in excess of 3·0 acres per head.

(ii) Attractiveness for private investment
Large private investors generally do substantial research before committing capital to an area. Retailers and those concerned with consumption would do straight-forward market research in spending capacity and accessibility. Employers would be concerned with level of skills and wage rates of the existing population. Both development and underdevelopment may be seen as a resource. In the case of the former a high level of public investment associated with established employment can serve as an incentive for an expanding, technological advanced concern which must have skilled labour. On the other hand if an employer wants to reduce labour costs and can readily train the necessary labour then an area of unemployment and low wages is more attractive. Less is known about the decision-making procedures of small businesses which move or expand. Much of the so-called 'inner city problem' is due to the loss of small concerns: some were inefficient and went bankrupt; some were efficient and moved away to new premises and some seem to have been killed by the eagerness of planners to disperse 'non-conforming uses'.

(iii) The socio-economic history of the area
Certain areas get labelled as deviant, difficult, run down, unsafe (Damer, 1974; Lloyd, 1975). Whether or not such labels are deserved, even to the smallest extent, the effect is to create a self-fulfilling prophecy. W. I. Thomas's adage that 'where men define situations as real they are real in their consequences' has enormous force in such matters as the distribution of investment where similar returns may be obtained in a number of different areas. There is some evidence to suggest that living in certain inner areas of cities is a source of discrimination in seeking employment.

These factors each deserve a substantial monograph to illustrate and discuss the complexity of the issues involved. The relative weighting of each possible factor in any one issue is obviously very difficult and I have by no means provided an exhaustive list. Students of 'community power' distinguish between three approaches; a one-dimensional view focusing on an issue and the behaviour of groups and individuals seemingly in conflict; a two-dimensional view which argues that only certain kinds of issues are considered under the first view and that potential 'key' issues are prevented from even getting on the agenda so that a strictly behavioural view is necessarily inadequate; and a three-dimensional view where real interests are not even articulated and the conflict is latent, consisting in a contradiction between the interests of those exercising power and the *real interests* of those they exclude. According to Lukes (1974), who makes these distinctions, the views on power themselves reflect values positions on the part of the analyst. *Liberals* take people as they are and see their preferences reflected by their political participation; *reformists* follow liberals in seeing people's interest reflected in what they want to prefer but do not accept the efficacy of the existing political system and recognize that interests may be revealed in more indirect or anti-political ways; and, lastly, *radicals* argue 'that men's wants may themselves be a product of a system which works against their interests' (Lukes, 1974, p. 34). As Lukes reminds us, if one believes in a system characterised by total structural determination, there would be no place for power understood in a context of social relationships.

Clearly one of the major problems facing those holding to a structural or institutional model of power is how to explain things that do not happen which determinism would appear to determine or which seem counter to the interests of the dominant class. Typically, there are two ways of sliding out of such difficulties: the first is to claim that the non-decision or event is not vital to the interests of the dominant class—or certainly not in the long term; the second is to argue that mistakes or concessions take place as part of a price which has to be paid for social stability. Such arguments do become rather metaphysical and need not detain us here. However, it is worth recognizing that pluralists, élitists, structuralists, and any other category which claims strength in the field are equally in disarray. All theorists face considerable difficulty in developing a position which can be sustained over time. The pluralists are in the worst position for they have little but *ad hoccery* within the *status quo*; the élitist or radical class analysts are in a plausible position when inequality is sustained and the structuralists, too, have their day in specific conjunctures. Slow and systematic shifts away from dominant class interests to those of the organized working class cause trouble to all theoretical positions. It is easier to explain the inadequacy of ameliorism than its potency. Apart from some brilliant exceptions (Wiles, 1977) the study of power and resource allocation lacks comparative analysis which is still one of the best tools available to social science. Perhaps the most useful line of approach to these general problems has been developed by Offe (1975).

Labour Markets as Fundamental Resource Allocators

In all market societies wages and salaries remain the basic resource and their availability varies between labour markets and therefore localities. How are these resources allocated? If employers perceive such payments as a cost to be met out of profits, then evidently it is in their interests to reduce payments or employees or both. A discussion in *The Times* during October 1977 which was stimulated by two articles by the editor, focused on the low productivity of British industry in comparison with its rivals. Over-manning is said to be one of the chief causes of our present difficulties and it is therefore argued to be in the nation's interest to increase unemployment as a step towards increasing productivity and the re-deployment of the displaced labour. An alternative view sees management as the source of our current difficulties and claims that the inherent injustice of the present range of wage differentials produces an aggressive or over-defensive trades-union movement. At a more abstract level it is argued that there is bound to be a tendency for the rate of profit to fall in a developed capitalist economy since, whilst it may be necessary to invest more capital in machines and raw materials than in labour, the former are less able to produce the amount of sur-plus value which can be extracted from labour (Gamble and Walton, 1976). The final reports of the British Community Development Programme made direct links between broader economic changes or what is commonly called 'crisis' and local services and facilities or the social wage (C.I.S./C.D.P., 1975; C.D.P., 1977). The debate about the relationship between levels of state expenditure and this 'crisis' of capitalism is largely due to the contribution of O'Connor (1973) which has stimulated a useful discussion (Gough, 1975; Fine and Harris, 1976; Mingione, 1977).

In the light of these discussions the previous work on local decision makers 'running' a town overtly or covertly seems curiously inadequate and dated. The liberal-pluralist conception of all sorts of interests and factions slogging it out in some kind of public arena is evidently extremely limited. If we take the example of Universities currently facing the problems of reduced Government support in real terms, it is evident that all the Faculty in-fighting to retain posts or to shift burdens elsewhere may lead to certain real outcomes and have considerable individual importance. However, nothing done within the Institution can affect the salaries of the teachers or the level of the capital grant each receives.

An alternative theory that the world capitalist crisis is responsible for every-thing from dirty streets to the closure of teacher-training colleges is similarly inadequate. It is virtually impossible to prove or to disprove any position based on a variant of Marxist analysis. Such an analysis is certainly hopelessly inade-quate in explaining differences in real income and living conditions between the same social category in different societies. More plausible is the softer version of the structural-determinism thesis which focuses on the class relations of specific societies, recognizing empirical diversity and not necessarily prejudging the out-come of conflict in the manner of certain Marxist teleological reasoning (Wright, 1976). However, it is hard to see how such an approach helps very much in handling specific issues in local-resource allocation. There seems to be no clear evidence to suggest that, for example, Labour-controlled councils are all markedly more progressive in distributing resources than those councils overtly supporting the interests of business and property owners. Indeed there is some evidence to suggest that authoritarian systems of allocation are *more* likely in long-standing Labour controlled Councils (Dennis, 1970).

But local labour markets and local-government delivery systems help to determine local life chances and it would be absurd to argue that *all* decisions are ultimately geared to the long-term interests of capital or the business interests alone. It is not difficult to point to many issues which have been dominated by a small and vociferous minority and have prevented a particular development from taking place. Various urban road proposals come readily to mind.

Neither market distribution nor rational redistribution alone can answer the old questions of who gets what, when and why. The growing professionalization and bureaucratization of the state administrative structure is evidently important. Authoritarian allocation can be as dominating as rampant market forces and it is not unreasonable to argue that self-management in industry would be easier to achieve than self-management of public services and facilities. Thus I would have a personal bias towards those theories which start from a basic assumption that there will always be scarce urban resources and facilities and that how these are controlled and distributed will always be a contentious political issue. Even Marx recognized that the differences between town and country might take longer to overcome than the achievement of a classless society. Indeed I suspect that he would see inevitable inequalities in the territorial division of labour as part of the realm of necessity.

Whether the position I adopt is termed managerialist, corporatist, or something else is less important than the essential understanding that specific *agents* ultimately control and allocate resources. States may attempt to centralise in the interests of equality or efficiency, but discretion must still remain at all levels. Administrative complexity has reached such a level that information overload is in danger of smothering the centre. This puts more discretion to the local level. Attempts in Eastern Europe or the Soviet Union to control centrally have illustrated some of the problems (Konrad and Szelenyi, 1977; Wiles, 1962). Maintaining flexibility becomes very difficult as rules proliferate to cover a range of contingencies. I consider that my position is strengthened by those who adhere to a variant of the 'crisis of capitalism' thesis. Assuming that unemployment is becoming more or less endemic, then the management of everyday life passes to some degree from employer or provider. In early industrial society the rhythm of the factory or mine dominated local committees. Now, one feels, different rhythms apply. The days and hours in which the agents of local delivery systems call or open their offices are crucial. The times of doctors' consulting hours, school hours and holidays, days for collecting supplementary benefit, times for registering, paying, being inspected or visited, and many other fixtures determine the daily routines of perhaps a majority of the population. Children, women without paid employment, old people, the permanently or temporarily unemployed, the ill or handicapped comprise a majority of the population in most areas. The State in some form or other will manage the flow of resources into the majority of these people's households (Castells, 1977).

Thus the questions I find interesting relate less to the metaphysical issues of ultimate interests but more to the day to day questions which seem to be as much a matter of style as of resources. Perhaps I can illustrate my point by outlining a research project which, as far as I know, has not been done. What can one learn by investigating the different *styles* of management of different institutions and societies? Taking the allocation and management of housing as an example one could compare a local authority, the Church Commissioners and a large private landholder in Britain and then in, say, Czechoslovakia compare enterprise-owned and State-owned housing to discover whether a different politico-economic system provides a greater difference in style of management than may be found within a society. Evidently management must take place in capitalist, corporatist, state socialist, and, indeed, in 'true' socialist societies, although we have no knowledge of these. Only by comparing existing systems can we hope to recognize the various factors and processes at work which we would have to live with or to overcome in a different system (Scase, 1977).

It may be objected that the main productive decisions are still made in the private sector in Britain and it is here that the interests of capital prevail. I wonder. First it is evident that all is not well with British industry despite being virtually free from corporation tax. Secondly it is at least arguable that managerial decisions are less rational and profit-conscious than appears from the text books. Finally, there is considerable inertia built into the system and neither firms nor workers are as mobile as the theory of the free market would suggest. Hence I would argue that locational and resource allocating decisions are more frequently made on a principle of *bargaining* rather than a crude response to the needs of 'the market' or 'the system'. As Wiles (1962) has shown managers have their own interests to pursue under state socialism and the same is true under capitalism. The logic of the political economy of capitalism may be quite different from the individual strategies of the agents working the system. There seems to be no room for informal activities in so much of formal Marxist analysis.

I am arguing that resources are allocated in all advanced societies through a system of managerial bargaining. Certainly there are exceptions, from lotteries and premium bonds at one level to the market in rare objects at the other. But in the middle are organizations and sets of social relationships which constrain and limit the operation of any pure logic whether capitalist, socialist or anything else. This is messy; it does not fit the neat theoretical packages of the text books. However, it is most people's experience that that is how resources are allocated in practice in local government or in industry (Abell, 1978; Downs, 1967).

Geographers who want to understand why the scarce resources are distributed as they are will not get the answer from the distributions in themselves, although they may certainly provide some clues; nor will abstract socio-economic models provide the answer. The allocations are made by agents in organizations: the intentions may be various but the social processes remain the same. Increasingly the production of roads, clinics, schools, social workers, and much else is determined by the State. The demand for these resources exceeds supply and probably always will. Someone has to invent rules and apply them: no matter what the macrostructure the socio-political processes of intra- and inter-organizational conflict will prevail (Collins, 1975, ch. 6).

I end where I began. There will always be scarce resources and societies will always be unequal. Demands for increasing material prosperity and higher levels of service delivery systems produce larger and more complex organizations to administer them. Once the organizations are in existence the inevitable socio-political consequences follow. Organizations are essentially bargaining systems and, to extend Michels's phrase 'he who says organization says bureaucracy and he who says "factors in resource allocation" says organization.'

References

Abell, P. 1978 *Organizations as Bargaining and Influence Systems*, Vol. II, Heinemann, London.

Bahro, R. 1977 'The Alternative in Eastern Europe', *New Left Review* 106. 3–37.

Boggs, C. 1976 *Gramsci's Marxism*, Pluto Press, London.

Castells, M. 1977 'Towards a Political Urban Sociology' in Harloe, M. (ed.), *Captive Cities*, Wiley, London, 61–78.

C.D.P. Inter-Project Editorial Team 1977 *The Costs of Industrial Change*, Home Office, London.

C.I.S./C.D.P. 1975 *Cutting the Welfare State (Who Profits?)*, Anti Report No. 13 Counter Information Services, C.D.P. Information and Intelligence Unit, London.

Collins, R. 1975 *Conflict Sociology*, Academic Press, New York, San Francisco, London.

Crozier, M. 1964 *The Bureaucratic Phenomenon*, Tavistock Publications, London.

Damer, S. 1974 'Wine Alley: the Sociology of a Dreadful Enclosure', *Sociological Review*, 22(2). 221–48.

Dennis, N. 1970 *People and Planning*, Faber & Faber, London.

Department of the Environment 1977 *Unequal City*, Final Report of the Birmingham Inner Area Study, H.M.S.O., London.

Djilas, M. 1957 *The New Class*, Thames & Hudson, London.

Downs, A. 1967 *Inside Bureaucracy*, Little, Brown & Co., Boston.

Fine, B., and Harris, L. 1976 'State expenditure in advanced capitalism', *New Left Review*, 98. 97–112.

Gamble, A., and Walton, P. 1976 *Capitalism in Crisis: Inflation and the State*, Macmillan, London.

Giddens, A. 1971 *Capitalism and Modern Social Theory*, Cambridge University Press, London.

Glasgow Media Group 1977 *Bad News*, 2 vols., Routledge & Kegan Paul, London.

Gough, I. 1975 'State expenditure in advanced Capitalism', *New Left Review*, 92. 53–92.

Heclo, H., and Wildavsky, A. 1974, *The Private Government of Public Money*, Macmillan, London.

Hegedus, A. 1976 *Socialism and Bureaucracy*, Allison & Busby, London.

Klein, R., Buxton, M., and Outram, Q. 1976 *Constraints and Choices: Social Policy and Public Expenditure 1976*, Centre for Studies in Social Policy, London.

Konrad, G., and Szelenyi, I. 1977 'Social Conflicts of Underurbanization' in Harloe, M. (ed.), *Captive Cities*, Wiley, London, 157–174.

Lenski, G. 1966 *Power and Privilege*, McGraw-Hill, New York, London, etc.

Lewis, J. 1975 'Variations in Service Provision: Politics at the Lay-Professional Interface' in Young, K. (ed.), *Essays on the Study of Urban Politics*, Macmillan, London.

Lindberg, Leon. N., Alford, Robert, Crouch, Colin, and Offe, Claus (eds.) 1975 *Stress and Contradiction in Modern Capitalism*, Lexington Books, Farnborough, England.

Lloyd, J. 1975 'The Labelling of Small Heath: The Role of the Press', Unpublished thesis, City of Birmingham Polytechnic.

Lukes, S. 1974 *Power; a Radical View*, Macmillan, London.

Mandel, E. 1975 *Late Capitalism*, New Left Books, London.

Michels, R. 1949 *Political Parties*, Free Press, Glencoe, Illinois, (originally published in German in 1911).

Miller, A. S. 1976 *The Modern Corporate State*, Greenwood Press, Westport, Connecticut, and London.

Miller, D. 1976 *Social Justice*, Clarendon Press, Oxford.

Mingione, E. 1977 'The Crisis, the Corporations, the State', *International Journal of Urban and Regional Research* (2). 370—8.

Moore, Barrington, Jnr. 1967 *Social Origins of Dictatorship and Democracy* Allen Lane, Penguin Press, London.

O'Connor, J. 1973 *The Fiscal Crisis of the State*, St. Martin's Press, New York.

Offe, C. 1975 'The Theory of the Capitalist State and the Problem of Policy Formation' in Lindberg, L. N. *et al.* (eds.), *Stress and Contradiction in Modern Capitalism*, Lexington Books, Farnborough, 245—259.

Pahl, R. E. 1977a 'Stratification, the relation between states and urban and regional development', *International Journal of Urban and Regional Research*, 1(1) 6—18.

—— 1977b ' "Collective Consumption" and the State in Capitalist and State Socialist Societies', Chapter 9 in Scase, R. (ed.), *Industrial Society: Class, Cleavage and Control*, George Allen & Unwin, London.

—— 1977c 'Managers, Technical Experts and the State: Forms of Mediation, Manipulation and Dominance in Urban and Regional Development' in Harloe, M. (ed.), *Captive Cities*, Wiley, London, 49—60.

Pickvance, C. G. 1977 'Marxist approaches to the study of urban politics: divergences among some recent French studies', *International Journal of Urban and Regional Research* 1(2). 219—55.

Plamenatz, J. 1975 *Karl Marx's Philosophy of Man*, Oxford University Press, Oxford.

Polanyi, K. 1957 *The Great Transformation*, Beacon Press, Boston, (first published 1944).

Poulantzas, N. 1975 *Classes in Contemporary Capitalism*, New Left Books, London.

Sahlins, Marshall D. 1963 'Poor Man, Rich Man, Big-Man, Chief: Political Types in Melanesia and Polynesia', *Comparative Studies in Society and History* 5. 285—303.

Scase, R. 1977 *Social Democracy in Capitalist Society*, Croom Helm, London.

Selznick, P. 1949 *T.V.A. and the Grass Roots: A Study in the Sociology of Formal Organization*, University of California Press, Harper Torchbook Edition, 1966, New York.

Thompson, J. D. 1967 *Organizations in Action*, McGraw Hill, New York.

Weber, M. 1968 *Economy and Society*, 3 vols., ed. Roth, Guenther, and Wittich, Claus, Bedminster Press, New York.

Wiles, P. J. D. 1962 *The Political Economy of Communism*, Basil Blackwell, Oxford.

—— 1977 *Economic Institutions Compared*, Basil Blackwell, Oxford.

Winkler, J. T. 1978 'Corporatism', in P. Abell, *Organizations by Bargaining and Influence Systems*.

Wright, E. O. 1976 'Class Boundaries in Advanced Capitalist Societies', *New Left Review* 98. 3—41.

4

THE ECONOMIC BASIS OF SOCIAL PROBLEMS IN THE CITY

Roger Lee

But what use is it to lament a historical necessity? (KARL MARX)

Despite its grand title, the objective of this essay is extremely limited. It is merely to ask a few questions concerning the assumptions made about the nature of economy and society and thereby of the city in the analysis of urban society and in the study of urban problems. The argument is that in so far as economic analysis penetrates the study of urban society it may do so by assuming one of three concepts of economy; and the study of 'social problems' itself imposes a fragmented view of society as it involves an inadequate concept of economy. More specifically the intention is to draw distinctions between productive and reproductive, individualistic and structural and universal and historic views of the economy and to discuss their relationship with the 'problem' approach in social science. It is argued that the study of social problems (inside or outside cities) is dominated by productive, individualistic and universal viewpoints and that not only does this delimit and define the nature of social problems but also conditions the societal response to them.

The intention then, is to provide from an 'economic' standpoint a critical perspective on the study of 'social' problems in the 'city'. It is essentially a background essay, rather than a substantive contribution and is concerned not with individual studies of social problems but with the nature of the theoretical and conceptual bases that lead simultaneously to the recognition of some problems and to the failure to recognize others.

Space and Problems in Societal Analysis

It is the contention of what follows that the very notions of 'social problems in cities' or 'urban problems' and allied perspectives like those of inequality and welfare are inadequate starting points for the understanding of contemporary society. The problem approach, like that of the spatially-based approach to the study of society, artificially constrains subsequent analysis unless it is concerned in essence with the fundamental problem of *social reproduction*. Just as it is no longer acceptable in any critical and scientific analysis of society to indulge in the fetishism of space—to consider spatial matters as a field of inquiry distinct from the political economy of society as a whole—so too a problem approach is ideological as it isolates and thereby defines a series of 'problems' through which the social system is perceived. Problems, rather than society, become the objective of analysis.

The fetishism of space enables the spatial analyst to sidestep the central theories and themes of the study of society by redefining those theories and themes in terms of the tangible reality of two dimensional space. This means that no questions need to be asked of the theory employed. Rather the available theory is used as a toolbox, or perhaps (more accurately) as a bran-tub, in which the spatial analyst rummages and finds pieces of theory that may be modified to provide a two dimensional basis for analysis. But unless great persistence characterizes the searcher for theory, no more than a disjointed view of the totality of that theory is appreciated and the underlying assumptions binding the bits of theory together are ignored in the anxiety to find, unwrap and rework the bit of theory selected for use. So spatial redefinition, far from providing an extra dimension to political economy, subverts it by locating analysis at the superficial level of tangible reality. In so doing, it creates a separate set of spatial problems for solution which are regarded as having a degree of autonomy and so justify a separate form of analysis.

The problem approach is also subversive because, by focusing attention upon particular outputs from or responses to societal processes, it provides a limited and disjointed perspective on the integrated and holistic nature of these processes. Social problems may be defined in terms of deviance which makes explicit the assumption of a 'normal' society against which deviance may be measured. Alternatively it may be argued that social problems are an output of a societal system and are the antithesis of social well-being. It is possible to conceive of a spectrum with social well-being at one end and social ill-being at the other. Whilst the precise specification of the variables and the make up of the social indicators used to define social conditions on this spectrum may provide the basis for innumerable academic disputes, there is substantial agreement amongst workers in this field (most if not all of whom live and work in advanced capitalist societies) as to what may be meant by social well-being and hence ill-being (see Chapter 2).

Now, it is not the intention here to dispute either that something called social ill-/well-being can be measured by certain variables or that substantial inequalities exist in their distribution. Nor is it the intention to discuss the arguments that the economy is moving society in one direction or another along the spectrum. Rather it is the notion of social problems as an appropriate starting point for the critical, realistic, and humanitarian analysis of contemporary society that is at issue.

In the first place the recognition and identification of problems, defined in the sense outlined above, is a function of the social environment. Thus the notion of social justice for example, which forms a basis for the identification of problems and a blueprint for their solution, is essentially distributive in character. It either avoids the issue of the class relationships of production in advanced capitalist society or assumes that they do not exist. Both state intervention in social consumption and the complex exchange relationships which seem to dominate life have moved contemporary society further away from a direct confrontation with the conditions of production.

This was less so with, for example, the concern for urban sanitation and public health during the last quarter of the nineteenth century. Mechanized production in the factory system involved the spatial concentration of labour and the consequent growth of urbanization underlain by the concentration of ownership in the means of production and the division of labour. This necessitates a separation between place of work—the place at which surplus value is produced—and the place of consumption and reproduction. Thus the reproduction of labour power takes place within the domestic economy, itself increasingly penetrated and regulated by the capitalist market economy. To function effectively—that is to maintain the processes of consumption and reproduction or to house and contain surplus labour—the domestic economy requires certain use values in the built environment. But in capitalism labour power is a commodity like any other and the objective of capital is to extract the maximum surplus value. The environment beyond the factory gate is not of immediate concern to industrial capital, especially in conditions of a substantial and geographically displaced reserve of labour continuously available for use. Thus the problem arises with capital in general, if not with certain specific capitals, that the urban environment cannot be used by labour as a means of its own reproduction and, instead of providing the means of consumption *for* labour, it assists, unproductively, in the more rapid consumption *of* labour. In this way the 'urban problem' of the nineteenth century, recognized initially by individual reformers and then necessarily taken up by the state and later by property capital as suburbanization was exploited as a means of the expanded reproduction of capital, was concerned less with distributive justice than with the central problem, starkly expressed, of the long-term reproduction of labour and the maintenance of both the means of consumption and social order.

Secondly the analysis of society, undertaken from the standpoint of particular problems, is essentially reformist and necessarily involves a particular and partial view of social process. Attention is fixed upon isolated effects rather than on the nature of the underlying structure. Indeed, unless the analysis is consciously revolutionary, the objective of studying problems is to help to maintain the social *status quo*. Given such a perspective, societal structure can hardly be questioned at all or at most questioned only in respect of the particular problems under investigation. Thus some of the characteristics of societal structure may be involved in the explanation of problems. But these characteristics are normally considered in terms of their distributive implications, either as 'problems' in themselves—poverty, inequality, unemployment—or as producers of unequal urban environments conducive to the generation of social problems such as crime. In this way the distributive attributes of society are blamed for, or defined as, social problems and societal allocative processes are seen in this context rather than as an integral part of the process of societal reproduction. By concentrating upon individual problems and upon distributive characteristics at the outset, the implicit assumption is that the underlying structure is not a problem or is at most a given to be modified but not replaced.

Furthermore, although the problem approach has the potential of involving the underlying structure and dynamic of human society, its concern is less with such notions (except in so far as they can be used as an explanation of particular problems) than with the definition of solutions to the problem. This can easily lead to a concern for ideal-type solutions which are, by definition, removed from underlying structures. To base the analysis of social problems upon the notion that men make the history they choose cannot provide a satisfactory framework for the analysis of social problems, except in a historically non-existent society. To argue that such an approach provides an ideal, independent of any kind of social context, is merely to excuse its use now by appeal to the coming of a never-never land in which individuals live outside any form of society. The concrete contradictions which confront Marx's theory of liberation need no elaboration here. However, attempts are currently and bravely being made to overcome such contradictions by theorists in some of the countries of eastern Europe—notably Yugoslavia and Czechoslovakia. Alexander Dubček's 'socialism with a human face' was a practical attempt to do this but such a fundamental threat to the reproduction of a centralized Soviet hegemony could not be tolerated.

The problem approach then, like the spatial approach, enforces a blinkered view of societal process. It subverts any attempt to approach the totality of society, as it starts with a set of outputs or responses which are, perforce, concerned with individuals and groups and not with the operation of the societal system considered as a whole. The similarities between the procedures adopted by the spatial approach and the problem approach in urban analysis may be demonstrated in Figure 4.1. In both sequences of inquiry two critical stages limit the fields of investigation. The first is the initial choice of the object of study or

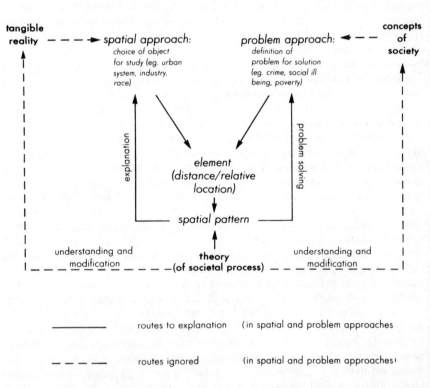

Figure 4.1 Procedural similarities between spatial and problem approaches in urban analysis.

the definition of problem. Tangible reality, or at least that which is capable of spatial representation, limits the former whilst the definition of a problem is a function of the concept of society adopted. Secondly the object of study is spatial pattern, the objective is description and explanation. The analyst reaches into the theory bran-tub for an analytical basis and it is at this point that an understanding of process is precluded because only bits of theory are used and because there are in fact several alternative theories (or bran-tubs).

It is only by attempting to understand concepts of society through the totality of alternative theoretical constructs, developed to provide understanding, that the limitations of particular concepts of society can be discerned or the super-ficiality of tangible reality realised. But spatial explanation and problem solving intensify the preclusion of a comprehension of process. Explanation and prob-lem solving feed back to reinforce the spatial and problem approaches without questioning the concern for tangible reality or the concepts of society adopted. In this way understanding, gained through a holistic appreciation of societal process, is prevented.

Thus it is possible to conceive of ever more elaborate and sophisticated spatial analysis or problem solving which moves further away from reality and prevents understanding, rather as neo-classical concepts of the economy have moved mainstream economics away from reality during the past hundred years or so. A first step in preventing this undesirable consequence is a fuller appreciation of the relationships between theory, image, and reality in generating concepts of reality and society. This is vitally necessary as both the problem and spatial approaches imply the acceptance (often without critical thought) of particular views of the nature of economy and, in consequence, of social process and particular modes of problem delimitation.

Alternative Concepts of Economy

Economic analysis is no stranger to the analysis of urban society. Theories relat-ing to the spatial structure of systems of cities are based upon economic con-cepts, as are most if not all theories of the internal structure of the city. More recently social ecology has been giving way to economy in the analysis of social problems in the city. This development implies a recognition that problems, whether on a personal or on a spatial dimension, may be explained by the extern-ally imposed processes of societal resource allocation rather than by internal processes of self generation. But this perspective brings its own limitations: the economy is seen as a black box which either creates problems like poverty and unemployment directly or creates the unequal social conditions in which urban problems are induced. In either case the separation of the 'economy' and the 'urban' is implied and the assumption is that solutions to urban problems are to be found by manipulation within the black-box economy.

One response to this has been to question the autonomy of the urban with respect to the economy. The quantitative growth of urbanization in western Europe, especially during the nineteenth century, was accompanied by the qualitative decline in the significance of urban autonomy and merchant capital in a societal system which had come to be based upon industrial and finance capital. The recent utterances of Manuel Castells and others on this theme were predated by some sixty years when Vidal de la Blache noted that the dominant societal force had become that of industry. The implication here is that just as it is necessary to base the analysis of French society before, say, 1870 upon the structure of rural economy and society—a point missed by most nationally orientated economic historians of France—so too is it necessary to understand the structure and dynamics of industrial capital to make sense of society in the succeeding period.

Despite this plea to treat history as it is made, as it *is*, rather than as it appears to be, the rise of neo-classical economic theory from the 1870s and of locational analysis a century or so later switched the image of society from one of structure and conflict to organization and equilibrium; from reality rooted in the relations of production to appearance based upon the relations of exchange.

The market economy

Thus conventional, market-based economic analysis insists upon a universal and hence a-historic approach. This reduces economy from a complex structure characterized by particular social relations and located within clearly defined historical epochs to an organizational system designed to ensure the satisfaction of individual wants and needs and hence to maximize individual utilities and social welfare. It becomes irrelevant to talk of 'clearly defined historical epochs' and 'particular social relations', as attention is shifted from an understanding of their complex but specific characteristics to an analysis of a universal, organizational theory of economic behaviour.

The essence of the universal market economy is that individual consumers or consumer households use their income, derived in the main from productive activities, to express their wants and needs by distributing their income in the various markets for goods and services offered to them. Their tendency is to distribute income such that the satisfaction derived from the last unit of expenditure in a particular market is equal to that derived from expenditure in other markets. At this point satisfaction (and even human happiness and well-being) are maximized. Individual firms or groups of individual firms act within these constraints in order to maximize profit or some other objective. Thus the individual agents of consumption and production which are seen to make up the economy differ in terms of goals and constraints only. But the essential point is that the view of society presented by the market economy is individualistic: it builds up a theory of economy by aggregating the behaviour of individuals. The individual economic agents are the prime movers; they are the cause of economic activity.

Economic activity is defined solely in terms of exchange relations—the market. Although mainstream economists distinguish between pre- and post-Keynesian economic theory, the emphasis on the market remains in both; only the scale, from micro to macro—from a concern with individual behaviour to aggregate behaviour—has changed. The state intervenes to modify market conditions in order to induce a desired change in the aggregate exchange relations between individual economic agents—the controllers and motivators of economic activity. So the power of the market, and of the individual within it, remains. But as the individual is the prime mover in the market economy, the system does depend upon consistent and system-rational behaviour. This is assumed by many analyses of urban processes, like the residential location decision, and the responses to the deficiencies of this approach have varied from behaviouralism to the notion that individuals may be constrained by other individuals or institutions.

Thus, within the concept of the market economy, there is no basis, other than that of market failure, for explaining malfunctions, save individual insufficiency or deviance. The analyst is forced into an individualistic position as the market economy denies the existence of autonomous social structures which guide and constrain the economic process. The critical question is whether such a body of theory is an acceptable basis for an understanding of society. But the problems approach has no way of assessing the nature of this theory. Where it adopts such a concept of the economy it does so in innocence of the social structures (or rather the lack of them) implied by it. Furthermore when other concepts of economy are adopted, the influence of the market economy is so pervasive that certain characteristics, like the notion of the autonomous individual, are transferred with impunity to the new concept, so reproducing certain features of the old in the new.

The welfare economy

The individualistic character of the market economy is replaced in the welfare economy by a concern for individuals and groups of individuals defined in terms of their distributive relations (one aspect of exchange relations) within society. But the welfare economy adopts universal rather than historic categories as its basic building blocks and so is unlikely to be able to elucidate the real nature of societal allocative processes. Indeed the welfare economy is both historically non-existent and socially incomprehensible.

Looked at from the perspective of the welfare economy, economic activity is a unilinear process producing certain levels of human well- or ill-being. The mobilization of factors of production and the process of production, distribution, and consumption follow sequentially and lead to the production of well-being. This process of production is a technical and a socially neutral matter in the welfare economy as it does not involve a consideration of the social relationships in production. It is concerned simply with the technical processes involved in the production of social well-being which is an end in itself, although the capability of human beings, in the transitive sense, is a function of the state of social well-being. Thus the welfare economy is simply a linear extension of Adam Smith's dictum that '(C)onsumption is the sole end purpose of all production' and it is located firmly within the individualism which forms the basis of his theoretical scheme.

In this crucial sense the welfare economy is essentially a productive rather than a reproductive system and so is fundamentally flawed as a perspective on real societies. The process of production is geared to the output of goods designed to satisfy human wants and needs. This is the objective of the system, the characteristic by which it is judged. Even the reproductive implications of the level of well-being produced by the economy for the reproduction of labour power are interpreted as a productivity effect. Indeed it is implied by the welfare economy that change may be consciously implemented and guided by plans designed to redress the mismatch between achieved and desirable levels of the output of well-being, defined in terms of a social welfare function. This is perfectly feasible within the logic of the welfare economy because its output is its objective. There are no reproductive structures which constrain the implementation of change. Such an emphasis upon production enables the use of a wide variety of theory to explain aspects of the process of production of social well-being without having to consider the internal and holistic structure of the bits of theory adopted. Would that the economy were susceptible of so straightforward an analysis.

The model of social change implied by the model is also beguilingly simple. Given that the welfare economy is output orientated, designed to satisfy human wants and needs, the extent to which it does so may be evaluated. Policy can then be designed to improve the performance and can be implemented by appropriate modifications to the economic process. However this reveals another fundamental weakness of the concept of the welfare economy. Its starting-point is the identification of problems which may be eradicated in a somehow better society. It therefore involves conscious change as an integral part of its structure. Thus the welfare economy clearly implies either the establishment of centralized social and economic management and power to change or the transition to a state of utopian anarchy in which selfless, humanitarian values prevail. How such a society is to come about is not made clear and neither does the welfare economy have a theory of the state. No institution to induce change is defined and so it follows that the relationships between such an institution and the society in which it is located cannot be made clear.

The mode of production

The assumptions of universality and individualism and the notion of a productive, output-orientated economy defined in terms of exchange relations are all challenged by the consistent and holistic application of structural analysis to society. Structural analysis is based upon the notion of a mode of production, with its philosophical basis in historical materialism. This is not concerned, as is often asserted, to reduce social process to a naive form of economic determinism. It is an attempt to approach the totality of social existence by providing a set of concepts through which societal process may be grasped as a whole rather than as a loosely linked set of social, economic and political factors. Thus the economy is interpreted not as a universal mechanism, capable of adjustment by intervention, but as a complex structure of interrelated social and material conditions. Analysis undertaken from this point of view is concerned with the structures men build to provide a basis for continuing to live and work together. Such structures are not universally present in time and space and must be reproduced in order to provide the structural basis for the production of the means of social reproduction.

Thus consumption, or the satisfaction of human wants and needs, which is the motivating force of the market economy and the objective of the welfare economy, is not an end in itself. It is part of production in the process of social reproduction. Consumption is essential to the process of reproduction and, although made possible by production, necessary consumption is also vital to it in order to reproduce both labour and the means of labour. Consumption and production are therefore inseparable and the circuit P–Cn–P, where P represents production and Cn necessary consumption, must exist in all societies. It is, simply, the most direct statement of the law of social reproduction and directly contradicts the notion that the sole objective of production is consumption. The fact that in urbanized societies with a highly developed division of labour, the organization of the relationships between production and consumption is based upon exchange relations does not make the social implications of production and consumption themselves any less fundamental, just less apparent. Furthermore the enjoyment of consumption by an individual does not make consumption a less necessary aspect of the production process.

One implication of the law of social reproduction is the necessity for the production of a surplus. This is a structural necessity and provides the constraints within which exchange relations may operate. Thus the wage level must be high enough to ensure the reproduction of the labour force, either by recirculation or by replacement and low enough to leave a sufficient amount to cover the productive consumption of the means of production. The market can work only within these limits, which are defined in terms of the social and material relations of production. Now the variety of historical conditions under which the surplus may be produced and appropriated for reproductive purposes can neither be contained within one universal model of economic activity such as that implied by the market economy nor can it be comprehended by adopting a productive, output-orientated welfare economy. The critical concept is that of the social relations of production which, wherever a surplus is produced by one group in society and appropriated by another, are based upon a class structure.

In the capitalist mode of production (CMP) the class structure is based upon property over the means of production, whereas in feudal or slave economies class relations are rooted in direct relations of domination by one group over another. Class relations constrain the development of the forces of production and it is the nature of the class relations of the CMP which account for its potential for growth, unsurpassed by precapitalist modes of production. This potential is created by the dialectical relationships between freedom and constraint in the existence of capital and labour within the CMP. Thus, only when labour has been separated from (made free of) the means of production and freed from direct relations of domination are both labour and capital socially free to make possible their combination at the highest possible level of the development of the forces of production. Only when they are free will such a combination be feasible, but more important, only in such conditions of freedom will such a combination be necessitated. Individual capitals (productive combinations of labour and capital) will, under conditions of free wage labour and privately owned capital, be forced to sell in order to buy and thereby to survive and to reproduce. The conditions of competition which are produced by such a structure (they are not the cause of it) also ensure that expansion and in consequence concentration and centralization of individual capitals are necessitated to ensure their survival. But by maintaining the extraction of surplus value such developments also reproduce capital itself.

Repetition of the circuit of industrial capital (Fig. 4.2) involves the continual

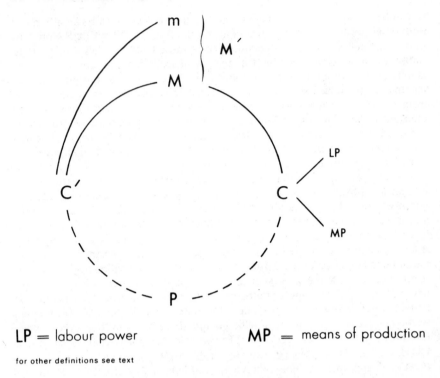

LP = labour power   **MP** = means of production

for other definitions see text

Figure 4.2 The circuit of industrial capital.

reproduction of production and the realization of the surplus in the form of surplus value (m). Money capital (M) is exchanged for the commodities of labour power (LP) and the means of production (MP) which combine in production (P) to produce commodity outputs (C'), themselves converted back to money by the final sale or realization. The value of the commodity outputs C' contains surplus value (m) defined in commodity terms as C'–C and in money terms as M'–M. If M' is capitalized and advanced the circuit grows through the process of expanded reproduction. But the circuit of industrial capital reproduces capital in a more fundamental way. The circuit involves the purchase of the commodity labour power and so presupposes the existence of a 'free' class of labourers. The latter receives its value for labour (the value necessary to ensure reproduction) and is, therefore, forced continually to re-enter the market. Fixed capital remains with the capitalist whilst the circulating surplus is reconstituted and reproduced as capital so maintaining the divorce between labour power and the means of labour. In this way not only is the material base of the CMP reconstituted but also its social relations are continuously reproduced. Furthermore expanded reproduction implies the expanded reproduction of capitalist social relations as the CMP invades pre-capitalist modes of production.

If any contact with reality is intended it is clearly impossible to conceive of the economy either as a mechanical system motivated by individuals and automatically reproducing the conditions of its social existence through the market mechanism, or as a system directed by unidentified social engineers. By placing their analyses at the level of the individual in the sphere of exchange relations, the market and welfare conceptions miss the essence of economy and so adopt inadequate concepts of society. Economies are social structures maintained and changed by the ability of human labour to produce a surplus. It follows that the interdependent material forces and social relations of production under which the surplus is produced and used in the process of social reproduction should form the basis of societal analysis.

Societal structure and social problems

The place of the analysis of social problems in urban society may be clarified by reference to Figure 4.3. These admittedly crude and schematic summaries demonstrate that the only concept of economy in which the problem approach is central and indeed essential is that of the welfare economy with its associated notion of socially-engineered history. The concept of society implied is that of a mechanism designed to recognize and rectify deficiencies in the production of well-being; 'problems' occur when ill-being is produced instead. The concept of well-being provides the welfare economy with its own internal definition of problems which may also be evaluated against a social welfare function. As the welfare economy is an open-ended, linear mechanism, rather than a closed structure with its own internally driven laws of motion, the cause of problems may be traced back to their origin and rectified by appropriate social engineering. In short the welfare economy exists to serve the individual and places him at the centre of economic history as he becomes perfectly capable of controlling his own destiny.

The major difference between the market economy and the welfare economy is that the former removes the need for social engineering. History is non-existent because the market economy is a universal construct and because the process of marginal adjustments within the market ensures, in theory at least, both partial equilibrium in particular markets and general equilibrium throughout the economy. Indeed the movement from conditions of disequilibrium towards equilibrium provides the only dynamic within the market economy and general equilibrium is, in effect, its reproductive basis. Thus, by the pursuance of self-interest on the part of the individual units that make up the market economy it tends, more or less automatically, towards a position of stable societal equilibrium in which, by definition, each individual unit maximizes its own well-being, measured in its own terms.

By contrast the concept of the mode of production defines the economy in reproductive rather than productive terms: in terms of societal structure rather than of the individual. Its concern is with the structure and reproduction of the societal system as a whole. Social problems become significant only insofar as they threaten reproduction. To do this they need to attain the dimensions of a social movement of some kind or to involve so many individuals that the reproductive basis of society is undermined. The essential point however is that problems are perceived, defined and assessed from the perspective of reproductive reality and in that context rather than as a condition which provides both the stimulus for and the basis of social action designed to remove it.

a) market economy: no history

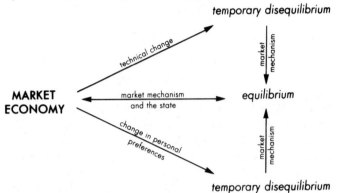

b) welfare economy: socially-engineered history

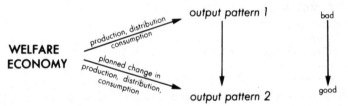

c) mode of production: history

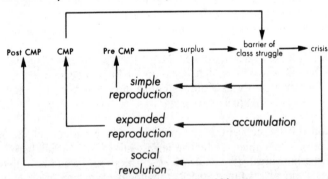

Figure 4.3 Economy, society and history.

Such a perspective of reproductive holism also prevents the simplistic distortions of the gatekeeper or managerial approach to the understanding of contemporary society. Here the process of reproduction is reinterpreted as the behaviour of a few significant institutions, ranging from multi-national corporations to local authorities and building societies, and of their staff—the so-called 'urban managers'. The implication of this mode of analysis is clear. The economy is shielded from suspicion and its agents may be blamed for adopting what are for the most part perfectly rational and fair courses of action in the process of reproduction. And, of course, the reformist potential of such an approach is both clearly significant and susceptible to analysis using the criteria of the welfare economy. This no doubt contributes to its appeal but it is fundamentally misleading. Individual institutions are simply agents of the underlying economic process. They may modify particular aspects of that process but as agents they cannot change it or be held responsible for it. It may be possible to understand individual institutions in the context of the economy as a whole but it is absurd to conduct an analysis in the opposite direction.

It is the process of social reproduction not the welfare or behaviour of individuals or institutions that provides the only satisfactory vantage point from which to perceive society as a whole. The most serious problem that can threaten any mode of production is that of non-reproduction. This may involve biological annihilation but more important in terms of world history are the processes of penetration and overthrow of one mode of production by another and the internal crises which promote social revolution and the transition from one mode to another. Issues such as the problems of old age, crime, race, health and health care, education, housing, poverty, and unemployment—all characteristic of advanced capitalism, but defined in individualistic and distributional terms in both the market economy and the welfare economy—are subsumed by this over-arching 'problem' of social reproduction.

Thus old age is a problem in terms of its effect upon local and economy-wide activity rates and in its implications for the financing of social services by the local and national states; crime becomes a serious matter if it takes the form of substained civil disruption or threatens by its size to break down a legal system that legitimizes property rights; the problem of race and racialism is not that of exploitation and segregation but of its potential to break down existing political institutions; health and health care do not confront the source of social pathology in the economy but are measured in terms either of the costs of the reproduction of labour and the maintenance of a growing non-productive sector of the population or of the profitability of high technology medical engineering and the production of synthetic drugs; education is an economic and political process concerned not with access to a critical understanding of society but with the production of skilled manpower; housing involves the contradiction of sheltering the labour force in the right place whilst facilitating the circuit of finance capital; and poverty and unemployment are not aberrant outputs, but inherent features of a dynamic mode of production based upon private property and the extraction of surplus value in the process of production. The problem they represent is that of ideological justification and the maintenance of legitimacy.

What, then, is the objective of the 'problem approach'? If containment, management, amelioration, and the preservation of what is, then the social achievements may be substantial although the intellectual achievement may be so limited as to be invisible. If understanding, criticism and change, the objective is unattainable as the perspective is simply incapable of critical insight.

Capitalism and Contemporary Urbanization

It remains to outline the implications of the foregoing for the analysis of contemporary urban society. Urbanization is a function of the nature of the mode of production and of the level of its development. Thus the mass physical urbanization that so distinguished social conditions in western Europe in the 150 years or so following the outbreak of the industrial revolution was the direct consequence of the production and reproduction of the CMP and of the productive forces unleashed by its widespread development. The generalized development of capitalist relations of production freed labour from ownership and from the direct social relationships characteristic of pre-capitalist social formations. The emergence of the factory system which was both cause and consequence of the quest for relative surplus value necessitated the spatial concentration of labour and so promoted mass physical urbanization sustained by the symbiotic relationships of labour and capital in the CMP. The 'urban problems' associated with this rapid development are both well documented and, in many areas, awaiting 'solution'.

The present century has seen a gradual reversal of the process of mass physical urbanization. This has been the result not merely of the greater spatial flexibility stemming from the growing sophistication of communications, mass and personal transport systems and of ever more spatially tolerant sources of energy and their systems of delivery, but from a change in the social relationships within capitalism. The continuing concentration and centralization of capital have now passed the point at which the narrow spatial coincidence of an individual capital and its source of labour is the norm. Individual capitals are now, like capitalism has always been, geographically unconstrained. Labour is exploited by non-local capitals which organize their production on an international scale. As a result the reproductive conditions of the local circuit of capital are much less significant in advanced capitalism than they were in the era of competitive capitalism. In the nineteenth century physical urbanization was a major control on the circuit of industrial capital; in the present century corporate structure has become a major influence upon urbanization.

The organization of production now resembles a gigantic version of the putting-out system. A small number of centres of finance and industrial capital are responsible for directing the spatial structure of the circuit of capital at an international scale, just as merchant capital controlled production in the hinterlands of the pre-industrial city. As a result the autonomy of the pre-industrial city is being recreated in the contemporary world city, but the basis of that autonomy is fundamentally different. It now rests upon the integration of the city with the whole economy, rather than upon the independence of the pre-industrial city from the essentially agricultural and locally-organized economy. But this integration itself implies separation as local conditions of production are only tenuously connected to individual world cities through the international network of the production and circulation of surplus value.

The urban consequence of the centralization and concentration of capital is momentous. The city, as the manifestation of industrial capital—which is essentially what most major western European cities are, including national capitals and long-established major urban centres like London and Paris—is undergoing fundamental change. No longer necessary as the spatial mainstay of capital, the big city is redundant. Cities are, increasingly, the location of surplus labour and, at the same time, the locus of the twentieth-century socialization of the conditions of nineteenth-century industrial urbanization. Whole areas of cities are now irrelevant to the expanded reproduction of capital: their 'problems' are not local, not to do with the malfunctioning of an economic system, not even the consequence of active exploitation. They are the result of the consumption of the urban instruments of production to the point of redundancy.

The societal problem *of* the city subsumes social problems *in* the city which are, to a greater or lesser extent, simply the surface manifestations of a structural process of change which can be understood only at the level of the mode of production. To constrain analysis at the level of 'problems' within highly restricted concepts of society is to indulge in obfuscation of a significance which can be measured only in terms of the number of people whose reality is distorted by it.

Further reading

The problem approach in geography is well exemplified by the spate of literature which emerged during the first half of the present decade. An early collection of such essays was edited by M. Albaum, *Geography and Contemporary Issues* (John Wiley, 1972). Until recently the issues dealt with in this diverse range of literature lacked any kind of theoretical framework. This gap has now been filled by David Smith, who has incorporated the concern for social well-being into the theoretical framework of welfare economics: 'Who gets what, *where* and how: a welfare focus for human geography' (*Geography*, 59. 389–97, 1974); *Human Geography: A Welfare Approach* (Edward Arnold, 1977). In so doing Smith succeeds not only in explaining and applying the concept of the welfare economy to an understanding of society but extends the concept to a variety of geographical scales.

An attempt to outline the role of the market economy in structuring social reality is made by B. W. Hodder and Roger Lee, *Economic Geography* (Methuen, 1974) whilst Peter E. Lloyd and Peter Dicken, *Location in Space: A Theoretical Approach to Economic Geography* (Harper & Row, 1977) adopt a market view of the economy and in addition their central concern is with space and spatial structure. By contrast Sue Himmelweit, 'The basic unit of analysis is the individual' in F. Green and P. Nore (eds.), *Economics: An Anti Text* (Macmillan, 1977), provides a critique of the individualism and universality of the market economy. One of the clearest statements elucidating the lack of structural understanding in bourgeois economics is contained in R. Brenner's 'The origins of capitalist development: a critique of neo-Smithian Marxism' (*New Left Review*, 104, 1977, 25–92).

The concern to separate the 'urban' from the 'economic' has been given prominence recently as a result, in part, of the writings of Manuel Castells *The Urban Question* (Edward Arnold, 1977). See, for example, the set of essays edited by Michael Harloe, *Captive Cities* (John Wiley, 1977). However, the lack of

62   Social Problems and the City

autonomy of the urban has for long been clearly recognized amongst a small group of scholars from Frederick Engels, *The Condition of the Working Class in England* (Panther, 1969) to Gareth Stedman Jones, *Outcast London: A Study in the Relationship between Classes in Victorian Society* (Clarendon Press, 1971).

The last word should, perhaps, be left with Karl Marx. His insights into the nature of the Industrial Revolution, *Capital*, volume 1, parts 3, 4 and 7 (Penguin/ NLR, 1976), clearly demonstrate the nature of the capitalist economy as a process of expanded reproduction.

Acknowledgements

If this paper has any merit it is due less to its author than to its critics. The editors of this volume both combined tolerance with rigour and, as ever, David Smith's many penetrating comments were far clearer to me than appears from my translation of them.

PART TWO

ANALYSES OF URBAN SOCIAL PROBLEMS

The aim in this second part of the book is to illustrate ways in which geographical approaches have been used in the study of social problems in the city. A process of selection in providing case studies was inevitable and some of the criteria used in this process can be identified. Firstly, as the title of the book suggests, the emphasis is upon social problems rather than those which might, in a narrow sense, be termed economic. There are many studies by geographers and other social scientists which investigate, for example, the decline of manufacturing industry and employment in the inner city (Gripaios, 1977) or the changing patterns of office location (Daniels, 1975); whilst these are related to social problems, they draw essentially upon a rather different set of concepts and literature. Secondly, the contributions in this part of the book are substantially based upon British cities. An original desideratum was that each chapter should have a strong empirical content in which the ways in which a geographical approach could be applied to a real problem could be demonstrated. Whilst all contributors refer to empirical work on British cities, the extent to which they take the form of detailed case studies does vary considerably. Thirdly, there was a conscious attempt on the part of the editors to invite contributors who would reflect different persuasions and styles rather than a consensus of a particular kind. Our justification would be, as argued in the introduction to Part One, that consensus does not exist and the representation of a diversity of analytical perspectives accurately depicts the state of the art. There are, therefore, contributions which clearly reflect different political stances and value judgements; some contributors who maintain faith with traditional methods of analysing and interpreting spatial patterns, others who regard such spatial outcomes as incidental and focus their analysis upon socio-political processes operating at a macro-scale. There are contributions that seek primarily to present the geographical data base as the scenario of an urban problem, others that focus upon academic diagnosis and yet others which seek to prescribe local solutions in policy terms. The variety that exists in this section both reflects contemporary research activities and illustrates the wealth of possibilities contained within the broad limits of a geographical approach.

The individual chapters in Part Two examine some of the key social problems which exist in British cities. Housing is both a social and a physical problem. Whereas many social problems are only visible at particular times, substandard housing and the bad built urban environment are clearly observable in the inner areas of cities. Substandardness is a relative concept both temporally and culturally, and actual housing standards have changed dramatically over the past century. Largely due to the obvious evidence of urban blight provided by the slums of the nineteenth century and fears of its social repercussions, policies for improvement have a long heritage. Brian Robson examines some of the key features of change, both in terms of housing standards and of policies, and identifies the main directions in which geographical research into housing is proceeding. Closely allied to the early awareness of bad urban environments was an awareness of their links with ill health and disease. When Dr. Snow constructed his famous map of cholera cases in London in the 1840s, he was using a basic geographical tool and providing a significant precedent. John Giggs traces the ways in which geographers and other social scientists have developed the study of ill health, both physical and mental, into a sophisticated and diverse research field. From basic spatial ecologies of illness, to analyses of disease diffusion processes, to appraisals of the efficacy of health care delivery systems, the scope for research in a rapidly expanding field of urban-medical geography is evident.

If the apparent association of ill health and level of urbanization has long been recognized, so has that between the growth of cities and the increase in crime. David Herbert examines some of the spatial qualities of urban crime as portrayed by data on both offences and known offenders. Whilst the 'structural' antecedents of much urban crime are recognized, the local environment provides the immediate interface of pattern and interaction. Russell Murray and Fred Boal have a related brief in their analysis of urban violence, a form of crime which has shown particularly startling rates of growth in recent years. They suggest a typology of acts of violence, provide a close scrutiny of the relevant sociological theories and focus upon the terrorism in Belfast as an example of one of the most recent and alarming expressions of urban violence. Murray and Boal also refer to Lambert's (1970) Birmingham study in which the extent to which coloured immigrants were offenders and propagators of urban violence was examined. This finding proved largely negative and the ethnic theme receives detailed treatment in the chapter by Philip Jones. Here the establishment of the basic facts of immigration and ethnic minority areas is a significant contribution. Birmingham provides a case study in which the form and intensity of spatial segregation amongst the variety of ethnic minorities can be demonstrated. The relationship of this segregation and its underlying processes to the urban morphology of Birmingham and the related administrative and planning policies is scrutinized in detail and the integration model is discussed.

A sharp contrast in style, emphasis, and perspective is provided by Bill Williamson and David Byrne in their essay on educational disadvantage in an urban setting. Their objectives in the chapter are to examine the spatial distribution of education opportunities and to discuss the significance of spatial inequalities for theories of educational disadvantage. With a basic belief in the necessity for radical change rather than any kind of liberal reform, Williamson and Byrne advocate far-reaching redistribution of power. From this critique of the present system and the use of facts to demonstrate disadvantages, they turn to the interpretative mode of Marxism both to illustrate the depth of the problem and to indicate proper directions for change. In the last essay in this section, Steven Pinch retains the prescriptive impetus but his emphasis is less upon radical change than upon reform of allocative systems in order to meet societal needs. Set in the framework of territorial justice, his study of London seeks to identify needs, measure provision and to discuss the reasons for such 'mismatches' as occur. Territorial justice, although focussing upon inequalities at a local environment level, does demonstrate how a spatial perspective can both identify the spatial outcomes of a problem and locate its origin in societal allocative systems.

The contributions in this section of the book seek to demonstrate some of the characteristics of contemporary research and have therefore a strong academic content. They also seek however to illuminate the problems and to assess the value of those policies which exist in a critical and constructive way. These sets of researches seek to combine sound conceptual frameworks and academic methodologies with insights which both contribute to the better understanding of social problems in cities and offer the prospect of a prescriptive role.

References

Daniels, P. W. 1975 *Office Location: An Urban and Regional Study*, Bell, London.

Gripaios, P. 1977 'The closure of firms in the inner city, a south-east London case study. 1970–75', *Regional Studies*, 11. 1–6.

Lambert, J. 1970 *Crime, Police and Race Relations*, Oxford University Press, London.

5

HOUSING, EMPIRICISM, AND THE STATE

B. T. Robson

'The housing problem' has only come within the purview of geography very recently. Earlier interest in housing was of an indirect and incidental kind. Concern about the distribution of different types of houses and of different housing environments, for example, has been at the base of much of the research on urban residential ecology; and urban geography has considered the effects of government policy in altering the spatial patterns of low-cost housing through large-scale programmes of redevelopment and resettlement, through the building of New Towns or through regional economic programmes. In such work, the focus on housing has been indirect and largely descriptive. More recently, interest has focused more narrowly and more directly on housing itself; on its production and distribution and hence on the nature and workings of the housing system and the spatial effects and determinants of housing policy. Such spatial differences will form the latter part of this chapter; its earlier part will look at the nature of the housing problem and the condition of housing in Britain and at the various philosophies of research through which the housing system has been studied.

The 'problem' of course is no new thing, despite the flurry of governmental and academic concern in the last few years. The housing problem in contemporary Britain has not suddenly become critical: it is less like a heart attack than like a perpetual nagging ulcer—basically irremediable, its worst symptoms can at least be ameliorated. That housing has come to figure so large amongst the list of social problems might appear odd, given the enormous funds of money and resources which have been poured into new infrastructure and the improvement of the existing stock over the last half century. Public expenditure on housing—in the form of fixed capital formation, subsidies, and improvement grants—formed over 1 per cent of Gross Domestic Product in the 1920s when state house building got under way and today has risen to 4 per cent (D.O.E., 1977b, part 1, pp. 39–42). To this, of course, should be added the sums involved in private house purchase and the loss to the public purse of tax relief on mortgage interest. That there should still be a housing problem despite the resources which have been devoted to solving it and despite the mountains of written analysis, technical reportage, and popular advice which have been strewn in the path of policy makers, says much about both the nature of the political system through which housing is produced and distributed as well as about our expectations of what houses are wanted and needed. As with so much of social life, the critical element is less the measurable improvements that have occurred and more the felt reaction to those changes.

Absolute Improvement

The fact of absolute improvement is hard to refute. Not only is the country now better housed in terms of the conventional measures of over-crowding, but the individual houses themselves are of a standard unthought of by the slum and 'rookery' dwellers in the early years of the century. The percentage of people living at densities of over 1·5 per room, which had been 18·6 in 1931, had fallen to 2·9 by 1971 and the trend of average space standards has shown a long-term rise in total floor space even though not in the living space of bedrooms and living rooms (Hole, 1965). In the public sector, the series of recommended or statutory minimum standards—from Tudor Walters to Parker Morris together with the various Housing Manuals and Circulars—have helped to ensure such gradual improvement even though it has been interrupted by the setbacks of periodic economies. For example, the average three-bedroom council house had a floor area of 750 square feet at the end of the 1930s; under Bevan in the 1950s the figure had risen to over 1000; but after 1952, in a period of rapid expansion of the public sector, it fell back to 950. In the private sector, in which Parker Morris standards are not mandatory, there has been a recent economizing

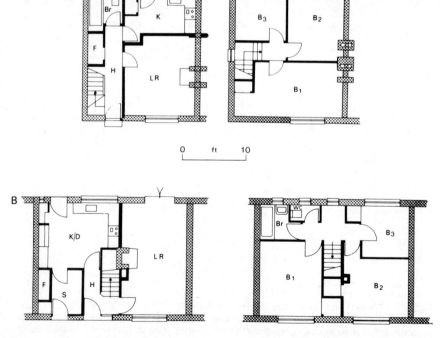

Figure 5.1 Typical plans of local authority houses in (A) the early 1930s and (B) the early 1950s. In the former, the kitchen has a gas cooker, solid-fuel copper, sink, and dresser. Indoor W.C. and bath are provided, but no wash-basin or hot-water system.
Source: Cleeve Barr, 1958, Figs. 13, 22, and 23.

as builders have counteracted the effects of rising land costs by allowing for less extensive provision of space (Thomas, 1973). It has, however been in the provision of equipment and services in which the most dramatic improvements have occurred. Now that recent council housing offers a wide range of modern cooking and living facilities, it is easy to forget that the provision of such basic equipment as a fixed bath was only made a statutory requirement for all new houses in 1936 and that wash-basins only became general in the post-war period. Something of such changes can be seen, for example, in a comparison of a typical 'non-parlour' house of the early 1930s with a characteristic design of the 1950s (Figure 5.1). In the former, even though an internal bath and W.C. are provided, there is neither wash basin nor hot-water system, only a copper in the kitchen.

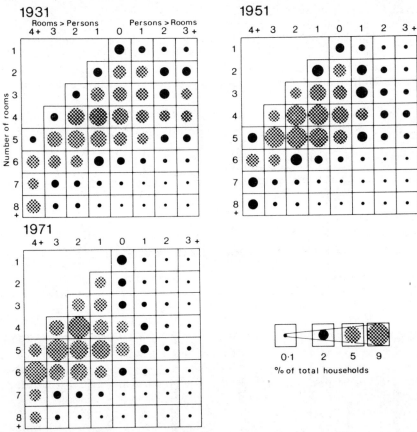

Figure 5.2 Houses and households in England and Wales, 1931–71. The vertical axis shows the number of occupied rooms per household; the horizontal axis shows the number of rooms in relation to persons in each household, ranging from an excess of 4 or more rooms to a deficit of 3 or more. The symbols in the matrix show the percentage distribution of households. No allowance has been made for changes in the Census definition of houses and households.
Source: Census Housing Tables.

To get a clearer impression of such changes, Figure 5.2 attempts to show the national trends for all houses in terms of the sizes of houses and their fit to households. The progression has obviously been towards a smaller range of sizes, towards a larger *average* size of houses and towards smaller households living in them. The housing and demographic changes are not entirely unrelated. Much of the demographic change is 'natural' in that the birth-rate has fallen dramatically and with it has fallen the size of the average completed family, but some of the change in household sizes has itself been the product of more and better houses which have enabled the 'fission' of households which would otherwise have been forced to live together so as to conceal a large 'potential' demand. In terms of the national stock of houses all commentators are agreed that there has been improvement across the country as a whole. For the first time this century there is now a crude surplus of houses over households, although the surplus may be real or imagined depending upon the extent of 'concealed' households and the size of the stock required to allow the necessary levels of mobility (Whitehead, 1977). The recent Green Paper (D.O.E., 1977b) offers some short-term projections of such national accounting tables (Table 5.1) which suggest the continuing

Table 5.1

D.O.E. projection of households and dwellings, England and Wales, 1971–1986 (thousands)

		1971	1976	1981	1986
(a)	Dwellings	17,024	18,086	19,216	20,352
(b)	Households	16,750	17,574	18,304	19,029
(c)	Excess of (a) over (b)	274	512	912	1,323
	Of total dwellings:				
(d)	Second house	150	150	175	200
(e)	Singly occupied	15,934	16,911	17,824	18,704
(f)	Shared	300	250	180	125
(g)	Vacant	640	775	1,037	1,323
(h)	Percentage vacant*	3·2	3·8	4·9	6·0

* Vacant percentages are calculated after the subtraction of a constant number (100,000) of dwellings not previously occupied.
Source: D.O.E., *Housing Policy: Technical Volume*, Part 1, Tables III.31 and 32

decline of shared dwellings and an increasing percentage of vacant houses which can accommodate mobility. Even though it is emphasised that such projections are as likely to be too high as too low and even though the demographic trends, the rates of headship formation, and the reaction of the building industry to higher rates of vacancy are all slippery imponderables, the trend towards a healthy surplus seems undoubted.

Relative Deprivation

Given these changes, to call housing one of the most pressing problems may seem extreme. The problems, however, lie in the uneven supply of housing in different parts of the country, in the demonstrable inequities of its distribution between different groups of the population, and in the frustrated expectations of large numbers of households, frustrations which are merely heightened by any improvement of the average figures. The first two of these points are addressed directly in the body of this paper. The third is one which must underlie any consideration of the social significance of housing since feelings about standards of accommodation are part of the general pattern of rising expectations which has characterized the whole range of social life in the post-war period. The loosening of the hierarchical structure of society, the changes in education which have accompanied this, and the wider public education which has increased the awareness of the standards and life styles of others, all have helped to broaden people's frameworks of reference and have therefore helped to exacerbate feelings of relative deprivation and to make households less content with whatever housing they have. Likewise, the involvement of the state in its welfare capacity has increased people's expectations of what is due to them as of right. Furthermore, in a period of 'consumerism', the material possession represented by a house and its contents has come to assume more importance for a wider range of households. When virtually all housing was rented and when the prevailing ethos provided a sop to poverty by extolling the spiritual rather than the material, housing counted less in the scale of merit. With over half of the population now being 'owners' and with taxation laws encouraging the maximization of expenditure on housing and housing services, the strategy of accumulation and of the purchase of housing for its exchange value rather than its use value has come to assume an undeniable logic.

Undoubtedly, many households still live in appalling housing conditions. Despite the massive efforts of the last few decades and the general improvement in the standards of *new* houses, the older stock includes many ill-equipped and inadequate houses. While some 44 per cent of dwellings are post-1945, no less than one-third of the stock was built before 1914 and it is overwhelmingly in these older houses that facilities are lacking. Even though less than 10 per cent of houses now lack an indoor toilet, for example, this percentage figure means in absolute terms over 1½ million dwellings. Yet the inequalities of housing have grown less. Figure 5.2 illustrates the case from the viewpoint of house size. As a specific example, one might quote Hole and Attenburrow's average per capita space figures of 192 square feet for a Parker Morris council house in the 1960s as against 185 square feet for a selection of private houses and compare both figures with the standard 'gentleman's house' of the 1870s with its 352 square feet (Hole and Attenburrow, 1966, p. 52). Likewise, Davidson's (1976) study of social deprivation in Hull shows that, while many social indicators demonstrate over time a complex pattern of relative convergence towards and divergence from the average values for the whole city, the indices of housing disadvantage show a consistent pattern of convergence. But while the inequalities have grown less and the average provisions raised, the awareness of inequalities has grown. With a larger proportion of the population being better housed, the remaining, and still large, numbers of ill-housed and homeless feel the inadequacy of their accommodation even more. Even if, by absolute standards, the very worst conditions were 'solved', a new set of 'very worst' would automatically be created. Dealing as one is with relative and with rising expectations the problem of housing, like the poor, will ever be with us. Housing is so closely connected with patterns of poverty that so long as income and wealth are unequally distributed so will there be inequality in housing and so will there be frustration with whatever standards of physical accommodation are at or below the average. No level of housing provision is likely to dampen the feelings of deprivation and unfairness so long as housing is produced and distributed within a market economy in which money rather than 'need' determines access to housing. Expectations have been socialized, but the economy is still orientated to the market. The housing problem emerges from the inevitable tensions generated by this contradiction.

Philosophies of Research

It is from these sets of contradictions that much of the geographical research on housing has proceeded. It has been riven with views as opposed and contradictory as are those within housing policy itself. The thrust of research has moved away from the micro-economic approaches of economists such as Evans (1973), Ball and Kirwan (1975), or Whitehead (1975), or of geographers such as Wilson (1974), all of which started with the assumption of interdependence between demand and supply in a market situation. Against the background of the flux and restructuring of the philosophy of the social sciences (Bernstein, 1976), recent research has stressed the essentially political nature of housing and its provision. There have been three notable strands involved as spring-boards for the work: first is social ecology with its concern for the evolution of geographical patterns of residential differentiation; second is conflict theory and the managerialism thesis; and third is what might be called the French connection, the reinterpretation of Marxist concepts from writers such as Castells (1977) and Lojkine (1976). The three have overlapped and the work, while having proceeded from different origins, has tended to point in similar directions: by emphasizing the importance of constraints rather than choice in access to housing; by illustrating the role of conflict rather than consensus in the goals and interests of the groups involved; and, taking this somewhat further, by arguing that class interests lie at the base of much of the system through which housing is produced and distributed.

Social Ecology

The three starting-points have, however, given rise to different sets of substantive topics. The most directly continuous line from the work of social ecology has focused on household mobility (Herbert, 1973) and the way in which the flux of movement perpetuates or changes patterns of social areas. Pritchard's study of Leicester provides a historical backdrop which demonstrates the fall in rates of mobility produced by the operation of the housing market (Pritchard, 1976). In contrast to the high turnover of the nineteenth century, rates after the first world war fell and have not since risen to their former levels. It is to the changes in tenure and housing law that he turns to explain these changes: to the effects of council tenancies and their constraints on transfers and of local residence requirements; to the discouragement to move through protected tenancies in the residual rented sector; and to the transfer costs associated with changing house for owners. These same constraints apply with equal force to longer-distance moves usually associated with a change of job (Johnson *et al.*, 1974). An alternative way of looking at mobility which has stressed even more strongly the constraints of the housing market is the study of chains of movement associated with vacancies (Gray, 1977; Watson, 1973). These studies have suggested the inappropriateness of a pure concept of residential filtering as a mechanism whereby households can progressively improve their housing and have also shown that the combined effects of demolition and council housing have produced in Britain chain lengths considerably shorter than those in America.

Managerialism

The second starting-point has prompted work on the nature and effects of the institutions which control the workings of the housing market and, in Pahl's terminology, act as 'gatekeepers' who determine access to housing (Rex and Moore, 1967; Pahl, 1975). It is in this work that the role of conflict has been most directly addressed and three topics have dominated the geographical research. First is the allocation policy of local authorities. Despite the emergence, since 1919, of council housing as the second arm of housing, the state has never convincingly determined what its role as a major provider of housing should be. At a national level, the fluctuations in emphasis between the provision of houses either to rehouse slum-clearance families on one hand or for 'general' needs on the other and the use of the public construction of houses as an economic regulator both suggest the conflict between the interpretation of the state as a provider of decent housing as a general right and as an inferior form for the needy. This dichotomy of views has coloured local allocation policy as much as national provision. Local authorities have seen the need to reconcile their statutory obligations to rehouse certain categories such as slum-clearance households, with their perceived role as providers of good housing for those in 'need' and both of these with their desire to make the most efficient use of their existing stock and to preserve as best they can the quality of that stock. Public housing has therefore been seen variously as an investment and as a form of social welfare and this has led to controversy over the selection and allocation policies of the authorities concerned. When housing was manifestly market dominated and income was the principal criterion of access the situation was at least unambiguous. Now, in the public sector, the combination of state subsidies, the relatively small variance in rents which is produced through 'pooling', the lower debt charges on older houses and the higher charges on recent houses, and the effects of rent and rate rebates and Supplementary Benefit have all combined to make household income less of a constraint on the type of house which a household can occupy. But if this suggests that 'need' should be the sole criterion which local authorities should consider, many of them would argue that the definition of need is a task of no small dimensions and one unlikely ever to produce a universally acceptable form of measure and that furthermore they must make the best use of their existing stock. If many families refuse to live in the less popular accommodation then only by allocating 'problem' families or households low on the points scheme to such stock can it be used to the communal good. Bird, for example, shows that in Newcastle, while half of the tenants live in flats, less than 30 per cent of those asking to transfer wished to live in flats (Bird,

1976, p. 30). It is considerations such as these, allied to the composition of the stock and the waiting list, that produce such wide variations in the periods that families have to wait before being rehoused (Dennis, 1970). Certainly, as Gray (1976) has shown, the respectability and rent-paying ability of prospective tenants are paramount in determining both whether a family gets a house and what type that accommodation will be. One can cite this as evidence of the inappropriateness of the criteria used and criticize the training of the house visitors who select tenants (English *et al.*, 1976), but what basically is at fault is the lack of a clear social goal. For the individual, the needs of the family should predominate; for the community at large there is a stronger case for making most efficient use of resources. The latter view has rarely been more clearly underlined than by the number of councils who have demolished or who are considering demolition of blocks of flats of only a few years standing. The recent recommendations of the Green Paper—that the local-residence require-ment should be abolished and that local authorities' allocation schemes should be published (D.O.E., 1977a, pp. 79—80)—might at least make more public the nature of the process even if not helping it to move to one based on social need rather than ability to pay for or to use accommodation to good effect. The results of such allocation policies have been that it is in the privately rented sector, not the council sector, that the very poorest households are still found and that the 'top' third of the local authority households have higher incomes than the 'bottom' third of owner occupiers.

A second focus on institutional behaviour and outcomes has been on the allocation of improvement grants in terms both of its connection with 'gentrifi-cation' and the social change of local areas (Hamnett, 1973) and the criteria used in their allocation. Here again it has been shown that it is not the area and the households in greatest need who are given the greatest assistance. In the declara-tion of General Improvement Areas, for example, Duncan has shown how local authorities have veered away from areas with high proportions of coloured households and of the very worst housing conditions with the aim of selecting those areas most likely to show to best effect the impact of improvement (Duncan, 1974). Bassett and Hauser (1975) have shown that the take-up of standard and discretionary grants in Bristol has been disproportionately low in certain of the inner areas in which 'objective' measures of poor housing suggest that the need is greatest.

A third topic has been the granting of mortgages in the private sector. Barbolet's (1969) early suggestion that building societies gave differential treat-ment to white- and blue-collar applicants for mortgage finance helped lead the way to the wider questions of building-society policy which have been taken up vigorously by many of the geographical studies of local housing markets. The 'red lining' of districts—the demarcation of whole areas of houses within which mortgages are not advanced—has been extensively documented (Boddy, 1976; Weir, 1976) and the restriction of mortgages to safer investments—to relatively new and more expensive houses—has been shown by Duncan (1977), amongst others. Building societies, estate agents, and the other professional bodies involved in the purchase and exchange of houses provide an institutional frame-work in which to varying degrees it is the constraints on the way in which the actors within the system operate rather than the choices of consumers which provide the background to what houses are bought and who has access to them, in the private no less than in the public sector (Williams, 1976; Harloe *et al.*, 1974).

Political Economy

These studies of the institutions that determine access have overlapped in many cases with the third starting-point, the more overtly radical approaches which have broadened the base of their concern to look at the underpinnings of the whole structure of the housing system. The argument here is that class interests or the financial structure of society are the determinants of the whole nature of the supply and allocation of housing (Harvey, 1973). The latter argument, for example, suggests that, whether in the public or the private sector, money and the finance market determines who gets what and what types of houses are produced when. Developers as a whole, whether concerned with housing or with office development, are prompted by the same rationale (Ambrose and Colenutt, 1975). Need rather than profitability gets short shrift. In this view the building societies, for example, can be seen not in terms of their self-image as the benign non-profit-making agencies whose function is to spread the benefits of ownership on the one hand and of small-scale saving on the other to as wide a variety of households as possible, but as institutions which generate a secondary circuit of capital which is borrowed on a short-term and lent on a long-term basis so as to make possible the primary circuit of capital between producers and buyers within the economy at large (Boddy, 1976). They act in harness with the 'exchange professionals'—the solicitors, estate agents, and valuers—to maintain profits for the economy as well as themselves (C.D.P., 1967a). Red-lining in the private sector and clearance in the public can be seen as necessary planks in a system which requires that the demand for new housing be maintained even if the transfer of fixed capital to the suburbs which this entails produces the contradiction that it undermines central city investment on which many of the organs of the finance market place heavy reliance.

What has been learned from such work has taken geography into unfamiliar realms and has begun to lay the foundations for a political economy of housing— the siting of problems within an analysis of the central economic and political dynamic of society—the aim indeed of the Political Economy of Housing Workshop which, together with the Community Development Project reports, has produced some of the most lively if polemical debate on the nature of housing and the state (P.E.H.W., 1975, 1976; C.D.P., 1976a, 1976b). Out of such work has come a much clearer picture of the political nature of housing, of the redistributional effects of the housing system and of the limits to the incrementalist managerial solutions which have tried to improve the workings of the system by smoothing the bottlenecks of allocation or by softening the impact of financial constraints in the production of houses. Valuable as the managerial study of housing is, it has tended to concentrate on the outcomes of the system and to regard the institutions which have been studied as given. While the 'radical' approaches as yet appear to have expended most energy in saying what theory *ought* to be or in adding a further twist to the saga of Castell's views on

Poulantzas's views on Althusser's views on Marx (Harloe, 1977), the aim is that of developing a framework which will show how the structure of the state, of finance, or of ideologies affect the way in which institutions develop, the manner in which the urban managers evolve their goals and policies, of how the resulting constraints affect the pattern of housing opportunities and disadvantages. It is clearly in the development of some more robust theoretical frameworks that one of the future foci of activity in the whole field of housing will lie. Only then will the unasked questions about the *meaning* of housing become realistic. Equally, only then will the studies of individual institutions lose some of their journalistic muck-raking air. It is at this broad level of investigating the role of the state and of class interests that one thrust of research seems likely to move and, for it, further international comparisons of alternative national systems of housing may well help to develop a research framework for the study of meaning in housing.

Future empirical work

In terms of the more traditional empirical theory, the singular contribution of geography to future research would seem still to lie in studying the regional and local incidence of housing conditions. Most of the existing research has been at the level of single authorities in which specific institutions have been studied or the failures of such area policies as General Improvement Areas or Housing Action Areas have been considered. Yet one of the most striking omissions has been of the role and impact of planning decisions and of the ideology of planning, topics which obviously need to be couched within the framework of ideas about class interests. At present the field of urban politics is dominated by the concepts of pluralism derived from the community power studies of America. In Britain it seems that local communities play a more subdued role and the attempts to develop a theory of urban political behaviour appropriate to indigenous local government is only just emerging (Newton, 1975). As yet there are simply a number of essentially local studies of particular issues in specific towns (Davies, 1972; Dearlove, 1973; Dennis, 1972; Elkin, 1974; Newton, 1976). With its emphasis upon the spatial externalities involved in the outcomes of local planning decisions (Cox, 1973) and of the notions of spatial justice (Massam, 1975; Smith, 1977), geographical contributions to the theory and to the empirical study of local politics and planning as it affects housing are as yet curiously under-developed. The example of high-rise housing is a pertinent illustration of a substantive topic which illustrates the way in which, despite the additional expense involved in building additional stories, housing policy has produced, through the now largely defunct industrialized building techniques, housing which has proved not to meet the wants of households who have been allocated to it (Sutcliffe, 1974). Dunleavy, for example, uses the case of Ronan Point in the London borough of Newham as an illustration of the role of non-decisions in determining political outcomes and of the power of a local authority over its client population (Dunleavy, 1977). The conjunction of a stronger theoretical framework and of a direct involvement in the study of local issues of political conflict seems a probable direction in which geographical work on housing and the local environment might move.

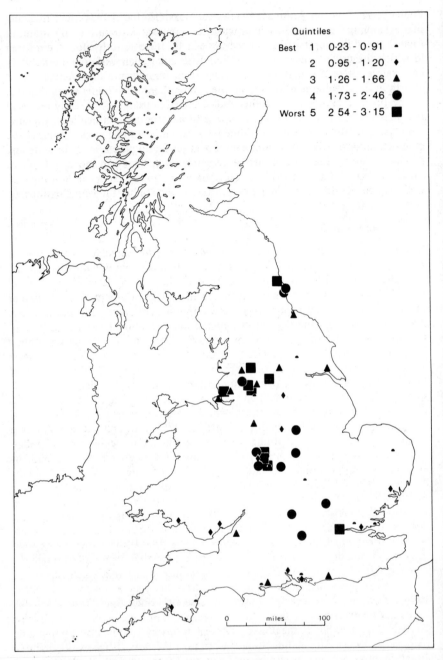

Figure 5.3 Percentage of households living at or more than 1·5 person per room in 1971. The towns shown are those with populations ⩾ 100,000 in 1971 and are listed in Fig. 5.4. *Source*: 1971 Census.

At the national scale there is a yet more obvious focus for future research since there is still a pressing need for more comparative information on variations in the supply of housing which are produced by local conditions and the local interpretation of national policy. The existence of such variation D.O.E. has been made clear by the D.O.E. study of social indicators which suggested not only that even the most spatially concentrated housing problems were not found exclusively in the areas of 'multiple deprivation'—that most of the deprived households do not live in deprived areas—but that at the national level London and Clydeside are abnormally ill housed (Holtermann, 1975). Such national variations can be illustrated by a variety of indicators: Figure 5.3 suggests the variation in degrees of overcrowding in the largest authorities in 1971 and Figure 5.4 shows

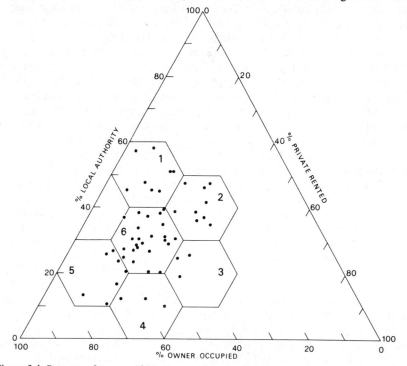

Figure 5.4 Patterns of tenure, 1971. Towns with populations ≥ 100,000 in 1971 are shown. They are grouped into 6 crude classes shown in the numbered hexagons which combine varying proportions of the three tenures.

Group 1: Basildon, Dudley, Sunderland, Thurrock, Walsall, Warley, West Bromwich, Wolverhampton.

Group 2: Hull, Liverpool, Manchester, Newcastle, Norwich, Nottingham, Salford, Sheffield, South Shields.

Group 3: Brighton, Greater London, Oxford.

Group 4: Bournemouth, Southend, Torbay.

Group 5: Blackburn, Blackpool, Bolton, Luton, Nottingham, Poole, Solihull.

Group 6: Birkenhead, Birmingham, Bradford, Bristol, Cardiff, Coventry, Derby, Havant & Waterloo, Huddersfield, Ipswich, Leeds, Leicester, Newport, Oldham, Plymouth, Portsmouth, Reading, St. Helens, Southampton, Stockport, Stoke, Swansea, Teeside, York.

the variations in patterns of tenure. London's position, with large numbers of privately rented houses and high levels of crowding, is largely explained by the high cost of land which, as Stone (1970) shows, makes the capital so considerable a drain on the national resources. It is partly explained too by the differential migrational flow of the young and single to the capital. The case of London is undoubtedly atypical, a fact which must rob much of the research based on the capital of its generality. Similarly there are differences between its large-scale landlordism and the greater tendency in the provinces for landlords to operate on a small scale and be more prepared to settle for returns based on the historic value of the capital invested in housing. Since houses are locationally immobile whereas population is not, the scope for studying regional variations in the national picture is considerable. National house-condition surveys and most of the official literature ignores the regional differences which have come to assume ever more importance in the housing problem. The closest approximations to such work are local studies, which suffer in comparative terms because they look at different topics in different places, or the few more consciously comparative studies which look at selected topics such as allocation policy (Niner, 1975).

The bases of any such comparative study would have to include consideration, first, of the patterns of existing resources, second of population and demographic characteristics, and, third, of the policy and goals of local authorities. On the first, variations in stock include not only the common measures of existing conditions, but also the historical residue of the building efforts of local authorities which have left local councils so differently placed with regard both to the composition of their housing and to the costs which they must meet from rents, rates, and central subsidy. The financial underpinnings of council housing depend so critically on central subsidy that variations, either regionally or by categories of cities, must directly influence the scope of a given council. Changes in the basis of the calculation of the rate-support grant since 1974, for example, have had the intended or unintended effect of increasingly favouring London and to a lesser extent the larger cities at the expense of the 'shire' counties (Jackman and Sellars, 1977). A recent report from voluntary housing agencies suggests that London has received disproportionate shares both of finance for housing-association rehabilitation and of money for local-authority house improvement (*Sunday Times*, 25 Sept. 1977). The second element, demographic change, has become especially critical in a period when housing has moved into an overall surplus nationally and falling birth-rates have made a nonsense of so many of the earlier projections of population growth. The greater shortages of the south (Table 5.2) are largely a product of migration and, as the critical problems become ones of providing specialized housing for the aged and handicapped or for the single, the young, the unmarried mother, so local population projections which include age distributions and other categorical breakdowns become ever more vital in determining what is needed in a particular area (Gilg, 1977). London's disproportionate share of such migrational flows is one instance; the development of a 'costa geriatrica' on the south coast is another (Law and Warnes, 1976).

The third element, local-authority policy, is perhaps the most difficult of all, involving as it does much of the question of meaning discussed earlier. The

Table 5.2
Regional Housing Need, 1976

	Percentage excess of dwellings over households	Percentage excess of dwellings when concealed households are included	Percentage excess of dwellings with allowance for 4 per cent vacancies
North	+6·1	+3·7	+0·3
Yorks and Humber	+4·2	+2·0	−1·0
North-West	+3·8	+1·2	−1·6
E. Midlands	+2·6	+0·1	−3·1
W. Midlands	+6·5	+4·2	+1·0
East Anglia	+4·6	+2·5	−0·6
South-East	+1·8	−0·6	−2·1
G.L.C.	+1·1	−1·6	−1·3
South-East	+4·5	+2·1	−0·6
Wales	+6·5	+3·3	−0·1
England and Wales	+3·7	+1·3	−1·2

Source: Whitehead (1977).

national policy debate on the illogicalities of the respective subsidies paid to owners and tenants, on the roles of council housing and owner occupation, on ways of easing the first-time buyer onto the housing ladder, can all be interpreted very differently by different authorities. Such variation brings into play the theme of local autonomy since local authorities cannot be seen simply as organs of the centre. The variations in patterns of expenditure and the delivery of goods and services is considerable (Boaden, 1971; Davies, 1968) and the controversy over the 1972 Finance Act centred precisely on this topic which has been a bone of contention since central influence began to be exerted in the nineteenth century. Local autonomy is reflected in variations in such substantive topics as the levels of rents, policy over the sale of council houses, the involvement of a direct works department, as well as the vigour with which council housing is produced. The task of exploring local policy differences must involve looking at the ideology of local authorities—a task far more complex than simply the differences between the political perspectives of Labour and Conservative councils as work by one of my own research students, Mr. J. J. Snewin, is showing for Bradford and Nottingham—but also the structure of committees, the influence of individuals and interest groups. It is clear that even in such centrally guided policy as the slum-clearance drive of the 1960s, the scope for local interpretation of central directives was considerable, as English *et al.* (1976) suggest in their comparison of centralized procedures of authorities such as Manchester with decentralized authorities such as Liverpool and Leeds. The recent decision to give block allocations for housing expenditure appears merely to exacerbate this conflict between central and local interpretations (Harrison and Webber, 1977). So long as there is local variation in the interpretation and execution of central policy and so long as there are marked variations in population composition and the existing housing stock, so is there scope for empirical geographical study to complement the non-spatial literature on housing.

Housing research appears to have been and seems likely to continue to be two-pronged and to stem from the widening schism between two main philosophies of the social sciences. On the one hand is the question of meaning and the exploration of the frameworks of the social formation through which institutions emerge to control the production and consumption of housing. On the other is the variety of empirical questions about the management and the more efficient and humane supply of houses, with its view of the housing problem as a localized one, localized either to particular areas or to particular target populations. Recent debate has shown the necessity of the former approach, since any social-science research cannot escape from the values and ideology which from the matrix within which it is couched and needs to make more explicit and more robust these values and the theoretical framework from which it operates. Yet the latter empirical work is also needed to continue to prod the pragmatic management of the policy makers, unable to await the resolution of academic debate or the improbability of a restructuring of state ideology, into directions which might improve the access to housing of the powerless and disadvantaged. The distinctively spatial contribution of traditional liberal geographers would be to this latter approach, but already geographers have made a vigorous contribution to the former theoretical debate on *espaces et sociétés* and it is to be hoped that they will continue to do so in a variety of epistemological moulds.

References

Ambrose, P., and Colenutt, B. 1975 *The Property Machine*, Penguin Books, Harmondsworth.

Ball, M., and Kirwan, R. 1975 'The economics of an urban housing market: Bristol area study', *Research Paper*, 15, Centre for Environmental Studies, London.

Barbolet, R. H. 1969 'Housing classes and the socio-ecological system', *University Working Paper*, 4, Centre for Environmental Studies, London.

Bassett, K., and Hauser, D. 1975 'Public policy and spatial structure: housing improvement in Bristol' in Peel, R., Chisholm, M., and Haggett, P. (eds.), *Processes in Physical and Human Geography*, Heinemann, London, pp. 20–66.

Bernstein, R. J. 1976 *The Restructuring of Social and Political Theory*, Basil Blackwell, Oxford.

Bird, H. 1976 'Residential mobility and preference patterns in the public sector of the housing market', *Transactions of the Institute of British Geographers*, N.S. 1, 20–33.

Boaden, N. 1971 *Urban policy-making: Influences on County Boroughs in England and Wales*, Cambridge University Press, Cambridge.

Boddy, M. 1976 'The structure of mortgage finance: building societies and the British social formation', *Transactions of the Institute of British Geographers*, N.S. 1. 58–71.

Castells, M. 1977 *The Urban Question: A Marxist Approach*, Edward Arnold, London (English translation).

Cleeve Barr, A. W. 1958 *Public Authority Housing*, Batsford, London.

Community Development Project 1976a *Profits against Houses: An Alternative Guide to Housing Finance*, C.D.P. Information and Intelligence Unit, London.

— — 1976b *Whatever Happened to Council Housing?*, C.D.P. Information and Intelligence Unit, London.

Cox, K. R. 1973 *Conflict, Power and Politics in the City: A Geographic View*. McGraw-Hill, New York.

Davidson, R. N. 1976 'Social deprivation: an analysis of intercensal change' *Transactions of the Institute of British Geographers*, N.S. 1. 108–17.

Davies, B. P. 1968 *Social Needs and Resources in Local Services*, Michael Joseph, London.

Davies, J. G. 1972 *The Evangelistic Bureaucrat: A Study of a Planning Exercise in Newcastle upon Tyne*, Tavistock, London.

Dearlove, J. 1973 *The Politics of Policy in Local Government: The Making and Maintenance of Public Policy in the Royal Borough of Kensington and Chelsea*, Cambridge University Press, Cambridge.

Dennis, N. 1970 *People and Planning: The Sociology of Housing in Sunderland*, Faber & Faber, London.

— — 1972 *Public Participation and Planners' Blight*, Faber & Faber, London.

Department of the Environment, 1977a *Housing Policy: A Consultative Document*, Cmnd. 6851, H.M.S.O., London.

— — 1977b. *Housing Policy: Technical Volumes*, 3 parts, H.M.S.O., London.

Duncan, S. S. 1974 'Cosmetic planning or social engineering: improvement grants in Huddersfield' *Area*, 6. 259–71.

— — 1977 'Housing disadvantage and residential mobility', *Working Paper*, 5, Urban and Regional Studies, University of Sussex.

Dunleavy, P. 1977 'Protest and quiescence in urban politics: a critique of some pluralist and structuralist myths', *International Journal of Urban and Regional Research*, 1. 193–218.

Elkin, S. L. 1974 *Politics and Land Use Planning: The London Experience*, Cambridge University Press, Cambridge.

English, J., Madigan, R., and Norman, P. 1976 *Slum Clearance: The Social and Administrative Context in England and Wales*, Croom Helm, London.

Evans, A. W., 1973 *The Economics of Residential Location*, Macmillan, London.

Gilg, A. 1977 'The housebuilder's hazards', *Guardian*, 9 Sept. 1977.

Gray, F. G. 1976 'Selection and allocation in council housing', *Transactions of the Institute of British Geographers*, N.S. 1. 34–46.

— — 1977 'Housing chains and residential mobility in an urban area' Unpublished Ph.D. thesis, University of Cambridge.

Hamnett, C. 1973. 'Improvement grants as an indication of gentrification in Inner London', *Area*, 5. 252–61.

Harloe, M. (ed.) 1977 *Captive Cities: Studies in the Political Economy of Cities and Regions*, Wiley, London.

— — Issacharoff, R., and Minns, R. 1974 *The Organisation of Housing: Public and Private Enterprise in London*, Heinemann, London.

Harrison, A., and Webber, R. 1977 'Capital spending on housing: control and distribution', *CES Review*, 1. 31–6.

Harvey, D. W. 1973 *Social Justice and the City*, Edward Arnold, London.

Herbert, D. T. 1973 'Residential mobility and preference: a study in Swansea', *Special Publication*, 5. 103–21, Institute of British Geographers, London.

Hole, W. V. 1965 'Housing standards and social trends', *Urban Studies*, 2. 137—46.
—— and **Attenburrow, J. J.** 1966 *Houses and People: A Review of User Studies at the Building Research Station*, H.M.S.O., London.
Holtermann, S. 1975 'Areas of urban deprivation in Great Britain: an analysis of 1971 Census data', *Social Trends*, 6. 33—47.
Jackman, R., and Sellars, M. 1977 'The distribution of RSG: the hows and whys of the new needs formula', *CES Review*, 1. 19—30.
Johnson, J. H., Salt, J., and Wood, P. A. 1974 *Housing and the Migration of Labour in England and Wales*, Saxon House, Farnborough.
Law, C. M., and Warnes, A. M. 1976 'The changing geography of the elderly in England and Wales', *Transactions of the Institute of British Geographers*, N.S. 1. 453—71.
Lojkine, J. 1976 'Contribution to a Marxist theory of capitalist urbanization', in Pickvance C. G. (ed.), *Urban Sociology: Critical Essays*, Tavistock, London, 119—46.
Massam, B. 1975 *Location and Space in Social Administration*, Edward Arnold, London.
Newton, K. 1975 'Community politics and decision-making: the American experience and its lessons' in Young, K. (ed.), *Essays on the Study of Urban Politics*, Macmillan, London, 1—24.
—— 1976 *Second City Politics: Democratic Processes and Decision-making in Birmingham*, Oxford University Press, London.
Niner, P. 1975 'Local authority housing policy and practice: a case study approach', *Occasional Paper*, 31, Centre for Urban and Regional Studies, Birmingham.
Pahl, R. E. 1975 *Whose City? And Further Essays on Urban Society*. 2nd edn., Penguin Books, Harmondsworth.
Political Economy of Housing Workshop 1975 *Political Economy and the Housing Question*, Conference of Socialist Economists, London.
—— 1976 *Housing and Class in Britain*, Conference of Socialist Economists, London.
Pritchard, R. M. 1976 *Housing and the Spatial Structure of the City: Residential Mobility and the Housing Market in an English City since the Industrial Revolution*, Cambridge University Press, Cambridge.
Rex, J., and Moore, R. 1967 *Race, Community and Conflict*, Oxford University Press, Oxford.
Smith, D. M. 1977 *Human Geography: A Welfare Approach*, Edward Arnold, London.
Stone, P. A. 1970 *Urban Development in Britain: Standards, Costs and Resources, 1964—2004*, Cambridge University Press, Cambridge.
Sutcliffe, A. 1974 *Multi-storey Living: The British Working-Class experience*, Croom Helm, London.
Thomas, R. 1973 'Housing trends and urban growth' in Hall, P., Thomas, R., Gracey, H., and Drewett, J. R., *The Containment of Urban England*, vol. 2, Allen & Unwin, London, 246—94.
Watson, C. J. 1973 'Household movement in West Central Scotland: a study of housing chains and filtering', *Occasional Paper*, 26, Centre for Urban and Regional Studies, University of Birmingham.
Weir, S. 1976 'Red-line districts', *Roof*, 1. 109—14.
Whitehead, C. M. E. 1975 *A Model of the New Housing Market in Great Britain*, Saxon House, Farnborough.
—— 1977 'Where have all the dwellings gone?', *CES Review*, 1. 45—53.

Williams, **P. R.** 1976 'The role of institutions in the Inner London housing market: the case of Islington', *Transactions of the Institute of British Geographers*, N.S. 1. 72–82.

Wilson, **A. G.** 1974 *Urban and Regional Models in Geography and Planning*, Wiley, London.

6

HUMAN HEALTH PROBLEMS IN URBAN AREAS

John A. Giggs

Despite immense progress in medical care, health education, and living standards during the past 200 years, man is still vulnerable to a multitude of physical and mental illnesses. In western countries virtually all the severely disabling and killing communicable diseases which were endemic during pre-industrial and early industrial times have largely been eradicated. Today a variety of non-communicable and 'social' ills constitute the most important human health hazards. Whilst heart disease, cancer, and mental disorders are now the leading causes of disability and death in most western countries (Howe, 1972a, 1977; Howells, 1975; Ford, 1976), the British Secretary of State for Social Services recently stated that 'mental illness is a major social problem, perhaps the major health problem of our time' (D.H.S.S., 1975a).

Even today very little is known about the nature and aetiology of many human diseases. Their study has long been an important field though traditionally one in which disciplinary boundaries have been blurred. (Ehrman *et al.*, 1972; Moos and Insel, 1974; Rutter and Madge, 1976). Thus many social scientists have used the principles and methods of epidemiology, ecology, and geography to demonstrate that the distribution of most diseases varies enormously over the entire range of spatial scales, ranging from international to local (i.e. intra-urban) levels. Particular attention has been devoted to the supposedly inimical effects of rapid urbanization and living in large cities upon human behaviour (Barker, 1968; Altman, 1975; Moos, 1976; Porteous, 1976). Social stress, social disintegration, and coping problems are claimed to be endemic in large cities (Glass and Singer, 1974, Harrison and Gibson, 1976). A limited amount of epidemiological research in western countries has shown that morbidity and mortality rates for many physical diseases do tend to be higher among urban rather than rural populations. Furthermore, the rates in very large cities are usually higher than those in smaller urban and suburban settlements (Berry and Horton 1974; Rose, 1976). For mental (i.e. behavioural) disorders however, the evidence is conflicting, primarily because of important regional variations in diagnostic and treatment practices and facilities (Lin, 1970; Kaplan, 1971; Srole, 1972).

Although a number of geographers have made important contributions to the understanding of human health problems our efforts have been modest when compared with those of workers in related sciences. During the past twenty-five years, however, the spatial study of human health problems has expanded and now embraces several conceptual frameworks which overlap numerous disciplinary boundaries. Although Pyle (1976) and others (McGlashan, 1972; Hunter, 1974; Learmonth, 1975; Smith, 1977) have provided useful reviews of these conceptual and methodological developments, we currently lack an adequate comprehensive and rigorous synthesis of the field.

The specific purpose of the present chapter is to provide a review of both existing research and current trends in the spatial study of human health problems within urban areas. The review is necessarily selective and is focused upon spatial studies of the health problems of western cities.

Useful guidelines concerning the main roles of a geographical perspective in this field have been provided by Armstrong (1972), Grundy and Grundy (1974), and Shannon and Dever (1974). These authors suggest that the relevant area for research can be expressed in a simple health system model which comprises three interacting elements, namely:

1. The spatial patterning of ill health and mortality.
2. The spatial patterning of the physical and human environmental characteristics which adversely affect man's state of health.
3. The spatial patterning and use of the main elements of the health care delivery systems developed to combat diseases and the environmental hazards which affect man's health.

This model provides a useful framework for a review of the main foci of spatial research into health problems at the intra-urban level.

The Spatial Patterning of Ill Health and Mortality

Workers from many disciplines have recognized that many diseases, behavioural disorders, and mortality rates display areal distribution patterns. Natural and social scientists have found that both epidemiological and geographical analysis are relevant and often prove useful in contributing to our understanding of these problems. Regrettably, however, the scientific value of much of the intra-urban work which has been completed to date has been limited by a number of important technical problems.

The scientific investigation of the spatial patterning of ill health and mortality is heavily dependent upon the availability of accurate standardized data and the application of the appropriate methods of epidemiological and spatial analysis. However, the problems of defining and measuring health and ill health are still key issues in clinical and epidemiological research. It has been suggested that physical and mental health are essentially social concepts determined by the values of individuals (Sells, 1968; Macklin, 1972; Cooper and Morgan, 1973; Wing, 1976; Smith, 1977). In consequence, attention has been focused upon attempting to measure and classify the varying degrees and kinds of ill health. Unfortunately, there are still considerable temporal and regional variations in the definition and classification of diseases and behavioural disorders. The issue is of particular importance with respect of mental disorders (Wing, 1971; Cooper et al., 1972; W.H.O., 1973; Kendell et al., 1974). Fortunately the prospects for serious comparative research have brightened considerably because clinical workers are now devoting greater attention to the issue of diagnostic standardization (W.H.O., 1965; Kendell, 1975).

The identification and enumeration of sick individuals presents additional difficulties for the medical geographer. The true prevalence of specific health problems can rarely be gauged precisely because the declaration of many kinds of physical and behavioural ills is influenced by social factors (Bastide, 1972;

Pyle, 1973). The scale of the problem can be illustrated with respect to psychiatric problems where differing case-finding and recording methods produce contrasting levels of morbidity. In the U.S.A. and the U.K. approximately 2 per cent of the population are in touch with the psychiatric services within a specific year and may be regarded as seriously mentally ill (Wing, 1976). Over the same period 10–25 per cent of the population complains of relatively minor and transient problems (i.e. of mental ill health) to their general practitioners (Shepherd et al., 1966; Mazer, 1969; Goldberg and Blackwell, 1970). A further (unknown) proportion of undeclared mental illness exists among persons whose behaviour is 'socially deviant' (e.g. alcoholics, drug addicts, parasuicides). The levels of un-declared psychiatric morbidity vary considerably both between and within cities and can only be measured via expensive community surveys (Taylor and Chave, 1964).

Data sources for health problems also vary markedly in quality and complete-ness. Mortality statistics, obtained from death certificates, are reasonably reliable and have been used extensively in the geographical study of disease (Banta and Fonaroff, 1969; Howe, 1972b). In contrast, morbidity data are uneven in quality and are generally published only in highly aggregated form (e.g. for the former County Boroughs, Metropolitan Boroughs, and Administrative Counties in the U.K.). Furthermore, information is usually only published for persons who have attended hospitals and related units. In some countries (notably the U.S.A.) the problems of data acquisition are further exacerbated by the fact that separate statistical banks are kept by private and public hospitals. In consequence, labor-ious cross-checking is essential to obtain a complete record and to avoid duplica-tion (Levy and Rowitz, 1973). Even in the U.K., where health care is provided almost entirely by the National Health Service, centralized case registers are a comparative novelty, particularly for the psychiatric services (Wing and Bransby, 1970; Baldwin, 1971; Hall et al., 1974). Centralized computer-based linked record systems are being established in many countries (Spitzer and Endicott, 1975) which will enable researchers to identify far more quickly the appropriate cases. Unfortunately these registers rarely contain address codes which will enable geographers to assign the relevant cases quickly to desired spatial units (e.g. enumeration districts, census tracts and wards) suitable for detailed intra-urban spatial analysis.

For most diseases and behavioural disorders the risk of morbidity and mortal-ity increases with age. Furthermore, exposure to the disease environment is also highly selective in terms of other important demographic attributes e.g. sex, nativity, marital status, social class, education, and occupation. Detailed popula-tion census data are therefore essential so that the population 'at risk' to a specific disease can be employed in the calculation of accurate morbidity rates (Learmonth, 1975). In many countries adequate census data are not available for detailed intra-urban research. Even in the U.K. unpublished census data for enumeration districts has only been available since 1961. Unfortunately this potentially valuable detailed areal framework has been altered drastically in subsequent censuses (i.e. in 1966 and 1971), so that it is virtually impossible to study the changing spatial patterns of ill health and mortality at the most detailed ecological level.

The scale and complexity of these problems account in large measure for the relatively small amount of research undertaken to date in this field at the intra-urban level. Nevertheless, the findings of existing studies have generally been significant and certainly provide a conclusive case for further research.

The methods employed in mapping health problems and mortality in cities vary considerably. A few workers have demonstrated that simple dot maps are often extremely effective devices for showing the spatial patterning of disease morbidity and mortality (Snow, 1965; Gilbert, 1958; Pyle, 1973). More commonly, however, workers have calculated and mapped crude or standardized rates for urban sub-areas. The kinds of sub-areas employed often vary enormously in size between cities, so that detailed comparisons are difficult. Thus the intra-urban spatial patterning of suicide has been studied at spatial scales ranging from enumeration districts in Brighton (Bagley et al., 1973) to Metropolitan Boroughs in London (Sainsbury, 1955). The effects of using different spatial scales are obviously important (Dever, 1972).

Virtually all the research published to date can be classed as static or 'period picture' in character. Truly dynamic studies are extremely rare and cover very limited periods of time. Data are usually collected for a single year (Levy and Rowitz, 1973) or aggregated for a number of consecutive years (Faris and Dunham, 1939). These are then used to calculate disease *incidence* rates (i.e. the number of new cases occurring within the defined population over the relevant period—Faris and Dunham 1939, see Fig. 6.1) or disease *prevalence* rates (i.e. the total number of cases occurring within the defined population over the relevant period—Bagley *et al.*, 1973—and see Fig. 6.2). A few workers have investigated the distribution of specific health problems and mortality rates over time. Thus Sainsbury (1955) and Whitlock (1973) have shown that the distribution of suicide rates in London remained remarkably stable at four points in time over a period of forty years. In contrast, Pyle (1973) used a succession of maps to show that a measles epidemic diffused rapidly throughout Akron over a period lasting barely eight months. Substantial changes in the distribution of several important kinds of mental disorders have occurred over a period of forty years in Chicago (Faris and Dunham, 1939; Levy and Rowitz, 1973). Similar trends have been identified in Liverpool for mental deficiency (Castle and Gittus, 1957; Liverpool District Council, 1973) although diagnostic categories here have changed over four decades (see Fig. 6.3).

The possibilities of rigorous comparative research in this field are immense, but largely undeveloped. There are very few published comparative studies of the spatial patterns of specific forms of ill health and morbidity between several cities (Schroeder, 1942; Howe, 1972b). Even here the analysis is essentially visual and descriptive. The development of adequate generalizations and spatial models of diseases in cities awaits the application of the range of sophisticated statistical techniques now employed by urban social geographers (Herbert and Johnston, 1976).

A similar situation exists in those studies which identify the spatial patterns of several different kinds of ill health and mortality within individual cities. In most cases the authors are content merely to compare distribution patterns visually but Pyle and colleagues (Pyle and Lashof, 1969; Pyle and Rees, 1971) have used factor analysis to identify statistically and spatially distinct clusters (or *syndromes*) of disease and mortality in Chicago (see Fig. 6.4). Even here, however, the spatial properties of the disease syndromes are not identified by statistical methods.

The assessment of the spatial relationship between measures of ill health and other forms of social defect constitutes another potentially important avenue for

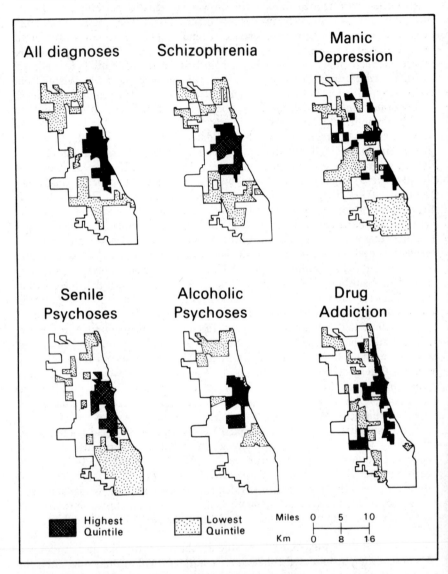

Figure 6.1 The distribution of severe mental disorders in Chicago.
Source: Faris, R. E. and Dunham, H. W., 1939, pp. 32, 47, 67, 113, 120, and 136.

research. Academic interest in this topic is strong and is based primarily upon the sociological concepts of *anomie* and *social disorganization* (Giggs, 1970; Herbert, 1976). The statistical and spatial relationships between rates of ill health, mortality, and other social problems (e.g. crime and delinquency) have

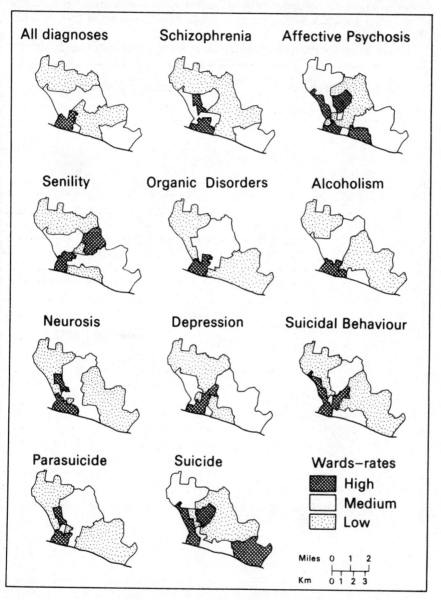

Figure 6.2 The distribution of psychiatric morbidity and mentality in Brighton.
Source: Data in Bagley, C. *et al*., 1973.

been demonstrated in a number of studies (Castle and Gittus, 1957; Bagley *et al.*, 1973). Recent geographical interest in this subject hinges upon identifying intra-urban variations in *social well-being*, or more specifically, *social malaise* (Smith, 1973; Boal *et al.*, 1978). Local Government Departments in the U.S.A. and U.K. are also beginning to map health and other social indicators as a prelude to formulating structure plans and new forms of social services (Smith, 1973; Webber, 1975).

Finally, a neglected methodological issue deserves special attention. In virtually

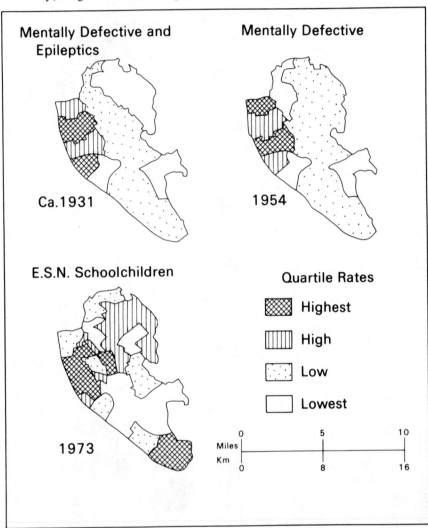

Figure 6.3 The distribution of mental deficiency in Liverpool, 1931, 1954, and 1973.
Source: Data in the Liverpool District Council Social Survey, 1973; see also Castle, I. M. and Gittus, E., 1957, Table V, Fig. 1.

all the intra-urban studies of disease mapping which have been published to date the significance of the findings have not been tested statistically. Yet the issue is of fundamental importance in epidemiology. Thus Cooper (1973, 401) has stated that 'The basic aims of epidemiology are to estimate rates of inception and

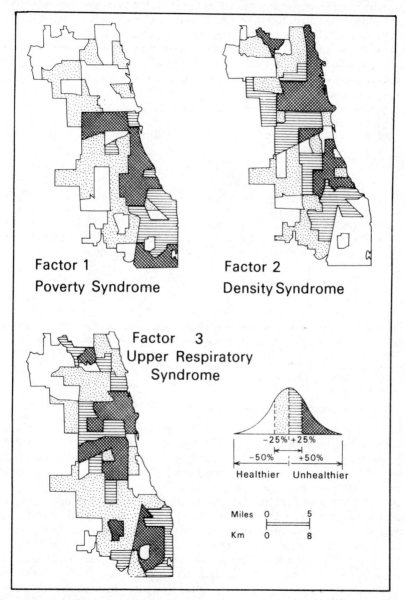

Factor 1
Poverty Syndrome

Factor 2
Density Syndrome

Factor   3
Upper Respiratory
Syndrome

−25% +25%

−50%   +50%

Healthier   Unhealthier

Miles   0   5

Km   0   8

Figure 6.4 The distribution of disease morbidity and mortality syndromes in Chicago.
Source: Pyle, G. F. and Rees, P. H., 1971, Fig. 2.

prevalance in populations, *and to test for differences between the rates for defined subgroups'* (my italics). It is probable that many of the seemingly important intra-urban variations in the incidence of specific diseases and mortality could be statistically insignificant. A number of statistical techniques (e.g. chi-squared) could be used as appropriate tests. Patno (1954) has produced probability maps to show the distribution of cancer morbidity among white men and women in Pittsburgh. More recently, Giggs *et al.* (1978) have employed the same method in a study of the distribution of primary acute pancreatitis in the Nottingham Defined Population Area (see Fig. 6.5).

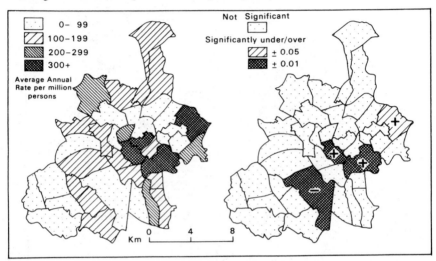

Figure 6.5 The distribution of primary acute pancreatitis in the Nottingham Defined Population Area.
A. Average annual attack rates per million persons: 1969–76.
B. High and low probability rates.

Environmental Health Hazards and Causal Research

For some workers the identification of the spatial patterning of specific health problems has been an end in itself. Others have used these maps to identify populations and environments which require special attention within the framework of developing local health-service systems. Most commonly however, disease and mortality mapping has merely formed the first stage in a range of more comprehensive investigations (Learmonth, 1975; Pyle, 1976). Most of the social scientists working in this field have subsequently attempted to identify those components of the urban environment which are hazardous to human health and well-being. They have also frequently used geographical methods of study in their attempts to determine particular aspects of disease causation. Several types of spatial 'disease-environment' analysis now exist. Some forms of associative study rely simply (but often very effectively) on cartographic comparison (McGlashan, 1972). Most, however, are based upon formal statistical testing. The available evidence suggests that the problem of disease aetiology is processual and multidimensional in character and that we need to exploit the full range of approaches currently available. The major findings of the spatial investigations of disease-environmental relationships within cities are presented below.

Physical Environments: Natural and Man-made

The relationships between climate and human behaviour and health have attracted the attention of researchers from many disciplines since the early nineteenth century (Howe, 1972a), though the rigorous scientific investigation of the relationships between climatic variables and many forms of disease morbidity and mortality at the intra-urban level has barely begun.

In the man-modified climates of large urban areas mortality rates have been most extensively studied in relation to the unfavourable effects of heat. In the United States high (i.e. 'excess') mortality rates have been associated with summer heat waves in several metropolitan areas (e.g. Oechsli and Buechley, 1970; Schuman, 1972). Within these large urbanized areas marked spatial variations in mortality rates have been identified. These correlate significantly with spatial variations in temperature. Thus in New York (Schuman, 1972) the areas of high mortality coincided with the heat island in the central core of the city. Here, mortality rates were very high among the poor, the elderly, the physically handicapped, and those persons with circulatory diseases. In the cooler suburbs, in contrast, mortality rates were considerably lower.

Within urban areas the adverse effects of weather upon human performance and health have also been investigated in relation to air pollution (Stern, 1968). Most large cities are important industrial regions and consequently have a variety of pollution-generating activities. The burning of fuel to create heat and power is the major contributor to atmospheric pollution. Industries, domestic sources, and motor vehicles release vast quantities of toxic gases, liquid droplets, and particulates into the atmosphere. These primary elements frequently combine to form secondary pollutants (e.g. the smog found in London and Los Angeles). There are pronounced seasonal, diurnal, and spatial variations in the concentration of these atmospheric pollutants. Under calm conditions and during temperature inversions, pollution concentrations can reach lethal levels. The problems are particularly severe near generating factories, in the city centre, and near major roads (Detwyler, 1972, pp. 69–96).

The findings of numerous epidemiological studies suggest that atmospheric pollution is significantly associated with many aspects of morbidity and mortality (Goldsmith, 1968; Ford, 1976, pp. 3–34; Moos, 1976, pp. 175–210). Gastrointestinal and respiratory complaints are common in most cities and they often assume serious, debilitating, forms (e.g. chronic bronchitis and emphysema). Many deaths from non-malignant and malignant diseases of the respiratory tract and some forms of cardiovascular disease have been positively correlated with atmospheric pollution. Thus in Greater Manchester Wood *et al.* (1974, p. 56) found that total mortality rates, and bronchitis and emphysema mortality rates by local authority areas (1970 figures) correlated strongly with winter average smoke concentration (1963–4 figures). The study thus shows that the adverse effects of pollution on health are subject to time lag.

There is also evidence to suggest that atmospheric pollution can adversely affect man's behaviour and mental health. The effects of carbon monoxide and ambient airborne lead have been examined in some depth. Ambient air lead is particularly harmful to young children (i.e. 1–6 years) because long exposure at high levels results in blood-lead absorption rates which can cause brain damage. Young children living in residential areas adjacent to major traffic arterials are particularly vulnerable.

Other forms of pollution are also damaging to health. The adverse effects of water pollution, in particular, are well known. In nineteenth-century British and North American cities many people died as a consequence of epidemics resulting from drinking contaminated water (Snow, 1965; Rosenburg, 1962). Despite the provision of effective sanitation some forms of disease found among city dwellers can still be attributed to water-borne factors. Thus Pyle and associates (Pyle and Lashof, 1969; Pyle and Rees, 1971) have shown that high rates of infectious hepatitis are found in areas close to tracts of polluted open water in Chicago (Fig. 6.4).

One of the most important stressors and pollutants in contemporary urban areas is noise. The effects of noise produced by factories, vehicular traffic, and aircraft on people have been analysed. Comprehensive reviews of the literature have been provided by Moos (1976, pp. 175–210) and McLean and Tarnopolsky (1977). In extreme cases (e.g. in some factories) noise levels can be loud enough to damage the hearing mechanism permanently. More commonly, however, exposure to loud and permanent noise produces anxiety and irritation. The problem is particularly acute near airports. Wood et al. (1974) identified the 'noise surface' of Manchester's Ringway Airport. The surface was elongated in the direction of the runways, and noise levels decayed exponentially with distance. Responses from the resident population ranged from 'intrusive' or 'annoying' in peripheral areas to 'very annoying' in localities fringing the airport. On the other hand, results of American studies published to date are very mixed (e.g. Burrows and Zamarin, 1972). It seems therefore, that people differ considerably in terms of their perception of aircraft noise and their consequent subjective and behavioural reactions.

The pollutants discussed here have traditionally been studied individually. However, they unquestionably interact and overlap spatially within large urban areas, creating environments of strongly contrasting health risk. This pattern has been demonstrated in Philadelphia (McHarg, 1969) and Greater Manchester (Wood et al., 1974). In an essentially exploratory study, Wood et al. aggregated six measures of pollution and calculated a *composite pollution index* for each of the seventy-one local authority areas. The pattern is mapped in Figure 6.6. The areas of high overall pollution were around Salford C.B. in the centre of the conurbation and around Wigan in the west. The lowest overall pollution rates were recorded on the north-eastern (Pennine) and southern (Cheshire) fringes of the region. The highest levels of atmospheric pollution were generally found in areas with populations of low socio-economic status. High concentrations of summer smoke and winter sulphur dioxide pose serious threats to health.

The physical condition of housing is one influence determining the physical and mental health of residents (Ittelson, et al., 1974; Schorr, 1963; Girt, 1972; Taylor, 1974). It is also recognized, however, that such factors as self-perception, residential satisfaction, and subjective stress are important health determinants. Several studies of the negative human consequences of large-scale urban change have demonstrated the impact of these influences. Thus the comprehensive planned destruction and renewal of slum neighbourhoods by city planning departments has incurred tremendous social and health costs. Gans's study (1962) of the Italian community in the West End of Boston has shown how a well-organized social environment was disrupted by well-intentioned planners. The psychological and health costs incurred by the forcibly relocated residents of the area have been explored by Fried (1963), and Wilner and Walkley (1963).

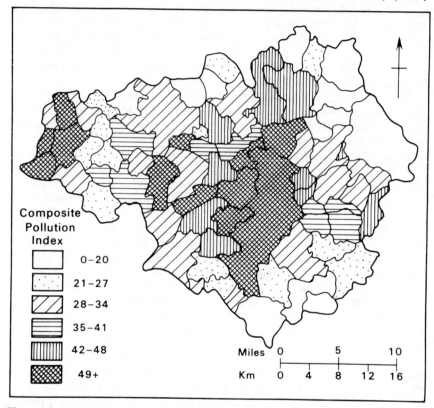

Figure 6.6 The distribution of population in Greater Manchester.
Source: Wood, C. M. et al., 1974, Fig. 31.

The impact of housing design and layout on spatial proximity, socializing patterns, and health in new residential areas has also been explored, but only in a piecemeal and preliminary fashion. In Britain Taylor and Chave (1964), Hare and Shaw (1965) and Taylor (1974) have examined the distribution of mental disorders among local-authority-housing tenants. The results tend to vary considerably between study areas and even within study areas over quite short periods of time (Taylor, 1974, 325–92). The experience of living in high flats on the mental health of residents has recently attracted considerable popular and scientific attention. It has been suggested that there exists a 'tower block neurosis' (Allen, 1973). The results of most epidemiological investigations have, however, been inconclusive (Bagley, 1974).

Many of the physical and social ills of the city have been attributed to high population density and overcrowding. Unfortunately the precise definition of the elements of density and crowding is very difficult. Investigations have used contrasting measures which vary considerably in methodological sophistication. It is therefore essential to clarify precisely which measures of density and crowding are associated with the specific dependent variables featured in each study. In most cases the measures of density indicate a physical condition involving limited space (e.g. persons per room/dwelling unit/acre; dwellings per acre). In contrast it has been suggested that crowding should include the additional requirement of *perceived* spatial inadequacy (Stokols, 1972). In most studies, however, the number of persons per unit of space has been used as a measure of both density and crowding (Zlutnick and Altman, 1972).

Several studies have shown that some measures of density and crowding are closely associated with measures of disease morbidity and mortality (Schmitt, 1966; Pyle and Lashof, 1969). Other studies of the relationships between mental health and density/crowding have produced conflicting results. Galle and colleagues (1972) demonstrated that there was no significant statistical relationship, a finding which has been corroborated by Hare (1956a, b). Areas with high admission rates to mental hospitals appear to be characterized by large proportions of persons living alone in 'rooming-house' environments. Other recent studies of crowding have suggested that it does not appear to be deleterious to human health and happiness. The findings of Booth and colleagues (1976) are particularly important because their investigation was based on the study of individuals and families in their home settings rather than gross ecological units (i.e. census tracts and communities).

The evidence provided by existing research thus shows that pathological health and behavioural conditions are not uniformly correlated with high population densities and crowding. Indeed, for some forms of mental illness it would appear that low population density and under-crowding (i.e. isolation) are important precipitating factors. Freedman (1975) has argued that crowding in cities has many positive benefits and that many people thrive in crowded inner-city environments. The available evidence suggests, therefore, that people adapt effectively to high-density living conditions. In consequence they do not appear to experience levels of density-related physical and social morbidity which are significantly higher than those found among people living in suburban and rural settings.

The Social Environment

It has long been recognized that the distribution of most physical and mental illnesses varies considerably between social groups. Numerous epidemiological studies have shown that the health status of populations differs markedly according to life style (i.e. age structure and life cycle), socio-economic and minority status, and variations in community homogeneity and stability (Bastide, 1972; Arieti, 1974, 1975; Ford, 1976; Moos, 1976).

Within urban areas epidemiologists have generally adopted the familiar ecological perspective. Selected elements of the social environment have been obtained from census sources and averaged for particular spatial subdivisions. In the earlier ecological studies the spatial units employed were usually the large preconceived 'natural' or functional areas of the city (e.g. Faris and Dunham, 1939). Subsequently administrative subdivisions—notably census tracts or wards—were favoured (e.g. Patno, 1960). More recently epidemiologists have followed social area analysts and factorial ecologists, often using even smaller spatial units (e.g. street blocks or enumeration districts) to identify uniform social areas (e.g. Stockwell, 1963a, b; Taylor, 1974). Morbidity and mortality rates for many diseases and mental disorders have been found to vary significantly among social areas defined in this fashion.

The evidence provided by most of these ecological studies suggests that socio-economic status has the strongest bearing on health differentials. City-wide studies have shown that disease mortality and morbidity rates generally exhibit a strong inverse relationship with social class (Ellis, 1958; Patno, 1960; Stockwell, 1963a, b; Griffiths, 1971; Pyle, 1973; Wood et al., 1974). In addition, several investigators have specifically defined poverty areas in many North American cities and compared their health status with that of the rest of the urban population (Hochstim et al., 1968; Struening et al., 1970; Sparer and Okada, 1974). In every case the populations of the inner-city poverty areas had grossly excessive rates for such problems as infant and neonatal mortality, maternal mortality, syphilis, tuberculosis, and cancer of the cervix. Of particular interest is a study made by Pyle and Lashof (1969). Their factor analysis of nineteen health measures for the seventy-five community areas of Chicago produced a 'poverty syndrome' dimension which accounted for 39·8 per cent of the total variance. Nine measures of ill health were strongly associated with poverty areas, namely gonorrhoea, illegitimate births, diarrhoea, premature births, syphilis, measles, poisonings, tuberculosis, and infant mortality (Fig. 6.4).

Similar relationships have generally been found for mental subnormality and mental disorder. In almost every ecological study of these major problems the highest rates for hospitalized persons have been concentrated in low income, inner-city residential areas (Faris and Dunham, 1939 (see Fig. 6.1); Bagley et al., 1973 (see Fig. 6.2); Lei et al., 1974). In Britain the distributional patterns tend to be more variegated because high rates for mental subnormality and mental disorder are often found in suburban post-war local-authority housing estates (Castle and Gittus, 1957; Taylor, 1974). For a few mental disorders—notably manic depression—the socio-economic correlates are not statistically significant. Several studies attest to this fact (Faris and Dunham, 1939; Bagley, et al., 1973; Levy and Rowitz, 1973; Taylor, 1974).

Many epidemiological studies have emphasized the importance of differences in life style upon the health status of urban populations. These differences are chiefly functions of age and life-cycle attributes. The spatial patterning of many morbidity and mortality rates within urban areas is thus partly a function of the varying age structures of the populations living within particular localities. It might therefore be expected that mortality and morbidity rates would generally tend to be highest in census tracts where the population is predominantly elderly.

The evidence suggests, however, that age and socioeconomic attributes are inter-dependent variables. Thus the health status of elderly populations tends to be poorest in areas of low socio-economic status. (Faris and Dunham, 1939; Bagley *et al.*, 1973). Similarly the rates for disease morbidity and mortality, and for mental subnormality among children are highest in poverty areas (Pyle and Lashof, 1969; Lei *et al.*, 1974).

The incidence of disease and behavioural disorders also varies considerably according to marital status. For many mental disorders, morbidity rates are generally low among married persons and high for single persons and those who have experienced traumatic events e.g. bereavement, divorce, and unstable family settings (Bastide, 1972). These groups are considerably over-represented in the inner residential areas of most cities. The findings of most factorial ecological studies confirm the existence and significance of this structural dimension and its related spatial patterning (Herbert, 1972; Herbert and Johnston, 1976). The inner-city neighbourhoods are distinguished by large proportions of single, widowed, separated, and divorced persons, and economically active married women. In contrast, the populations of the suburbs are characterized by high proportions of married persons and dependent populations (i.e. children and married women engaged in home duties).

It is a well-documented fact that rates of disease morbidity and mortality and of mental subnormality and disorder vary considerably among social groups identified by such traits as race, ethnic status, nationality, and religion (Bastide, 1972; Ford, 1976) and are substantially greater among foreign-born persons and ethnic racial minorities than among the host population (Bagley, 1968; Giggs, 1977).

The ecological analysis of intra-urban differentials in the physical health of minority and host populations is a comparatively recent phenomenon. A small number of studies published since the early 1960s provide a modest amount of information concerning the nonwhite minorities in North American cities. Most of this research has been conducted within the broader context of 'poverty area' analyses (e.g. Hochstim *et al.*, 1968; Struening *et al.*, 1970; Sparer and Okada, 1974). In these investigations analysis is restricted to highly aggregated figures for minority and host populations in poverty and non-poverty zones in each city. Pyle and Lashof (1969) provide a more detailed analysis for the seventy-five community areas of Chicago. Despite the comparatively crude analytic methods and coarse spatial frameworks employed in these studies, the findings are both dramatic and depressing. In every case the morbidity rates for most chronic diseases (e.g. tuberculosis and venereal diseases) and mortality rates (especially infant, neonatal, child, and maternal mortality) were substantially higher among non-whites than among whites. In central Chicago the average life expectancy among negroes was ten years shorter than that for whites and the total death-rate was 25 per cent higher (de Visé, 1969, iii). In some localities the morbidity and mortality rates are similar to those in some of the world's poorest countries.

It is possible that some part of the differences in morbidity and mortality rates experienced by minority and host populations can be attributed to genetic variation. However, most authorities have argued that race/ethnic differences *per se* are probably rather minor at the intra-urban level (Conover, 1971). They suggest that the differentials are probably primarily functions of social environmental factors. The findings of the various poverty area studies cited above demonstrate that most non-whites are found at the bottom end of the socioeconomic scale, where the impact of chronic disease is most pronounced. Several authors have identified an important variant of the minority status division. This is a form of social isolation which appears to have significant implications concerning mental health. In their ecological investigation of Chicago, Faris and Dunham (1939) discovered that rates for many severe forms of mental disorder were higher for blacks, whites, and foreign-born persons living in areas in which they constituted only a small proportion of the total population. Thus negroes living in predominantly white neighbourhoods had a schizophrenia rate 32 per cent above that found among negroes living in predominantly negro areas (see also Mintz and Schwartz, 1964).

Numerous epidemiological studies have shown that residential mobility appears to have important repercussions upon the health status of urban populations (Miller, 1975, 996–1006). Many physical and mental health problems appear to be more prevalent in areas of high residential mobility than in areas where residential stability and social cohesion are marked (Leighton, 1974). These relationships are most pronounced and persistent in central city ghettoes and 'rooming-house' areas (Faris and Dunham, 1939; Levy and Rowitz, 1973; Bagley, 1974). High rates for depression, emotional and physical illnesses have also been recorded for new local authority housing estates in Britain (Hare and Shaw 1965; Bagley, 1974; Taylor, 1974), and rapidly growing private suburbs in the United States (Gordon et al., 1960). An interesting exception to these findings is provided by Lei et al. (1974). Their study of mentally retarded persons in Riverside, California, illustrated that the highest rates were clustered in areas of *greater* duration of residence.

Environment–Health Relationships: The Search for Causes

It has thus been established that morbidity and mortality rates for most diseases and mental disorders vary considerably within cities. Furthermore, these rates appear to be systematically related to readily identifiable elements of the physical (i.e. natural and man-made) and social environment. The establishment of specifically *causal* links between ill health, mortality, and environmental correlates is, however, a difficult task. For many physical and mental disorders it is usually the case that pathogenesis is rarely related to a single environmental phenomenon. More typically, morbidity and mortality are functions of several interacting phenomena. Even where these can all be identified, it is rarely the case that appropriate (i.e. quantified) data is available, or that the relative significance of these factors can be assessed (Pyle and Rees, 1971). An additional complication is provided by the fact that the disease-producing episodes frequently precede notification by fairly long periods of time. In such cases, correlation of morbidity/mortality- environmental factors at the time of notification will yield erroneous results.

In consequence, there are very few spatial analyses at the intra-urban scale which successfully demonstrate causal relationships. A recent study of measles in Akron, Ohio (Pyle 1973), illustrates the problems involved in aetiological research at the ecological level. The study is valuable because it demonstrates the merits and limitations of several analytical techniques. Age-specific attack rates for children aged under ten years were calculated and mapped for the city's fifty-nine census tracts for the years 1965, 1966, 1969, and 1970. The four maps displayed one common feature, namely a concentration of the highest attack rates in the central and south-eastern parts of the city. However, when the distribution of high-rate areas was compared with that of the actual communities containing the highest numbers of children aged less than ten it was discovered that the relationship was completely inverse. The tracts with the largest number of potentially vulnerable children were located in the city's higher income suburban fringes.

A simple regression analysis did not provide an explanation but the issues were partly resolved in an investigation of temporal aspects of the spread of the 1970 epidemic. Measles data for the date of reporting, age, and address of the children affected were used to identify and map the distribution of fourteen generations in the epidemic between late November 1970 and late May 1971. The epidemic originated in a poverty area in south-eastern Akron (see Fig. 6.7). Thereafter clear patterns of contagious diffusion were discernible, firstly in the city core, then in the transitional residential areas and subsequently in suburban tracts. During the last three months of the epidemic (generations eight to fourteen) the number of cases diminished due to natural causes and the activity of public health inoculation teams. However, many of the cases in the final generations of the outbreak were pre-school children located in the initial generating area. Pyle asserts that this pattern of reinfection at the point of origin (high-rate 'poverty' areas) reflects patterns of measles spread which precede the availability of vaccine.

Although the measles epidemic in Akron was a minor problem, Pyle concluded that it raises important issues for health-care policy and behavioural research. Despite the development of an elaborate and sophisticated health-care system within the United States, the delivery of necessary services to persons with health problems is imperfect. In this specific instance the appropriate vaccines were relatively expensive, and price therefore presented a barrier to the diffusion of inoculations to the entire population 'at risk'. In addition it would appear that behavioural patterns among low-income groups in relation to health-care treatment affected both the availability of measles vaccine and their willingness to accept it as a protective measure.

Ecological research into the aetiology of mental handicap and mental disorders is hampered by even greater problems. The absence of universally accepted diagnostic criteria seriously inhibits comparative research. Furthermore, there is little unequivocal scientific evidence for specific aetiological factors for most forms of mental disorder. Even in the case of schizophrenia (one of the severest, most easily recognizable, and intensively studied mental disorders) opinion is divided as to whether it is exclusively the product of inherited constitutional factors, individual experiential defects, social factors, or some combination of these factors (Giggs, 1973, 1975a, b).

The first major ecological study documenting the spatial patterning of treated mental illness raised several issues which remain unresolved. Faris and Dunham

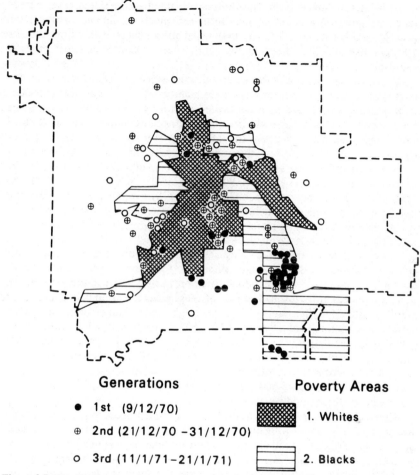

Generations

●   1st (9/12/70)

⊕   2nd (21/12/70 –31/12/70)

○   3rd (11/1/71–21/1/71)

Poverty Areas

1. Whites

2. Blacks

Figure 6.7 The distribution of poverty areas and the early generations of a measles epidemic in Akron.
Source: Pyle, G. F., 1973, Figs. 6 and 10.

(1939) showed that the incidence of several forms of severe mental illness was highest in the centre of Chicago and decreased progressively towards the periphery (see Fig. 6.1). They suggested that the uneven spatial distribution of mental disorders (and particularly schizophrenia) within the city could be accounted for by two interpretations. The first (often termed the 'breeder' hypothesis) attributes causal roles to the poor social climate and housing conditions found in central residential areas. The second view (usually termed the 'drift' hypothesis) assigns causality to defects of the individual. Thus genetically and psychologically vulnerable persons move (or drift) down the social ladder and from random locations to specifically low status inner city residential areas. Here they are admitted to hospital for the first time, thus inflating local admission rates. Numerous investigators have since attempted to assess the relative importance of these hypotheses within both ecological and individual frameworks (Taylor, 1974; Moos, 1976). The available evidence suggests that both processes are operative and that their relative significance varies both between cities and over time.

The most convincing evidence for the influence of social-housing environmental factors in precipitating (perhaps even causing) mental disorders comes from studies which have been conducted within both individual and ecological frameworks. This is particularly true of studies of attempted suicide and suicide. For more than twenty years the Maudsley Monograph *Suicide in London* (Sainsbury, 1955) has been the most authoritative and generally emulated investigation of the contribution of certain environmental factors to the incidence of suicide in urban areas. Thus Whitlock (1973), McCulloch and colleagues (1967, 1972), and Morgan and colleagues (1975) have emulated and extended his methods in studies of suicidal behaviour in London, Edinburgh, and Bristol, whilst Bagley and colleagues (1973, 1976) have investigated the incidence of attempted and completed suicide in Brighton.

Bagley and Jacobson (1976) have tested the hypothesis that four apparently phenomenologically distinct kinds of suicide (depressive, socio-pathic, physical illness, and 'residual') vary significantly in prevalence between three ecologically contrasted areas in Brighton. The first of these areas consisted of the four central wards of the city. High rates of social disorganization and poor housing characterized this area in 1966 (Bagley *et al.*, 1973). The second set consisted of four middle-class wards, and the third of thirteen 'intermediate' wards. A chi-squared analysis revealed that two of the four categories of suicide varied significantly, (P < 0·01) across the three ecologically contrasted areas. Thus 'sociopathic' suicide occurred predominantly in the four central wards, and 'physical illness' suicide in the three middle-class wards.

These exploratory studies of the typology and incidence of suicide at contrasting spatial scales provide useful guidelines for future epidemiological research into the aetiology of mental disorders. Their findings suggest that further research is needed to determine whether the methods have wider applicability. It is certainly true that significant advances in specifically *causal* research will depend heavily upon carefully devised longitudinal investigations of the life histories of both hospital patients and control populations and not exclusively upon cross-sectional, aggregate (i.e. ecological) investigation. However, 'life-event' research is fraught with difficulties, since the onset of mentally disordered behaviour is often insidious and progressive in character, rather than florid (i.e. reactive). It will certainly require collaboration with colleagues in the relevant fields, and the application of methods which are new to geographers (Smith, 1977).

The Geography of Health Care in Cities

The bulk of geographical research into urban health problems has been focused upon the ecological approach to the spatial distribution of diseases and their possible causes. Until recently very little attention has been paid to the third important component of medical geography, namely the spatial analysis of health care, behaviour, and planning. In recent reviews of the limited urban geographical literature in this field, Pyle (1971, 1974) and Shannon and Dever (1974) have shown that 'The spatial element, synonymous with the geography of health care, is an important part of the economic, the sociological, the epidemiological, the behavioural (psychological), and other factors that constitute the systems of health care' (Shannon and Dever, 1974).

Three major components of health-care provision have thus far been identified and explored at the intra-urban level. The first component embraces the organization of the supply elements of the urban health-care system. This field of study includes the structure and spatial patterning of the various resources (i.e. physicians, clinics, and hospitals) which make up the system. The second component comprises studies of patient utilization of the various medical services, and the influences which affect their spatial behaviour. The third perspective is concerned with identifying patterns of inequity in the supply and use of services, and in planning 'optimal' structural and spatial health-care systems. Almost all of the research into the geography of urban health care has been done in the United States. Furthermore, very little attention has been paid to mental health services at the intra-urban scale (Giggs, 1975b; Smith, 1977). Our knowledge in this important field of medical geography is therefore extremely incomplete and localized.

The Intra-urban System of Medical Services

The findings of a limited number of empirical studies suggest that the medical services within urban areas in the United States form a spatial hierarchy, ranging from the office of a single physician to the largest hospital (Morrill and Earickson, 1968, 1969; Shannon et al., 1975).

The supply of primary physicians—the basic stratum of the health-care system—has been declining rapidly for several decades. The losses can be partly attributed to the fact that even community-based doctors are tending to specialize. In consequence, the supply of primary physicians has not kept pace with population growth. Thus, according to one study (Joroff and Navarro, 1971), even the affluent United States has only half the number of physicians required to furnish good medical care according to prevailing physician standards. In many metropolitan areas in the United States the number of primary physicians has actually declined over the past forty years. Within the urbanised area of Boston, for example, the population increased by 30 per cent between 1940 and 1961, whereas the number of physicians fell from 2887 to 1812, a net loss of 37 per cent (Robertson, 1970).

The problems arising from the general shortage of primary physicians are exacerbated by their extremely uneven spatial distribution within metropolitan communities. This phenomenon has been investigated in detailed studies of Buffalo, Rochester, Syracuse (Terris and Monk, 1956), Chicago (Rees, 1967; de Visé, 1969, 1971, 1973; Elesh and Schollaert, 1972), Los Angeles (Norman, 1969), Boston (Dorsey, 1969; Robertson, 1970; Navarro, 1971), Cleveland (Bashshur et al., 1971), and Pittsburgh (Kaplan and Leinhardt, 1973). In these studies the relative maldistribution of physicians between one area and another has been expressed in terms of a population–physician ratio. Despite the problems involved in using this admittedly simple index it is evident that there are often massive differentials in the distribution (and hence availability) of primary physicians over very short distances within large urban areas. Thus in Chicago S.M.S.A., in 1970, the physician–population ratio ranged from 1·13 per 1,000 in the city to 0·81 per 1,000 in the outlying counties. At a more detailed spatial scale the disparities reached even greater levels. A ratio of 15·42 per 1,000 was found around the teaching hospitals in the Central Area of Chicago. In the more typical residential areas the ratios ranged from 0·51 per 1,000 in the predominantly low-income negro inner city to 1·70 in the affluent white suburbs of North Cook (de Visé, 1971).

The studies cited above also reveal that the marked differentials in the spatial distribution of physicians are increasing rather than diminishing over time. A pronounced centrifugal movement is discernible. Thus physicians (and especially the general practitioners) are leaving the inner-city neighbourhoods and establishing offices in the suburbs.

Economic variables have been invoked by many authors as being the most influential considerations in the physician's decision to locate or relocate his practice. Dorsey (1969) provides a useful example. He analysed the distribution of physicians in Boston and Brookline in 1940 and 1961 according to five speciality classes and location of practices, and the average levels of income, occupation, and education of the residents of the census tracts in which their offices were located. By 1961 the highest socio-economic tracts, with 40 per cent of the 1960 population, contained the offices of 51·5 per cent of the general practitioners, 90·2 per cent of the internists, pediatricians, and obstetricians-gynaecologists, and 93·5 per cent of the other community-based specialists. Other studies support the view that many private physicians (and particularly those with some measure of specialism) are being attracted to the higher income suburbs located on the fringes of metropolitan areas and de Visé has also claimed (1969) that the very low fees allowed for treating public-aid recipients, and the low medical purchasing power of the near poor, have provided important push forces upon physicians practising in the inner-city communities and (1971, 1973) that some of the black communities of inner Chicago are now almost devoid of primary physicians. Kaplan and Leinhardt (1973), however, suggested that the main factors affecting physician-office location in Pittsburgh were proximity to short-term hospitals and the presence of large tracts of commercially zoned land (i.e. major shopping centres and the C.B.D.). The effect of income was found to be neutral, for physicians' offices were scarce in both high- and low-income neighbourhoods.

Earickson (1970) has demonstrated that the pattern of physician location in Chicago is hierarchical and conforms closely with the pattern of retail business in general. A similar hierarchical pattern has been identified for hospitals in Chicago (Morrill, 1966; Morrill and Earickson, 1968) and Cleveland (Shannon et al., 1975). The hospitals in both cities have been classified according to size (number of beds) and levels of service offered (range of facilities, number of intern-resident programmes, total services, and number of medical staff). Several discrete hierarchical levels were identified, ranging from large teaching and research hospitals to small unspecialized community hospitals.

When these groups are mapped (Fig. 6.8) it is apparent that there are striking variations in their distribution. The higher-level specialized hospitals are concentrated in the downtown and university areas, near the centres of population and transport. In contrast, the small community hospitals are mainly scattered and located in suburban tracts. Although the older central hospitals are the largest and most specialized, there has been a gradual expansion of hospital capacity in the suburbs which has closely followed population growth (Earickson, 1970; Pyle, 1971).

Variations in the Use of Medical Services

Research into the patterns and determinants of patient use of physicians and hospitals is a fairly well-developed facet of medical geography. Geographers and other social scientists have paid particular attention to the spatial interactions of patients, physicians, and hospitals. The main starting-point for most of their investigations has been an attempt to describe patient travel patterns to medical-care facilities. Straight-line distance or travel time have been used as measures of distance between patients and the physician's office or the hospital. Variants of the gravity model have then been used to describe these travel patterns (Morrill and Earickson, 1968; Shannon *et al.*, 1969, 1973; Morrill *et al.*, 1970). The evidence suggests that patient movements to medical-care facilities reveal a fairly regular pattern. The rate of use of physicians and hospitals usually varies inversely with distance.

The explanatory power of most of these variants of the gravity model varies considerably. Detailed studies of actual patient-trip and facility-use patterns have shown that important irregularities exist. Morrill and Earickson (1968) have found that hospital size is an important attribute in understanding service areas. Schneider (1967) has demonstrated that direction is an important distorting influence. In areas with a number of hospitals of roughly comparable size and service status the service areas tend to be elongated in the direction of the fewest intervening opportunities.

The spatial and institutional organization of health services in cities also affects their patterns of utilization. Physicians and hospitals vary considerably in terms of level of specialization and locational preferences. The concentration of specialized physicians and medical services in large teaching and research hospitals located near city centres usually extends and distorts patient travel patterns (Morrill and Earickson, 1968; Shannon *et al.*, 1975—see Fig. 6.8). Further distorting influences are provided by a range of restrictive institutional influences. Although Chicago had eighty hospitals in the late 1960s they were not equally accessible to all Chicagoans. Very few hospitals provided free (i.e. public) or subsidized services for poor persons. Others cater almost exclusively to minority groups defined in terms of occupations, age, race, and religion (e.g. Roman Catholic and Jewish hospitals). In consequence, there were significant intra-urban differentials in terms of both spatial and social access to necessary medical services. The medical travel patterns of most minority groups were therefore frequently more extended and directionally biased than those of the majority of Chicagoans (Earickson, 1970; Morrill *et al.*, 1970). Similar findings have been reported for trips to both physicians and hospitals in Cleveland (Bashshur *et al.*, 1970, 1971).

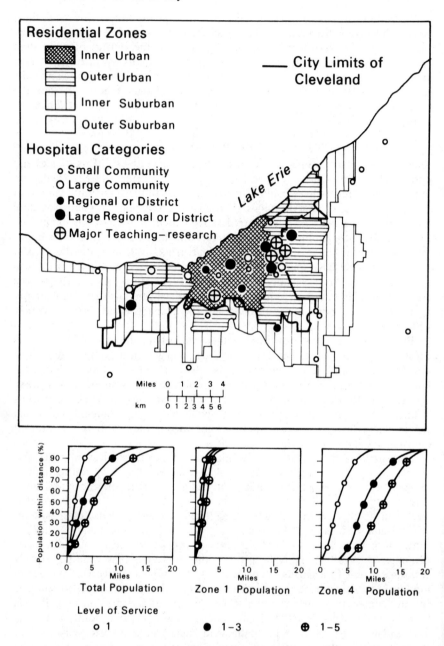

Figure 6.8 The distribution of hospitals and differential accessibility patterns in Cleveland. *Source*: Shannon, G. W. *et al.*, 1975, Figs. 2, 3, and 4 by permission of the Association of American Geographers.

Physicians also exert a considerable influence on patient-to-hospital travel patterns. Most of the persons who require medical attention at a hospital are usually admitted after consulting their physician. In the United States most patients therefore tend to go to the hospital to which their physician is affiliated. In many cases this is not the nearest hospital that a patient could visit from home (Earickson, 1970; Morrill et al., 1970). Physician referral practices can have important repercussions for the health of patients. Indeed, Hobbs and Acheson (1966) have found that perinatal mortality in the Oxford Record Linkage Study (O.R.L.S.) area in 1962 was profoundly influenced by general practitioner referral decisions. In medical practices with ready access to local G.P. obstetric units the percentage of pregnant women referred to specialist (i.e. consultant) care decreased with increasing distance from consultant units. Perinatal mortality rates were significantly higher among women who had not been referred to consultant care, and especially so among high-risk women who lived a long way from consultant units.

Social and demographic characteristics of the population have also been found to affect the utilization of health services. Social-psychological factors such as the influence of neighbours and friends are important (Suchman, 1964). In addition the nature and frequency of utilization varies significantly with age, social class, race/ethnicity, mobility, and religion (Anderson, 1973). Social groups defined by these important traits are very unevenly distributed within large urban areas. In consequence, differential spatial behaviour vis-à-vis medical services tends to distort the relatively simple idealized distance-decay models of patient travel patterns to physicians and hospitals. Economic and social constraints frequently combine to provide a deleterious pattern of medical facility utilization among the poor, the aged, and minority groups. These large disadvantaged groups tend to visit physicians much less frequently than higher-income white Americans. Frequently they live in inner city neighbourhoods adjacent to large hospitals and specialist physician quarters. These facilities are, however, economically and socially inaccessible to them. The poor and non-white populations in many cities are often obliged to undertake long, expensive, and time-consuming trips to distant hospitals (White, 1968; Bashshur et al., 1970, 1971; Earickson, 1970; Morrill et al., 1970; Perkoff and Anderson, 1970; Weiss and Greenlick, 1970; Bice et al., 1973; McDonald, 1973; Sparer and Okada, 1974; Shannon and Spurlock, 1976). In most cases they arrive at hospital in a chronically ill condition and use emergency services. Mortality rates are consequently high (de Visé, 1969).

New Perspectives: attempts to optimize, evaluate, and plan health services
Although medical care systems are now more complex and sophisticated than ever before it is apparent that they still have many shortcomings. Even within the confines of the relatively small but well-served metropolitan areas there is substantial inequality in geographical access to medical care. The identification of structural and spatial imperfections in the general efficiency of existing systems of medical care (Gross, 1972) has prompted social geographers to offer solutions to these defects. These include attempts to measure the locational efficiency of medical-care-distribution patterns (Schneider 1967; Morrill and Earickson 1968, 1969; Morrill and Kelley 1970; Shannon et al., 1975) and to

delineate efficient medical-service areas which possess a minimum of overlap and duplication (Schneider and Symons, 1971).

Some geographers and epidemiologists have adopted what Pyle (1974, 165–6) terms a 'disease-categorical' approach to medical-care assessment and planning to make allocations to future treatment facilities on the basis of community need (Pyle 1971, 1974). Similar work has been done for mental disorders, but only on a very modest scale. Thus Gardner (1967) used the Psychiatric Case Register for Rochester (Monroe County, New York) to show disparities in the provision of psychiatric services for populations in middle-class and lower-class districts.

In order to assess the service needs of the population in a particular locality, medical administrators need information about its social structure, the prevalence and distribution of morbidity, and the existing service-utilization patterns. In the field of mental health the necessity for these requirements has been appreciated only in the past decade. In the United States the National Institute of Mental Health has sponsored the publication of a number of reports which specifically adopt modified forms of social-area analysis and factorial ecology as methods for identifying intra-urban variations in socio-demographic and environmental characteristics. These are recommended as a framework for identifying areas of need for different forms of mental health service (Redick et al., 1971; Goldsmith and Unger, 1972).

At the purely local level in the United States and the United Kingdom, information relating to changes in morbidity patterns and the utilization of psychiatric medical services is obtainable only from the few areas where cumulative, computer-based case-registers exist (Monroe et al. (eds.), 1967; Wing and Bransby (eds.), 1970; Hall et al. (eds.), 1974; Spitzer and Endicott, 1975). Accurate comparative epidemiological research in this field, therefore, is still not possible. We require classificatory schemes which give standardized information relating not only to disease definition and genesis, but also to treatment patterns and recovery processes. Unfortunately the problems associated with these essential prerequisites are still being addressed (Kramer, 1976).

The limited data resources that are available have been exploited by researchers concerned with monitoring and evaluating the major changes which have occurred in psychiatric services since the early 1950s. The face of psychiatry in western countries has changed dramatically. The use of custodial institutions (i.e. the mental hospitals) as the primary mode of care is giving way to a variety of community-based services (e.g. psychiatric units in general hospitals, community mental-health centres, day-patient centres, clinics, and welfare agency services). In both the United States and the United Kingdom there has been considerable regional variation in both the rates and degrees of adoption of these new forms of treatment (D.H.S.S., 1969, 1975a, b; Arieti, 1974, 1975). In both countries medical administrators have given little weight to research findings when planning the growth and development of these services. Given the scale and economic and social costs of these changes, systematic research into the working of contemporary psychiatric services is therefore essential. To date there has been little evaluative research concerning these important changes (Hare and Wing, 1970; Wing and Hailey (eds.), 1972; Cooper and Morgan, 1973; Wing and Hafner (eds.), 1973). Geographers have a valuable part to play in this research. Any assessment of the impact and effectiveness of existing and proposed components of the community mental-health-care system which claims to be comprehensive will need to incorporate a critical review of its spatial structuring and operation.

References

Allen, T. 1973 'A Tale of High Living', *Guardian*, 11 January.
Altman, I. 1975 *The Environment and Social Behavior,* Brooks/Cole Publishing Co., Monterey, Calif.
Anderson, J. G. 1973 'Demographic Factors Affecting Health Services Utilization: A Causal Model', *Medical Care*, xi (2). 104—20.
Arieti, S. (ed.) 1974 *American Handbook of Psychiatry*, 2nd edn., Vol. ii, Basic Books Inc., New York.
—— 1975 *American Handbook of Psychiatry*, 2nd edn., Vol. vi, Basic Books Inc., New York.
Armstrong, R. W. 1972 'Medical Geography and Health Planning in the United States: Prospects and Concepts' in McGlashan, N. D. (ed.), *Medical Geography: Techniques and Field Studies*, Methuen & Co. Ltd., London, pp. 119—29.
Bagley, C. 1968 'Migration, Race and Mental Health: A Review of some Recent Literature', *Race*, 9 (3). 343—56.
—— 1974 'The Built Environment as an Influence on Personality and Social Behaviour: A Spatial Study' in Canter D. and Lee T. R. (eds.), *Psychology and the Built Environment.* The Architectural Press Ltd., Tonbridge, 156—62.
—— and **Jacobson, S.** 1976 'Ecological Variation of Three Types of Suicide', *Psychological Medicine*, 6. 423—7.
—— **Jacobson, S.,** and **Palmer, C.** 1973 'Social Structure and the Ecological Distribution of Mental Illness, Suicide and Delinquency', *Psychological Medicine*, 3. 177—87.
—— **Jacobson, S.,** and **Rehin, A.** 1976 'Completed Suicide: a Taxonomic Analysis of Clinical and Social Data', *Psychological Medicine*, 6. 429—38.
Baldwin, J. A. 1971 *The Mental Hospital in the Psychiatric Service: A Case-Register Study*, Oxford University Press for the Nuffield Provincial Hospitals Trust, London.
Banta, J. F., and **Fonaroff, L. S.** 1969 'Some Considerations in the study of Geographic Distribution of Disease', *Professional Geographer*, 21. 2. 87—92.
Barker, R. 1968 *Ecological Psychiatry*, Stanford University Press, Stanford.
Bashshur, R. L., Shannon, G. W. and **Metzner C. A.** 1970 'The Application of Three-Dimensional Analogue Models to the Distribution of Medical Care Facilities', *Medical Care*, 8. 5. 395—407.
—— 1971 'Some Ecological Differences in the Use of Medical Services', *Health Services Research*, 6 (1). 61—75.
Bastide, R. 1972 *The Sociology of Mental Disorder*, Routledge & Kegan Paul, London.
Berry, B. J. L., and **Horton, F. E.** 1974 *Urban Environmental Management: Planning for Pollution Control*, Prentice-Hall, Englewood Cliffs, 295—340.
Bice, T. W., Rabin, D. L., Starfield, B. H., and **White, K. L.** 1973 'Economic Class and Use of Physician Services', *Medical Care*, xi (4). 287—96.
Boal, F. W., Doherty, P., and **Pringle D. G.** 1978 *Social Problems in the Belfast urban area: an exploratory analysis*, Occasional Paper No. 12, Department of Geography, Queen Mary College, University of London, London.
Booth, A. 1976 *Urban Crowding and its Consequences*, Praeger, New York.

Burrows, A. A., and Zamarin, D. M. 1972 'Aircraft Noise and the Community: Some Recent Survey Findings', *Aerospace Medicine*, 43. 27–33.

Castle, I. M., and Gittus, E. 1957 'The Distribution of Social Defects in Liverpool', *Sociological Review*, 5. 43–64.

Conover, P. W. 1971 'Social Class and Chronic Illness', Paper presented to the Southern Sociological Society.

Cooper, B. 1973 'Epidemiological Psychiatry', *Psychological Medicine*, 3. 401–4.

—— and Morgan, H. G. 1973 *Epidemiological Psychiatry*, C. C. Thomas, Springfield, Illinois.

Cooper, J. E., Kendell, R. E., Gurland, B. J., Sharpe, W., Copeland, B. R. M., and Simon, R. 1972 *Psychiatric Diagnosis in New York and London*, Maudsley Monograph No. 20, Oxford University Press, London.

Detwyler, T. R. 1972 *Urbanization and the Environment: The Physical Geography of the City*, Duxbury Press, Belmont, Calif.

De Visé, P. 1969 *Slum Medicine: Chicago's Apartheid Health System*, Community and Family Study Center, Report no. 6, University of Chicago, Chicago.

—— 1971 'Cook County Hospital: Bulwark of Chicago's Apartheid Health System and Prototype of the Nation's Public Hospitals', *Antipode*, 3 (1). 9–20.

—— 1973 'Misused and Misplaced Hospitals and Doctors', *Commission on College Geography Publications. Resource Paper No. 22*, Association of American Geographers, Washington, D.C.

D.H.S.S. 1969 'A Pilot Survey of Patients Attending Day Hospitals', *Statistical Report Series, No. 7*, Department of Health and Social Security, H.M.S.O., London.

—— 1975a *Better Services for the Mentally Ill*, Department of Health and Social Security, H.M.S.O., London.

—— Welsh Office 1975b Censuses of: A. Patients in Mental Illness Hospitals and Units in England and Wales at the end of 1971. B. Mental Illness Day Patients in England and Wales at April, 1972, *Statistical and Research Report Series, No. 10*, H.M.S.O. London.

Dever, G. E. A. 1972 'Leukemia in Atlanta, Georgia', *Southeastern Geographer*, 12. 91–100.

Dorsey, J. L. 1969 'Physician Distribution in Boston and Brookline', 1940 and 1961, *Medical Care*, vii (6). 429–40.

Earickson, R. 1970 *The Spatial Behaviour of Hospital Patients. A Behavioural Approach to Spatial Interaction in Metropolitan Chicago*, Department of Geography: Research Paper No. 124, The University of Chicago.

Ehrman, L., and Omenn, G. S. (eds.) 1972 *Genetics, Environment and Behavior*, Academic Press, New York.

Elesh, D., and Schollaert, P. T. 1972 'Race and Urban Medicine: Factors Affecting the Distribution of Physicians in Chicago', *Journal of Health and Social Behavior*, 13. 236–50.

Ellis, J. M. 1958 'Socio-Economic Differentials in Mortality from Chronic Diseases', in Jaco, E. G. (ed.), *Patients, Physicians and Illness*, Free Press, New York, 30–7.

Faris, R. E., and Dunham, H. W. 1939 *Mental Disorders in Urban Areas*, University of Chicago Press, Chicago.

Ford, A. B. 1976 *Urban Health in America*, Oxford University Press, New York.

Freedman, J. L. 1975 *Crowding and Behavior*, Viking Press, New York.

Fried, M. 1963 'Grieving for a Lost Home', In Duhl, L. J. (ed.), *The Urban Condition*, Basic Books, New York, 151–71.

Galle, O. R., Gove, W., and McPherson, J. M., 1972 'Population Density and Pathology: What are the Implications for Man?', *Science*, 176. 23–30.
Gans, H. 1962 *The Urban Villagers*, Free Press, New York.
Gardner, E. A. 1967 'The Use of a Psychiatric Case Register in the Planning and Evaluation of a Mental Health Program', in Monroe, R. R. *et al.* (eds.), *Psychiatric Epidemiology and Mental Health Planning*, Psychiatric Research Report No. 22, The American Psychiatric Association, Washington, D.C., 259–81.
Giggs, J. A. 1970 'Socially disorganised areas in Barry: a multivariate analysis', in Carter, H. and Davies W. K. D. (eds.), *Urban Essays: Studies in the Geography of Wales*, Longman, London, 101–43.
— — 1973 'The Distribution of Schizophrenics in Nottingham', *Trans. Inst. Brit. Geogr.* 59. 55–76.
— — 1975a 'The Distribution of Schizophrenics in Nottingham: A Reply', *Trans. Inst. Brit. Geogr.* 64. 150–6.
— — 1975b 'Small Area Studies and Psychiatric Epidemiology', paper presented to the Social Geography Study Group, Institute of British Geographers, 29 May, at City of London Polytechnic.
— — 1977 'The Mental Health of Immigrants in Australia', in Bowen, M. (ed.) *Australia 2000: The Ethnic Impact*, Proceedings of the First National Conference on Cultural Pluralism and Ethnic Groups in Australia, University of New England, Armidale, 256–66.
— — *et al.* 1978 'The Distribution of Primary Acute Pancreatitis in the Nottingham Population Area', unpublished discussion paper.
Gilbert, E. W. 1958 'Pioneer Maps of Health and Disease in England', *Geog. Journal*, 124. 172–83.
Girt, L. 1972 'Simple Chronic Bronchitis and Urban Ecological Structure', in McGlashan, N. D. (ed.), *Medical Geography: Techniques and Field Studies*, Methuen, London, 211–33.
Glass, D., and Singer, J. 1974 *Urban Stress*, Academic Press, New York.
Goldberg, D. P., and Blackwell, B. 1970 'Psychiatric Illness in General Practice', *British Medical Journal*, 2. 439.
Goldsmith, J. R. 1968 'Effects of air pollution on human health', in Stern, A. C., (ed.), *Air pollution*, 2nd edn., Academic Press, New York, 547–615.
Goldsmith, H. F., and Unger, E. L. 1972 *Social Areas: Identification Procedures Using 1970 Census Data*, Laboratory Paper no. 37. Mental Health Study Center. National Institute of Mental Health.
Gordon, R. E., McWorter, J. E., and Gordon, K. K., 1960 Coronary Artery Disease in a Rapidly Growing Suburb, *J. Med. Soc. New Jersey*, 57. 677–83.
Griffiths, M. 1971 'A Geographical Study of Mortality in an Urban Area', *Urban Studies*, 8 (2), 111–20.
Gross, P. F. 1972 'Urban Health Disorders, Spatial Analysis, and the Economics of Health Facility Location', *International Journal of Health Services*, 2. 1. 64–83.
Grundy, F., and Grundy, P. F. 1974 *Community and Social Services*, H. K. Lewis & Co. Ltd., London.
Hall, D. J. *et al.* (eds.) 1974 Proceedings of the Conference on Psychiatric Case Registers at the University of Aberdeen, March 1973. *DHSS Statistical and Research Report Series No. 7*, H.M.S.O., London.
Hare, E. H. 1956a 'Mental Illness and Social Conditions in Bristol', *Brit. J. Prev. Soc. Med.* 9. 191–5.

Hare, E. H. 1956b 'Family Setting and the Urban Distribution of Schizophrenia' *J. Ment. Sci.* 102. 753–60.

— and Shaw, G. K. 1965 *Mental Health on a New Housing Estate*, Oxford University Press, London.

— and Wing, J. C. (eds.) 1970 *Psychiatric Epidemiology*, Oxford University Press for the Nuffield Provincial Hospitals Trust, London.

Harrison, G. A., and Gibson, J. B. (eds.) 1976 *Man in Urban Environments*, Oxford University Press, London.

Herbert, D. T. 1972 *Urban Geography: A Social Perspective*, David & Charles, Newton Abbot.

— 1976 'Social Deviance in the City: A Spatial Perspective'. In Herbert, D. T. and Johnston, R. J. (eds.), *Social Areas in Cities,* Vol. 2, *Spatial Perspectives on Problems and Policies*, John Wiley & Sons, London, 89–122.

— and Johnston, R. J. 1976 *Social Areas in Cities*, Vol. 1, *Spatial Processes and Form*, John Wiley, New York.

Hobbs, M. S. T., and Acheson, E. D. 1966 'Perinatal Mortality and the Organisation of Obstetric Services in the Oxford Area in 1962', *British Medical Journal*, 1. 499–505.

Hochstim, J. R., Athanosopoulos, D. A., and Larkins, J. H. 1968 'Poverty Area Under the Microscope', *Amer. J. Publ. Hlth.* 58 (10). 1815–27.

Howe, G. M. 1972a *Man, Environment and Disease in Britain*, Barnes & Noble, New York.

— 1972b 'London and Glasgow: A Comparative Study of Mortality Patterns', in Adams, W. P. and Helleiner, F. M. (eds.), *International Geography, 1972*, University of Toronto Press, Montreal, 1214–17.

— (ed.) 1977 *A World Geography of Human Disease*, Academic Press, London.

Howells, J. G. (ed.) 1975 *World History of Psychiatry*, Bailliere Tindall, London.

Hunter, J. M. (ed.) 1974 *The Geography of Health and Disease*, Studies in Geography No. 6, Department of Geography, University of North Carolina at Chapel Hill, N.C.

Ittelson, W. H. *et al.* 1974 *An Introduction to Environmental Psychology*, Holt, Rinehart & Winston, Inc., New York.

Joroff, S., and Navarro, V. 1971 'Medical Manpower: A Multivariate Analysis of the Distribution of Physicians in Urban United States', *Medical Care*, ix (5).

Kaplan, B. H. (ed.) 1971 *Psychiatric Disorder and the Urban Environment*, Behavioural Publications, New York.

Kaplan, R. S., and Leinhardt, S. 1973 'Determinants of physician office location', *Medical Care*, xi (5). 406–15.

Kendell, R. E. 1975 *The Role of Diagnosis in Psychiatry*, Blackwell Scientific Publications, London.

— Pichot, P., and Cranach, M. von 1974 'Diagnostic criteria of English, French, and German psychiatrists', *Psychol. Med.* 4. 181–6.

Kramer, M. 1976 'Issues in The Development of Statistical and Epidemiological Data For Mental Health Services Research', *Psychological Medicine*, 6. 185–215.

Learmonth, A. T. A. 1975 'Ecological Medical Geography', *Progress in Geography*, Vol. 7, Edward Arnold, London, 202–26.

Lei, Tzuen-Jen, Rowitz L., McAllister, R. J. and Butler, E. W. 1974 'An Ecological Study of Agency Labelled Retardates', *Amer. J. Ment. Deficiency*', 79. 22–31.

Leighton, A. H. 1974 'Social Disintegration and Mental Disorder' in Arieti, S. (ed.) *American Handbook of Psychiatry*, 2nd edn., Vol. ii, Basic Books Inc., New York, 411–23.

Levy, L., and Rowitz, L. 1973 *The Ecology of Mental Disorder*, Behavioral Publications, New York.

Lin, Tsung-Yi 1970 'Effects of Urbanization on Mental Health', *Ekistics*, 29 (172). 205—8.

Liverpool District Council 1973 Unpublished Social Survey Data, Liverpool District Council, Liverpool.

Macklin, R. 1972 'Mental Health and Mental Illness. Some Problems of Definition and Concept Formulation', *Philosophy of Science*, 39. 341—65.

Mazer, M. 1969 'Psychiatric Disorders in the General Practices of an Island', *Medical Care*, vii (5). 372—8.

McCulloch, J. W., and Philip, A. E. 1972 *Suicidal Behaviour*, Pergamon, Oxford.

—— Philip, A. E., and Carstairs, G. M. 1967 'The Ecology of Suicidal Behaviour', *Brit. J. Psychiat.* 113. 313—19.

McDonald, A. D. 1973, 'Physician Service in Montreal before Universal Health Insurance', *Medical Care*, xi (4). 269—86.

McGlashan, N. D. (ed.) 1972 *Medical Geography: Techniques and Field Studies*, Methuen & Co. Ltd., London.

McHarg, I. 1969 *Design with Nature*, Natural History Press, Garden City, New York.

McLean, E., and Tarnopolsky, A. 1977 'Noise, discomfort and mental health. A review of the socio-medical implications of disturbance by noise', *Psychol. Med.* 7 (1). 19—62.

Miller, W. B. 1975 'Psychological and psychiatric aspects of population problems' in Arieti, S. (ed.), *American Handbook of Psychiatry*, 2nd edn., Vol. vi, Basic Books Inc., New York, 978—1019.

Mintz, N. L., and Schwartz, D. T. 1964 'Urban Ecology and Psychosis', *Int. J. Soc. Psychiat.* 10. 101—18.

Monroe, R. R., Klee, G. D., and Brody, E. B., (eds.) 1967 *Psychiatric Epidemiology and Mental Health Planning*, Psychiatric Research Report No. 22, The American Psychiatric Association, Washington, D.C.

Moos, R. R. 1976 *The Human Context, Environmental Determinants of Behavior*, Wiley, New York.

—— and Insel, P. M. 1974 *Issues in Social Ecology: Human Milieus*, National Press Books, Palo Alto, Calif.

Morgan, H. G., Pocock H., and Pottle, S. 1975 'Urban Distribution of Non-fatal Deliberate Self-harm', *Brit. J. Psychiat.* 126. 319—28.

Morrill, R. L. 1966 *Historical Development of the Chicago Hospital System*, Chicago Regional Hospital Study Working Paper No. 1.2, Hospital Planning Council of Chicago, Chicago.

—— and Earickson, R. 1968 'Variations in The Character And Use of Hospital Services', *Health Services Research*, 3. reprinted in Bourne, L. S. (ed.), *Internal Structure of the City*, 1971, Oxford University Press, London, 391—9.

—— and Earickson, R. J. 1969 'Locational Efficiency of Chicago Hospitals: An Experimental Model', *Health Services Research*, 4. 128—41.

—— and Kelley, M. 1970 'The Simulation of Hospital Use and the Estimation of Locational Efficiency', *Geographical Analysis*, 2. 293—300.

—— Earickson, A. J., and Rees, P. 1970 'Factors Influencing Distances Traveled to Hospitals', *Economic Geography*, 46. 161—71.

Navarro, V. 1971 'The City and the Region', *American Behavioural Scientist*, 14 (6). 865—92.

Norman, J. C. 1969 *Medicine in the Ghetto*, Appleton–Century–Crofts, New York.

Oechsli, F., and Buechley, R. 1970 'Excess Mortality Associated with Three Los Angeles Hot Spells', *Environmental Research*, 3. 277–84.

Patno, M. E. 1954 'Geographic Study of Cancer Prevalence Within an Urban Population', *Public Health Reports*, 69, 8. 705–15.

—— 1960 'Mortality and Economic level in an Urban Area', *Public Health Reports*, 75. 841–51.

Perkoff, G. T., and Anderson, M. 1970 'Relationship Between Demographic Characteristics, Patient's Chief Complaint, and Medical Care Destination in an Emergency Room', *Medical Care*, 8. 4. 309–23.

Porteous, J. D. 1976 *Environment and Behaviour: Planning and Everyday Urban Life*, Addison-Wesley Publishing Co., Reading, Mass.

Pyle, G. F. 1971 *Heart Disease, Cancer and Stroke in Chicago: A Geographical Analysis with Facilities, Plans for 1980*, Department of Geography, Research Monograph No. 134, University of Chicago.

—— 1973 'Measles as an Urban Health Problem: The Akron Example', *Economic Geography*, 49. 344–56.

—— 1974 'The Geography of Health Care' in Hunter, J. M. (ed.) *The Geography of Health and Disease*, Department of Geography, Studies in Geography no. 6, University of North Carolina at Chapel Hill, 154–84.

—— 1976 'Introduction: Foundations to Medical Geography', *Econ. Geogr.* 52. 2. 95–102.

—— and Lashof, J. 1969 'The Geography of Disease and Death in the Two Chicagos' in De Visé, P. *et al.*, *Slum Medicine: Chicago's Apartheid Health System*, Chicago, University of Chicago Community and Family Study Center, 1–16.

—— and Rees, P. H. 1971 'Problems of Modeling Disease Patterns in Urban Areas: The Chicago Example', *Economic Geography*, 47. 475–88.

Redick, R. W., Goldsmith, H. F., and Unger, E. L. 1971 *1970 Census Data Used to Indicate Areas with Different Potentials For Mental Health and Related Problems*, National Institute of Mental Health, Mental Health Statistics, Methodology Series C, no. 3, U.S. Government Printing Office, Washington D.C.

Rees, P. H. 1967 *Movement and Distribution of Physicians in Metropolitan Chicago*, Chicago Regional Hospital Study, Working Paper No. 12.

Robertson, L. S. 1970 'On the Intraurban Ecology of Primary Care Physicians', *Soc. Sci. and Med.* 4. 227–38.

Rose, G. A. 1976 'Epidemiological Evidence for the Effects of the Urban Environment' in Harrison, G. A. and Gibson, J. B. (eds.), *Man in Urban Environments*, Oxford University Press, London, 205–16.

Rosenburg, C. E. 1962 *The Cholera Years*, University of Chicago Press, Chicago.

Rutter, M., and Madge, N. 1976 *Cycles of Disadvantage*, Heinemann, London.

Sainsbury, P. 1955 *Suicide in London*, Maudsley Monograph No. 1, Chapman & Hall, London.

Schmitt, R. C. 1966 'Density, Health and Social Disorganisation', *J. Amer. Inst. Plann.* 32. 38–40.

Schneider, J. B. 1967 'Measuring the Locational Efficiency of the Urban Hospital', *Health Services Research*, 2. 154–69.

—— and Symons, J. G. 1971 *Regional Health Facility System Planning: An Access Opportunity Approach*, Discussion Paper No. 8, Regional Science Research Institute, Philadelphia.

Schorr, A. L. 1963 *Slums and Social Insecurity*, U.S. Dept. of Health, Education, and Welfare, Washington, D. C.

Schroeder, C. W. 1942 'Mental Disorders in Cities', *American Journal of Sociology*, 48. 40–7.

Schuman, S. 1972 'Patterns of Urban Heat-wave Deaths and Implications for Prevention: Data from New York and St. Louis during July, 1966', *Environmental Research*, 5. 59–75.

Sells, S. B. (ed.) 1968 *The Definition and Measurement of Mental Health*, U.S. Government Printing Office, Washington, D.C.

Shannon, G. W., and Dever, G. E. 1974 *Health Care Delivery: Spatial Perspectives*, McGraw-Hill Book Co., New York.

Shannon, G. W., and Spurlock, C. W. 1976 'Urban Ecological Containers, Environmental Risk Cells, and the Use of Medical Services, *Economic Geography*, 52 (2). 171–80.

Shannon, G. W., Bashshur, R. L., and Metzner, C. A. 1969 'The Concept of Distance as a Factor in Accessibility and Utilization of Health Care', *Medical Care Review*, 26. 143–161.

—— Skinner, J. L., and Bashshur, R. L. 1973 Time and Distance: The Journey for Medical Care', *International Journal of Health Services*, 3. 2. 237–43.

—— Spurlock, C. W., and Skinner, J. L. 1975 'A Method for Evaluating the Geographic Accessibility of Health Services', *Professional Geographer*, 27. 1. 30–6.

Shepherd, M., Brown, A. C., and Kalton, G. W. 1966 *Psychiatric Illness in General Practice*, Oxford University Press, London.

Smith, C. J. 1977 'The Geography of Mental Health', *Commission on College Geography Publications. Resource Paper No. 76–4*, Association of American Geographers, Washington, D.C.

Smith, D. M. 1973 *The Geography of Social Well-Being in the United States*, McGraw-Hill Book Co., New York.

Snow, J. 1965 *Snow on Cholera: Being a Reprint of Two Papers*, Hafner Publishing Co., New York, originally published 1849–55.

Sparer, G., and Okada, L. M. 1974 'Chronic Conditions and Physician Use Patterns in Ten Urban Poverty Areas', *Medical Care*, 12. 7. 549–60.

Spitzer, R. L., and Endicott, J. 1975 'Computer Applications in Psychiatry' in Arieti, S. (ed.), *American Handbook of Psychiatry*, Vol. vi, 2nd edn., Basic Books Inc., New York, 811–39.

Srole, L. 1972 'Urbanization and Mental Health: Some Reformulation', *American Scientist*, 60. 576–83.

Stern, A. C. (ed.) *Air Pollution*, Academic Press, New York, 2nd edition.

Stockwell, E. G. 1963a 'A Critical Examination of the Relationship between Socio-Economic Status and Mortality', *American Journal of Public Health*, 53. 956–64.

—— 1963b 'Socio-Economic Status and Mortality', *Connecticut Health Bulletin*, 77. 10–13.

Stokols, D. 1972 'A Social-Psychological Model of Human Crowding Phenomena', *J. Amer. Inst. Plann.* 38. 72–83.

Struening, E., Rabkin, J. B., and Peck, H. B., 1970 'Context and Behaviour: A Social Area Analysis of New York City', in Brody, E. (ed.), *Behavior in New Environments*, Sage Publications, Beverly Hills, Calif., 203–15.

Suchman, E. A. 1964 'Sociomedical Variations Among Ethnic Groups', *Amer. J. Sociol.* 70. 319–31.

Taylor, Lord S., and Chave, S. 1964 *Mental Health and Environment*, Little, Brown, & Co., Boston.

Taylor, S. D. 1974 'The Geography and Epidemiology of Psychiatric Disorders in Southampton', unpublished Ph.D. thesis, University of Southampton.

Terris, M., and Monk, M. 1956 'Recent Trends in the Distribution of Physicians in Upstate New York', *American Journal of Public Health*, 46. 1. 585–91.

Webber, R. J. 1975 *Liverpool Social Area Study, 1971 Data: Final Report*, PRAG Technical Paper TP14, Centre for Environmental Studies, London.

Weiss, J. E., and Greenlick, M. R. 1970 'Determinants of Medical Care Utilization: The Effect of Social Class and Distance on Contacts with the Medical Care System', *Medical Care* 8. 6. 456–62.

White, E. L. 1968 'A Graphic Presentation of Age and Income Differentials in Selected Aspects of Morbidity, Disability and Utilization of Health Services', *Inquiry*, 5. 18–24.

Whitlock, F. A. 1973 'Suicide in England and Wales 1959–63', Part 2: 'London', *Psychological Medicine*, 3. 411–20.

Wilner, D., and Walkley, R. P. 1963 'Effects of Housing on Health and Performance', in Duhl, L. (ed.), *The Urban Condition*, Simon & Schuster, New York, 215–28.

Wing, J. K. 1971 'International Comparisons in the Study of Functional Psychoses', *British Medical Bulletin*, 27. 77–81.

–– 1976 'Mental Health in Urban Environments', in Harrison, G. A. and Gibson, J. B. (eds.), *Man in Urban Environments*, Oxford University Press, London, pp. 304–28.

–– and Bransby, E. R. (eds.) 1970 *Psychiatric Case Registers D.H.S.S. Statistical Report Series, No. 8*, H.M.S.O., London.

–– and Hafner, H. (eds.) 1973 *Roots of Evaluation: The Epidemiological Basis for Planning Psychiatric Services*, Oxford University Press for the Nuffield Provincial Hospitals Trust, London.

–– and Hailey, A. M. (eds.) 1972 *Evaluating a Community Psychiatric Register: The Camberwell Register 1964–1971*, Oxford University Press for the Nuffield Provincial Hospitals Trust, London.

Wood, C. M., Lee N., Luker, J. A., and Saunders, P. J. W., 1974 *The Geography of Pollution: A Study of Greater Manchester*, Manchester University Press, Manchester.

W.H.O. 1965 *International Statistical Classification of Disease, Injuries and Causes of Death*, 8th Revision, World Health Organization, Geneva.

–– 1973 *The International Pilot-Study of Schizophrenia*, World Health Organisation, Geneva.

Zlutnick, S., and Altman, I. 1972 'Crowding and Human Behaviour', In Wohlwill, J. F., and Carson, D. H. (eds.), *Environment and the Social Sciences: Perspectives and Applications*, American Psychological Association, Washington, D.C.

7

URBAN CRIME: A GEOGRAPHICAL PERSPECTIVE

David T. Herbert

Crime and delinquency qualify, on any criteria, as social problems and there is a considerable research literature which testifies to the links between urbanization, the growth of cities, and increasing crime rates (Scott, 1972). As regular annual increases in crime rates, especially those for violent offences, have become a feature of advanced western societies, so crime and delinquency have become regarded as urban phenomena. Although criminology is a long established field of study, crime remains one of the least understood of social problems, particularly in the key contexts of causality and prevention. There are many theories of criminal behaviour (see Mannheim, 1965; Taylor, Walton, and Young, 1973) but none of these has gained more than partial acceptance. Even the 'facts' of crime are of highly debated reliability. The representativeness and adequacy of official statistics, their method of collection, the variations in recording practice over time and space, and the diversity of interpretations, are all questioned by analysts of the statistical returns (Hindess, 1973).

Given the nature of the social problem and the reliance by the vast majority of researchers and analysts upon official sources of statistics, it was perhaps inevitable that the mainstream of criminological research should be in the logical positivist tradition. Laws and the socio-legal systems which produce them are, by and large, conservative and seek to protect the interests of 'society'. Crime is therefore seen as a 'deviant' form of behaviour seeking to disrupt existing order and consensus. Over time, the emphasis in positivist attempts to characterise the 'criminals' has shifted progressively from cruder forms of determinism, such as that associated with Lombroso (1968), to more systematic measurement of individual physiological traits and somato-typing (Sheldon, 1949; the Gluecks, 1950, 1952). Whilst these forms of positivism have concentrated upon factors 'internal' to individuals, others have pointed towards the conditioning circumstances in the local environments in which individuals were placed and to the acquired characteristics of the local group *per se*. This ecological tradition (Shaw and McKay, 1942; Morris, 1957) endures and provides one link with a geographical perspective on crime in an urban environment.

Most social theories relating to crime and delinquency have only an incidental interest in the local environment as a point of reference (Herbert, 1977b). Both social disorganization and anomie, for example, relate an individual's disposition towards criminal or delinquent behaviour to underlying structural conditions—the nature of the encompassing social system and the individual's place within it. Shaw and McKay's (1942) brand of ecological analysis had a strong empirical content, which has been continued in more recent studies (Lander, 1954; Chilton, 1964) and even in those sub-cultural investigations (Cohen, 1955;

Downes, 1966) which are linked with the Chicago tradition. Their main focus of attention however was the reference group in social rather than in geographical space. Although these relatively neglected themes of spatial ecology and the associated local environment fall most clearly within the remit of any geographical approach, it is increasingly evident that these cannot form the exclusive terms of reference for the geographer. As with other types of urban problem, the pattern of crime in itself is merely the spatial outcome of a complexity of social processes. It is in the processes at a variety of scales, from resource allocation systems of policing practices, labelling and intra-urban migration, that some of the more telling contributions to the study of urban crime may be developed. The more general movement away from a preoccupation with pattern and the local environment, which is identified by Hamnett (1979) has been paralleled in criminological research. For the self-styled 'new criminologists' (Taylor, Walton, and Young, 1973), the trend has been partly a reaction against the positivist tradition but is more explicitly a radical critique which is neo-Marxist in its interpretation, 'for us, as for Marx . . . deviance is normal in the sense that men are consciously involved in asserting their human diversity . . . the task is to create a society in which the facts of human diversity, whether personal, organic or social, are not subject to the power to criminalise' (Taylor, Walton, and Young, 1973, 282). This wider debate in criminology has parallels in changing geographical views on social theories (Eyles, 1974) and in the emergence of a radical geographical perspective (Peet, 1977). The radical critique has found some direct expression in the geography of crime in the exchange between Peet (1975, 1976), Harries (1975), and others. Peet's prescriptions for a radical geographical approach to urban crime are generalist in the sense that they could apply equally to many other kinds of social problems. Such problems are seen as results of the system of material production and the origins of the class struggle, 'The geography of crime is thus the predictable spatial manifestation of contradictions inherent in the capitalist mode of production' (Peet, 1976, p. 99). The value of this particular debate has been to remind geographers of the broader canvas against which any patterns of crime need to be viewed and to encourage a wider perspective for study.

Whilst there is evidence that geographers have shown awareness of the need for this wider perspective, there is as yet little empirical research aimed at this broader structural context. Herbert (1977b) identified what he termed the 'antecedents' of crime patterns as key areas for future research by geographers. These antecedents fall into several categories. They include, for example, what has been termed the social formation, that is the nature of the encompassing society with its values and traditions and the allocative systems by which resources and funds are distributed. All of these contribute to the persistence of societal inequalities and to the occurrence of localized concentrations of disadvantage. For crime studies, the socio-legal system is an 'antecedent' in its role as the critical structural element from which definitions of criminal behaviour, sanctions on such deviance, and statistical records of crime and delinquency proceed. Nearer the ground, police activities at the point of contact with law breakers strongly influence any pattern of urban crime which may emerge.

Whilst the possibilities of research into these antecedents of spatial patterns of crime can be recognized, they so far remain largely untested. There is the radical critique referred to above, there are more general studies of urban allocative systems (Boddy, 1976; Gray, 1976) but most reported research has focused upon the spatial outcomes of criminal behaviour, upon patterns and processes in the local environment. It is upon these latter studies that this discussion of the evidence for a developing geographical approach to urban crime must therefore concentrate. The intention is to examine the ecological tradition as it has been developed in the criminological literature and to test some of its main hypotheses. A second objective is to consider developments in the analysis of what is termed the 'offence-prone' environment, that is those parts of the city in which *offences* are most likely to occur. Finally, with examples drawn from a research project based upon Cardiff, the scope of spatial analyses of offender data will be analysed and the concept of the 'problem estate' will be examined.

The Ecological Tradition

Of the various traditions within criminological research, that which contains the most explicit links with a spatial analysis of urban crime is found in the ecological mode of analysis. Examples of intra-urban analysis are found in the nineteenth century, but it was the work of Shaw and McKay (1942) which gave form to this type of investigation. Although much of this work was not conducted by geographers *per se*, the relevance of a spatial perspective was accepted by its practitioners. Both areal and ecological analyses were evident, the former concerned with the distribution of offences and offenders, the latter with the relationships between crime rates and environmental measures. These analyses relied heavily upon official crime statistics and also upon other published sources of aggregate data, notably the Census. In using crime statistics, ecological studies have usually, though not consistently, distinguished between offence rates and offender rates. Offence rates, relating to where offences occur, pinpoint 'prone environments'; offender rates, relating to where offenders live, identify those population groups from which known offenders are drawn. As ecological analysis rests upon the calculation of rates for small areas, it is vulnerable to the 'ecological fallacy' and other problems of statistical association (Gordon, 1967). Whilst technical procedures to improve the quality of interpretation do exist (Blalock, 1964), the limitations of this scale of analysis must always be acknowledged.

The 'traditional' areal hypotheses which emerged from the work of Shaw and McKay were few and simple. They observed that both offence and offender rates were higher amongst population groups in central zones of the city and decreased progressively towards peripheral zones; the gradient principle replicated this zonal generalization. More recent American studies (Schmid, 1960) have tended to confirm this 'model' in general terms, though studies elsewhere in the world have provided less support. Basically any spatial pattern of crime reflects its 'antecedents', the social formation and the general urban structure which emanates from it. To the extent that these antecedents differ, so will the generalized spatial distribution of crime differ. In Britain, for example, a larger governmental commitment towards public-sector housing has led to fundamental changes in the arrangement of urban residential areas. Urban population groups have been redistributed from inner cities to peripheral estates and have taken their behavioural characteristics with them. The distribution of offender rates in the typical British city (Herbert, 1977a) now shows clusters of high scores in both central and peripheral locations.

Generalizations upon the spatial distribution of crime at a city-wide scale will vary with time, place, and culture-context. Such generalizations are of interest, but have limited practical value or meaning.

Whilst the areal hypotheses were derived mechanically by mapping crime statistics and generalizing upon the observed patterns, the ecological hypotheses were more directly concerned with the question of the relationship between crime rates and the urban environment in which they occurred. In a series of analyses using crime and census variables derived for small areas, the ecologists employed a variety of statistical techniques to measure this relationship. Shaw and McKay (1942) suggested that the main correlates of delinquency rates in Chicago were substandard housing, poverty, foreign-born population, and levels of mobility; some studies before this and a great many since have identified statistical groupings of a similar kind. Schmid (1960) used a multivariate analysis based upon a large number of variables, and listed low social cohesion, weak family life, low socio-economic status, physical deterioration, mobility, and personal disorganization as the social characteristics of crime areas in Seattle. Wallis and Maliphant (1967) relied upon the simpler procedure of examining pairwise correlations but suggested links between delinquency rates and over-crowding, substandardness, population decline, non-white residents, and low socio-economic status in London. Most of these analyses of aggregate data would acknowledge that a statistical association is not necessarily a causal one and have looked at more general hypotheses to provide explanations. For Shaw and McKay, for example, social disorganization theory provided the key and although criticized (Mays, 1963), it did find recent support in the work by Baldwin and Bottoms (1976). For purposes of discussion, three ecological hypotheses will be identified and two of these tested with empirical data.

The first hypothesis, for which no further empirical evidence will be offered here, is that proposed by Lander (1954) as a result of his study of Baltimore. Lander used a number of correlational and regression techniques to analyse associations between delinquency rates and seven social variables (education, rent, overcrowding, non-white, substandardness, foreign-born, and owner-occupance). His hypothesis, from the results of this analysis, was that the concept of anomie was a valid explanatory basis for the incidence of delinquency in Baltimore. Lander based this hypothesis upon the observed links between high delinquency rates and percent non-white (positive) and level of owner-occupance (negative) and, also, from observation of the nature of an area's ethnic mix. Some debate has been generated by Lander's findings and methodology (Chilton, 1964; Gordon, 1967), but whether a complex sociological theory such as that of anomie can be proven or otherwise by ecological analysis is doubtful and this particular hypothesis has not been explicitly supported in replicative research.

A second hypothesis and one which has found most general support in ecological analyses is that of the effect of 'poor environment'. Statistical studies using indicators of built environmental disadvantage such as substandard housing, and social problems such as unemployment and poverty have demonstrated their correspondence with high rates of delinquency. There is ample evidence that simplistic interpretations of links between bad housing and crime are misplaced but correlates with measures of bad social environment are more persistent. Table 7.1 provides an example of evidence supportive of the poor environment hypothesis. These figures are drawn from a detailed statistical analysis of Cardiff data (Herbert, 1977a) in which, for the regression part of the study which is reported here, delinquency rate formed the dependent variable and sixteen independent variables were derived from census data. Before the regression analysis was applied, the sixteen independent variables were subjected to a varimax rotation in factor analysis and the derived factor scores formed the input to regression. This procedure has the advantage of ensuring the statistical independence of the 'independent' variables. As Table 7.1 shows, step one, identifying the most closely linked independent variable, designated a factor positively associated with unemployed males and overcrowding, and negatively associated with owner-occupance and high social status. From the evidence in this table, high delinquency rates occur in those parts of the city that suffer poor built environments, as indicated by lack of amenities and fixed baths, and poor social environments, as indicated by high levels of unemployment, of shared dwellings and overcrowding. As the ordering of factors in Table 7.1 suggests, deficiencies in the social environment are of greatest significance and these findings, generally supportive of the poor environment hypothesis, are typical of many research findings.

The third hypothesis is of more recent origin, though some of the earlier evidence can be discerned in Lander's study of Baltimore (1954). Baldwin and Bottoms (1976), with some reference to an earlier concept developed by Rex and Moore (1967) proposed a 'housing class' hypothesis on the basis of their empirical study of Sheffield. This hypothesis suggests that crime rates are lower in owner-occupier tenure groups than in rented tenure groups. On examining the proposition that this variation was simply a reflection of social class differences, Baldwin and Bottoms found that, for adult male offenders, the link between tenure group and offender rates remained even when socio-economic status differences were controlled. They concluded that in considering the pattern of adult male offender rates, 'It is essential to bear in mind type of tenure area in addition to social class' (Baldwin and Bottoms, 1976, p. 111).

It was possible to test this hypothesis using data for Cardiff in 1966 and 1971. Using the procedure adopted by Baldwin and Bottoms (1976), enumeration districts in Cardiff were classified as owner-occupied, local-authority-rented, private-rented, or mixed. This procedure involved, for designation of the first three categories, the requirement that over one half of households should fall into the particular tenure group. Table 7.2 shows the distribution of mean offender rates for three sub-groups by the four classes of tenure type in Cardiff. In each case it is clear that offender rates in the owner occupier group are well below city averages and are substantially below those recorded for other tenure groups. Highest offender rates occur in the private-rented sector (though it should be noted that the number of enumeration districts in this group is small) and are also relatively high on local-authority estates.

Table 7.1
Delinquency rates and social variables: a regression analysis (Cardiff, 1971)

Regression step	Factor	High Loadings	Standard Error	Cumulative R^2	Regression Coefficient	Standard Error
1	3	+ overcrowding unemployed males – owner occupiers Social Class 1 + 2	1·72	·15	·71	·16
2	5	+ unemployed males foreign born	1·60	·27	·71 ·64	·15 ·15
3	2	+ no amenities no fixed bath shared dwellings – Social Class 1 + 2	1·51	·36	·71 ·64 ·54	·14 ·14 ·14

N.B. The independent variables are varimax scores from Factor Analysis of the sixteen socio-economic-demographic measures derived from the Census.

Table 7.2
Offender rates* by housing (tenure) class in Cardiff

1966	council	rented	owner-occupied	mixed	all districts	overall S.D.**
No. of EDs	28	6	74	11	119	
Male 10–19	29	45	18	33	23	20
Female 10–19	5	50	5	12	8	24
Male 15–19	46	60	27	34	34	37
1971						
No. of EDs	28	14	64	13	119	
Male 10–19	40	59	24	39	33	29
Female 10–19	11	13	6	12	9	11
Male 15–19	63	90	35	66	51	47

* Offender rates = number of known juvenile offenders per 1,000 population at risk.

** S.D. = standard deviation

On the straightforward comparison of mean offender rates, therefore, the Cardiff evidence is supportive of that reported for Sheffield, it remains, however, to test the independence of the relationship from socio-economic status. Table 7.3 records the results of testing the partial correlation coefficients among five variables, three of which described tenure groups and two the social-class composition of the enumeration districts. Table 7.3 does reveal some limited support for the 'housing class' hypothesis. At the 5 per-cent level, the correlation between low delinquency rates and owner-occupance remains significant when social class differences are controlled. This is true of three of the offender rates, but none of these relationships remains significant at the 1 per-cent level and neither of the two rented tenure groups holds significant correlations with offender rates when social class is controlled. The limited-housing-class hypothesis which can be supported from this statistical analysis, is that owner-occupiership appears to have some influence upon offender rates regardless of social-class variations. This influence, by implication, is one which deters criminal behaviour but although plausible reasons could be formulated for this—ownership of property places the interests of people on the side of maintenance of law and order, such areas are more benevolently viewed by law enforcers—these can only be conjectural from evidence at this scale of analysis.

Table 7.3
Partial correlations: offender rates/tenure.social class

		1. 4	2. 5	3. 5
a. all offenders	10—19	—·20*	·06	·11
b. male ofenders	10—19	—·20*	·00	—·04
c. female offenders	10—19	—·12	·15	—·02
d. male offenders	15—19	—·22*	·08	·08

* significant at the 5 per-cent level.
1. Owner occupiers   2. Council tenants   3. Private renters
4. High social class   5. Low social class

Ecological analysis, though possessing a useful role in identifying the contextual circumstances in which crime and delinquency are likely to occur and therefore suggesting ameliorative measures, does suffer severe problems in the extension of statistically measured associations into theoretical constructs. Taylor (1973) was critical of ways in which ecologists had yielded to the temptation to progress from observations on characteristics of urban life to theories, which view offenders as products of particular local environmental features. What is not understood is how these environments look to the offenders themselves. The Chicago ecologists saw dereliction, diversity, and transience as underpinnings of delinquency, Fyvel (1961) suggested that modernity, uniformity, and stability had similar effects. Both were objective analyses of local environments, more significant may have been the subjective images of youths themselves. Again, it is critically important to remember that whilst local environment may provide clues or pointers, it is in itself merely one expression of the encompassing societal structure which provides the broader frame of reference.

Identifying the Offence-Prone Environment

One of the more promising potential avenues through which geographers may develop their contribution to criminological research lies in the detailed analysis of offence—as opposed to offender—patterns. As the Brantinghams (1975a, pp. 11–12) recently suggested, 'The empirical study of crime is approaching its two hundredth year. One of the most interesting current thrusts in criminology returns us to concerns which marked the early phases of the systematic study of crime, namely the distribution of crime in space and what that implies for crime prevention.' This concern for detailed study of criminal behaviour in its environmental context finds support in Newman's (1972) essay on 'defensible space' and the possibility of prevention through design. Some of the 'new' ideas have pedigrees in the ecological tradition and in architectural determinism, but are none the less capable of restatement and qualification.

There are two broad areas of central interest to geographers in the context of offence patterns. One involves the characteristics of the urban environment within which offences occur. These characteristics are primarily physical; the qualities of design, layout, and accessibility of buildings, but may also include ways in which local space is controlled and observed. Studies of the urban environment in these terms have sought to assess the extent to which opportunities for crime are offered and to consider changes in design which might diminish the vulnerability of particular localities. The second area of interest concerns the behavioural features of the offence environment. How far do offenders travel in order to commit offences? What paths do they follow? How do offenders perceive their opportunity environment? How do victims perceive the hazards of their local environments and react to them?

Oscar Newman (1972) was instrumental in focusing attention upon environment as a conditioner of offence behaviour. As Mawby (1977a) has indicated, Jane Jacobs (1961) initially produced some of the ideas, such as the relevance of residents' attitudes toward control, though her work was largely impressionistic. Newman produced empirical evidence from surveys of American public-housing projects to support his contention that areas will be generally well defended if they are visible to possible witnesses, if a community spirit is developed whereby neighbours are encouraged to guard neutral territory, if design is such that a constant stream of potential witnesses is present and if private territory is clearly demarcated, physically or symbolically (Newman, 1972). Whilst Newman's methodology and the vagueness of his concepts have been criticized (Mawby, 1977a), his work has played a part in rekindling interest in studies of offences rather than of offenders.

Several recent studies have examined the offence environment at a micro-level. Pablant and Baxter (1975) tested three main hypotheses related to the incidence of school vandalism: that low vandalism rates would typify schools with high levels of aesthetic appeal and good maintenance, with a location in diverse and active neighbourhoods, and with 'visible' sites. From the empirical evidence available to them, Pablant and Baxter were able to support these hypotheses. In another study, Leather and Matthews (1973) examined the local circumstances under which vandalism appeared to thrive and their findings, similarly, gave support to Newman's general ideas.

More critical, however, have been Mawby's comments (1977a, 1977b) derived from an empirical study of Sheffield. Using data for four estates, labelled council housing (CH) and council flats (CF) with high (H) or low (L) *offender* rates, it was found that when rates per 1,000 for residential *offences* were calculated, a contrasted pattern (CHH 85.1; CHL 23.7; CFH 29.9; CFL 20.2) appeared. The fact that the highest offence rate was recorded for low-rise housing contradicted one of Newman's central ideas. More importantly, Mawby noted that Newman had failed to clarify some of his concepts; individual components of the built environment could, for example, have more than one role, dependent upon the ways in which they were perceived by offenders. A garden could in itself present opportunities for theft, it could however also act as a barrier to the house or even diminish the visibility factor for the burglar. In another reported investigation, Mawby (1977b) obtained data on twenty-seven telephone kiosks in Sheffield which had above average vandalism rates. His evidence suggested that a number of available hypotheses for high rates of vandalism, such as adjacency to high-rise flats could be discarded, but that when levels of usage were controlled for, a relationship did exist between visibility and vandalism. Mawby did therefore, support one of the defensible-space concepts, but again commented upon its ambiguity. Greater use of public space provides more 'witnesses' and increases its visibility, but it also provides more potential offenders. Visibility may have protected kiosks in Sheffield, but those which were most publicly sited had higher vandalism rates simply through greater usage.

Offender behaviour has received an increasing amount of research attention in recent years, though the theme is, as yet, not well developed. Suttles (1968) and Turner (1969) both examined the distances travelled to commit offences and suggested that a distance-decay feature was evident. Other studies (Haring, 1972) have investigated other characteristics of this 'journey-to-crime' pattern. Although Scarr (1972) hypothesized a cycle through which a burglar might move in planning and carrying out a burglary, there is limited evidence of the ways in which offenders perceived their environments. Reppetto (1974) questioned a sample of convicted burglars and listed apparent affluence, lack of police control, ease of access, and isolation as the main desiderata. Carter (1974) produced empirical evidence that criminals discriminated amongst areas on the bases of familiarity and excitement. P. L. and P. J. Brantingham (1975a, 1975b) studied relationships between residential burglary and urban form in more objective ways and speculated that the border blocks of definable neighbourhoods were particularly vulnerable targets.

The type of study discussed in this section is less concerned with what 'produces' the offender, than with what 'produces' the particular location at which he commits his offence. Here, at least, most of the relevant factors are found in the local environment itself rather than in the broader framework of societal structure. Research has primarily sought to isolate the relevant facets of the built environment but has also recognized that social usage of these facets and the social values attached to them have central relevance. What these facets are and how they interact with offender behaviour are questions which deserve closer attention from geographers and other social scientists.

Patterns of Offender Residence

Much research in the ecological tradition has been concerned with patterns of known offender residence. This research has identified distinctive concentrations of offenders in particular districts of the city and has offered tentative theories on relationships between the offender and his urban environment. To a large extent this relationship is unreal; local environment is merely an intervening variable between the individual and the social formation of which he is part, and most researchers have acknowledged this fact. It remains a possibility, however, that part at least of the explanation for the uneven spatial distribution of urban offenders is a function of the local circumstances. Whilst the social formation produces general conditions of inequality and disadvantage and contributes towards more particular conditions of personal individual circumstance, the local environment or 'neighbourhood' retains significance on several counts. It contains, for example, the immediate 'cues' to which the individual responds and, in particular, it houses some of his most significant reference groups. Areal analyses have consistently shown that known offenders are highly clustered in particular neighbourhoods in ways which cannot be explained by objective social indicators (Herbert, 1976; see also Murray and Boal, 1979). Again, because of these typical local concentrations, there tend to emerge 'problem areas' for which ameliorative measures as part of an area policy may be an urgent need. The contention is, therefore, that whilst broader research avenues are acknowledged, there is some residual value in exploring the offender/local environment relationship. Two possibilities are examined here. The first, which proved largely negative, was concerned with analysis of offender distribution at a micro-scale; the second, which was more positive, investigated a problem area as a social milieu.

Distribution of individual offenders

Whilst many researchers have obtained detailed information on individual known offenders, areal hypotheses have typically been formed for aggregate data sets using rates for small areas such as wards or census tracts. There are of course constraints of confidentiality on the identification of individuals and their precise addresses which has influenced the way in which research has proceeded and results reported. For some districts in Cardiff, however, data sets on individual offenders were collected and although, in graphical presentation, locations of individual residence have here been deliberately blurred to prevent identification, sufficient detail remains for *within* neighbourhood patterns to be observed.

These individual patterns for two 'delinquency areas' in Cardiff (Herbert, 1977a), derived from data for one year, are presented in Figures 7.1 and 7.2. Each figure is divided into three maps, the first of which shows the basic distribution, the second shows a 'generalized' pattern obtained from use of a simple centrographic technique, and the third investigates some of the possible and 'real' linkages among individual offenders. The basic distributions (Figures 7.1a and 7.2a) show that there is an uneven spread of offenders over the two estates; the patterns mainly are composed of clusters around particular streets. Figures 7.1b and 7.2b generalize upon the form of these point patterns. After super-

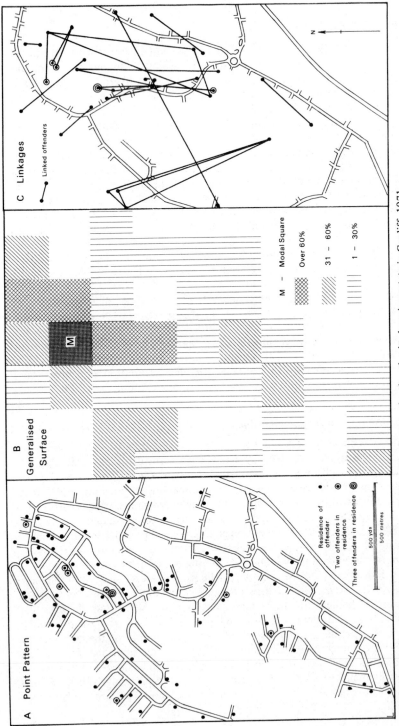

Figure 7.1 Distribution of known juvenile offenders in a post-war local authority housing estate in Cardiff, 1971.
A. Point pattern distribution by residence. B. Generalized surface using the modal square technique. C. Known linkages amongst offenders.
Figure 7.2 (*see opposite*) Distribution of known juvenile offenders in an inter-war local authority estate in Cardiff, 1971. A. Point pattern distribution by residence. B. Generalized surface using the modal square technique. C. Known linkages amongst offenders *and* hypothesized groupings from cluster analysis.

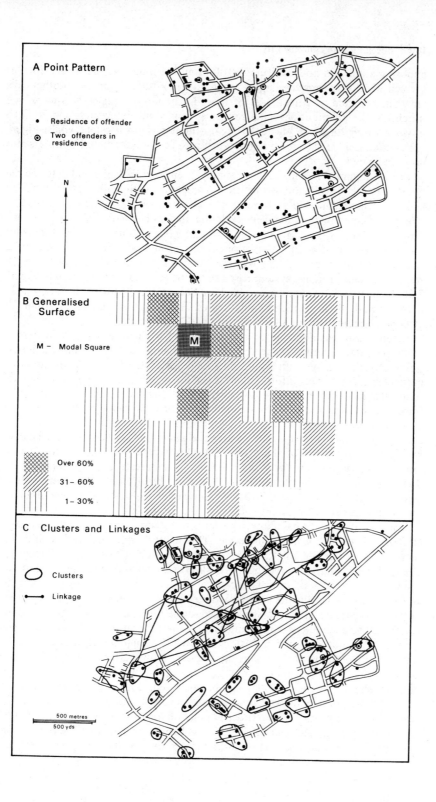

A Point Pattern

- • Residence of offender
- ⊚ Two offenders in residence

N

B Generalised Surface

M – Modal Square

M

Over 60%

31– 60%

1– 30%

C Clusters and Linkages

⬭ Clusters

•—• Linkage

500 metres

500 yds

imposing a uniform grid over the distribution, the modal square is identified as the cell which contains the largest number of points. Occurrences in other cells are then depicted as percentages of those in the modal square. This technique simplifies the distributions and confirms their general features; Figure 7.1b shows a strong 'regional' cluster in the northern part of the estate, whilst Figure 7.2b contains a modal square in the north-west sector but emphatic clusters also occur elsewhere.

So far, Figures 7.1 and 7.2 have simply been used to depict and describe the point patterns. The hypothesis which was examined with the use of Figures 7.1c and 7.2c was that *within* each estate the social networks of offenders would be strongly affected by their detailed residential locations. Figure 7.2c, for example, shows the form of associations which should exist within the estate if distance was the sole criterion for interaction. Each offender residence was allocated a grid co-ordinate reference and was used as the input to a cluster analysis (the Ward hierarchic grouping system based upon the error sum of squares). In Figure 7.2c the initial 167 input observations have been reduced to fifty clusters, which, if the hypothesis is correct, should correspond with local 'gangs' or groups of offenders occupying particular territories within the estate.

Information was available to test the reality of these groups or clusters in social interaction terms. Some data in the file indicated actual links amongst offenders, specifically, with whom they were associated in the commission of a particular offence. This information on real linkages was by no means complete. Associates in the offence were not always named and some names could not be traced to addresses, but it does provide sufficient evidence to show that the initial hypothesis was not tenable. Those links which are shown in Figure 7.2c are rarely contained within the marked clusters and associates are found in widely separated parts of the estate. Clusters were not derived in Figure 7.1c but the linkages clearly show that distance at this scale is not a major factor. Some 'groups' are widely dispersed, others are highly localized, whilst others combine both of these characteristics. Households with more than one offender sometimes appear to have some focality in the delinquent network.

The Cardiff data set has allowed patterns of offender residence to be depicted and considered at an individual scale. This in itself is a rare quality and the exercise has confirmed what the few comparable studies have suggested (Morris, 1957), namely that there are highly localized clusters within estates. The estate shown in Figure 7.1 was 'known' to contain particular black spots by its residents and by agencies within the city and these did in fact emerge in the objective mapping. There are of course special hazards at this scale of analysis. In a data set limited to delinquents, for example, the detailed location of the total population at risk is not known and clusters of offenders could merely reflect concentrations of youths in the relevant age groups. It was clear from this analysis, however, that the simple hypothesis that location and distance affected groupings of offenders at this scale, could not be sustained. Spatial analysis *per se* may provide some pointers towards processes of social interaction but unless allied to direct survey analysis of the offender population, of their activities, contacts and images, it is unlikely to lead to clear comprehension of the processes underlying the patterns, or indeed of the patterns themselves. For the youth in an estate, residence is but one spatial point of reference. There are other shared points of conflux, such as school and club, which are strongly relevant to patterns of human association. Again, non-spatial parameters are obviously important, evidence from the Cardiff data showed a clear banding of associates by age groups. In conclusion, therefore, the individual data do reveal localized clustering within estates—the delinquent groups, however, are not closely coincident with small territories within the area; and it is residence within the estate *per se*, with its associated sharing of local facilities and institutions, which seems to provide the most relevant spatial reference group.

Problem estates

Having pointed to the significance of the residential *area*, a second hypothesis can be formed in relation to its role. This is that particular residential areas within a city, by virtue of reputations and an ethos which they have acquired over time, are the most likely to foster the continuance of a delinquent tradition. Research experience relating to the emergence and persistence of problem areas (Damer, 1974) and to attempts by social geographers to demonstrate a 'neighbour-hood effect' (Johnston, 1976) are relevant to this hypothesis which will be tested by reference to one estate in Cardiff.

Urban criminologists have consistently verified the fact that, from official statistics, both known offenders and offences are disproportionately concentrated in particular parts of the city. Observations of this kind were made upon Liver-pool in the mid-nineteenth century (Tobias, 1976), were formalized into the delinquency area concept in Chicago in the 1930s (Shaw and McKay, 1942), and have continued to find confirmation in recent studies (Baldwin and Bottoms, 1976). Whilst many past studies have characterized delinquency areas as part of the inner city, a more recent British phenomenon has been the emergence of comparable areas in peripheral urban locations. These peripheral areas inevitably coincide with large local-authority estates, most typically of inter-war construction. Baldwin (1975) suggests that in Sheffield the continuing problem of criminality remained, for the most part, on those estates built in the 1930s or earlier; these are the 'problem estates' and are so regarded by local population, local agencies, social workers, and police. Police attitudes may contribute to the persistence of such areas in that they are likely to patrol most intensively local-ities where they *expect* to find trouble-makers. Other studies (Wilson, 1963; Damer, 1974) have suggested a number of conditions which may lead to the emergence of such problem estates. These include the role of the local authority as a rehousing agent, the self-selection process which occurs amongst tenants in respect of particular estates, and the 'labelling' process by which an estate acquires or reinforces its bad image.

The Ely estate, which in 1971 comprised 4,200 dwelling units and housed over 14,000 people, qualifies for the description of a problem area on a number of counts. It was, on the basis of mapping offender residences from several data sources (see Herbert, 1976, 1977a), a delinquency area. It possesses a poor reputation within Cardiff, as will be shown, and the emergence of this reputation can be traced over time. Land for the new estate was acquired in 1920 and by 1929, 3,412 dwellings had been completed. A chronic problem was the lack of facilities and the estate remains poorly served in this respect. Largely as a result of changing standards over time, the houses compare unfavourably with those on newer estates; many of the first-phase dwelling units in Ely, for example, have no inside toilet. First occupants of Ely were drawn from the crowded area of the inner city, principally from the districts of Grangetown, Splott, and Canton, These people were often Catholics and from the most substandard parts of the old city. 'They were not "Chapel" or "Church" and attended Catholic schools. They had strange names that all began with O' or Mac', they belonged to large families, they tended to be poorly dressed and were dangerous if provoked. Their homes were often the rent collector's nightmare, and occasionally poverty would drive them to bizarre behaviour' (Denning, 1973). There was a record of minor gang warfare in these early days, and a well-documented incident of vandalism involving newly planted trees. Ely, then, grew with problems, some were the production of inadequacies of design and provision, others were imported with sections of its early population. It has a reputation as a problem estate which matches its modern high relative rates of delinquency, 'Ely, one of the largest housing estates in Cardiff, does not have a lot going for it. It has poor social facilities for young and old, not enough open space, traffic problems and poor shopping. Among the key problems facing the district are truancy, vandalism and delinquency' (South Wales Echo, 1975).

This historical material provides partial support for the hypothesis concerning delinquent traditions in particular estates; more direct evidence was obtained from a direct survey of residential areas in Cardiff (Herbert, 1976). Respondents drawn from six contrasted areas in the city were asked to name any three Cardiff districts to which they would definitely not wish to move. As Figure 7.3 shows, Ely was by far the least favoured of the council estates with 46 per cent of respondents including it in their nominations. Amongst respondents from the four low-income areas in the sample, excluding Ely, nominations rates for Ely ranged from 51 to 74 per cent. When asked to give reasons for their nomination of the single least desired area, comments made in respect of Ely related to its remoteness, the fact that it was 'very rough' and 'dirty' and, for one at least, it was a 'little Chicago'. Ely is now clearly stigmatized as a problem estate in Cardiff, though it is of course in no way comparable to the bad areas of places like Glasgow and Belfast. Social processes mentioned earlier, such as housing policy and tenant selection, are likely contributory mechanisms and although there is a reasonable level of satisfaction amongst Ely residents, to outside eyes the image is bad and observable behaviour is confirmatory (see also Damer, 1974).

The next question which arises in relation to the hypothesis for this section concerns the 'climate of opinion' within Ely and the significance this might have in understanding its high modern levels of delinquent behaviour. To probe this question, further data from the Cardiff survey are used and another council estate, Mynachdy, is used as a basis for comparison. Mynachdy, from official statistics, had a very low delinquency rate and, from Figure 7.3, did not figure prominently in nominations for 'undesirable' residential areas. Anecdotal evidence from the survey suggested that it was one of the most desirable council estates and possessed a good 'image'.

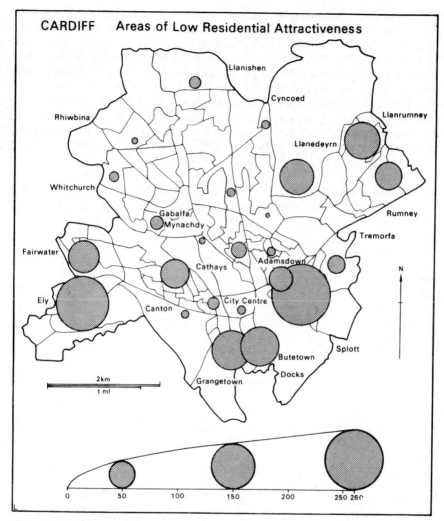

Figure 7.3 Residential areas of Cardiff nominated on the basis of low residential attractiveness.

Table 7.4 summarizes information obtained from questions designed to investigate the personal social environments of the two estates (Herbert, 1975). Table 7.4A shows responses to questions on ways in which people perceived their estates as places where offences occur and as places where offenders live, in both cases relative to other Cardiff districts. Results show strong contrasts between the two estates with, in Ely, a considerable awareness of the bad image of the district. Table 7.4B explores parental attitudes towards education as a criterion for assessing good, positive home influence. It is clear that if interest in education and schooling is a measure, Ely parents provide a poor social environment for their children. They are little involved in school activities, have low educational aspirations for their children, and 80 per cent of their children who had left school had done so without formal qualifications. Table 7.4C compares parental control on the two estates by comparing stated responses to misbehaviour (see Herbert, 1976 for further detail). Ely parents make much less use of verbal sanctions and more use, markedly so in the case of truancy, of the institution as a surrogate for parental responsibility. Finally in Table 7.4D, when parents were presented with a checklist and asked to define serious misbehaviour, it is clear that, at the margins of right and wrong, Ely parents tended

Table 7.4

Two estates compared

A. Perceptions of estate as (a) place where offenders live
                         (b) place where offences occur

| | Mynachdy | | Ely | |
	a	b	a	b
much better	14	16	0	0
better	38	40	6	4
average	45	41	53	56
worse	1	1	33	31
much worse	0	0	1	3
don't know	2	2	7	6

B. Parental involvement in education

| | Mynachdy | Ely | | Mynachdy | Ely |
	attend evening classes			have contact with school	
yes	35	20	very much	22	1
no	65	80	some	35	32
			not much	25	32
			none	18	35

| | Mynachdy | Ely | | Mynachdy | Ely |
	aspirations for children			actual qualifications	
none				59	83
C.S.E.	13	36		1	0
Trade	7	7		24	8
G.C.E./O.N.D.	10	40		12	7
A level/H.N.D.	0	2		1	1
College/Degree	70	15		3	1

C. Sanctions used

| | Mynachdy | | Ely | |
	generally	for truancy	generally	for truancy
physical punishment	19	11	21	10
verbal	51	53	23	13
deprive of privileges	28	13	43	3
institutional	6	20	15	49
ignore	8	3	21	21

D. Acts which would be reported

	Mynachdy	Ely
drinking under age	36	47
taking money from a child	50	40
taking from school	57	31
not paying on bus	38	17
damaging public property	80	73
taking drugs	91	94
taking from cars	82	85
taking from shops	88	92
attacking strangers	89	97

N.B. All figures in Table 7.4 are percentages: chi-squared tests on the original data showed significant differences between the two areas on these tabulations. (See Herbert, 1976, for more detailed statistical analysis.)

to have more lax standards and codes of behaviour. At all points in this table which tests a number of attitudes indicated by the research literature as related to the incidence of delinquent behaviour, Ely compares unfavourably with Mynachdy.

There is sufficient evidence to suggest that the hypothesis nominated for this section can be sustained. Although the historical evidence is fragmentary, there are numerous clues to the understanding of Ely's early acquisition of a poor reputation and its persistence over time. The survey data which have been used are strongly indicative of a general (though not of course universal) set of values within the estate which underpins its measurably high rates of delinquents and delinquent behaviour. The comparison with Mynachdy is pertinent in that by many objective criteria, such as occupational characteristics and demographic structure, the two estates are similar. There are differences in the incidence of delinquency however, and there are related differences in the personal social environments.

Conclusions

This essay has considered the level of awareness of the spatial qualities of urban crime which exists in the criminological literature and has explored a number of ways in which geographical approaches might be developed. There is in the literature both a set of simple spatial generalizations, developed in the context of the western city, and a group of ecological hypotheses which can, with the caveats accepted at this scale of analysis, still find verification in modern studies. The two ecological hypotheses tested in this study, relating to 'poor environment' and 'housing class', both found qualified support. Aggregate analyses of data sets on both offences and offenders will doubtless continue and will fulfil a useful though limited role in the study of urban crime.

Whilst these more 'traditional' exercises in spatial ecology are unlikely to provide significant advances along research frontiers, the thrust of much recent research is that the encompassing of a behavioural perspective may provide important new insights. In this chapter it was demonstrated that a simple 'spatial' hypothesis based upon place of residence of individual offenders could not be supported. It was suggested, however, that if this detail of spatial data could be matched with social data relating to the spatial behaviour, attitudes, and images of individuals, the results could have been rewarding. At the neighbourhood scale of analysis, the successful hypothesis relating to the problem estate indicated the reality of a 'neighbourhood effect' and the potential link between personal social environments and delinquent behaviour. Similarly, in the promising research areas of the offence-prone environment, details of design, built form, accessibility, and offence-commission behaviour are likely to provide good avenues for progress.

All of this centres on the quest to authenticate a particularly geographical approach to the study of urban crime, and the contention is that this can be shown and that 'space' does matter. In itself of course this is an over-restricted perspective. On the one hand, urban crime, perhaps more than any other single theme, has demonstrated the need for an interdisciplinary view. If there is a definable 'geographical' view, it is still best seen as part of that broader framework. Again, as acknowledged at the outset, the fact of urban crime is the product of complex processes and local environment is but one outcome of a 'system'. The facts that local concentrations of urban crime exist and that urban environment is the immediate interface for offenders and offences justifies continuing research in this mode. The value of such research must however, always be seen in the context of the wider structural origins of many urban problems and indeed of many disadvantaged individuals in urban environments.

References

Baldwin, J. 1975 'Urban criminality and the problem estate', *Local Government Studies*, 1. 12–20.

— — and Bottoms, A. E. 1976 *The Urban Criminal*, Tavistock, London.

Blalock, H. M. 1964 *Causal Inferences in Non-experimental Research*. Univ. of North Carolina Press, Chapel Hill.

Boddy, M. J. 1976 'The structure of mortgage finance: building societies and the British social formation', *Transactions, Institute of British Geographers*, N.S. 1. 58–71.

Brantingham, P. J., and Brantingham, P. L. 1975a 'The spatial patterning of burglary', *Howard Journal*, xiv. 11–23.

— — 1975b 'Residential burglary and urban form', *Urban Studies*, 12. 273–84.

Carter, R. L. 1974 *The Criminal's Image of the City*, University microfilms, University of Oklahoma.

Chilton, R. J. 1964 'Continuity in delinquency area research: a comparison of studies for Baltimore, Detroit and Indianapolis', *American Sociological Review*, 29. 71–83.

Cohen, A. K. 1955 *Delinquent Boys*, Free Press, Chicago.

Damer, S. 1974 'Wine Alley: the sociology of a dreadful enclosure', *Sociological Review*, 22. 221–48.

Denning, R. 1973 *Growing up in Ely* in Williams, S. (ed.), *The Cardiff Book*, Vol. 1, 149–56. Williams, Cowbridge.

Downes, D. M. 1966 *The Delinquent Solution*, Routledge & Kegan Paul, London.

Eyles, J. D. 1974 'Social theory and social geography' in Board, C., Chorley, R. J., Haggett, P., Stoddart, D. (eds.), *Progress in Geography*, 6. 27–87.

Fyvel, T. R. 1961 *The Insecure Offenders*, Penguin, Harmondsworth.
Glueck, S. and Gleuck, E. 1950 *Unravelling Juvenile Delinquency*, The Commonwealth Fund, New York.
—— 1952 *Delinquency in the Making*, Harper, New York.
Gordon, R. A. 1967 'Issues in the ecological study of delinquency', *American Sociological Review*, 32. 927–44.
Gray, F. 1976 'Selection and allocation in council housing', *Transactions, Institute, of British Geographers*, N.S. 1. 34–46.
Hamnett, C. 1979 'Area based explanations: a critical appraisal' in Herbert, D. T. and Smith, D. M. (eds.), *Social Problems and the City: A Geographical Approach*, 244–257, Oxford University Press, London.
Haring, L. L. (ed.) 1972 *A Summary Report of Spatial Studies of Juvenile Delinquency in Phoenix, Arizona*, Arizona State University (mimeo).
Harries, K. D. 1975 'The geography of crime: a political rejoinder', *Professional Geographer*, 27. 280–2.
Herbert, D. T. 1975 'Urban deprivation: definition, measurement and spatial qualities', *Geographical Journal*, 141. 362–72.
—— 1976 'The study of delinquency areas: a social geographical approach', *Transactions, Institute of British Geographers*, N.S. 1. 472–92.
—— 1977a 'An areal and ecological analysis of delinquency residence: Cardiff 1966 and 1971', *Tijdschrift voor Economische en Sociale Geografie*, 68. 83–99.
—— 1977b 'Crime, delinquency and the urban environment', *Progress in Human Geography*, 1. 208–39.
Hindess, B. 1973 *The Use of Official Statistics in Sociology*, MacMillan, London.
Jacobs, J. 1961 *Death and Life of Great American Cities*, Random House, New York.
Johnston, R. J. 1976 'Political behaviour and the residential mosaic' in Herbert, D. T. and Johnston, R. J.: (eds.), *Social Areas in Cities*, Vol. 1, 65–88, Wiley, London.
Lander, B. 1954 *Towards an Understanding of Juvenile Delinquency*, Columbia University Press, New York.
Leather, A., and Matthews, A. 1973 'What the architect can do: a series of design guides' in Ward, C. (ed.), *Vandalism*, Architectural Press, London, 117–72.
Lombroso, C. 1968 *Crime, its Causes and Remedies*, Patterson, Smith, Montclair, New York (first published 1911).
Mannheim, H. 1965 *Comparative Criminology*, Routledge & Kegan Paul, London.
Mawby, R. I. 1977a 'Defensible space: a theoretical and empirical approach', *Urban Studies*, 14. 169–79.
—— 1977b 'Kiosk vandalism: a Sheffield study', *British Journal of Criminology*, 17. 30–46.
Mays, J. B. 1963 'Delinquency areas: a re-assessment', *British Journal of Criminology*, 3. 216–30.
Morris, T. P. 1957 *The Criminal Area: A Study in Social Ecology*, Routledge & Kegan Paul, London.
Murray, R., and Boal, F. W. 1979 'The social ecology of urban violence' in Herbert, D. T. and Smith D. M. (eds.), *Social Problems and the City: A Geographical Approach*, 139–157, Oxford University Press, London.
Newman, O. 1972 *Defensible Space*, Macmillan, New York.

Pablant, P., and Baxter, J. C. 1975 'Environmental correlates of school vandal-ism', *Journal, American Institute of Planners*, 42. 270–9.
Peet, R. 1975 'The geography of crime: a political critique', *Professional Geographer*, 27. 277–80.
—— 1976 'Some further comments on the geography of crime', *Professional Geographer*, 28. 96–100.
—— 1977 'The development of radical geography in the United States', *Progress in Human Geography*, 1. 240–63.
Reppetto, T. A. 1974 *Residential Crime*, Ballinger, Cambridge, Mass.
Rex, J., and Moore, R. 1967 *Race, Community and Conflict*, Oxford University Press, London.
Scarr, H. A. 1972 *Patterns of Burglary*, U.S. Department of Justice, Washington.
Schmid, C. F. 1960 'Urban crime areas', *American Sociological Review*, 25. 527–54 and 655–78.
Scott, P. 1972 'The spatial analysis of crime and delinquency', *Australian Geographical Studies*, 10. 1–18.
Shaw, C. R., and McKay, H. D. 1942 *Juvenile Delinquency and Urban Areas*, Chicago University Press, Chicago.
Sheldon, W. 1949 *The Varieties of Delinquent Youth*, Harper, New York.
South Wales Echo, 1975 Thomson Press, Cardiff.
Suttles, G. C. 1968 *The Social Order of the Slum*, Chicago University Press, Chicago.
Taylor, I., Walton, P., and Young, J. 1973 *The New Criminology*, Routledge & Kegan Paul, London.
Taylor, L. 1973 'The meaning of environment', in Ward, C. (ed.), *Vandalism*, Architectural Press, London.
Tobias, J. J. 1976 'A statistical study of a nineteenth century criminal area', *British Journal of Criminology*, 14. 221–35.
Turner, S. 1969 'Delinquency and distance', in Sellin, T. and Wolfgang, M. E. (eds.), *Delinquency: Selected Studies*, Wiley, New York.
Wallis, C. P., and Maliphant, R. 1967 'Delinquent areas in the county of London', *British Journal of Criminology*, 7. 250–84.
Wilson, R. 1963 *Difficult Housing Estates*, Tavistock, London.

8

THE SOCIAL ECOLOGY OF URBAN VIOLENCE

R. Murray and F. W. Boal

Notwithstanding the title, this chapter is concerned with violence as a social problem rather than with all behaviour that might be classified as violent; the two are not synonymous. If violence is defined as behaviour that injures people, then it is clear that there are instances of such behaviour that are not generally regarded as constituting a social problem. Indeed, the terms 'violence' and 'social problem' are usually employed tautologically; injurious behaviour that is seen as legitimate, and thus not creating a problem, is not defined as violent.

Motor accidents are now the major cause of sudden death and injury; even in contemporary Northern Ireland more people are killed by motor vehicles than by bomb or bullet. Nevertheless, society accepts this with equanimity. Violence, as a social problem and as the subject of this chapter, means criminal acts directed against people—murders and assaults of various forms. Violence against the person, particularly its more publicized manifestations—football hooligans, muggings, terrorists, racial conflicts—is increasingly regarded by the public and by policy-makers as a major urban problem.

Difficulties of Measurement

Since the problem, as popularly defined, is one of criminal behaviour, practically all studies of violence have been based on analyses of events recorded by the police or on the study of people convicted by the courts. While such sources are obviously the most convenient, if not the only practicable, source of data, they have major shortcomings which may be taken into account in any evaluation of research findings (Walker, 1971).

  a. Not all acts of violence are officially recorded. The victims may be unable or unwilling to report the incident (cf. Amir, 1971). The police may decide to overlook certain types of violence such as domestic assaults or teenage brawls. To tackle this problem some researchers have employed 'victim surveys' (e.g. Hauge and Wolf, 1974; McDonald, 1969).
  b. Similar incidents may be classified differently in different police areas or at different times. Even if consistently applied the official system may not be suitable for research purposes; the researcher may need to examine the original police reports and reclassify each case using his own system (e.g. McClintock et al., 1963).
  c. Official sources can only provide information on the subset of violent offenders who are convicted; these may constitute only an unrepresentative sample of the people who commit violence.

There is one further problem with the use of official statistics, a paradoxical one that particularly affects researchers in Britain: there are not enough recorded acts of violence! The problem is especially acute for geographers using small areal units such as enumeration districts; because of the rarity of violent events among the criminal statistics, very many areas may contain no incidents at all, or very few, unless a long time span is taken.

Epidemic

Epidemiology of Violence

A prerequisite for the study of any phenomenon is its epidemiology. In this case it is the description of the characteristic features of offences of violence and of the people who commit them. For this purpose a valid system of classification is of crucial importance. As McClintock (1974) points out:

Criminological research which was focused on descriptive and classificatory analyses of criminal behaviour has given proof that even within the more restricted legal groups of crime, such as sex offences, robbery, violent crime, fraud or burglary, there are variations of such substantially different behaviour that, as regards both theory and criminal policy, it is very dubious whether such legal categories have any meaning or use as descriptions of social reality. (p. 40)

Without such a system it is doubtful whether any real progress can be made towards an understanding of the nature of violent acts or of the reasons why people commit them. Otherwise the researcher is dealing with a set of categories which do not differentiate in any meaningful manner; within each category there is likely to be a mixture of cases with different roots.

Many attempts have been made to produce classification systems with a higher level of validity than those employed in the official records. McClintock *et al.* (1963), for example, used a sixfold system to classify the circumstances of the offences in their study of crimes of violence against the person without theft:

  I Attacks in order to perpetrate a sexual offence
 II Attacks on police officers or on civilians intervening to prevent a crime
III Attacks arising from domestic disputes, quarrels between neighbours or between persons working together
 IV Attacks in or around public houses, cafes, etc.
  V Attacks in thoroughfares and other public places
 VI Attacks in special circumstances

A more comprehensive system (including property violence) has recently been proposed by Hadden and McClintock (1970).

In practice, however, most researchers have simply made use of official categories, despite their recognized shortcomings; some have even amalgamated these categories to yield a single category of violent crime. There has been a tendency in recent years, however, in American urban studies, to recognize a distinctive category of collective or social violence. Although the criteria for differentiating this from other acts of violence may be ambiguous an extensive literature has been produced on urban riots, the most common urban manifestation of such violence. Janowitz (1969) distinguishes between two types of riot— 'communal' and 'commodity'—with different geographical implications. The former (in the U.S.A.) involve clashes between whites and blacks and are usually triggered by white reaction to black 'encroachment' on white spheres of control. Commodity riots, on the other hand, are largely confined to black groups. Although they generally begin as a reaction to some police action they do not involve clashes between blacks and whites. Once begun the riot is aimed mainly at property and retail establishments; any violence is aimed at the security forces and is generally incidental to the destruction and looting of property.

From the many studies of the epidemiology of violence, collective and other, a fairly coherent picture has emerged concerning where violence chiefly occurs, the form it takes, and the characteristics of the people who commit it.

The Geography of Violence

Violent acts tend to be more local, in the sense of being committed in or near to the offender's home, than other crimes. Baldwin and Bottoms (1976), for example, found that 'over 60 per cent of such offences [in Sheffield] were committed within one mile of the offender's residence' (p. 81). (This may, however, simply reflect the limited opportunities for mobility of young working-class males.) There is thus a high degree of correspondence between offender and offence areas. Studies in a large number of western cities have consistently found that violent crime is most often found in urban areas characterized by: low income; physical deterioration; dependency; racial and ethnic concentrations; broken homes; working mothers; low levels of education and vocational skills; high unemployment; high proportions of single males; overcrowded and substandard housing; low rates of home ownership; multiple occupancy of dwellings; mixed land use; high population density. In practice these attributes tend to be highly correlated, particularly in the absence of any public sector housing, and the areas concerned are almost invariably found in the inner city; many studies have reported a gradient of violence from the inner city to the suburbs.

In Britain five post-war studies have examined intra-urban variations in violent crime: McClintock et al. (1963) in London using police subdivisions as the area unit (Fig. 8.1); McClintock and Avison (1968) in English conurbations using entire police-force areas; Lambert (1970) in one police division of Birmingham using enumeration districts; Brown et al. (1972) in a 'Northern town' using enumeration districts; Baldwin and Bottoms (1976) in Sheffield using enumeration districts. In general these studies have confirmed that areas of poor, private housing with high levels of poverty and migrant populations have the greatest incidence of violent crime. They have noted, however, that domestic violence shows a greater geographical spread than other forms, with suburban council estates, for example, showing moderately high levels. Most of the violence that occurs in such areas is of this type with attacks on strangers being quite rare; this may, however, simply reflect the low density of public houses on council estates.

The spatial patterning of collective violence varies with the circumstances of the rioting. Communal riots generally take the form of attacks by one group upon the territory of another and the violence is thus concentrated at the interfaces between different areas; most of the clashes between Protestant and Catholic in Belfast over the last hundred years or so have followed this pattern (Boal and Murray, 1977).

One feature of such rioting in Belfast is that certain key locations, particularly

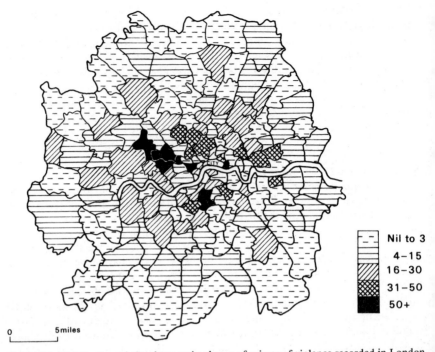

Figure 8.1 Distribution of the three main classes of crimes of violence recorded in London in 1960.
Source: McClintock, F. H. et al., 1963, Map III, p. 203, by permission of Macmillan, London and Basingstoke.

along the line dividing the Catholic Falls and Protestant Shankill areas, have been the foci for battles in every outbreak since the middle nineteenth century, despite their change from fields to residential areas. In the rioting in the early years of the present 'troubles' it was found that participants were in fact travelling to such sites from other areas of the city. With the development of more organized urban guerrilla warfare in the city the locations of incidents have become more scattered; the mobility provided by the motor car is a key element in this. The recent clashes in England between National Front supporters and their opponents apparently represent a new variation on this theme. A 'Front' march, usually involving people bussed in from other areas, is in itself grounds for conflict with left-wingers, also bussed, regardless of its location; Grimshaw (1960) noted this phenomenon in relation to the Negro Civil Rights protests in America in the late 1950s. We might use the term 'floating interface' to describe this situation of transitional territoriality; the precise location may often be determined by police tactical decisions.

   In commodity riots, however, such as those in many American Cities in the 1960s, the focus of the rioting, and hence of whatever violence occurs, lies within the territory of the rioting group or in neutral commercial areas.

The Nature of Violence

Despite public anxiety aroused by the dramatic examples of violence, such as murder and apparently unprovoked attacks on innocent bystanders, these are a relatively minor component of violent crime which, in turn, is only a small fraction of all offences; crimes of violence, of all forms, make up less than 5 per cent of all offences known to the police in England and Wales, and the level has changed little for many years (Klein, 1972).

Thus McClintock (1963) and his colleagues, in the most detailed and comprehensive British study into the circumstances of violent crimes, found that in 1960 the breakdown of such crimes, using the classification system described above, was as follows (as percentage of all violent offences):

I	Violent sex offences	6·0
II	Attacks on police etc.	12·1
III	Domestic disputes etc.	30·8
IV	Public house and cafe fights	19·7
V	Street attacks	29·7
VI	Miscellaneous attacks	1·7

Similarly, of 562 disputes studied by Lambert (1970) (where the police were called but brought no charges), 53 per cent were between members of the same family or neighbours and another 17 per cent between landlord and tenant. Allowing for all the problems of definition, reporting, and recording, it seems safe to conclude that most violence is unpremeditated and occurs in the context of an argument or dispute, not as an adjunct to some other crime such as rape or theft; the consumption of alcohol is often important in this respect. In Britain acts of violence rarely involve weapons but in the U.S.A. the ready availability of firearms is reflected in their frequent use even in domestic incidents.

Riots, not surprisingly, tend to produce more serious violence since a main intention, particularly in communal riots, is to inflict injury. Where weapons are plentiful and the security forces fail or refuse to intervene effectively such riots have led to casualties on the scale of open warfare. Commodity riots usually have lower levels of violence against the person because the target is property; since, however, commodity riots are a more recent feature than communal this difference probably also reflects more sophisticated police tactics.

The Violent Offender

The typical offender, as far as can be judged from samples of convicted persons, is

(i) young—the incidence of convictions for violence is highest among the 17—21 age group and is disproportionately high between the late teens and the early thirties.

Currently the rate for the 14—17 age group, in both the U.S.A. and Britain, is increasing most rapidly and now approximates that for the 17—21-year-olds. McClintock *et al.* (1963) noted that offenders whose violence occurred in the context of a domestic dispute were, on average, older than other violent offenders. Despite their youth, however, violent offenders tend to be older than persons convicted of theft offences.

(ii) male—more than 90 per cent of offenders are male. Again domestic violence, such as homicide or cruelty to children, shows the greatest deviation from this level.

(iii) working class—offenders are disproportionately drawn from the semi-skilled and unskilled social classes. A high proportion are found to be unemployed or in casual employment at the time of their crimes; many display an erratic employment history.

Researchers in the U.S.A. have consistently found higher rates of violent crime amongst blacks, even when social class differences are taken into account. British studies have been less clear cut. McClintock *et al.* (1963) concluded:

In each of the three years [examined for the study] the Irish immigrants and others born overseas were responsible for a substantial number of the crimes in each class of violence. Between 1950 and 1957 a considerable increase in the number and proportion of violent offenders not born in the United Kingdom occurred in all classes of offence except in that of violent sexual offences (Class I). A finding of outstanding significance is that in 1960 more than 4 in 10 of those convicted of crimes of violence which arose from domestic disputes, etc. (Class III) were immigrants—mainly from the West Indies and the Irish Republic. Of almost equal importance is the fact that more than 3 in 10 of those convicted of attacks on police, etc. (Class II) were also immigrants. A great deal of the violence committed by those born in the Irish Republic was associated with heavy drink. (p. 127)

However, Lambert (1970), in a study which was concentrated on the links between crime and race, found that West Indians, and to an even greater extent Asians, had disproportionately low rates of all forms of crime. His analysis of the minor disputes showed that only for one type—disputes with neighbours or fellow tenants—were West Indians more likely to become involved than native English; their rates for family disputes and quarrels in pubs/cafés, etc. were, if anything, lower.

As far as their home circumstances are concerned, violent offenders are more likely to come from a broken home in their childhood, to be divorced or separated, to be from an overcrowded home, to lack a permanent home.

The American urban riots of the mid-60s have been extensively researched and a consistent picture of the typical rioter has emerged. Like the individual offender described above, the rioter is a young male of low social class. He is, however, better educated than his non-rioting neighbours, although more likely to be in an unskilled job, and more politically aware. They have a greater sense of personal efficacy but believe they cannot attain their goals through conventional non-violent means (Caplan, 1970).

Theories of Violence

The researcher seeking explanations for these observations regarding violent behaviour is faced with a wide choice of theories. This is not surprising since there are many different forms of violent behaviour. It may even be that the same behaviour will require different explanations for different social groups; a psychological theory for an act committed by a member of a non-violent culture, a sociological one for the same act committed by someone from a violent sub-culture (Ferracuti and Wolfgang, 1963). As yet, the nearest approach to a general theory of violence, other than genetic theories (e.g. Ardrey, 1966; Lorenz, 1966), is the frustration-aggression hypothesis (Dollard *et al.*, 1939) but it is now clear that frustration is not a sufficient condition for violence (Berkowitz, 1969); furthermore, the concept of frustration has often been so widely stretched as to lose all validity.

If we confine ourselves to theories advanced to account for intra-urban variations in violence then at least six major theories are involved:

(i) Differential opportunity—this relates to the observation that certain types of micro-environment (e.g. pubs/cafés/underpasses/deserted streets, etc.) have significantly higher rates of violence because of the opportunities they present for disputes to arise, for robberies to occur (Angel, 1968; Newman, 1973); facilities, such as football grounds, which attract large numbers of young, working-class males are particularly important (cf. Banfield, 1968). Intra-urban variations in violence arise because of the distribution of such locations.

(ii) Differential drift—this assumes that there are people with violence-prone life-styles or personalities. Rejected by or unable to live in most areas, they tend to drift into the inner city. The recent British studies, beginning with Lambert (1970), have focused attention on the role of the housing market in this process, particularly, because of the importance of the public sector, on council allocation policies and procedures. 'By making decisions to allocate a family to a particular area, we are likely to be either increasing or decreasing the factors associated with a brush with the law . . ..' (Brown *et al.*, 1972, 265; cf. Gray, 1976; Duncan, 1976)

(iii) Violent sub-culture—this theory argues that in certain areas, or in certain groups in these areas, a sub-culture develops which rejects the majority culture and its values. Instead it encourages, or at least condones, the use of violence as a legitimate form of behaviour. Thus, residents of such areas who engage in violence are simply acting in a normal fashion (Wolfgang and Ferracuti, 1967). The main use of this theory has been to account for adolescent violence, particularly that involving gangs. Thus Miller (1966): 'Gang members fight to secure and defend their honor as males; to secure and defend the reputation of their local area and the honor of their women; to show that an affront to their pride and dignity demands retaliation' (p. 112).

(iv) Social alienation—the residents of certain areas, particularly if they belong to a minority ethnic group, or some other under-class, are alienated from society. This leads to feelings of powerlessness and hostility which increase the likelihood of violence.

(v) Stress—a state of stress arises when the demands made on an individual or group exceed their resources: this can arise from excessive demands or inadequate resources or both (Lazarus, 1966). The term 'resources' applies to a wide range of factors such as income, education, social skills, housing, friends, and so on. Similarly, the demands can be very varied—anything that requires the individual or group to adapt their behaviour.

The argument that people who are stressed are more likely to resort to violence to resolve their problems is used by Lambert (1970):

Many of such incidents [minor disputes] reveal the effects of overcrowding in poor standard housing. Such conditions provoke argument and hostility among and between tenants and neighbours; many family disputes suggest how the comforts and stability of normal home relations break down under the strain of living in rooms and lodgings and substandard housing. (p. 129)

(vi) Frustration/relative deprivation—in one form or another this has been the major theory of violence for many years. Put very simply, frustration occurs when an individual or group is prevented from satisfying some need or desire that it expected to gratify. A closely related but separate theory is that of relative deprivation or social comparison (Festinger, 1954; Runciman, 1966). Like the frustration and stress theories, its essential feature is a gap between two sets of conditions. Here the divergence is between what people have or the treatment they receive, and the situation of another group whom they regard as socially equivalent. The greater the gap, the higher the level of discontent and the greater the probability of violence.

(vii) Disorganization—since the pioneering work of the 'Chicago school' of urban ecologists, most explanations of areal differences in violence (and many other social problems) have been based on the disorganization model. 'Divorce, crime, delinquency, war, narcotics use, suicide, personal violence, alcoholism, and other social problems have been seen as resulting from the fragmentation of the usual bonds between people that society depends upon for its persistence and stability' (Lowry, 1974, p. 139).

The disorganization of people, and of communities, is supposed to arise because certain areas have very heterogenous and rapidly changing populations and are thus unable to form 'normal' stable social structures that are deemed necessary for adequate socialization.

(viii) Differential policing/labelling—recent explanations of areal variations in violence have stressed that these differences are based on official statistics. They argue that the 'true' levels of violence (i.e. including all the unrecorded events) do not vary so markedly between areas but that instead certain areas, because of the character of their residents or because of the reputation they have acquired, are subject to more intensive police activity (e.g. Werthman and Piliavin, 1967).

In particular, there are persistent allegations in both England and America that the police treat black youths, especially when they seem to be doing nothing, as miscreants. Encounters between two groups, police and youths, with very different perceptions, can create violent incidents (Toch, 1972).

Clearly, many of these theories are not necessarily mutually exclusive; some may prove to be merely different interpretations of the same factor. One can, perhaps, distinguish two main types of theory:

(a) Reactive theories—stress; frustration; relative deprivation; alienation. These explain behaviour as a reaction to features of the physical or socio-economic environment.

(b) Learning theories—violent sub-culture; disorganization. According to these, violence arises because people have learnt the wrong forms of behaviour or failed to learn the right ones (from the perspective of the majority) or have adapted to the circumstances of their environment by learning more appropriate forms of behaviour.

An alternative classification scheme for these theories of violence would yield the following:

(a) Environmental theories—stress/frustration/deprivation/sub-culture/opportunity/disorganization. The source of the violence lies in the immediate environment.

(b) Structural theories—drift/labelling/alienation. The source lies in the wider socio-economic structure of society and the way in which certain social groups are treated.

Furthermore, it is clear that we are not faced with deciding which is the single 'right' or 'best' theory. It will undoubtedly prove necessary to have different theories for different behaviours or situations. Indeed it may well be that explanation lies in the interaction between, or the accumulation of, a number of psychological and socio-economic processes. For example, what is important is not that deprived people 'drift' into bad housing, or that bad housing is stressful, but that the people who are least able to cope with the strains of bad housing are the very people who, because of the operation of the housing system, are most likely to be forced into such housing. Similarly, frustration on its own is not enough to cause violence but the chance of violence is greatly increased if the frustrated person lacks alternative modes of resolving his frustration because of lack of economic or social power, because of inadequate social or verbal skills or simply because of inebriation.

The Geographical Contribution

Although geographical theories of urban structure and processes are incorporated in explanations of urban violence and have been used, as have techniques of spatial analysis, to guide research, geographers, as such, have not been directly involved in this field. All the studies of areal differences have been conducted by criminologists/sociologists. Thus when we speak of the geographical contribution, we are concerned with the contribution of areally based research. This leads us to the question: to what aspect or aspects of urban violence should such research be primarily directed? In the past its role has been to shed light on the problem of violent behaviour, to provide a fuller understanding of why individuals commit violent acts; that, at any rate, has been the criterion against which it has been evaluated.

Set against that standard, areal studies have been of relatively little value. Most, and this applies particularly to the American literature, have been exercises in correlational epidemiology; they have tried to identify those physical or social features of areas that correlate most highly with the level of violence. The failure of such research to contribute to an understanding of violent acts is due to two factors. One is the ever-present problem of the 'ecological fallacy' (Robinson, 1950), the inability to translate areal correlations into individual ones. Perhaps more importantly, areal studies have employed very crude measures of the key phenomena.

Most theories of violence are mediational theories, that is, they can be reduced to the form:

$$A \rightarrow B \rightarrow C$$

where A represents some dimension of the environment, such as bad housing, poverty or ethnic affiliation, and C represents behaviour—in this case, violent behaviour. It is postulated that A does not lead directly to C but to some intervening factor, usually psychological or sociological, such as stress, frustration or alienation; C is then a response to B. Indeed, as we have argued earlier, the process will usually be even more complex with a number of variables intervening between A and B and B and C. This complexity, however, is not reflected in areal research; instead they have simply used readily available measures (usually census material) as crude surrogates for the supposed intervening variables (e.g. population mobility as an index of social disoranization) and related these to equally crude official crime statistics. The consequences of this approach for any advance in understanding the roots of violence is demonstrated by the poignant conclusions of Brown et al. (1972): 'The main features associated with offences against the person appear to be rented council houses, unemployment and poverty. This could be explained in terms of anomie, working-class culture, sub-culture or differential association' (p. 264). Or frustration or relative deprivation or stress . . . The point is that there is no attempt to probe the crucial intervening variables although many of them, according to theory, should be as much attributes of an area as its population density or percentage unemployed. Furthermore, the characteristics that are measured are, in geographical terms, those of site; aspects of situation are generally ignored. There is no attempt to put the area in the wider social or urban context.

It is doubtful, therefore, whether the traditional areal or ecological approach can make any important contribution. On the whole it has produced nothing in the way of social or psychological processes that generate violent behaviour that could not equally well have been, and were, derived from case studies of violent offenders. Baldwin (1975) in a critique of British areal studies of crime, has suggested ways in which the areal approach might be made to contribute to the study of behaviour. He argues that 'researchers should attempt to move beyond straightforward descriptive analyses either towards more detailed examinations of particular hypotheses or else towards the more qualitative and penetrative observational studies of particular social areas' (p. 224). In the latter context the particular value of the ecological method would be to identify areas which had similar population and environmental characteristics but which differed in their levels of violence; in the past the search for significant correlations tended to submerge such observations. Research along these lines is now being incorporated in the Sheffield Study on Urban Social Structure and Crime (Baldwin and Bottoms, 1976).

Although such modifications, which lead to the use of areal studies as just the starting-point of research, clearly constitute an improvement over the traditional approach, they are still concerned primarily with unravelling the processes that produce violence. We would suggest, however, that the causation of individual behaviour is only one facet of the problem of violence and that a separate and more relevant goal for geographical research is the question of why there are areal variations in the levels of violence, in the sense that the residents of certain areas seem to commit more acts of violence than those of other areas. This distinction between these two aspects of violence is particularly relevant if we are concerned with violence as a social problem. Regardless of the overall level of violent crime in society it is surely an affront to widely held views of social justice that the incidence is markedly higher in certain areas. As we have seen, violence is a particularly local crime. If an area contains a high proportion of people committing violent acts, then it will be, overwhelmingly, their relatives and fellow-residents who will suffer; such victims are, simultaneously, least likely to be able to escape to a safer area (Droettboom *et al.*, 1971). Thus, reducing the level of violence in such high-risk areas is a legitimate end in itself apart from any wider goal of reducing its overall level.

In effect, we are arguing that the primary contribution of the geographical perspective on the problem of violence is to develop an understanding of violence as geographical phenomena. If, in so doing, it sheds light on the processes underlying individual behaviour, then this is all to the good, but that should not be its objective nor the criterion by which it is judged. Its aim should be to unravel the processes by which the various factors identified in other studies as contributing to acts of violence come to be more intense or prevalent in certain areas.

A Study of Birmingham

One recent important British study which has attempted such a study of differences in violence is that by Lambert (1970). He took a sector of Birmingham, stretching from its apex at the edge of the city centre to the suburbs, that constituted one police division. It was selected because it contained a wide range of housing types and included a significant proportion of the city's major immigrant groups.

The sector was divided by Lambert into three concentric zones and then further subdivided into eleven areas 'which seemed to be distinctive geographical, housing type, or broadly 'cultural' districts' (p. 13). (Although enumeration district boundaries were incorporated, the identification of areas seems to have proceeded on a subjective basis.)

The conceptual basis for the study was as follows

But if, as can be shown, various kinds of crime and disorder are persistently more prevalent in some kinds of areas than others, such findings can add to our understanding of crime as a social phenomenon and reflect the kind of security and stability, the kind of quality of community that exists in areas of a city. Such findings may also deepen our awareness of the meaning and causes of crime and throw some light on its due social treatment.

If crime is the result of certain typical living conditions, a study of these conditions is necessary for an understanding of comparative rates of involvement in crime of different categories of persons (p. 91).

Lambert was concerned with all aspects of crime and disorder, but in his analysis treated certain categories, such as violence, separately. In general his findings regarding violence, which included an analysis of minor disputes which had merely been noted by the police without any charge being preferred, were similar to those of McClintock *et al.* (1963). Incidents of violence were relatively rare events and most arose from domestic disputes or arguments in the street or public houses (usually associated with drunkenness). The highest rates occurred in the areas with the highest proportions of privately rented housing, partly because many involved disputes between landlord and tenant or between tenants in multi-occupied dwellings (Fig. 8.2). There was a tendency for members of different ethnic groups to be more involved in certain types of incident.

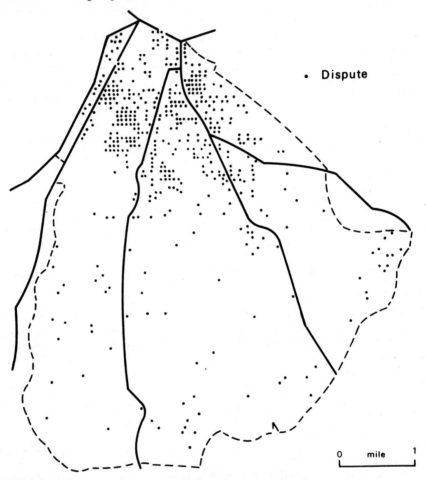

Figure 8.2 Locations of minor disputes in south-west Birmingham, November 1966 to February 1967.
Source: Lambert, J. R., 1970, Map 11.

Lambert then goes on to examine the processes by which different areas generate or attract crime. In relation to the latter he shows how the level of violent incidents arising from street disorders is closely related to the distribution of public houses. He is mainly concerned, however, with the way in which violence grows out of the way of life imposed upon the residents of certain areas.

Overcrowding and poor living conditions provide hostility between landlords and tenants, place great strains on the stability of personal relations, and can lead to argument, fighting, and violence. The nature of crime and disorder is that it underlines the stark reality of the disorganisation and instability which are features of conditions in such areas. The security and stability reflected in the data from [areas of owner-occupation] and from the outer area of the division highlight the inequalities and conflicts that are visible in the city.

He then proceeds to discuss, with particular reference to immigrant groups, the wider social and economic processes which generate such inequalities in living conditions and which assign certain social groups, usually those least able to cope, to the areas of greatest housing stress. In this respect he draws heavily on the 'housing classes' model advanced by Rex and Moore (1967). Lambert's final summing-up crystallizes the essence of the geographical perspective:

The nature of crime and its uneven distribution between discrete areas require that crime statistics and interpretations of rates of crime and criminality be treated with caution. The processes whereby areas of crime are created are not random. Clearly, if crime is a feature of certain areas and is local in character, the status of the population in those areas will be reflected in the statistics. The processes whereby certain groups come to live in certain neighbourhoods are not random. The processes reflect the variations in the wealth, the status, the power of the various groups. Comparative rates of crime between classes and between ethnic groups can only be meaningful in relation to those variations and when crime is related to those processes. Crime can only be understood in relation to the sociology of urban society. (pp. 282–3)

Territorial Violence in Belfast

The most dramatic form of urban violence today is undoubtedly that associated with the urban guerilla; few western nations have been free of this phenomenon in recent years. The violence associated with such conflict is generally of a social rather than individual nature. People kill or are killed because they belong to a certain social category; the left attack members of the 'establishment'—politicians, businessmen, the security forces—the right chooses its victims from intellectuals and trade unionists. Membership of the 'wrong' group can be sufficient grounds for assault.

For generations there has been conflict in Northern Ireland between the two major indigenous groups, usually labelled 'Protestants' and 'Catholics'. This conflict periodically erupts in social violence as in the present 'troubles'. The study of certain aspects of such disturbances can further our understanding of the processes linking geography and violence that are of relevance to other societies.

Despite the evidence that most acts of violence are between people known to one another there is no doubt that the main cause of public anxiety about violence is the fear of attack by a stranger, of being suddenly assaulted while going about one's daily life. In Britain and America such attacks are usually associated with theft of some form, the violence being secondary. Plain murder by a stranger is extremely rare.

The 'troubles' in Northern Ireland, however, have produced hundreds of such murders. It seems that in many cases, particularly within Belfast, the territorial geography of the area has been a key factor. One category of murder that demonstrates this is that of civilians killed in their homes. Between 1969 and October 1977 there were forty-six such murders in the city of Belfast, sometimes labelled 'doorstep murders' because in most the victim was shot on answering the door (*Belfast Telegraph*, 1975). Figure 8.3 shows the locations of these murders (some locations involve multiple deaths) and the distribution of Protestant, Catholic, and mixed areas in 1973.

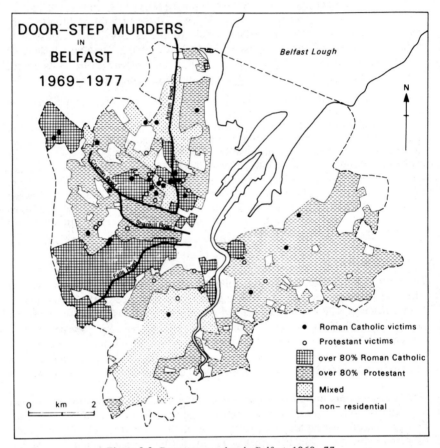

Figure 8.3 Doorstep murders in Belfast, 1969–77.

The most striking feature of the map, and the aspect we wish to examine, is the concentration in the area north of the Crumlin Road; this sector contains over half the murders. Furthermore, the deaths here are disporportionately of Catholics. Overall, the ratio of Catholic to Protestant victims is 2:1, in the north it is 3:1. This high incidence and ratio are due in part to the religious geography of the area.

The map shows one feature that distinguishes North Belfast. Unlike the rest of the city where there is a fairly tidy pattern of segregated and mixed areas (both usually found in large tracts) the north presents much more of a patch-work pattern. This facilitates sectarian murders in two ways. Firstly, the areas are relatively easy to penetrate; their smallness means that they are quickly traversed while, unlike the large ghettos to the south, there are few men to provide local defence. (One response of residents in these areas to the murder campaigns has been the construction of barricades.) Secondly, all possible target areas are near to secure areas such as the Shankill or Ardoyne. Murderers can very soon be back in the safety of their own territory.

The other distinctive feature of territoriality in North Belfast cannot be seen from the map but it is probably a more important factor in the pattern of murders than the first feature. In most of Belfast the residential pattern has remained remarkably constant for generations; the present troubles have merely reasserted the divisions. North Belfast, however, is in a state of flux. Since 1969 many Catholic families intimidated from further north have settled in the streets around the long-established Catholic areas of Ardoyne and New Lodge (Darby and Morris, 1974). They have been joined by the overspill of new households from the latter areas who are unable to move elsewhere safely. As a result many streets, particularly around the southern end of the Antrim Road, have 'gone' or are 'going' Catholic. Not surprisingly, many local Protestants, who regarded much of this area as their territory, feel threatened.

In addition to these domestic incidents many other cases of murder in Belfast since 1969 have their roots in the territoriality of the city. People have been murdered essentially because they were in the wrong place at the wrong time; people whose work took them into the other side's territory, who chose to journey through 'enemy' territory for some reason (a particular problem in West Belfast where the sectarian fragmentation makes it difficult to travel from one safe area to another without passing through or near danger zones), or who went to drink in the wrong pub.

Practically all studies of violence have treated it as the dependent variable, the consequence of other processes. Within an urban system, however, violence can also be an important factor in shaping spatial structure (Boal, 1972). The history of residential segregation in Belfast provides a classic example of this process. The periodic outbreaks of sectarian violence in the city and the enduring memory of them have been a powerful force maintaining high levels of ethnic segregation and territoriality (Boal et al., 1976, 1977). During years of peace the relaxation of tensions results in hundreds of families venturing out of segregated districts and thus increasing the degree of residential mixing. When strife recurs, however, these households are among the first victims; direct attacks or intimida-tion forces the local minority group to flee to the security of their co-religionists.

Between 1969 and 1973 at least 6,000 families moved within Belfast because of the 'troubles', 72 per cent moved to segregated areas, most of those moving to mixed areas being middle-class families leaving the 'ghetto' areas (Murray et al., 1975). For Catholics in particular their segregated areas, as the arenas for guerilla warfare, are still hazardous but it is clear that they are perceived as offering security, the feeling that one is at least safe from sectarian attack (Boal et al., 1976). The impact of violence on the urban fabric, and in turn on spatial processes, also extends into non-residential spheres, affecting the distribution and form of industry and commerce (Compton *et al.*, 1978).

In a context where the control of space is of crucial importance for the security it offers and the opportunities it provides, violence becomes a deliberate tool of social engineering. It is used, as in the case of North Belfast, both to defend space against invasion and to gain new territory; it is a means of ensuring social homogeneity. There have been examples in Belfast of orchestrated cycles of territorial violence which begin with group *A* forcing members of group *B* out of one area. These in turn are made room for by their co-religionists forcing members of group *A* out of another area; this cycle, in one form or another, has persisted for years. In such circumstances, where social conflict is endemic, it is often misleading to regard social violence as either a cause or an effect of social geography. It is both simultaneously, an inseparable component of the urban system.

With the heightening of racial tension within English cities it is likely that the processes linking social violence and social ecology will become more important there too; Murray and Osborne (1977) have discussed some of the possible consequences for public housing. It is already known that high levels of individual violence in certain areas, and their resultant reputations, can have wider social implications (cf. Damer, 1974).

The Future

There is now a greater awareness of the need for a geographical perspective to be concerned with ecological processes rather than with straightforward correlational epidemiology. An important example of research currently being undertaken is the Sheffield Study. The earlier stages of the Study (Baldwin and Bottoms, 1976), like the work of Lambert, emphasized the high correlation between levels of violence and privately rented housing; this tenure effect persisted even when differences in social factors such as levels of migration were taken into account. More significantly, in view of the continued decline in the private rented sector, they devoted particular attention to differences between areas within the public sector and the manner in which these may be related to the processes which lead to the creation of 'problem estates'. Further work in the Study is concentrating on selected areas of different tenure types and different levels of crime.

It is clear that research into the processes which generate areal differences in violence will require a higher level of theoretical and methodological sophistication than has generally been the case so far. More care will be needed in designing studies that allow for the explicit and relatively unambiguous testing of different theories or models. Measures of the various components, particularly the crucial hypothesised intervening variables, must be given greater priority; the use of census variables as surrogates can no longer be justified. And, finally, there will have to be more relevant systems for classifying and measuring different forms of violence to replace the current crude official indices.

In Britain the social scientists who have investigated violence have been mainly criminologists or psychologists. One consequence has been an almost total concentration on legally defined categories of behaviour, to the exclusion of other perspectives, and a tendency to regard violent acts as examples of deviant behaviour that can have no positive social functions. This has led, in turn, to the interpretation of violence as, essentially, a form of individual pathology. Although the role of social factors is acknowledged, the roots of violence are ascribed to flaws in the personality or behavioural repertoire of the individual. It is instructive to contrast this with much of the research on animal violence where the concern is with violence as a function of the population's interaction with its environment. Some members may be more susceptible to environmental pressure than others, some may exhibit more violence, but the concern of the ethologist is with the level of violence as a group characteristic, as a measure of its adjustment to the environment (Crook, 1970).

If the various theories advanced to account for intra-urban differences in violence have any degree of validity then it would seem that violence, particularly where it is not merely incidental to some other crime, is a neglected social indicator since it reflects an underlying state of profound social pathology. Self-directed violence, in the form of attempted suicide, is now generally interpreted as a cry for help; a high level of violence may be a community's cry for help. In this context, one aspect of violence that unfortunately seems likely to become increasingly significant in Britain is community or social violence. Even if it is not yet on the scale of that in Northern Ireland it is certainly on the increase in response to major problems in the field of ethnic relations; social violence, to echo Clausewitz, is merely the continuation of social conflict in other forms.

This shift in the interpretation of violence that is bound to accompany any emphasis on the geographical perspective has important implications for any policies concerned with tackling areal differences in violence. Even at this stage of research it seems clear that differences in violence essentially reflect wider social inequalities and can only be dealt with effectively by reducing those inequalities, by giving the residents of all areas adequate resources, in the widest sense of that term, for social and self-actualization.

It will also require the social scientists concerned to question the generally-accepted views of violence as a social problem. 'Social problems' tend to be construed in terms acceptable to those elements of society with the power to make definitions; as Deutsch (1973) points out, there is always an alternative perspective.

Suppose, in effect, that as social scientists we were consultants to the poor and weak rather than to the rich and strong. What would we suggest? Let me note that this would be an unusual and new position for most of us. If we have given any advice at all, it has been to those in high power. The unwitting consequence of this one-sided consultant role has been that we have too often assumed that the social pathology has been in the ghetto rather than in those who have built the walls to surround it, that the disadvantaged are the ones who need to be changed rather than the people and the institutions who have kept the disadvantaged in a submerged position. (p. 391)

Acknowledgement

We wish to acknowledge the cartographic assistance of Gillian Armstrong and Ian Alexander, both of the Department of Geography, The Queen's University, Belfast in the construction and presentation of the illustrations in this chapter.

References

Amir, M. 1971 *Patterns in Forcible Rape* University of Chicago Press, Chicago.
Angel, S. 1968 *Discouraging Crime Through City Planning*, Working Paper No. 75, Institute of Urban and Regional Development, University of California, Berkeley.
Ardrey, R. 1966 *The Territorial Imperative*, Atheneum, New York.
Baldwin, J. 1975 'British areal studies of crime: an assessment', *Brit. J. Criminol* 15. 211–27.
–– and Bottoms, A. E. 1976 *The Urban Criminal*, Tavistock, London.
Banfield, E. C. 1968 'Rioting mainly for fun and profit' in *The Unheavenly City*, Little, Brown & Co., Boston, 185–209.
Belfast Telegraph 'The doorstep murders', 7 Oct. 1975.
Berkowitz, L. 1969 'The frustration–aggression hypothesis revisited' in Berkowitz, L. (ed.), *Roots of Aggression*, Atherton, New York, 1–28.
Boal, F. W. 1972 'The urban residential sub-community–a conflict interpretation', *Area*, 4(3). 164–8.
–– and Murray, R. 1977 'A city in conflict', *Geographical Magazine* 49(b), March, 364–71.
–– Murray, R., and Poole, M. A. 1976 'Belfast: the urban encapsulation of a national conflict' in Clarke, S. E., and Obler J. L. (eds.), *Urban Ethnic Conflict: A Comparative Perspective*, University of North Carolina, Institute for Research in Social Science, Comparative Urban Studies Monograph Series No. No. 3, Chapel Hill.
–– Poole, M. A., Murray, R., and Kennedy, S. J. 1977 *Religious Residential Segregation and Residential Decision Making in the Belfast Urban Area* S.S.R.C. Project Report No. HR 1165.
Brown, M. J., McCulloch, J. W., and Hiscox, J. 1972 'Criminal offences in an urban area and their associated social variables', *British Journal of Criminology*, 12. 250–68.
Caplan, N. 1970 'The new ghetto man: a review of recent empirical studies', *Journal of Social Issues*, 26. 59–73.
Compton, P. A., Murray, R., and Osborne, R. 1978 'Conflict and its impact on the urban environment of Northern Ireland', *Proceedings of the 2nd British-Hungarian Geographical Seminar* (forthcoming).
Crook, J. M. 1970 'Social organization and the environment: aspects of contemporary social ethology', *Animal Behaviour* 18. 197–209.
Damer, S. 1974 'Wine Alley: the sociology of a dreadful enclosure' *Sociological Review* 22. 221–48.
Darby, J., and Morris, G. 1974 *Intimidation in Housing*, Belfast, Northern Ireland Community Relations Commission, Belfast.
Deutsch, M. 1973 *The Resolution of Conflict*, Yale University Press, New Haven.
Dollard, J., Doob, L. W., Miller, N. E., Mowrer, O. H., and Sears, R. R. 1939 *Frustration and Aggression*, Yale University Press, New Haven.
Droettboom, T. J. Jr., McAllister, R. J., Kaiser, E. J., and Butler, E. W. 1971 *Urban Violence and Residential Mobility*, University of North Carolina, Mimeo.
Duncan, S. S. 1976 'Research directions in social geography: housing opportunities and constraints', *Trans. Inst. Brit. Geogr.*, N.S. 1(1). 10–19.
Ferracuti, F., and Wolfgang, M. E. 1963 'Design for a proposed study of violence: a socio-psychological study of a subculture of violence', *British Journal of Criminology*, 3. 377–88.

Festinger, L. 1954 'A theory of social comparison processes', *Human Relations* 7. 117–40.

Gray, F. 1976 'Selection and allocation in council housing', *Trans. Inst. Br. Geog.* N.S. 1(1). 34–46.

Grimshaw, A. D. 1960 'Urban racial violence in the United States: changing ecological considerations', *American Journal of Sociology* 66. 2. 109–19.

Hadden, T. B., and McClintock, F. H. 1970 Social and legal definitions of criminal violence', *Proceedings of the Fourth National Conference on Research and Teaching in Criminology*, Cambridge (mimeo).

Hauge, R., and Wolf, P. 1974 'Criminal violence in three Scandinavian countries', *Scandinavian Studies in Criminology*, 5. 25–33.

Janowitz, M. 1969 'Patterns of Collective Racial Violence' in Graham, H. D., and Gurr, T. R. (eds.), *Violence in America: Historical and Comparative Perspectives*, Bantam Books, New York, 412–44.

Klein, S. 1972 'Crimes of violence against the person in England and Wales', *Social Trends*, 3. 53–4.

Lambert, J. R. 1970 *Crime, Police and Race Relations*, published for the Institute of Race Relations, London by Oxford University Press, London.

Lazarus, R. S. 1966 *Psychological Stress and the Coping Process* McGraw-Hill, New York.

Lorenz, K. 1966 *On Aggression*, Harcourt, Brace & World, New York.

Lowry, R. P. 1974 *Social Problems*, D. C. Heath, Lexington, Mass.

McClintock, F. H. 1974 'Facts and Myths about the State of Crime', in Hood, R. (ed.), *Crime, Criminology and Public Policy*, Heinemann, London.

– – and Avison, N. H. 1968 *Crime in England and Wales*, Heinemann, London.

– – Avison, N. H., Savill, N. C., and Worthington, V. L. 1963 *Crimes of Violence*, Macmillan, London.

McDonald, L. 1969 *Delinquency and Social Class*, Faber, London.

Miller, W. B. 1966 'Violent crimes in city gangs', *Ann. Amer. Acad. Polit. Soc. Sci.* 364. 95–112.

Murray, R., Boal, F. W., and Poole, M. A. 1975 'Psychology and the threatening environment', *Architectural Psychology Newsletter*, 5, Dec. 1975, 30–4.

Murray, R., and Osborne, R. 1977 'Horn Drive: a cautionary tale', *New Society*, 40. 106–8, 21 Apr. 1977.

Newman, O. 1973 *Defensible Space*, Architectural Press, London.

Rex, J., and Moore, R. 1967 *Race, Community and Conflict*, Oxford University Press, London.

Robinson, W. S. 1950 'Ecological correlations and the behaviour of individuals', *American Sociological Review*, 15. 351–7.

Runciman, W. 1966 *Relative Deprivation and Social Justice*, Routledge & Kegan Paul, London.

Toch, H. 1972 *Violent Men*, Penguin, Harmondsworth.

Walker, N. 1971 *Crimes, Courts and Figures*, Penguin, Harmondsworth.

Werthman, C., and Piliavin, I. 1967 'Gang Members and the Police' in Bordua, D. (ed.), *The Police: Six Sociological Essays*, Wiley, New York, 56–98.

Wolfgang, M. E., and Ferracuti, F. 1967 *The Subculture of Violence*, Tavistock, London.

9

ETHNIC AREAS IN BRITISH CITIES

P. N. Jones

The objective of this chapter is to consider the geographical distribution of coloured ethnic-minority populations in British cities, and their interrelationships with other components of the urban system. The extent of segregation, and its causation, is discussed initially within a national context, and with reference to general measurements. The example of Birmingham is then used to demonstrate how general indicators of trends in ethnic segregation find detailed geographical expression in a particular spatial context. The major national social issues arising from the predominantly inner-city concentration of coloured minorities are examined, again using Birmingham to illustrate both their derivation and proposed policy solutions. The chapter concludes with some suggestions for future research.

National Perspectives

Coloured ethnic minorities from the New Commonwealth,[1] number 1·77 millions in Great Britain, 3·3 per cent of the total popuation (O.P.C.S. Monitor, 1977). This population is ethnically heterogeneous, the term 'ethnic' being used to embrace groups of people characterized by racial, religious, or other cultural differences (Boal, 1976, p. 42). An approximate balance exists between West Indian and Asian[2] immigrants (Table 9.1) but census data give only a limited impression of the underlying ethnic diversity which has such important implications for the interpretation of residential patterns. Similar problems are presented by the distinctive phasing of immigration, since the major groups have had unequal lengths of time to adjust to British conditions (Table 9.1). Geographically, ethnic minorities are highly localized in regions where job vacancies for low-skilled labour were high, but which found difficulty in attracting white immigra-

---

[1] The New Commonwealth refers to territories of the Commonwealth other than the 'white dominions' of Australia, New Zealand, and Canada. A discussion of the technical problems concerning the use and interpretation of Census birthplace data is beyond the scope of this paper, but the topic is thoroughly treated in Immigrant Statistics Unit (1975). The paper uses a variety of data, and where statistical information is referred to, the terms 'coloured' or 'ethnic' denote estimates of the actual population of ethnic origin. Where crude unadjusted birthplace data are used, the term 'immigrants' is used; these data exclude children born in the U.K. to coloured parents, and may include a variable, but generally small, number of white persons. Pakistan is no longer a member of the Commonwealth, but it was included in the 1971 Census data.

[2] 'Asian' refers to people who derived either directly or indirectly (e.g. via East Africa) from the Indian sub-continent; this usage has become general in recent years, as Tinker (1977) points out.

Table 9.1

Great Britain: Population of Ethnic Origin 1971 and date of arrival

| Birthplace | Numbers[1] | Percentage[1] | Arrivals by end 1961 percentage[2] | |
			Males	Females
India	384,000	29	41	34
Pakistan*	169,000	13	29	7
African CW	157,000	12	16	11
American CW	548,000	41	70	54
Other Areas	73,000	5	–	–
Coloured New				
Commonwealth	1,331,000	100	–	–

* Including Bangla Desh; CW – Commonwealth
Sources: Immigrant Statistics Unit, 'Country of Birth and Colour', *Population Trends*, 2, 1975, pp. 2–8;[1] Lomas, 1974, Table 1.5, p. 35.[2]

tion; the problems were most acute in the large cities (Peach, 1966, pp. 158–9). In 1971 three-quarters of the population of New Commonwealth ethnic origin was found in the south-east, including Greater London, and the West Midlands (Immigrant Statistics Unit, 1975, 6); almost 70 per cent were resident in the six major conurbations alone (Lomas, 1974, pp. 51–2). Ethnic minorities are essentially a phenomenon of major cities, but the potential variety in city size, ethnic composition, local employment, and housing-market structures makes generalization difficult. Many important differences were revealed in a recent study of immigrants in four large cities (Lomas, 1975) and the following remarks, which relate mainly to very large cities, are not necessarily typical of all urban situations.

Racial Segregation in British Cities

Segregation: The Pattern and its Causes

Smith (1976, p. 17) has stated that '. . . the great unevenness of the geographical distribution . . . underlies all discussions and controversy about racial disadvantage and the policies required to deal with it.' Evidence from the 1971 Cenus, however, suggests that down to enumeration district level at least, ethnic minorities live in varying degrees of 'mixture' with the white population, and not in conditions of exclusive segregation commonly found with negroes in American cities (Morrill, 1965). In a national sample of 1,547 enumeration districts only one-quarter of New Commonwealth immigrants lived in districts where they formed over 20 per cent of the population (Smith, 1976, p. 17). An intermediate degree of segregation is also indicated by studies using indices of dissimilarity, which compare the distribution of two population sub-groups within any given set of areas.[3] The resulting statistic expresses the proportion of one population sub-group which would have to be redistributed in order to make it equal to the other. In cases where one population sub-group is compared with the total

[3] For a recent critique, and method of calculation, see Woods (1976).

population, the resulting index of dissimilarity is called a segregation index. Woods (1976) has demonstrated the depenence of these indices on the scale of areal units employed, but to date they form our only reasonably comparable measures. On a scale ranging from 0 (no segregation) to 100 (complete segregation), segregation indices calculated for major coloured immigrant groups in selected British cities were in the range 40 to 70 (Table 9.2). Considerable segregation thus exists, but it falls well short of the median index of 88 for negro segregation at a tract level in U.S. cities (Taeuber, 1965, p. 4).

Table 9.2
Segregation Indices in selected cities 1971 (Ward level)

Birthplace Group	Greater London[a]	City Birmingham[b]	Coventry[c]
West Indians	51*	50	34
Pakistanis	49*	⎫ 57	70
Indians	38*	⎭	59
African CW	38*	54	52

Sources: a. Peach, 1975; b. Woods, 1976; c. Winchester, 1974.
* Index of Dissimilarity with England and Wales born.

The factors leading to the segregation of coloured minorities in British cities can be grouped under two broad headings, internal (or sub-cultural) and external (or structural). The former stem from the social needs and desires of coloured minorities themselves, whilst the latter relate to their relationships with the wider society within which they find themselves—its economic structure, its institutional framework, and so on. Assessing the balance between these two broad groups of factors is not easy especially as both are constantly changing, but reference will be made to attempts to compare their relative strengths after the specific characteristics of both types of factors have been examined.

Segregation: Internal or Sub-cultural Factors

Coloured minorities are recently arrived immigrants, differing quite profoundly both from the host population and from one another in terms of basic cultural characteristics such as language, religion, social organization, and experience of an urban society. They need the support provided by both formal ethnic-oriented institutions and informal friendship and kinship ties, and these are cemented by the process of chain migration. Voluntary residential propinquity, leading to geographical concentration, is necessary for these functions to flourish, creating what Rex and Moore (1967) have called an ethnic 'colony'. The available statistical evidence indicates that a broad positive relationship exists between the degree of cultural and spatial 'separateness'. Thus West Indians, who are culturally the least dissimilar group from the white population, also have the lowest segregation indices; Pakistanis, culturally the most dissimilar, have the highest indices (Table 9.2). Moreover, in a recent P.E.P. study, Smith (1976, p. 17) has shown that 51 per cent of Pakistani immigrants and 39 per cent of Indian immigrants, but only 26 per cent of West Indian immigrants in a national sample of enumeration districts lived in districts with 20 per cent and over New Commonwealth-born.

Additional evidence of the strength of self-segregation forces is provided by the high degree of segregation *between* various groups. Peach (1975, p. 377) has drawn attention to high dissimilarity indices in London in 1971 between Pakistanis and West Indians (52), Indians and West Indians (50), and even between different groups of West Indians, such as 41 between Jamaicans and Trinidadians. An important internal factor is the high priority which Asian immigrants in particular grant to property ownership, for reasons of social status and financial economy (Community Relations Commission, 1976, p. 29). This has made Asian households reluctant entrants into local authority housing, and imposed a considerable restraint on their potential residential choice in British cities.

Segregation: External or Structural Factors

Although formal discriminatory barriers on racial grounds are illegal, coloured ethnic minorities have been handicapped in the housing market in a variety of ways (Burney, 1967). Within a 'mixed' housing market their predominantly low incomes hinder their ability to compete in the private sector, whilst institutional obstacles reduce their chances in the public sector. The concentration of coloured immigrants in occupations which are characteristically unattractive to white workers, often unpleasant in some form or another, and which are usually rewarded by low wages, has been highlighted in a recent report by the Unit for Manpower Studies (1976). Low incomes have in turn led to a general association of coloured immigrants with poor housing. In 1971 about one-third of New Commonwealth immigrants in Britain lived in the worst 25 per cent of enumeration districts classified in terms of four critical indicators of sub-standard housing (Holtermann, 1975, p. 43), and coloured households tend to occupy poorer quality housing overall (Table 9.3). This general relationship is even more pronounced in areas of high immigrant concentration, as Smith (1976, p. 239) has

Table 9.3
General Survey of Household Amenities

Ethnic Group of Household	Percentage of households with exclusive use		
	Bath	Hot Water	Inside W.C.
West Indian	73	80	75
Pakistani	61	67	48
Indian	78	81	67
White	91	92	87

Source: Smith, 1976, Table B88, p. 238.

demonstrated. This lowly economic status imposes real restrictions on coloured households' choice of housing in the private sector, and exerts a strong external barrier to movement into newer, better-quality, suburban housing. Such a movement is not however impossible, and, using both aggregate and individual household data, Lee (1977) has shown how residential segregation has been declining among London's West Indians as increasing numbers of households successfully compete in the wider housing market. Although many coloured households within the areas of high immigrant concentration do experience inadequate housing, they also enjoy the compensating social benefits of a closer community life.

A second set of external factors maintaining segregation are the various difficulties surrounding the entry of coloured immigrants into the public housing sector. In the earlier years of immigration the imposition of lengthy residence qualifications greatly reduced their chances of council housing, despite their working-class-occupational status. Whilst these barriers have obviously diminished in time, and West Indians in particular have become well represented (though still less than their economic status warrants) in council housing, it is still far from certain that complete equity of treatment of coloured and white households is the rule. The evidence of immigrants' experience in the public-housing sector so far has not been promising. Although housing allocation is a very complex procedure which places many *unintentional* disadvantages on coloured tenants, a recent study has shown that coloured tenants on Greater London Council estates were being disproportionately allocated to older, poorer-quality accommodation (Parker and Dugmore, 1976). The authors show (p. 64) that in the older, undesirable 'flatted' estates of Inner London about one-half of incoming tenants in 1974 were coloured, so threatening to re-establish and perpetuate a pattern of racial disadvantage within local authority housing. Moreover, instead of sharing the tendency of white families to move *out* of Inner London, coloured tenants are becoming geographically more concentrated and strongly localized *in* Inner London (Parker and Dugmore, 1976, p. 34).

Council housing theoretically has a critical role to play, because of the opportunities it provides for 'social engineering' in housing allocation, enabling coloured minorities to achieve greatly improved housing conditions and by-passing the market mechanisms of the private sector. Tentative government approval has recently been given to '. . . a balanced policy of dispersal by offering prospective tenants a choice of council dwelling over a wide area [which can help] to open up new possibilities to their coloured residents, and avoid the sorts of problems which might arise from their concentration in less desirable estates' (*Race Relations and Housing*, 1975, p. 12). Yet such attempts to break the association of coloured minorities with poor housing, however laudable in themselves, necessarily face the obstacles stemming from within the immigrants themselves— the fear of social isolation, and of rejection. As the P.E.P. study suggests, more positive action is essential in order to offer immigrants a balanced realistic choice, action which would involve actively *planning* for the creation of small communities of Asian and West Indian families on all types of estates in order to counteract the social disruption of dispersal (Smith, 1976, pp. 303–8).

To date, therefore, the balance of factors involved in the segregation of coloured minorities suggests that internal, or sub-cultural, factors are more powerful than the external factors, or structural constraints. The most elaborate test of this hypothesis has been made by Lee (1973), using a proximity model technique by which '. . . the expected number of West Indians in a ward [of Greater London] has been estimated on the basis of the similarity between the socio-economic characteristics of each ward and those of the West Indian population as a whole' (Lee, 1973, p. 484). The simulated distribution of the predominantly working-class West Indian population results in an index of dissimilarity of

28·0, compared with an actual index of 54·9 (Lee, 1973, p. 487). Therefore, although approximately one-half of the residential segregation of West Indians was accounted for by their socio-economic status, the remainder was due to specifically sub-cultural factors. Indeed, using a similar technique but a simpler estimating procedure, Peach *et al.* (1975) allocated even more weight to these internal, sub-cultural factors and correspondingly less to that of socioeconomic status. Although the balance between voluntary and imposed factors within the sub-cultural category cannot be ascertained, the high degree of segregation between otherwise similarly disadvantaged groups points towards voluntary clustering as the most likely hypothesis (Peach, 1975, p. 376). The consistent increases in observed segregation indices of Asian immigrant groups between 1961 and 1971 is a further pointer in this direction (Woods, 1976, p. 171; Winchester, 1974—5, p. 100).

The existence of residential segregation among coloured immigrants, and the causal factors behind this segregation, have been derived from studies using summary statistical procedures. It is necessary, however, to examine the detailed geographical expression of these indices in order to establish the nature of their relationship with the broader urban context and the degree to which generally observed trends find a response in particular spatial contexts. Birmingham has been chosen to examine some of these interconnections.

The Birmingham Case

Numerical, Secular, and Cyclical Background

Birmingham's coloured population in 1971 was 92,632, some 9·3 per cent of the total.[4] During the period of coloured immigration since 1950, neither the city, its coloured minority population, nor society's perceptions of the associated problems have remained static. Between 1945 and 1974 almost 58,000 houses were demolished, mostly in inner redevelopment areas, and 90,000 new houses built by the local authority alone, either inside the city or just beyond the boundary (*Birmingham Statistics*, 1976). Between 1961 and 1971 despite the influx of coloured immigrants, there was a net loss by migration of 18,000, representing a colossal demographic upheaval since the out-migrants were predominantly young and white. The ethnic composition of New Commonwealth immigration became more diverse, reflecting the phasing of immigration on a national level (Table 9.4). But in all groups there has been a steady demographic maturing as the early phase of 'single males' was transformed into a phase of 'family stabilization', a trend reflected in the pattern of housing demand. The perception of associated social problems has also changed. In the 1950s and early 1960s concern was focused on the association of coloured immigrants with multi-occupation, overcrowding, and related ills, summarized in the phrase 'Twilight Zone'. During the middle and late 1960s the rapid influx of Asian immigrants created major linguistic and cultural problems at a neighbourhood level. In the

---

[4] Throughout data and maps refer to Birmingham as it was constituted before the 1974 reorganization of local government.

Table 9.4

Birmingham—Birthplaces of persons born in the New Commonwealth

Birthplace	1961		1971		1961–71
	Number	Percentage of total	Number	Percentage of total	Percentage change of 1961 total
Africa	589	2·1	4,925	7·2	+736·1
America	16,290	57·1	25,365	37·1	+ 55·7
India, Ceylon	4,877	17·1	18,005	26·4	+269·2
Pakistan*	5,355	18·8	17,515	25·6	+227·1
Far East	288	1·0	1,095	1·6	+280·2
Cyprus, Malta, Gibraltar	1,145	4·0	1,415	2·1	+ 23·6
Total	28,544	100·0	68,325	100·0	+139·4

* Including Bangla Desh.
Source: Original statistics in General Register Office, *Census England and Wales County Report Warwickshire* (1963), Table 10, p. 23; Office of Population Censuses and Surveys, *Census England and Wales County Report Warwickshire Part I* (1972), Table 14, p. 45.

present decade, along with a greater concern for racial equality in its widest sense, has come an awareness of the *total* urban problems facing the inner city, in which the majority of immigrants live.

The Changing Spatial Distribution of Coloured Immigrants

Figures 9.1 to 9.3 give a general impression of the changing distribution of New Commonwealth immigrants (excluding Mediterranean territories) between 1961 and 1971, and are derived from Census data.[5] In 1961 at the 'pioneer' stage, a classic concentric distribution existed, about 1 to 1·5 km outside the Conurbation Centre, with a prominent sector break in exclusive Edgbaston. Densities within the belt were low, characteristically 50 or 100 per grid square, and there were many small inliers and interruptions. However high densities over 300 were found in three areas—Handsworth, Aston, and on the western edge of Balsall Heath around Calthorpe Park. The city outside this concentric belt was virtually unaffected, there being few outlying grid squares of significant concentration. By 1971 the concentric belt was more emphatically developed, having pushed outwards in a contiguous manner and also infilling many small interruptions (Figure 9.2). Furthermore, densities were far higher, being mostly over 200, and often over 500, Handsworth forming the largest single concentration of high density squares. The zone within this belt was still comparatively empty, and although outlying concentrations were more prominent (Gravelly Hill, Tyseley,

    [5] Because enumeration districts were not precisely comparable in all instances, separate dot distribution maps were prepared, and then transformed by the 1/3 × 1/3 km grid mesh. The grid is fine enough to preserve a useful degree of locational detail but also evens out minor boundary discrepancies. A constant set of equal-interval class divisions has been used in order to facilitate visual interpretation and comparisons. As the emphasis is on the general facts of the distribution a lower cut-off of 50 per grid square was adopted.

etc.), much of outer Birmingham was still devoid of coloured immigrants at this low level of concentration. Figure 9.3 further emphasizes the dominant role of the concentric belt in absorbing the bulk of intercensal population growth, with the most rapid increases focused in Handsworth, Balsall Heath, Small Heath, and Sparkbrook. Only local declines in the Calthorpe Park area, and a scatter of detached low value squares modify this generalization.

The map stresses the immense importance of the concentric belt for coloured immigrants in this period. The explanation basically lies in what Boal (1976, p. 59) has called the urban 'fabric', whereby the influence of urban morphology is expressed through the accessibility of particular housing types. The concentric belt coincides with the zone of pre-1919 by-law housing, which although variable

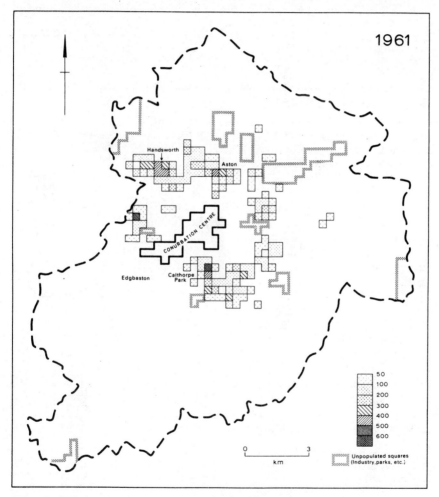

Figure 9.1 Birmingham: Density of coloured immigrants 1961.
Source: 1961 Census, Enumeration District Statistics.

in detail (Stedman, 1958) contains the lowest priced housing under present market conditions. Immigrants, faced with the disadvantages of low incomes and low eligibility for council housing, have been channelled into this zone. Initially this often meant poor rented accommodation in large, multi-occupied houses. Later this usually gave way to the purchase of smaller properties for family occupation. Before 1971 only limited numbers of coloured households were in council housing, largely as a result of renewal schemes, so their comparative absence from both innermost and outer Birmingham is understandable (Sutcliffe and Smith, 1974, p. 380). Moreover Asian immigrants, unlike West Indians, were slow to enter council housing (Select Committee on Race Relations and

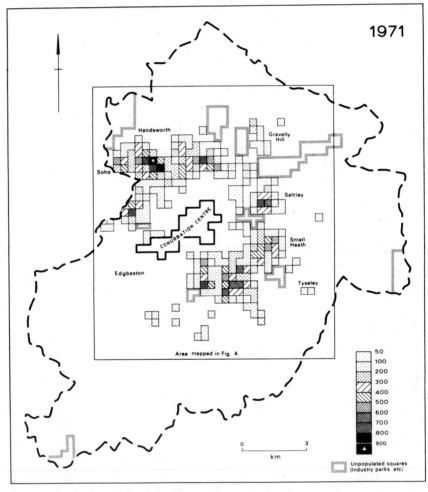

Figure 9.2 Birmingham: Density of coloured immigrants 1971.
Source: 1971 Census, Small Area Statistics.

Immigration, 1971, p. 117). From 1969 onwards the housing department's dispersal policy for coloured tenants would also have prevented concentrations developing in council estates.

Within the concentric belt immigrants are further concentrated by the forces of self-segregation, which are particularly effective for Asians. Many concentrations have developed as a 'spread' outwards from initial localizations in kernels of multi-occupied properties characteristically found around Victorian parks, such as Small Heath or Sparkbrook (Jones, 1967, pp. 21–3). Subsidiary concentrations beyond this concentric belt are invariably associated with outliers of pre-1919 housing.

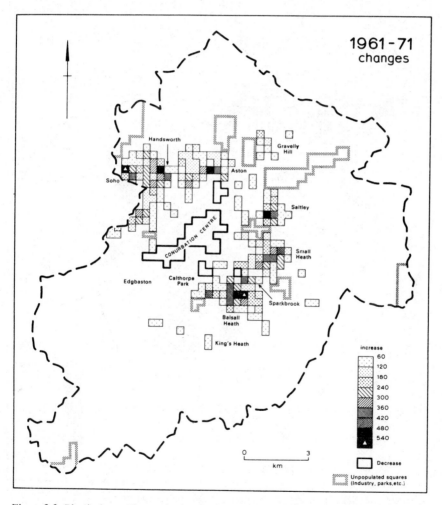

Figure 9.3 Birmingham: Changes in the density of coloured immigrants 1961–71.
Sources: 1961 Census, Enumeration District Statistics; 1971 Census, Small Area Statistics.

Coloured areas of the city in 1971

The proportion of the population with *both* parents born in the New Commonwealth is a good approximation of the coloured 'ratio' or proportion (Immigrant
Statistics Unit, 1975, p. 3): Figure 9.4 includes all enumeration districts in the
city with coloured ratios above the mean, but excludes special enumeration
districts and the conurbation centre. The spatial pattern derived from enumeration districts is fine in its detail, but a concentric arrangement of high values is
immediately apparent. In a number of small sub-nuclei there was a coloured
majority, and within all these areas some districts had even higher ratios. Their

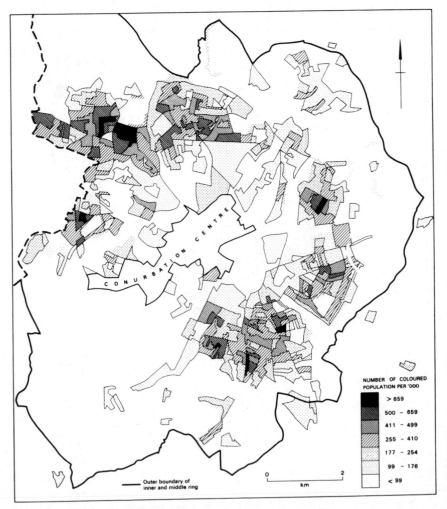

Figure 9.4 Birmingham: Distribution of the coloured population 1971.
Source: 1971 Census, Small Area Statistics as in Jones, P. N., 1976 by permission of the
Association of American Geographers.

Table 9.5
Population and Ethnic Composition of the Coloured Clusters 1971

Cluster	Total population	Percentage coloured	Persons born in NCW*		
				Percentage born in dominant Ethnic Groups by rank	
			Number	1st	2nd
South Birmingham	33,938	42·5	10,994	38·5 PAK	23·8 IND
Small Heath	16,239	37·8	4,920	56·4 PAK	23·2 IND
Saltley	8,201	41·3	2,697	75·1 PAK	19·6 WI
Summerfield	8,990	40·5	2,434	44·3 IND	42·3 WI
Handsworth	31,239	51·3	10,665	48·7 IND	40·5 WI
Aston	24,194	44·7	7,415	45·5 WI	24·3 IND
Total Clusters	122,801		39,125	33·6 WI	29·3 IND

* New Commonwealth, Key to abbreviations: PAK—Pakistani, WI—West Indian, IND—Indian.
Source: 1971 Census Small Area Statistics.

distribution was nevertheless fragmentary, with the notable exception of Hands-worth, and they formed intense local 'pockets' within a fairly extensive concentric belt. Some eighty enumeration districts had a coloured majority, containing one-quarter of the city's coloured population. Nine districts had ratios greater than 750 per thousand, but only contained 4 per cent. Although these ratios are below the levels established in the United States by Rose (1972) or Duncan and Duncan (1957), they represent a considerable increase over estimates based on the 1966 Census (Jones, 1970, p. 217).

An operational definition of 'coloured space' in Birmingham has to be broader than the 'majority districts', because the unstable social characteristics associated with population transition affect wider areas. The majority districts can be looked upon as forming the 'cores' of more extensive spaces defined empirically by the 255 ratio.[6] A set of territorially contiguous and relatively homogeneous enumeration districts results, which can be approximately termed 'Coloured Clusters'. These had a total population of 122,000, including almost 40,000 coloured immigrants (Table 9.5). The population of individual clusters varied from 8,000 to 38,000, with a coloured ratio generally in the range 40 to 45 per cent. The presence of a large coloured population is thus a dominant feature over quite extensive areas of the inner city.

The clusters are ethnically diverse. In 1971 Pakistanis were predominant in South Birmingham, Saltley, and Small Heath; Indians and West Indians were evenly balanced in the remainder (Table 9.5). This simplicity disappears when the data are mapped at enumeration district level using Weaver's combination-index technique[7] (Figure 9.5). In accordance with their greater social isolation, Pakistanis living in the clusters were geographically the most segregated, and one-quarter were resident in one-group Pakistani districts (Table 9.6). Saltley and Small Heath had especially large numbers of one-group Pakistani districts. In the northern and western clusters the even blend of Indians and West Indians was generally replicated in the predominance of two-group West Indian—Indian districts, with minor interruptions, including some Pakistanis in Aston, and limited areas of Indian or West Indian dominance. In contrast South Birmingham was particularly heterogeneous, and had a high proportion of three- and four-group districts. In 1971, despite the strong forces making for self-segregation, the ethnic groups had achieved limited success in creating a mosaic of ethnically homogeneous enclaves. The tendency was strongest amongst Pakistanis, but three-quarters still lived in districts which they 'shared' with other groups. But 1971 is but a stage in a developing process. In 1961 the numerical preponderance of West Indians was expressed in high levels of immigrant ethnic homogeneity over large tracts (Jones, 1967, pp. 15–7). Asian immigrants subsequently infil-

[6] Rose (1972) used 30 per cent to delimit the outer margin of his 'ghetto transition zone', since this was regarded as a significant 'threshold' by the white population under American conditions.

[7] The percentage breakdown of New Commonwealth immigrants by birthplace was calculated for each district, and tested against a succession of 'models' (e.g. one-group = 100 per cent from one country or region; two-group = 50 per cent from each of two regions or countries) in order to find the model which gave the lowest least squares deviation. The technique is fully outlined in Weaver (1954).

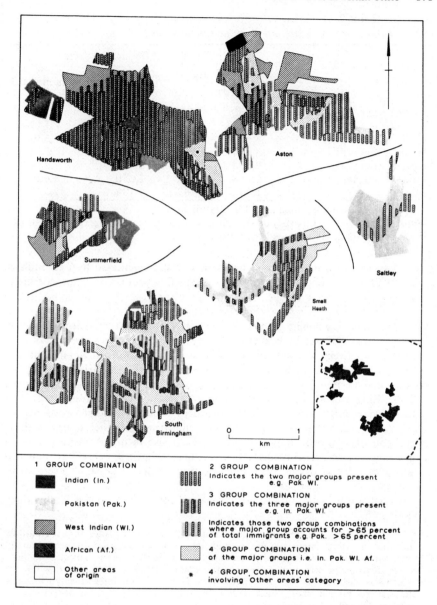

1 GROUP COMBINATION

Indian (In.)

Pakistan (Pak.)

West Indian (WI.)

African (Af.)

Other areas of origin

2 GROUP COMBINATION
Indicates the two major groups present e.g. Pak. WI.

3 GROUP COMBINATION
Indicates the three major groups present e.g. In. Pak. WI.

Indicates those two group combinations where major group accounts for >65 percent of total immigrants e.g. Pak. >65 percent

4 GROUP COMBINATION
of the major groups i.e. In. Pak. WI. Af.

* 4 GROUP COMBINATION
involving 'Other areas' category

Figure 9.5 Birmingham: The place of birth of the New Commonwealth-born population of the coloured clusters by combination index groups. The only five-group combination is shaded black.
Source: 1971 Census, Small Area Statistics as in Jones, P. N., 1976 by permission of the Association of American Geographers.

Table 9.6
Ethnic Group Combination in the Clusters 1971

Combination	Number of Immigrants from			
	Pakistan	India	West Indies	New Commonwealth
One Group:	2,676	1,237	1,836	5,982
Pakistani	2,620	198	427	3,311
Indian	23	898	104	1,141
West Indian	33	141	1,305	1,530
Two Group†	3,774	5,881	6,756	17,332
Three Group†	2,554	2,024	2,459	7,388
Four Group and Others	2,268	2,325	2,050	8,423
Total	11,272	11,467	13,137	39,125

† Involving Pakistanis, Indians and West Indians.
Source: The ANNALS of the Association of American Geographers, Vol. 66, 1976, P. N. Jones (reproduced by permission).

trated space which in most cases had been initially penetrated by West Indians. The evidence of population trends suggests this process was not complete.

Trends in Immigrant Population Distribution 1961–1971

It is proposed to examine these at three geographical levels, so that their continuity or otherwise can be evaluated. Figure 9.6 demonstrates the pronounced divergence between the net shifts[8] of West Indian and Asian immigrants at a ward level. Both record negative shifts in inner-city wards such as Edgbaston, Aston, and Deritend, where urban renewal clearance was extensive. Within the Middle Ring wards[9] where both groups are most highly concentrated, West Indians were shifting away from the majority, whereas Asians recorded massive positive shifts into all wards. In the outer suburban wards the pattern of shifts was again diametrically opposed. West Indians also recorded positive shifts in some inner wards, undoubtedly reflecting their willingness to use the municipal sector, since these wards were the location of major urban-redevelopment schemes.

A comparison with shifts in the total and Irish populations is illuminating,

[8] 'Net shifts' in the population of the various groups were calculated for each ward by comparing the actual intercensal change with the estimated change if the average rate of change for the group within the city had been maintained. It therefore indicates whether a ward is increasing or decreasing its share of the total population of a given group within the city, and as such is a measure of redistribution between wards rather than an index of numerical growth or decline as such. An account of its calculation, use, and further elaboration may be found in Hall *et al.* (1973).

[9] The terminology Inner, Middle, and Outer Ring is derived from the Bournville Village Trust's classic account (1941) of the city's concentric morphological and social structure. The Inner Ring is now almost completely redeveloped, the Middle Ring is dominated by pre-1919 by-law housing, and the Outer Ring corresponds to post-1919 suburbia. Ward boundaries do not match these 'ideal' types precisely, so that the data inevitably reflect some 'blurring' of the rings in wards such as Deritend or Sandwell; but on balance there is an acceptable degree of 'fit' for an overall impression.

since both displayed a huge flight from the inner wards particularly, and a substantial shift away from the Middle Ring Wards of high immigrant concentration
(Table 9.7). Both have large gains in the Outer Ring. West Indians recorded a

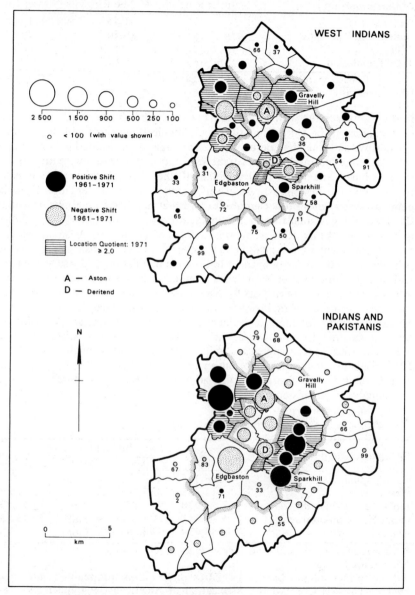

Figure 9.6 Birmingham: Net shifts of population by ward 1961–71. The thickened boundaries separate the Inner, Middle, and Outer Rings.
Source: Statistics supplied by Mr. A. B. Neale, City Statistician.

Table 9.7

Net shifts in population between major zones 1961–71

Birthplace Group	Inner Ring	Net shifts in Middle Ring	Outer Ring
West Indians	− 215	−1,453	+ 1,668
Indians and Pakistanis	− 4,483	+6,567	− 2,084
Irish	− 5,221	−3,539	+ 8,760
Total Population	−60,835	−9,807	+70,642

Source: Census ward statistics made available by A. B. Neale, City Statistician (Birmingham).

roughly similar trend, with a significant net loss in the Middle Ring, compensated by net gains in the Outer Ring. In detail, Middle Ring wards with West Indian net positive shifts tend to be on the outer margin, such as Sparkhill or Gravelly Hill. Although the absolute shifts of the West Indian population were numerically small (13 per cent of the 1971 population), they were demonstrably outwards to the suburbs. In contrast, Asian shifts appear as a 'counter-current' to the dominant 'flow' of all other groups, except that net losses were experienced in the Inner Ring wards. Clearly the momentum of ethnic minority population growth in the Middle Ring wards was maintained entirely by Asian immigrants. Indeed a gradient of assimilation and dispersal is evident. Irish immigrants display the greatest similarity in trend to the total population, and Asians the least. Irish and total population shifts were opposed in only seven out of thirty-nine wards, compared with twenty-six for Asians. West Indians were opposed in fifteen, the main divergence being in wards where West Indians recorded positive shifts against the trend for the total population. Net shifts of Irish and West Indians were similar in thirty-one wards, those of West Indians and Asians similar in only ten. West Indian and Asian shifts were therefore strongly dissimilar in 1961–71, only the former exhibiting a wider dispersal.

This fundamental divergence in Asian and West Indian trends is reflected in the population trends in the clusters[10] (Table 9.8). The 'white' population

Table 9.8

Population Changes in the Coloured Clusters 1961–71*

Birthplace Group	Population			
	1961	1971	Change	Percentage
Total population	166,315	139,861	−26,454	− 15·9
West Indians	11,885	13,769	+ 1,884	+ 15·9
Indians and Pakistanis	4,930	23,775	+18,845	+382·3
Other New Commonwealth[1]	541	3,426	+ 2,885	+433·3
Remainder (White)[2]	148,959	98,891	−50,068	− 33·6

* Adjusted for intercensal boundary changes.
[1] Including Africa.
[2] But also including British-born children of New Commonwealth ethnic origin.
Source: The ANNALS of the Association of American Geographers, Vol. 66, 1976, P. N. Jones (reproduced by permission).

[10] For details of the adjustments made to allow for intercensal boundary changes see Jones (1976).

declined sharply, and although West Indians increased slightly, in both absolute and relative terms Asian immigrants transformed the demography of the clusters between 1961 and 1971. The situation is that of 'polarization' (Peach, 1975), with coloured immigrants steadily becoming a higher proportion of a declining population in the inner city. The bulk of West Indian population growth occurred in those parts of the Inner and Middle Rings *outside* the clusters, although the fastest percentage increases were in the Outer Ring (Table 9.9). Asian increases were at a maximum in the clusters. Much of the West Indian increase, particularly in the Outer Ring, involved filtering into predominantly white areas. In 1971 one-fifth of West Indians lived in enumeration districts with below-average coloured ratios, compared with 11 per cent of Indians and only 5 per cent of Pakistanis.

Table 9.9
Changes in Immigrant Numbers 1961–71 (by Zones)

| City Zone | Immigrants born in | | | |
| | West Indies | | India and Pakistan | |
	Increase	Percentage	Increase	Percentage
Clusters	1,884	15·9	18,845	382·3
Remainder of Inner and Middle Ring	4,689	138·3	5,243	130·6
Outer Ring	1,700	266·1	755	76·1

Source: The ANNALS of the Association of American Geographers, Vol. 66, 1976, P. N. Jones (reproduced by permission).

This divergence was also reflected spatially. Figure 9.7 is based on exactly comparable sets of enumeration districts, which Woods (1974) has termed Amalgamated Areas, covering the concentric belt. The dominant category spatially is that in which the absolute numerical growth of Asians exceeds that of West Indians. In many parts of the south and east (e.g. Small Heath, Balsall Heath) West Indians declined whilst Asians increased. Tracts where West Indians increased more than Asians were generally confined to the *outer* margins of the concentric belt, suggesting that the longer-established West Indians were still pushing into new territory.

West Indians have therefore been dispersing, but not in sufficiently large numbers to change fundamentally the balance of immigrant population distribution. The dense concentration in the concentric belt of the Middle Ring wards still remains the primary geographical reality for coloured ethnic minorities in the city.

Social Problems and Policies

In this section the major social issues raised by the development of ethnic concentrations in British cities are outlined, and some of the alternative policy solutions discussed. The framework of the discussion is general, but illustrative examples are drawn from Birmingham in order to illustrate the vital local context of national issues.

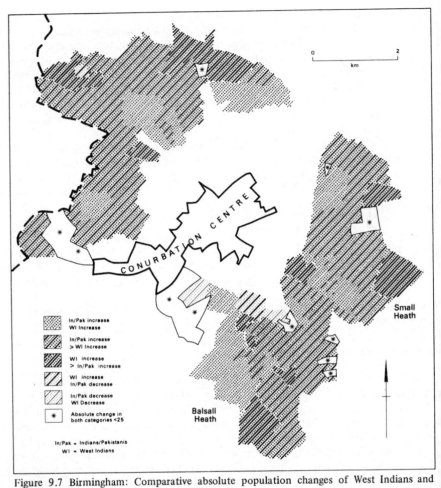

Figure 9.7 Birmingham: Comparative absolute population changes of West Indians and Indians–Pakistanis 1961–71 in the concentric belt.
Sources: 1961 Census, Enumeration District Statistics; 1971 Census, Small Area Statistics.

Ethnic Areas: Social Issues

In 1971 coloured minority populations in Birmingham were strongly associated with the Middle Ring of by-law housing, a residential zone which had been losing its attractiveness for the local white population for a considerable time. This was amply borne out by the population trends for the 1961–71 period. This segregation basically reflects the operation of processes which are national in scope, and Birmingham was not unique in the degree of segregation present in 1971 (Table 9.2). Nevertheless the considerable variability of immigrant concentration within this zone is due in part to the controls on the spatial diffusion of multi-occupation under the powers provided by the Birmingham Corporation Act 1965,[11] although

[11] The Birmingham Corporation Act, 1965, requires that houses in which there are

the impact is difficult to assess with precision. As the city stated in 1971, 'In the last four years [i.e. since 1965] the spread of multi-occupied houses has been greatly curtailed . . .', and according to the same evidence, over half of the 4,350 houses registered in multi-occupation were owned or occupied by coloured immigrants (Select Committee on Race Relations and Immigration, 1971, p. 275). Indeed a map of registered property in multi-occupation in 1970 indicates that the distribution pattern was strongly related to the 'urban fabric', suggesting that the main impact has been to restrict this form of housing to the kernel areas of large houses (City of Birmingham Structure Plan, 1973, p. 33). On the other hand not all properties are registered, despite a vigorous programme of control and inspection, and there has also been a rapid growth in 'non-registrable multi-occupation' at levels of occupance below the threshold of the 1965 Act, so that by 1970 an estimated 8,000–9,000 houses were in this category (Select Committee on Race Relations and Immigration, 1971, p. 275). It is in fact arguable that the search for new accommodation around the major kernel areas of multi-occupation has been accelerated by the high levels of successful prosecutions of owners of multi-occupied property for bad management and overcrowding.

In its basic elements, however, the geographical distribution of the coloured minority population in Birmingham exhibits a familiar parallelism with that observed in other British cities. Furthermore, the slowdown of physical clearance and renewal in the late 1960s in favour of rehabilitation and improvement has meant that a high percentage of the coloured population are living in what is, for the most part, a 'fossilized' housing zone. In Birmingham approximately two-thirds of the coloured population lived in proposed or declared General Improvement Areas (GIAs), where housing has a long life-expectancy and where little physical renewal is anticipated (Figure 9.8). A further fifth lived in scheduled clearance and renewal areas where substantial disturbance has been occurring in the 1970s; many of these disturbed will be coloured families, although much property will also be retained and rehabilitated (Jones, 1976, p. 101). A high proportion of the coloured households in these renewal areas who are affected by clearance will probably seek alternative private accommodation in the contiguous GIA areas, where leeway certainly existed.[12] Those affected families, particularly West Indian, who opt for council housing are likely to gravitate mainly towards inner Birmingham estates on the evidence of past trends (Select Committee on Race Relations and Immigration, 1971, p. 178). This is particularly likely since the relaxation of the city's originally rigid dispersal policy in 1975 (*The Times*, 1975). A rise in the coloured population in inner Birmingham during the 1970s can therefore be anticipated as a result of processes at work in both private and council housing markets. The numerical weight of this coloured

---

more than two separate occupances, or more than four individual lodgers, must be registered with the Corporation. 'Registration may be refused in cases where it is considered that the house is unsuitable for use in multiple occupation, the use would be detrimental to the locality, or the person in control is unsuitable' (City of Birmingham Structure Plan, 1973, p. 32).

[12]   28 per cent of all Asian households in the Small Heath Study Area had been resident less than two years i.e. approximately *since* the 1971 Census (Social and Community Planning Research, 1975, p. 141).

population will be reinforced by natural increase, especially as the ethnic balance of this increase within the immigrant population has swung decisively from a West Indian to an Asian dominance between 1966 and 1974.[13] The bulk of the coloured population is therefore undoubtedly firmly entrenched in the inner city, which itself has become the locale of a variety of problems.

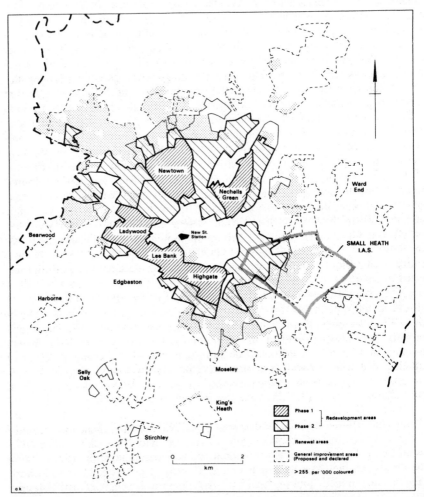

Figure 9.8 Birmingham: Distribution of coloured areas 1971 in relation to the major urban policy areas.
Sources: 1971 Census, Small Area Statistics; City of Birmingham Planning Department, as in Jones, P. N., 1976 by permission of the Association of American Geographers.

[13] In 1966 there were 2,188 births of West Indian parentage and 1,440 of Asian; by 1974 there were only 894 West Indian births and 2,350 Asian. (*Birmingham Statistics*, 1976, p. 47).

The concentration of coloured populations in the declining inner areas of British cities has been linked with a number of problems which were collectively examined by the Cullingworth Committee (Cullingworth, 1969). Foremost was the association of such concentrations with poor housing conditions and other indicators of social malaise. This association, although not necessarily a causal relationship, has nevertheless contributed to a stereotype of coloured immigrant inferiority. In Birmingham the evils of the worst types of multi-occupation were at the forefront of public and local authority concern in the earlier years of immigration, and were instrumental in the passing of the 'sanitary'-type legislation against multi-occupation. Although an appreciation of the material disadvantages faced by coloured immigrants has widened to include inadequacies in all types of housing tenure, and deepened with the realization that their deprivation is multiple and shared with a large segment of the white population, there is a danger of what Deakin (1970, p. 119) has called a 'ghetto psychosis' developing, particularly amongst the young. This is reinforced by the fact that ethnic concentration has been interpreted as a symbol of cultural isolation and withdrawal, which ultimately hinders integration into the wider society. This feeling was well articulated by a Birmingham councillor: 'What we want is not to establish the ghetto, which is a word that I hate, but we feel that the sooner people are integrated and dispersed the more likely they are to learn of the things due to them and mix in with the community as a whole' (Select Committee on Race Relations and Immigration, 1971, p. 197). On a more practical level, however, the problems created by immigrant concentration emerged in an acute form during the 1960s when Asian children with no knowledge of English began arriving in Britain to join parents already settled. This led to conflict situations between Education Authorities and parents of white children in many cities, and to the adoption of widely different responses, ranging from the dispersal of 'excess' coloured children, to the concentration of extra staff and resources on affected schools. The latter course was chosen by Birmingham in the face of considerable pressures from central government (Sutcliffe and Smith, 1974, pp. 381–6). This particular linguistic crisis has now subsided; in fact, it has been reversed in Birmingham, with the establishment of Asian-language classes for British-born children of Asian parentage (*Birmingham Mail*, 1974).

Despite the existence of these problems, it has become increasingly apparent that concentration itself is looked at in a different light by the coloured population, and that the relationship of the coloured population with the inner city is more complex than was previously thought. The Cullingworth Committee (Cullingworth, 1969) was perhaps the first body of an 'official' nature to stress the positive benefits which immigrants derived from concentration. The supportive role of immigrant concentration is vital for Asian immigrants in particular, for as a Birmingham Community Relations Officer pointed out: '. . . the Asians [in Birmingham] like to preserve their kinship ties, they have their own churches, their own cinemas, their own businesses and they pool their resources together . . . this provides security for them, especially as their English is not very good' (Select Committee on Race Relations and Immigration, 1971, p. 123). Whilst West Indians' ties are not as marked, they still exist. Moreover, insufficient attention has been given to the immigrants' own wants and appraisals when the housing market is examined. Although much of the housing bought is qualitatively deficient in the inner areas, work of social anthropologists such as Dahya (1974) and Jeffery (1976) indicates that Asian immigrants in particular have economic priorities which place cheapness of accommodation very highly indeed, especially in the early years of immigration. From their viewpoint, the assessment of 'poor' housing is clearly an ethnocentric one imposed from outside, rather than representative of its value to the immigrants themselves.

The role of immigrants in the inner city is indeed one which is in need of constant re-appraisal. Within Birmingham, for example, the variety of housing stock within the suburban girdle is very much greater than the almost uniformly bad housing of the inner redevelopment zones. That the physical potential of this housing is considerable is implicit in the designation, or intended designation, of most of this zone as GIAs. Moreover, although generalization is difficult in view of the heterogeneous nature both of the housing stock and the immigrants themselves, the specific relationships of the coloured population with the multiple deprivation of the inner city is not clear cut, because of basic demographic and economic contrasts with the indigenous white population. In recent years a stereotype of the 'inner city' as a deteriorating zone inhabited by a deprived population has emerged, even if doubts about its nature and universality have been voiced (Hall, 1977; Holtermann, 1975). The Birmingham Inner Area Study in Small Heath (Fig. 9.8) has shown that many symptoms of urban decay are recognizable, including a contracting industrial base, deficiencies in the urban infrastructure, and above-average numbers of disadvantaged individuals and families (Llewelyn-Davies et al., 1974a). It might appear, therefore, that the coloured population in this Middle Ring area is enmeshed in a hopeless web of deprivation, but this is not the case. Firstly, the geographical incidence of environmental deficiencies and individual deprivation is highly uneven, and a pronounced internal gradient exists within the Study Area, from the poorest conditions of severe multiple deprivation in the innermost zone, to the far superior conditions of the GIAs in the east. Coloured households are present in all three major zones of pre-1919 housing, and are not restricted to the poorest; indeed there was a tendency for Asian families to make 'upward' moves into the better housing of the GIAs (Llewelyn-Davies et al., 1974a, p. 21). Secondly, the study stresses the vital role of the coloured population (mainly Pakistanis but with some West Indians) as a dynamic replacement population. Although the coloured newcomers are of a similar socio-economic status to the white residents, they are much younger, have more children, more members of each household at work, record negligible unemployment, and have an average household income which is higher than white households (Social and Community Planning, 1975, pp. 20, 105–7). Furthermore they are not affected by the prevailing low 'white' image of the inner city, but generally express a high degree of satisfaction with both housing and area (Social and Community Planning, 1975, p. 51). If the experience of Small Heath can be taken as typical, and the Study Area was chosen to be representative, then the population transition in the Middle Ring is creating a younger, more satisfied community, committed to the area through house purchase. One of the future scenarios envisaged by the Study is that '. . . [Small Heath] will attract further immigration by Asians. While this would lead to an even greater concentration of Asians in this area and to a corresponding displacement of the indigeneous population, it could also result in a more stable, mostly home-owning and more self-reliant community with its own culture and identity' (D.O.E., 1977, p. 34). Whilst not wishing to minimize the prevalence of associated social problems such as house overcrowding, which derive mainly from the large families characteristic of the immigrant population, it is also apparent that the dangers of over-generalization in the other direction must also be avoided. Policies concerning immigrants and their residential patterns must be evaluated in relation to the needs and aspirations of the coloured populations themselves.

Present policies and alternative solutions

Three cornerstones of government policy have emerged. Firstly, it is recognized that concentrations of immigrants play a vital role in the life-style of ethnic minorities, and must not be deliberately dismantled. Secondly, immigrants, and their children, must be able to make a free decision to move out of areas of concentration when they perceive the need (*Race Relations and Housing*, 1975). In the public sector this definitively rules out such expedients as the compulsory dispersal of coloured tenants, which operated in Birmingham until 1975. In the private sector this freedom of choice will depend largely on the present and future income status of families, balanced by the strength of ethnic ties, sheltering under the anti-discriminatory umbrella of the Race Relations Acts. It does mean accepting the fact that, in the short term at least, concentrations may increase. Thirdly, the 'area enrichment' policy involves diverting financial resources to inner-city areas in order to improve housing, environmental, and other standards for all the population, whether coloured or white. For, in the words of the 1975 White Paper, '. . . the most important question is not that of concentration versus dispersal but of improving the housing, environment, educational and employment opportunities of the inner urban areas where large numbers of coloured families will continue to live for some time to come, whatever the rate of movement out' (*Race Relations and Housing*, 1975, p. 9). Consequently, finance has been provided for inner area refurbishment through a variety of agencies, ranging from the Urban Aid programme to the Housing Acts. In order that this policy based on freedom of choice can be made more effective and realistic in terms of meaningful improvements in the quality of life, a number of structural changes are necessary. The careful monitoring of council-housing allocation procedures within each local housing authority to ensure just allocation for coloured families is one obvious necessity, and a research study by C.U.R.S. on this topic in Birmingham has recently begun (*Birmingham Mail*, 1977). Immigrant house purchasers have been disproportionately severely affected by the drastic cut-backs in local-authority house mortgages in the last five years—as the Community Relations Commission (1976) has emphasized—and lending levels should be restored; 40 per cent of Birmingham's loans were to coloured immigrants in 1970 (Select Committee on Race Relations and Immigration, 1971, p. 174). The level of financial commitment incurred by house-owners in Housing Action Areas and similar area-based improvement policies can also be burdensome and difficult to comprehend for immigrant households, and a review of these is needed (Community Relations Commission, 1976; Llewelyn-Davies *et al.*, 1974b).

But the most fundamental changes in the present 'mixed' market situation are dependent on improvements in the financial resources available, both for individual households, and for area-based schemes. A major advance towards greater equality of job opportunities for coloured citizens in society as a whole would probably accelerate a wider suburban dispersal through income transmission effects (Deakin, 1970, p. 123). For the majority of immigrants in low-income jobs and resident in the inner cities, more immediate goals are the improvement of their personal income status and their shorter-term housing prospects. In the opinion of Llewelyn Davies and partners, the Department of Environment's Consultants in the Small Heath Inner Area Study, these essential aims can be achieved through a combination of national and local policy changes. Measures to channel more assistance to the lower-income purchasers of cheaper housing would benefit inner city residents and the status and quality of their housing. In this respect, the Consultants suggested restricting local authority mortgages to purchasers of pre-1919 property, and more generous tax concessions to low-income mortgagors (Department of the Environment, 1977, p. 24). Within the particular context of Birmingham, the Consultants drew attention to the huge disparity in capital expenditure in 1975–6 on new council housing (£34m), and on the Housing Action Areas and General Improvement Areas (£4m); a reduction of one-half in the new house construction programme could provide capital for accelerating inner city refurbishment, as well as financing schemes to provide new sources of much-needed employment (D.O.E., 1977, p. 26). Although there is ultimately no way that parts of modern city systems can be isolated and treated *in vacuo*, extra selective investment in inner cities and their populations is necessary. The eventual scale of this investment remains uncertain until the government has fully formulated its inner-city policy. Meanwhile racial minorities in inner Birmingham are part of a social and demographic succession, and, with appropriate forms of encouragement for their acknowledged entrepreneurial skills, they could yet form a vital component of its economic regeneration (Hall, 1977). The Asian clothing industry of East London already provides such an example (Unit for Manpower Studies, 1976, pp. 52–5).

Others would dispute this 'integrationist' approach to the problems of the racial minorities in British cities, and see them as another manifestation of the general pattern of class inequality and conflict within a capitalist society (Lambert and Filkin, 1971, p. 331). According to Harvey (1973, p. 137) the ultimate radical solution for this inequity lies in replacing the political and economic conditions which produced it; more specifically, property ownership and the market mechanism would be replaced by socialized controls over housing. However, whilst recognizing the dangers of underestimating the economic dimension of the problems facing racial minorities, it is unrealistic to envisage such revolutionary solutions ever being implemented within a British context.

Conclusion

Future years will witness the further growth of Britain's coloured population, almost entirely as a result of natural demographic processes, and most of this population will remain concentrated in our major cities. The single most important aspect of this growth will be the maturing of British-born coloured persons, since their experiences in areas such as employment and housing will provide the crucial testing ground in which the various perspectives of their role in British society will be measured. In the meantime there is much research that geographers can contribute and three areas are of most pressing urgency. In the field of residential patterns and processes, the scale and motivation of dispersal from ethnic concentrations needs careful evaluation at a household level. This dispersal process needs to be related to the aspirations of the various sub-groups of the immigrant population and to possible contrasts between first- and second-generation families and their varying abilities to compete in the different sectors of a highly complex housing market. A valuable start in this direction has been made by Lee (1977). The resilience, or otherwise, of the existing ethnic concentrations, and their interrelationships with the fluctuating housing and planning policies of the inner-city areas is another sphere of concern. Finally, the economic structure of ethnic areas has been neglected hitherto, and with it the opportunity, to study the growth of self-generated employment in retailing, warehousing, manufacturing, and other commercial activities. This is by no means an exhaustive list, but focuses on the more immediate spatial implications of the coloured minorities' wider relationships within society.

References

Birmingham Mail 1974 2 August; 2 December.
—— 1977 17 August.
Birmingham Statistics 1976 Vol. 18, 1973—5, Birmingham City Council, Birmingham.
Boal, F. W. 1976 'Ethnic residential segregation' in Herbert, D. T., and Johnston, R. J. *Social Areas in Cities*, Vol. I, *Spatial Processes and Form*, Wiley, London, 41—79.
Bournville Village Trust 1941 *When We Build Again*, Allen & Unwin, London.
Burney, E. 1967 *Housing on Trial: a study of Housing and Local Government*, Oxford University Press for the Institute of Race Relations, London.
City of Birmingham Structure Plan 1973 *Report of Survey: Housing*, Birmingham City Council, Birmingham.
Community Relations Commission 1976 *Housing in Multi-racial Areas*, Community Relations Commission, London.
Cullingworth, J. B. (Chairman) 1969 *Council Housing: Purposes, Procedures and Priorities*, H.M.S.O., London.
Dahya, B. 1974 'The nature of Pakistani ethnicity in British cities', in Cohen, A. (ed.), *Urban Ethnicity*, Tavistock Publications, London, 77—118.
Deakin, N. 1970 'Race and Human Rights in the City' in Cowan P. (ed.), *Developing Patterns of Urbanization*, Oliver & Boyd, Edinburgh, 107—29.
Department of the Environment 1977 *Inner Area Studies: Summaries of the Consultants' Final Reports*, H.M.S.O., London.
Duncan, O. D., and **Duncan B.** 1957 *The Negro Population of Chicago*, University of Chicago Press, Chicago.
General Register Office 1963 *Census 1961 England and Wales County Report Warwickshire*, H.M.S.O., London.
Hall, P., Thomas, R., Gracey, H., and **Drewett, J. R.** 1973 *The Containment of*

Urban England Vol. I, *Urban and Metropolitan Growth Processes*, Allen & Unwin, London.

Hall, P. 1977 'The inner cities dilemma', *New Society*, 39, 223–5.

Harvey, D. 1973 *Social Justice and the City* (Arnold, London).

Holtermann, S. 1975 'Areas of urban deprivation in Great Britain: an analysis of 1971 Census data', *Social Trends*, 6. 33–47.

Immigrant Statistics Unit 1975 'Country of birth and colour 1971–74', *Population Trends*, 2. 2–8.

Jeffery, P. 1976 *Migrants and Refugees*, Cambridge University Press, Cambridge.

Jones, P. N. 1967 *The Segregation of Immigrant Communities in the City of Birmingham, 1961*, University of Hull, Hull.

—— (1970) 'Some aspects of the changing distribution of coloured immigrants in Birmingham, 1961–66', *Trans. Inst. Br. Geogr.* 50. 199–219.

—— (1976) 'Coloured minorities in Birmingham, England', *Ann. Ass. Am. Geogr.* 66. 89–103.

Lambert, J. R., and Filkin, C. 1971 'Race Relations Research: some issues of approach and application', *Race*, 12. 329–35.

Lee, T. R. 1973 'Ethnic and social class factors in residential segregation: some implications for dispersal', *Environment and Planning*, 5. 477–90.

—— 1977 *Race and Residence: The Concentration and Dispersal of Immigrants in London*, Clarendon Press, Oxford.

Llewelyn-Davies, R., Watkins, Forester-Walker, and Bor, W. 1974a *Inner Area Study Birmingham Project Report*, Department of the Environment, London.

—— 1974b *Inner Area Study Birmingham Second Progress Report*, Department of the Environment, London.

Lomas, G. B. 1974 *Census 1971: The Coloured Population of Great Britain*, Runnymede Trust, London.

—— 1975 *The Coloured Population of Great Britain: A comparative Study of Coloured Households in Four County Boroughs*, Runnymede Trust, London.

Morrill, R. L. 1965 'The negro ghetto: problems and alternatives', *Geographical Review*, 55. 339–61.

Office of Population Censuses and Surveys 1972 *Census 1971 England and Wales: County Report Warwickshire*, H.M.S.O., London.

OPCS Monitor 1977 Ref. PP1 77/1, Office of Population Censuses and Surveys, London.

Parker, J., and Dugmore, K. 1976 *Colour and the Allocation of G.L.C. Housing: The Report of the G.L.C. Lettings Survey 1974–5*, Greater London Council, London.

Peach, G. C. K. 1966 'Factors affecting the distribution of West Indians in Great Britain', *Trans. Inst. Br. Geogr.* 38. 151–63.

—— 1975 'Immigrants in the inner city', *Geographical Journal*, 141. 372–9.

—— Winchester, S., and Woods, R. I. 1975 'The distribution of coloured immigrants in British cities', *Urban Affairs Annual Review*, 9. 395–419.

Race Relations and Housing 1975 Cmnd. 6232, H.M.S.O., London.

Rex, J., and Moore, R. 1967 *Race, Community and Conflict: A Study of Sparkbrook* Oxford University Press for the Institute of Race Relations, London.

Rose, H. M. 1972 'The spatial development of black residential sub-systems', *Economic Geography* 48. 43–65.

Select Committee on Race Relations and Immigration 1971 *Housing: Minutes of Evidence 8th and 9th February, 1971, Birmingham HC 228–V*, House of Commons, London.

Smith, D. J. 1971 *Racial Disadvantage in Britain*, Penguin, Harmondsworth.
— 1976 *The Facts of Racial Disadvantage*, P.E.P. London.
Social and Community Planning Research 1975 *Small Heath, Birmingham: A Social Survey*, Department of the Environment, London.
Stedman, M. B. 1958 'The townscapes of Birmingham in 1956', *Trans. Inst. Br. Geogr.* 25. 225–38.
Sutcliffe, A., and Smith, R. 1974 *History of Birmingham 1939–70*, Oxford University Press for Birmingham City Council, London.
Taeuber, K. E. 1965 'Residential Segregation', *Scientific American*, 213. 12–19.
The Times 1975 24 January.
Tinker, H. 1977 *The Banyan Tree*, Oxford University Press, Oxford.
Unit for Manpower Studies 1976 *The Role of Immigrants in the Labour Market*, Department of Employment, London.
Weaver, J. C. 1954 'Crop-Combination Regions in the Middle West', *Geographical Review*, 44. 177–81.
Winchester, S. W. C. 1974–5 'Immigrant areas in Coventry in 1971', *New Community*, 4. 97–104.
Woods, R. I. 1974 *The Stochastic Analysis of Immigrant Distributions*, University of Oxford School of Geography, Oxford.
— 1976 'Aspects of the scale problem in the calculation of segregation indices: London and Birmingham, 1961 and 1971', *Tijdschrift voor economische en sociale geografie*, 69. 169–74.

10

EDUCATIONAL DISADVANTAGE
IN AN URBAN SETTING

W. Williamson and D. S. Byrne

The title of this chapter reflects the two main themes with which we shall be concerned—the nature of disadvantage in education as a feature of modern capitalist society and the particular form of such disadvantage in urban social structures. Our aim is to describe the terms in which urban educational disadvantage has been typically understood, to describe the kinds of social policies which have evolved to deal with it and to evaluate the results of this work (both the theoretical results and the policy outcomes) with a view in particular to assessing just how far the urban-deprivation theories of the 1960s can cope with the very different complexities of the 1970s. We shall be particularly concerned to examine the spatial distribution of educational opportunities and to discuss the significance of spatial inequalities for general theories of educational disadvantage.

In the limited space available we cannot document our argument as fully as we might but our position is this: spatial structuring of educational opportunities in Britain is the outcome of social, economic, and political processes with historical roots which are part of the changing structure of a capitalist society. Measurable inequalities in the *distribution* of schools of different type and quality, in the *access* of different social groups to these schools, and in different potentialities of social groups to *control* their own educational destinies, are not the inevitable consequences of urbanism as such, but must be understood as the outcomes of the way in which a given social formation functions and changes. Urban structures of resource distribution and of life chances are features of the broader structure of society itself and in particular the distribution of power among different social groups in that society.

This broad orientation to the study of urban educational deprivation has many ramifications for the further development of social theory, social policy and, not least, social action. We shall discuss what these are and, in the course of doing so, set out what seem to us to be some of the most important steps in the development of current thinking about urban educational deprivation. Our broad assessment of much of this work is simply that it is confined to its own political context and reflects a now unjustifiable optimism that education can be used as a lever of change for social improvement in the most disadvantaged areas of modern cities. To argue this, however, is not tantamount to the claim that education is therefore unimportant. The danger in such a position is, in fact, already evident in the way in which, all over western Europe and the United States, education has become the 'cinderella' of social policy and public expenditure. What we shall try to argue is that change in education towards a more egalitarian distribution of resources and life chances, even on the terms in which they have been conventionally understood, is possible, justified, and urgently required, and that in the economic conditions of the 1970s radical change is needed simply to stand still.

These arguments are clearly contentious, complex, and overlaid heavily with political debate. But to pretend that in some way this is avoidable, that the questions with which we have to deal are purely technical, seems to us to be an equally strong political stance and perhaps even more pernicious than our own. The evolution of the ideas we shall now describe took place in a distinctive political environment in which they played a distinctive political and ideological role; not to alert people to this seems to us to be an act of great intellectual dishonesty.

In what follows we examine first the nature of research and the kinds of results which have been obtained in the general field of urban educational studies. We shall then examine the changed context of that work. Finally, we shall raise questions and discuss some of the answers which are becoming available about the kind of theorizing which now seems appropriate to make sense of the issues which had such a resonance in the late nineteen-sixties.

The Nature of Research into Urban Educational Deprivation

Before the impetus given to social research by the Plowden committee report, *Children and Their Primary Schools* (Central Advisory Council for Education, 1967), to focus on the characteristics of particular areas of cities where educational deprivation was severe, sociologists had been concerned with the broader relationships between social class background and educational opportunity. The nature of this work has been discussed extensively elsewhere by Banks (1976), Williamson (1974), and Tyler (1977). Before noting some of the results of this work some preliminary observations are necessary.

A concern with inequalities of educational opportunity had been an important feature of radical social reform in the inter-war period, particularly in the writings of Tawney (1931), although its roots go deep in the history of the British working class. In this respect the work on inequality can be seen as part of a much older tradition of social democratic politics and, as Morton and Watson (1971) have shown, even of 'liberal' politics. The research work and the tradition of which it is such a central part has, as one of its main thrusts, the aim of combating injustice so that more people, particularly the children of workers, can realize greater opportunities for their own social improvement. The main conviction of this political tradition is that important changes in society can be brought about within the framework of social democratic politics if, through research, imaginative propagandizing, and effective social policies, a way forward can be identified which large numbers of people can support. Economic growth, economic management, social justice, and the welfare state were some of the main preoccupations of this tradition and as Paul Addison (1975) has shown, such ideas reached their own high tide and became an important part of British socialism during the second world war. The issue was no longer whether people should exploit one another but how, as Keynes once put it, such exploitation should be regulated. The war, then, ushered in the era of reformed capitalism or, at least, the prospect of it. And the careful, empirical social investigations of post-war British social science, skillfully angled towards issues of social policy, are an integral part of this tradition, monitoring social change, probing the claims of politicians, and, increasingly during the 1950s and 1960s, probing 'the rotten underbelly of affluence' (Williamson, 1974, p. 6).

This 'social democratic' tradition has to be distinguished from the socialist alternative. Clearly the boundaries between the two perspectives are imprecise, and individuals such as Tawney express both perspectives, sometimes simultaneously. The essence of the difference for us is that the socialist tradition in the British Labour movement seeks to replace capitalism whereas the social democratic tradition seeks to establish a *modus vivendi* based on a regulation of market processes.

It had been very clear before the war that great social inequalities in educational opportunity existed among children from different social backgrounds. What the post-war studies revealed was that such inequalities showed a degree of intransigence which seemed immune to the effects of economic growth and the expansion of the education service. The *Early Leaving* report of 1954 (Central Advisory Council for Education, 1954) had identified a social-class gradient to school children leaving secondary schools before the full completion of their courses. And the later work of Douglas (1964) illustrated a continuing problem of early leaving into the 1960s. He found in a national survey of school children born in 1946, and studied on a longitudinal basis, that of the total of 64 per cent who left school early, 16 per cent were from upper-middle-class families compared with 77 per cent from lower manual groups. And he put his finger on one of the problems when he rejected the currently fashionable hypothesis (which is now becoming fashionable again) that such results reflected a basic pool of ability in the population. Douglas (1964, p. 160) writes: 'It has been said, however, that what is extracted from the pool depends much less on its content than on the effectiveness of the pump: it is clear from the present study that the pump is leaking badly at the points of secondary selection and school leaving.' The issues of what was in the pool and what was wrong with the pump have continued to be hotly debated and researched. Much of this work has been focused on two groups of problems and used to justify two broad thrusts of social policy. These problems are, respectively, the non-educational determinant of ability and the structure of school inequalities. And the policies they give rise to are, broadly, policies of positive discrimination and massive redistribution of resources and changes in the control of education.

The first group of problems concern what has come to be known as the non-educational determinants of ability and relate to those variables which describe different home conditions or cultural differences which bear upon the capacity of children to benefit from schooling. They include such factors as family size, social class, family attitudes, community organization, and patterns of child rearing and language use. All of these variables have been richly studied. In fact, we have elsewhere typified this tradition of research as the 'class-culture paradigm', in so far as it is concerned with the social determinants of educability and particularly as these are affected by social class factors. (Byrne, Williamson, and Fletcher, 1975). Indeed, the growing realization that the removal of financial barriers to secondary education does not of itself modify class gradients of opportunity was what initially led to demands for premature selection to be abolished, schools expanded, and comprehensive policies to be implemented in the belief that schools could play some role in overcoming these influences and thus give more children greater opportunities.

To talk about a particular research paradigm is not, however, to imply agreement among researchers. From an overall concern with the question of educability and differential ability, several explanations of educational inequality have emerged, each stressing the importance of different variables. Tyler (1977) has identified five such 'models' of explanation. These are (1) the meritocratic model which is concerned with intelligence and explains variations in educational achievement amongst different types of children as the outcome of different inherited abilities, (2) the class-conflict model which is concerned with the distribution of material inequalities in the belief that these dominate all other inequalities, (3) the traditional-élites model which explains inequalities as the outcome of interactions between hereditary and environmental factors which none the less favour those groups who are already well off, (4) the evolutionary-liberal model which posits little connection between intelligence and family background, and (5) the 'compensatory liberal' model which insists that changes in school environment and home environment can be effective in changing the educational outlook of working-class children (Tyler, 1977).

The search for the non-educational determinants of educability took an important step forward in the 1960s in the identification of distinctive cultures of poverty (Lewis, 1962, 1966, 1968) and of culturally deprived children (Riessmann, 1962) in particular areas of great cities. Such areas later became known in Britain as educational-priority areas (Central Advisory Council for Education, 1967; Halsey, 1972) and, a little later, as inner-city areas or 'twilight zones'. Social research into the supposed special problems of the inner city and the deprived urban child has increased remarkably in the ten years since the Plowden report was initially published. Much of this work has been extensively reviewed by Herbert (1976) and Robinson (1976).

Two key ideas of much of this research have been those of positive discrimination and some notion of the spatial concentration of deprivation in areas which have properties unique to themselves or, at least, thought to be unique. A landmark in this tradition of research in Britain is the work by Halsey and his colleagues on the education priority-area programme who carried out research work in Deptford, Birmingham, Liverpool, the West Riding, and Dundee. This group recommended the extension of the education-priority programme, on the grounds that positive-discrimination policies had small but beneficial results in terms of improving school performance. (Halsey, 1972). Their work lent support to such programmes as nursery education, a school–home visiting service, positive discrimination in such areas as pupil–teacher ratios, class sizes and resources. But perhaps its real importance lay in its exposition of a network of social pathologies which led to complex, self-defeating adaptations on the part of the people most affected by them. Through a concern, therefore, with ways in which the material circumstances of families influence the performance of children at school the whole vexed question of cognitive poverty is raised, inviting further studies of the special needs of special areas. This was very much the rationale behind the

Home Office's programme of studies known as the Community Development Project (1977) and of the Department of the Environment's later studies into the state of the inner cities (1977). In a specifically educational context it provided the rationale for much more highly focused studies of the learning difficulties of particular groups of children which showed that inner-ring children typically had parents who were almost wholly uninvolved in their education and whose contact with the school was almost negligible. An example is the study that Wilson and Herbert (1974) have carried out in Birmingham. More broadly this orientation has raised questions about alternative forms of schooling for areas of multiple deprivation, of new ways of relating home to school, of innovating in teaching methods and of coping with specially difficult children. Many of these issues are admirably discussed in *Education and the Urban Crisis* (Field, 1977).

But there is an inevitable tension in work of this kind which offers the prospect of a different approach to questions of educational deprivation in urban areas and of inequality in education more generally. The tension arises because the facts of poverty which the studies seek to understand can be related not simply to particular groups of disadvantaged people but to the organization of the economy and society itself. Halsey (1972, p. 7) was clearly aware of this himself when he noted once that 'Too much has been claimed for the power of educational systems as instruments for the wholesale reform of societies which are characteristically hierarchical in their distribution of chance of life.' And, a little later (1972, p. 17), he pointed out:

The poverties to which urban industrial populations are prone must be understood to have their origins in both situational and cultural characteristics of those minorities which suffer disadvantage and discrimination and to have their cures in both economic and cultural reform not only at the local or community level but also in the total structure of society.

From such an elevated perspective it is difficult indeed to be sanguine about the long-term importance of policies of positive discrimination aimed at the most deprived groups. In any case, as Jack Barnes has pointed out, the number of people who could be identified as educationally deprived is greater outside the inner-city area than inside it (Barnes and Lucas, 1974).

A further aspect of this tension concerns the focus of research. Research designed to explain the cognitive poverty of different social groups which focuses on the conditions of successful learning is not perhaps the best way to reveal those mechanisms of the social structure that lie behind given patterns of educational inequality. The issue of the spatial distribution of education resources and differences among regions of the country and local-authority areas in patterns of educational provision and educational policy illustrate the point quite well.

During the late sixties and early seventies several pieces of work documented massive spatial imbalance in educational resources and levels of educational provision and policy among regions of the country (Coates and Rawstron, 1971; Taylor and Ayres, 1969), within particular regions (Byrne and Williamson, 1971; Harrop, 1976), among local authorities themselves (Byrne, Williamson, and Fletcher, 1975), and within particular local authorities among schools themselves (Williamson and Byrne, 1977). What is more, some of this work, particularly that of Byrne, Williamson, and Fletcher, claimed to demonstrate a connection between such spatial inequalities (with their roots both in history and in a broader structure of social inequality) and different patterns of educational attainment. Much of this work has recently been reviewed by Eggleston (1977). It was, and still is, undoubtedly the case that different groups of children, even when they are from similar socio-economic backgrounds, through living in different local-authority areas or parts of towns, differ in their educational attainments, measured either in terms of the length of time they stay at school or in terms of the educational qualifications they eventually acquire. Such a spatial structuring of educational inequalities, of which the phenomenon of inner-city deprivation is only the tip of the iceberg, is related to local education-authority organization, resource levels, and politics, and is entrenched in the much larger system of local-authority financing through the rate-support grant which is controlled by central government. It reflects, therefore, a rather complex mechanism of the distribution of social income (i.e. the share of national income received by a person or group which is received as benefits or services) since educational life chances are an important determinant of income life chances at a later date.

Pahl has attempted to capture this structure in his concept of the socio-spatial system (1970) and Harvey has identified the problem of the distribution of social income as a key problem of territorial justice (1973). In Pahl's work, the notion of the socio-spatial system is designed to reveal something of the nature of urban systems which can be seen, partly at least, as mechanisms for the distribution of scarce resources. However, it is possible, as Byrne, Williamson, and Fletcher (1975) argued, to see such a mechanism as part of a wider system of production in a capitalist society. If this is right, then it is clear that the spatial structuring of educational advantage and disadvantage must be set in a much broader context and that changes in this structuring can only follow from a re-distribution of power so that hitherto disadvantaged groups can assume a much greater control of their own education and the resources given over to it.

This analysis is clearly contentious and might even be thought of as being ideological. But could not the same be said in reply to those who would seek to explain the distribution of educational disadvantage in our society in a way which simply takes the existing structure of power and control for granted and focuses attention on the most deprived groups? What is certain, however, is that explanations of educational disadvantage, and even different understandings of the concept of a socio-spatial system, reflect different sociological theories about how society as a whole functions and changes. Much of the debate in the 1960s and early 1970s about educational deprivation and its remedies can be seen as part of a longer tradition of what Popper once called 'piecemeal social engineer-ing' (Popper, 1957). The question which must be faced in the late 1970s is whether this approach, i.e. of piecemeal social reform and the politics with which it is associated can grasp the complexity of the problems involved or whether it simply performs an unintentional ideological role in giving the appear-ance that something can, in fact, be done when, quite possibly, the opposite is the case.

This reference to the 1970s is deliberate, for under the impact of economic and political changes important new constraints in education have to be faced.

The Changing Context of Educational Reform

Three themes illustrate the changed situation of education in the 1970s in comparison to the 1960s. The first is the economic crisis. The second is a kind of theoretical retreat from the education forum on the part of the social-democratic left. The final one is the changing nature of control in education.

The current economic crisis affects education directly in the way in which it acts on resources. The process is obvious but some of the effects may have been underestimated. Inflation erodes the value of current resources; public-expenditure cuts prevent future growth in education provision. But such processes and actions do not necessarily have uniform effects on all local education authorities or social groups. A recent study of Gateshead in the north of England showed that, under the impact of Government expenditure cuts, improvements in the education service which had begun in the 1960s could not be sustained. In 1976–7 the nursery programme was brought to a halt and capital expenditure to an abrupt stop (Bird, 1977). In 1976–7, following a year in which expenditure had, through inflation, increased in money terms by 23 per cent over the estimates, Gateshead was forced, through Government counter-inflation policies, to evolve expenditure estimates based on a policy of no further growth in education spending. As Bird (1977, p. 29) writes:

Gateshead's programme for growth in 1976–77 is 0 per cent. The Education Department has given priority of spending to staff and capitation allowances. The nursery programme has had to be halted. Capital expenditure on schools buildings has also come to an abrupt stop, with minor works receiving only £300,000, a drop in the ocean, and no major works given permission by the D.E.S.

Put another way, the possibility of Gateshead overcoming the problems of years of neglect, of low ratable values, and of low school attainment rates has been most severely affected although the very same changes will not affect richer local authorities to quite the same degree. The financial system, as Bird makes clear, does not allow Gateshead to compensate some of the poorer areas in the town for years of decay and poverty. During the 1960s Gateshead had managed to build twelve new primary schools and had managed, too, to build them in areas where overcrowding, unemployment, low socio-economic grouping, and numbers of children receiving free school meals were at their highest. But a quarter of Gateshead's primary schools were built before 1910 and are in areas where between 40 per cent and 75 per cent of the houses lack at least one of the three basic amenities (indoor toilet, bath, and/or hot/cold water).

Gateshead is only one of many urban local authorities whose capacity to improve old schools and halt decay is seriously eroded by expenditure cuts and inflation and who have taken the maximum they can from their own local taxes. And if Government expenditure estimates are to be believed, cuts in education are not simply emergency measures but will be a permanent feature of British social policy well into the 1980s.

Expenditure cuts are also related to our second theme, the retreat of the social democratic left or the collapse of a politics of change in education. We refer here to a situation where none of the major political parties regards increases in expenditure on education as an important political priority. Halsey (Bird, 1977, p. 1), reviewing the notion of positive discrimination in 1977 has written:

We live today under the sentence of death by a thousand cuts. In Education, the position is one of extreme relative deprivation, not only because of the financial background of a sudden halt to previously mounting largesse, but because of the collapse in the belief in education either as the best instrument for national production or the great redistributor of chances to the traditionally disadvantaged.

Much of this collapse of belief to which Halsey refers can be attributed to the work of some social scientists both in America and Europe which, while ostensibly radical, has none the less tended to portray inequalities in educational opportunity as simply derivative of larger inequalities and of being, therefore, unamenable to significant changes by educational means. Jencks *et al.* (1972) have argued this quite strongly in America and Boudon (1974) in France, although they would claim that their argument is applicable to all modern capitalist societies. The work of Jencks has been examined and evaluated elsewhere (Douglas, 1973; Byrne *et al.*, 1975) and need not concern us here except in so far as it contributes to a climate of pessimism about change in education. In particular, by seeming to demonstrate the ineffectiveness of the major tool of social democrats, public expenditure on education, Jencks's findings reinforced Conservative proponents of expenditure cuts and the inability of a Labour government to resist such demands. In retrospect, perhaps it will become clear that the optimism upon which both research and social policy thrived in the 1960s was an optimism of a precarious affluence no longer justified in the very different circumstances of the 1970s.

The third element of the current situation which prompts a theoretical re-evaluation of the education system concerns the issue of control in education which has itself become prominent in the 1970s. This is very well illustrated by Prime Minister Callaghan's 'Ruskin' speech in 1976. The demand, under pressure from a resurgent right, for a reassertion of the traditional curriculum and of industrial relevance as a central theme in educational processes might, on the face of things, seem to be concerned with enhancing productivity. However, such a position has to be carefully considered in the light of the trends in the character of the labour force required by a rapidly changing industrial structure. The extent of the de-skilling in the labour force which has already occurred is considerable but that which is projected is far greater. The Department of Employment (1975a) has projected that by 1981 there will be 530,000 fewer manufacturing jobs in the British economy than there are now. The total work force at this time, 1981, is now estimated to be 25 million, of which 4,526,000 will be skilled workers and 2,714,000 will be semi-skilled workers. Thus 28 per cent of the labour force will fall into these categories. In 1961 the comparable figure was 40 per cent. The number of projected skilled workers will thus have fallen by approximately 20 per cent over twenty years and the number of semi-skilled workers will have declined by 23 per cent (Department of Employment, 1975b).

It seems far more valid to regard these pressures for industrial relevance in the school curriculum as concerned with the functions of the educational system in controlling *and* containing working-class children. Schools and other institutions can then be seen to have functions of social control essentially the same as those of the old elementary schools but in very different circumstances. These functions have been correctly described as custodial rather than educational, and the processes of control referred to here are discussed in detail by Finn *et al.* (1977). Recent Marxist work in urban sociology and elsewhere does much to illuminate these issues and the final section of this article deals with such perspectives.

Marxism and a New Perspective

Urban studies as a whole have recently had to come to terms with a new Marxist urban sociology most generally associated with those writers based around the Centre de Sociologie Urbaine in Paris. Pickvance (1976) has described these new approaches as 'historical materialist'. Fred Gray (1976) recently attempted a statement of the central themes raised for our area of concern in a succinct summary of a materialist position on the education system. The qualification is necessary because Gray tends to take over the early Althusserian structuralism of many of the French Urbanists, an analysis (correctly in our view) criticized as over-deterministic and politically inept in terms of its under-rating of class struggle as a force in historical development. A similar point has been made by Erben and Gleeson (1977). But the themes Gray identified seem essential to an understanding of how spatially oriented research in education might proceed, first to clarify the problem and second to inform action.

These approaches see the city as 'the residential locale of the reproduction of labour power' and education as an institutionalized process emanating from the state and contributing to the reproduction of the capitalist relations of production. Gray (1976, p. 42) outlines this perspective as follows and we quote:

We can understand the continuing involvement of the State in the provision and financing of education in the following ways:
1. A response to the material conditions of production which has led to the progressive concentration of the workforce and the concomitant need to establish vast communal units of consumption to organise, control and manage the daily life of labour power.
2. A reaction to the inability of private enterprise, acting under the laws of 'free competition' and the search for profit, to provide education which is an indispensable functional element necessary for the reproduction of the social formation.
3. A mechanism maintaining and aiding the creation of scarcity (and the production of need) which is fundamental to the realisation of surplus value.
4. A mechanism to ensure the extended reproduction of labour power (through the education system's role as provider of 'technical skills and know-how') and the social relations of production (through the education system's role as dominant *ISA*, i.e. ideological state apparatus—Williamson and Byrne, 1977). This division into two functions is theoretically useful although in practice the two are intricately bound together.
5. A result of the social evolution of the social formation. The extended reproduction of the material means of production has led to a progressive and accelerating increase in the complexity of capitalist production and consump-

tion, and this, in turn, has required occupational and 'social' mobility and the development of new skills and abilities. Education acts to service the needs of the economy, and responds to and reflects changes in the capitalist conditions of production. In part this is expressed in the extraction and training of the 'most able' and suitable working class children and their placement in other social positions, although for the mass of the working class, education still functions to fit children to their class destiny (thus, just as the reproduction of the social formation requires the mobility of certain sections of the labour force, equally it requires a pool of low-paid unskilled and suitably motivated and 'trained' workers for the lowest end of the job-market).

However he does not deal in any detail with the location of the reproduction of labour power and it is our belief that it is by developing the emphasis on urban reproduction that the political potentials of radical research can be developed.

The first radical urbanist with a materialist perspective was Friedrich Engels, and the basis of the notion of the city as the residential locale of the reproduction of labour power lies in his *The Conditions of the Working Class in England in 1844*. To our minds there are two things that matter in taking forward analysis and action. The first is that there is something identified by Marx and Engels about the working class which is re-emerging, in so far as it was ever hidden, namely an account of the industrial 'reserve army'. The second is that in the 130 years since 1844 the urban situation has been the locale of the development of a form of working-class politics and consciousness which first began to assume significance in this country at the end of Engels's life and after Marx was dead. What is characteristic of twentieth-century urban politics, at least in Great Britain, is radical reformism as the dominant motif in urban working-class consciousness and, to a decreasing degree, in working-class organization.

It would take a great deal of ivory-tower isolation not to see that something is happening to the structure of the work-force in advanced industrial countries in the late 1970s, something rather unpleasant, to say the least. The most obvious manifestation in the U.K. is the emergence of circa 1½ million *recorded* unemployed. The U.K.'s unemployment rate of 6·4 per cent (as of October 1977) is, in fact, exceeded within Europe by Belgium at 8·5 per cent, Eire at 9·5 per cent and Italy at 7 per cent. Great care is needed, however, in interpreting these figures because of national differences in definition of unemployment. What is plainer is that between 1974 and 1977 the total number of unemployed in the E.E.C. has increased from 3,070,000 to 5,833,000 (*Sunday Times* 23 Oct. 1977, p. 8). In understanding this it helps to know something about 'The Structure of the Working Class and its Reserve Armies' the title of Chapter 17 of Braverman's *Labour and Monopoly Capital*. As Sweezy says in his introduction (Braverman, 1974, p. xii):

Harry Braverman's book is to be considered an invitation and a challenge to a younger generation of Marxist economists and sociologists to get on with the urgent task of destroying bourgeois ideology and putting in its place an honest picture of the social reality within which we are forced to live. . . . In this connection let me call attention to Chapter 17 . . . where the thesis is put forward that Marx's 'General Law of Capitalist Accumulation', according to which the advance of capitalism is characterised by the amassing of wealth at one pole and of deprivation and misery at the other, far from being the egregious fallacy which bourgeois social science has long held it to be, has in fact turned out to be one of the best founded of all Marx's insights into the capitalist system. How much more coherent and useful the voluminous literature of recent years on poverty and related questions would be if it had started from this solid foundation.

We are not going to attempt to summarize this important work here. One quotation will suffice (Braverman, 1974, p. 381):

Under conditions of capitalism, unemployment is not an aberration but a necessary part of the working mechanism of the capitalist mode of production. It is continuously produced and absorbed by the energy of the accumulation process itself. And unemployment is only the officially counted part of the relative surplus of working population which is necessary for the accumulation of capital and which is itself produced by it. This relative surplus population, the industrial reserve army, takes a variety of forms in modern society, including the unemployed; the sporadically employed, the part-time employed; the mass of women who as house workers, form a reserve for the 'female occupations' the armies of migrant labour, both agricultural and industrial, the black population with its extraordinary high rates of unemployment; and the foreign reserves of labour.

The theme of urban consciousness is rather more tendentious. A lot of urban writing from France to which we have referred, is structuralist and has no place for consciousness as a phenomenon that exists, let alone as something which is important. Even those Marxists concerned with consciousness have neglected the arena of reproduction for that of production. The generation of consciousness in the work place is an important theme. But in understanding working class politics the position of those groups organizing outside the work place, particularly in relation to the local state, (Cockburn, 1977) is crucial in the history of urban and working-class development. Radical reformism can indeed be crudely summarized as having the political objective of achieving socialism in reproduction through the agency of the state and without the transformation of the capitalist basis of production. As such it has not succeeded but the character of twentieth-century urban life in Great Britain at least (Northern Ireland is quite deliberately excluded) will not be understood without taking account of it and its products.

We need now to turn from abstraction to reality and to the reality of the educational system of Great Britain as it now stands in its urban context. In Scotland as well as England and Wales there has been an extensive re-organization of local government and in general the secondary educational system is organized on comprehensive lines. The educational system therefore appears to be more equal but important spatial inequalities remain. It might therefore be assumed that a radical research programme in education would, if spatially organised, be concerned with attempts to achieve 'territorial justice' (Davies, 1968). However, the issues which affect education are now obviously and openly bigger than 'equality' alone. The unskilled and semi-skilled working-class areas of the conurbations (in some places this means black areas, in others, e.g. Tyneside and Scotland, not) which typically nowadays are located in the worst of the public-sector housing stock (Byrne, 1976) are also the areas of massive youth unemployment. Braverman pointed out that in fact shrinkage or, as it is politely termed, 'natural wastage', in what some American writers call the primary labour force occurs far more through non-recruitment than through actual redundancy. The kids on the street corners in Sunderland and North Shields are the industrial reserve army.

The educational system relates to this reserve army in a number of important and specific ways. First it recruits it. Those without formal qualifications are more likely than others to experience immediate unemployment on leaving school and to experience unemployment more frequently as they grow older (Expenditure Committee, 1977). Second, the educational system polices the young reserve army. Normally this task falls to the Department of Employment rather than the Department of Education and Science and contemporary approaches are far less crude than the dole schools of the 1930s. The prospects are laid out' in some detail in the recent Holland report (Manpower Services Commission, 1977) but in essence the complex system boils down to inculcating the work ethic in school-leavers which schools themselves have failed to do and to keeping them off the streets, or, at least, to keeping alive the faint hope of work.

Now here is a social problem with an educational dimension and an urban context which affects directly the inner cities of current concern or the inner cities picked up and dumped on green fields by slum-clearance procedures (e.g. Kirby New Town or Killingworth New Town). What can spatial analysis say about this problem? On its own, nothing, but quite a lot of the information about the way in which these processes occur, if not why, is possibly opened up by a spatial viewpoint. Further knowledge of the 'how' is essential if analysis is to get out of Marxism's own ivory tower and become involved with the struggles of the poor in specific localities. In this country the educational system is typically spatially organized and to a degree, if by no means totally, it is spatially differentiated. Schools have catchment areas whether *de jure* or *de facto* and these can become barriers which divide children along social class lines. Of course the system is complex and internal mechanisms play a major role in differentiation, but as our Sunderland study (Williamson and Byrne, 1977) shows, geographical variation in the quality of schools, closely related to the spatial differentiation of residential areas on class lines *is* important in influencing patterns of educational attainment. What we discovered in a survey of secondary schools in the borough of Sunderland were some very high correlations between the level of provision among schools—measured by such factors as teacher/pupil ratios, range and level of examinable courses offered—and success rates in examination and in rates of staying on beyond the minimum leaving age. What is more the spatial distribution of school opportunities measured in these terms corresponded directly with the social background of their pupils. Some of the poorest children went to those schools that offered few opportunities for higher levels of attainment.

The mechanisms behind the process are subtle. In general it is that which contributes to a school culture, that which conditions teachers' expectations of pupils and pupils' and parents' expectations of the educational system. Clearly there are also direct and obvious resource constraints e.g. an accessibility to examination streams, even assuming such examinations to be on offer. These things discriminate against the poor. Now this discrimination is not of itself the 'cause' of the problem, which lies quite centrally in the capitalist relations of production. Neither will a campaign for educational reform do much about that base. However to think, as for example Gray seems to, that analysing the mechanisms of oppression does not matter so long as the basic relations are stated, is to fall straight into the structural trap of informed inactivity. Most poor working-class people are very well aware that the educational system offers little to their kids, but they do not know how this works. This explains why, for example, a lot of the hostility to radical teachers who attempt a purely educational solution to these issues often comes from the working-class parents. It is important that the system is 'unfair' in its own terms and that it is shown to be unfair. Anderson (1977) has recently written on the 'differentia specifica', of the consent won from the working class to the accumulation of capital in the West today as being a belief by the masses that they exercise *ultimate self-determination* within the existing social order. In a real sense, amongst the issues which must be posed as a challenge to this are those relating to distribution, access and the quality of local environment. These, the spatial outcomes of a system founded in the capitalist ethic, provide manifest evidence of unfairness and inequality; a spatial analysis has, therefore, a role to play.

References

Addison, P. 1975 *The Road to 1945: British Politics and the Second World War,* Jonathan Cape, London.
Anderson, P. 1977 'The Antimonies of Antonio Gramsci', *New Left Review 100,* 5–81.
Banks, O. 1976 *The Sociology of Education,* Batsford, London.
Barnes, J., and Lucas, H. 1974 'Positive Discrimination in Education; individuals, groups and institutions' in Leggatt, T. (ed.), *Sociological Theory and Survey Research,* Sage Publications, London, 43–109.
Bird, C. 1977 *'Gateshead', A Study of Educational Inequality,* North East Area Study Working Paper 43, University of Durham, Durham.
Boudon, R. 1974 *Education, Opportunity and Social Inequality,* Wiley, London.
Braverman, H. 1974 *Labour and Monopoly Capital,* Monthly Review Press.
Byrne, D. S. 1976 'Allocation, The Council Ghetto and the Political Economy of Marxism', *Antipode* March 1976, 24–9.
—— Williamson, W., and Fletcher, B. G. 1975 *The Poverty of Education. A Study in the Politics of Opportunity,* Martin Robertson & Co. Ltd., London.
—— and Williamson, W. 1971 'Some intra-regional variations in educational provision and their bearing on educational attainment: *the case of the North East,* in *Sociology,* 6 (January), 71–87.
Central Advisory Council for Education 1954 *Early Leaving,* H.M.S.O. London.
—— 1967 *Children and their Primary Schools,* H.M.S.O., London.
Coates, B., and Rawstron, E. M. 1971 *Regional Variations in Britain,* Batsford, London.
Cockburn, P. 1977 'Local state management and cities of people', *Race and Class,* xviii (4) 363–376.
Community Development Project 1977 *Gilding the Ghetto,* C.D.P. Information and Intelligence Unit, Home Office, London.

Davies, B. 1968 *Social Needs and Resources in Local Services*, M. Joseph, London.
Department of Employment 1975a *Department of Employment Gazette*, August.
—— 1975b *Department of Employment Gazette*, October.
Department of the Environment 1977 *A Policy for the Inner Cities*, H.M.S.O., London.
Douglas, J. W. B. 1964 *The Home and the School*, MacGibbon & Kee, London.
—— 1973 'A Blunt Instrument', *New Society*, 20 Sept., Vol. 25, No. 572, 717—18.
Eggleston, J. 1977 *The Ecology of the School*, Methuen, London.
Engels, F. 1968 *The Condition of the Working Class in England in 1844*, Blackwell, Oxford.
Erben, M., and Gleeson, D. 1977 'Education as Reproduction: a critical examination of some aspects of the work of Louis Althusser' in Young, M., and Whitty, G. (eds.), *Society, State and Schooling* Falmer Press, London, 73—93.
Expenditure Committee 1977 *The Attainment of the School Leaver*, H.M.S.O., London.
Field, F. 1977 *Education and the Urban Crisis*, Routledge & Kegan Paul, London.
Finn, D., Grant, N., and Johnson, R. 1977 'Social Democracy, Education and the Crisis', *Cultural Studies* 10. 147—44.
Gray, F. 1976 'Radical Geography and the Study of Education', *Antipode* (March), 38—44.
Halsey, A. H. 1972 *Educational Priority*, Vol. 1: *E.P.A., Problems and Policies*, H.M.S.O., London.
—— 1977 'Whatever Happened to Positive Discrimination?', *Times Educational Supplement*, 21, 4.
Harrop, K. 1976 'Education in the North—A Regional Profile and Comparison with other Regions', *Durham Research Review* (Autumn), 1—11.
Harvey, D. 1973 *Social Justice and the City*, Edward Arnold, London.
Herbert, D. T. 1976 'Urban Education: Problems and Policies' in Herbert, D. T., and Johnston, R. J. (eds.), *Social Areas in Cities*, Vol. 2, 123—58, Wiley, London.
Jencks, C., with Smith, M., Acland, H., Bane, M. J., Cohen, D., Gintis, H., Heyns, B., Michelson, S. 1973 *Inequality: A reassessment of the effect of family and schooling in America*, Allen Lane, London.
Lewis, O. 1962 *The Children of Sanchez*, Penguin, Harmondsworth.
—— 1966 'The Culture of Poverty', Scientific American, 215.4. 19—25.
—— 1968 *La Vida*, Panther, London.
Manpower Services Commission 1977 *Young People and Work*, H.M.S.O., London.
Morton, D. C., and Watson, D. R. 1971 'Compensatory education and contemporary liberalism in the United States: a sociological review', *International Review of Education*, Vol. 17, part 3, 289—305.
Pahl, R. 1970 *Whose City?*, Longmans, London.
Pickvance, C. G. 1976 *Urban Sociology: Critical Essays*, Tavistock Publications, London.
Popper, K. 1957 *The Poverty of Historicism*, Cambridge University Press, London.
Riessman, F. 1962 *The Culturally Deprived Child*, Harper & Row, New York.
Robinson, P. 1976 *Education and Poverty*, Methuen, London.
Tawney, R. H. 1931 *Equality*, Allen & Unwin, London.
Taylor, G., and Ayres, N. 1969 *Born and Bred Unequal*, Longmans, London.

Tyler, W. 1977 *The Sociology of Educational Inequality*, Methuen, London.
Williamson, W. 1974 'Continuities and Discontinuities in the Sociology of Education' in Flude, M., and Ahier, J. (eds.), *Educability, Schools and Ideology*, Croom Helm, London.
Williamson, W., and Byrne, D. S. 1977 'The Structure of Educational Provision: An LEA Case Study' in Raggatt, P. and Evans, M. (eds.), *Urban Education* 3, The Open University, Milton Keynes, 216–42.
Wilson, H., and Herbert, G. W. 1974 'Social Deprivation and Performance in School', Policy and Politics, 3.

11

TERRITORIAL JUSTICE IN THE CITY:
A CASE STUDY OF THE SOCIAL SERVICES
FOR THE ELDERLY IN GREATER LONDON

Steven Pinch

In recent years there has been a growing awareness of the geographical bases of inequality in our society. It would therefore seem to be no mere coincidence that policies designed to eliminate or ameliorate these inequalities have assumed explicit spatial dimensions. Thus, the allocation of resources within the public section is based increasingly on criteria which aim to discriminate between the needs of administrative areas (e.g. D.E.S., 1967; D.H.S.S., 1976). From a geographical point of view an 'ideal' distribution of resources might be one that is in direct proportion to the needs of the areas—a situation which has been termed 'territorial justice' (Davies, 1968). Yet, although geographers have devoted considerable efforts towards defining and measuring spatial variations in needs, with what have been termed 'territorial social indicators' (Smith, 1973; see Chapter 2), they have paid far less attention to the relationships between these needs and the spatial patterning of resources. This chapter is intended as a contribution towards redressing this imbalance. There are three main aspects: first an introduction to the idea of territorial justice, second an empirical illustration of the approach, and third an evaluation of the concept and its implications for the geographical analysis of social problems.

The Concept of Territorial Justice

The spatial analysis of welfare resource allocations across administrative areas has not formed a major research tradition within the social sciences. Principles appropriate for the distribution of public sector goods and services have frequently been discussed by economists and social administrators (e.g. Buchanan, 1968; Titmuss, 1968; Culyer, 1973; Williams and Anderson, 1975) but their spatial ramifications have usually been merely implicit. This lack of research can in part be attributed to the failure of geographers to bring their spatial perspective to bear upon these problems. Human geographers have been preoccupied with the allocation of industries, offices, shopping facilities, and transport networks, based upon traditional criteria of locational efficiency (such as least cost, maximum profit, or distance minimization), and until comparatively recently (e.g. Bassett and Hauser, 1975; Hodge and Gatrell, 1976; Massam, 1975; Morrill, Earickson and Rees, 1970; Shannon and Dever, 1972) have paid little attention to the allocation of social provisions such as housing, schools, health facilities, and personal welfare services, whose primary aim should be the satisfaction of social needs.

It is thus in the field of social administration that the spatial scrutiny of service provision has received most attention. Davies (1968) suggested that, since social justice is frequently defined as 'to each according to his needs', the territorial corollary of this must be 'to each according to the needs of the particular area'. If this normative principle were rigorously enforced this should produce: '. . . a perfect positive correlation between standards of provision and the index measuring the relative needs of each area for the service—the relative inequality of the standards indices being the same as that of the index of relative needs' (Davies, 1968, p. 39). Such a pattern of territorial justice *between* a set of administrative areas does not necessarily imply a situation of social justice amongst individuals *within* the areas. The bulk of published statistical information does not specify whether those in greatest need actually received the resources or services provided by the authority and a different scale of analysis is required to answer these questions. Nevertheless, it is at the scale of local authorities that many important decisions concerning levels of resource allocation are made and these demand detailed scrutiny at the inter-authority level.

In this context social justice and its geographical aspects are not used to encapsulate some absolute notion of a 'just' or 'ideal' society but are used as criteria for resolving specific issues of how resources should be allocated between competing groups or areas (Harvey, 1973). Davies (1968), for example, examined the extent of territorial justice in the education and personal social services administered by British local authorities. Many of the correlations between indices of needs and resources within these services were extremely small, suggesting considerable inequality in levels of provision amongst local authorities with similar estimated levels of need. Since this pioneering study the notion of territorial justice has been frequently used in discussions of social policy and the analysis of areal variations in local services has become relatively commonplace (Packman, 1968; Boaden and Alford, 1969; Davies, 1969; Oliver and Stanyer, 1969; Alt, 1971; Boaden, 1971; Davies, Barton, McMillan and Williamson, 1971; Nicholson and Topham, 1971; Cooper and Culyer, 1972; Davies, Barton, and McMillan, 1972; Nicholson and Topham, 1973; Noyce, Snaith and Trickey, 1974; Lewis, 1975; Karn, 1977). However, much less common are attempts to relate service variations to needs in the specific manner of Davies' approach. This may be related to the complex nature of the task, for although relatively simple in a conceptual and technical sense, evaluation of the degree of territorial justice displayed by a service involves many difficult inferential problems. These difficulties can best be illustrated with a particular example of the approach. In this chapter there is a comparison of the local social services for the elderly (such as home helps, meals-on-wheels, home nurses, and residential accommodation) provided by the thirty-two Greater London Boroughs (see Fig. 11.1) between 1965 and 1971.

The Measurement of Needs

To evaluate the extent of territorial justice first requires an empirical measure of needs for the services under examination. The concept of 'need' is inherently linked to inequality and refers to the adequacy of existing conditions in society

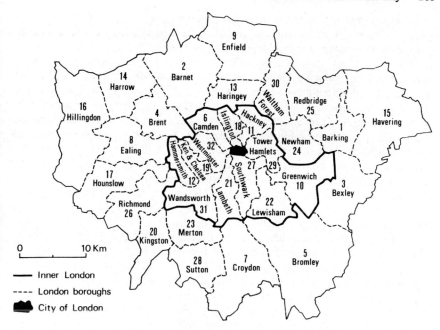

Figure 11.1 The Greater London Boroughs (numbers refer to alphabetical listing).

in relation to some socially acceptable norm (Cullingworth, 1973). It is thus a problem as perceived by someone, thereby reflecting their values. The multiplicity of individual preferences and values means that there is an enormous number of possible empirical measures of need. Bradshaw (1972), for example, has distinguished between the following types:

Normative needs—those which administrators, academics or professionals define as needs in a given situation.

Felt needs—those needs expressed by individuals through questionnaires or interviews.

Expressed needs—the results if felt needs are turned into actions, such as applications for a service, or demands for a service if none is available.

Comparative needs—those needs which may be ascertained by studying the characteristics of those in receipt of a service.

A basic distinction which emerges from this typology is that between the values of adminstrators, which are likely to be reflected in comparative needs, and the felt needs of the general public, which may or may not be expressed. The values of these groups can interact in complex ways to affect the degree of territorial justice. The demand for services (defined by expressed needs) may be determined to some degree by the supply of these services (defined by the normtive needs of professionals). For example, a lack of supply may inhibit demand for a service and it is not unknown for councils to restrict publicity for services when resources are insufficient to meet total demands (Karn, 1977). In contrast, generous provision may turn felt needs into expressed needs, as is frequently the case when siting of an old peoples home in an area stimulates applications for places (Parker, 1965; Sumner and Smith, 1969). Alternatively, a lack of supply may stimulate discontent and increase expressed needs for a service.

The concept of territorial justice implies a broad consensus between administrators and the general public over the criteria which give rise to needs and requires that these conditions be reflected in specifically tailored social indicators. However, the approach also recognizes that there are likely to be considerable differences both within and between the various sub-groups in different administrative areas. The responsibilities of local authorities for the welfare of the elderly are rather vaguely worded in the relevant legislation (Parker, 1965) and administrators in different authorities have varied enormously in the criteria they have used to define eligibility for their services. Administrators may thus underestimate the amount of felt need in an area, and in these circumstances to use actual service levels as indicators of need (e.g. Castle and Gittus, 1957; Hatch and Sherrott, 1973) may lead to considerable error.

The concept of territorial justice also recognizes the possibility of considerable variations between the felt needs of individuals living in similar conditions. It is therefore possible for needs as defined by administrators to exceed the definitions of the public but for considerable resistance to the uptake of services to restrict overall provision levels. The elderly are often the most resistant to what they regard as 'charity' but some studies suggest that there is often far more latent demand for social services amongst old people than can usually be met by existing resources (Harris, 1968; Hunt, 1970). Which of these complex factors is affecting the degree of territorial justice in a given situation can only be determined by more detailed study and is considered in the final section of this chapter.

Although local services are generally intended to aid those old people who are too frail or feeble to look after themselves (Parker, 1965), in effect, given shortages of resources, it is the absence or inability of relations to look after an aged person which becomes the most frequent and important qualification for a successful application to the services (Davies, 1968). Unfortunately, it is impossible to obtain direct and comprehensive information on the extent of areal variations in the availability of family care.

Davies overcame this problem by weighting the proportions of old people in each local authority in age, sex, and marital categories by nationally available information on the proportions in these categories in residential homes for the old and disabled. The rationale for this was that, since the probability of admission to a home increases greatly with age and single, widowed, or divorced status, the larger the proportions in these categories in each local authority area the greater should be the need for care. This produced a weighted population index to act as a measure of needs. A possible objection to this approach is the fact that it is based upon the actual services provided (i.e. comparative needs) which may not reflect needs measured in some other manner. These homes rapidly become congested with older infirm inhabitants and this may have excluded subsequent individuals in need because of an absence of family care (Davies, Barton, and McMillan, 1973).

This approach is, in any case, impractical in London because it does not take into account a second factor leading to the need for care—a low income and/or debilitating social circumstances. Indeed, Davies omitted this factor by constructing a socio-economic index and eliminating from his analysis those observations (mainly seaside resorts) whose old-age structures gave them high scores on the weighted population scale but whose social conditions did not suggest high needs. This left a set of county boroughs, relatively homogeneous in terms of social conditions, but differing in age structures. In direct contrast, Table 11.1 indicates that while the old-age structure of London boroughs displays relatively little variation, the differences in socio-economic composition are considerable and, clearly, cannot be ignored. The crucial question, therefore, is how important are areal variations in the ability of relatives to care for elderly members of their families in areas of widely differing socio-economic status?

Fortunately, two well-known studies have examined this question in areas of contrasting social status in Greater London. The first (Young and Wilmott, 1957) examined life-styles in the old borough of Bethnal Green, now part of the London borough of Tower Hamlets, an inner substantially low-class area. The second replicated the previous study in the substantially middle-class borough of Woodford and Wanstead (Wilmott and Young, 1960) which, under local government reorganization, now forms the western extreme of the borough of Redbridge. Table 11.1 indicates that, while these two boroughs have almost identical proportions of their populations above pensionable age, they differ by a factor of more than two in their proportions of economically active and retired males in the socio-economic groups of lowest status.

Although these studies revealed widely differing life-styles within the two boroughs, it was clear that the elderly members of the family were not deserted by their offspring in either area. Although there was a greater degree of separation of family members in the middle-class suburb, there was a tendency, as the parents grew older and their needs increased, for them to move closer to their offspring in order to receive help if necessary. Of those old people who were socially isolated (with less than three contacts per day), 11 per cent of pensioners were in this plight in Woodford, remarkably similar to the figure of 10 per cent for Bethnal Green. These results should be treated with some caution, not least because of the relatively small samples upon which they are based (Platt, 1971) and the fact that the original fieldwork is now over twenty years old, but similar findings have emerged from later studies (Tunstall, 1966; Shanas et al., 1968). It may be argued, therefore, that differences in the availability of family care will be negligible at a borough level and that social conditions should be most diagnostic of the *relative* needs of areas for social services. Recent evidence on the availability of family care from 'inner city' studies would suggest that the population decline of these areas is creating a growing residual population of socially isolated old people. If this is a widespread trend it would indicate a differential in the availability of family care which should be associated with deprivation in inner areas (see D.O.E., 1977).

Poor living conditions, a limited income, and a general lack of 'command over resources' will affect the needs of old people for local authority services in many ways. A number of these factors were incorporated into a composite index of needs using the variables listed in Table 11.2. Most individuals are faced with a

Table 11.1

The age and socio-economic structure of Greater London boroughs

	Percentage of Popuation		Percentage of economically active and retired males in socio-economic groups 7, 10, 11, and 15 in 1966
	above pensionable age in 1971	75 or over of single, widowed, or divorced status in 1971	
Barking	17·1	2·7	33·0
Barnet	17·9	3·3	14·2
Bexley	14·8	2·6	18·7
Brent	15·1	2·8	22·6
Bromley	15·9	3·4	14·8
Camden	17·0	3·7	23·1
Croydon	15·5	3·4	15·8
Ealing	15·9	3·2	21·4
Enfield	17·7	3·6	18·5
Greenwich	16·2	3·4	26·2
Hackney	16·5	3·4	29·0
Hammersmith	17·4	3·7	26·1
Haringey	16·3	3·4	22·8
Harrow	17·2	3·1	13·9
Havering	12·2	2·4	20·4
Hillingdon	14·1	2·5	18·7
Hounslow	15·6	3·0	21·0
Islington	15·6	3·3	32·1
Kensington and Chelsea	14·6	3·6	18·1
Kingston upon Thames	17·8	3·7	14·3
Lambeth	15·5	3·3	26·3
Lewisham	16·7	3·6	25·3
Merton	18·7	3·8	17·4
Newham	15·6	3·0	35·1
REDBRIDGE	17·2	3·5	15·7
Richmond upon Thames	19·1	4·3	15·3
Southwark	16·4	3·5	32·6
Sutton	18·4	3·6	14·8
TOWER HAMLETS	16·7	3·4	37·3
Waltham Forest	18·5	3·7	22·7
Wandsworth	17·0	3·9	23·2
Westminster	17·8	3·6	21·9

Note: Socio-economic groups 7, 10, 11, and 15 = personal service, semi-skilled manual, and unskilled manual workers.
Sources: 1966 and 1971 Census.

drop in income upon retirement but the effects of this decline are likely to be greatest amongst those who have worked in the poorly paid occupations and have had less opportunity to provide themselves with alternative means of income, apart from state welfare, upon retirement (Townsend, 1962). The incidence of infirmity and chronic illness is greater in low status households

(Office of Population Censuses and Surveys, 1973) and this should also be reflected in variable 1, the percentage of economically active and retired males in personal service, semi-skilled, and unskilled manual employment. Other factors related to poor living conditions are the standardized mortality rate (variable 2), the bronchitis mortality rate (variable 3), and the infant mortality rate (variable 4). Low social class also frequently entails a higher incidence of unemployment (variable 5) and fewer cars (variable 6). The elderly frequently live in the poorest quality housing and this is measured by the percentage of households without exclusive use of a hot-water tap, fixed bath, or inside W.C. (variable 7). Finally, there is a measure of the greater incidence of pensioners living alone in some inner-city areas (varable 8).

Table 11.2

Social Conditions variables and correlation matrix for Greater London boroughs

Variable

1. Percentage of economically active and retired males in socio-economic groups 7, 10, 11, and 15 (personal service, semi-skilled manual workers and unskilled manual workers) in 1966.*
2. Standardized death rate (Triennial average 1970–71).†
3. Bronchitis mortality rate in 1971.†
4. Infant mortality rate in 1971.†
5. Percentage of males of working age unemployed in 1971.‡
6. Percentage of households without a car in 1966.*
7. Percentage of households without exclusive use of hot water tap, fixed bath and inside W.C. in 1971.‡
8. Percentage of persons above pensionable age living alone.‡

Sources: *1966 Sample Census; †1971–72 Statistical Review of England and Wales; ‡1971 Census.

Correlation Matrix (N = 32)

	1	2	3	4	5	6	7	8
1	1							
2	·92	1						
3	·70	·70	1					
4	·71	·68	·53	1				
5	·82	·78	·53	·80	1			
6	·77	·72	·39	·77	·95	1		
7	·63	·49	·27	·70	·82	·92	1	
8	·55	·55	·21	·62	·88	·92	·85	1

As might be expected, the correlation matrix in Table 11.2 shows that these variables are all highly interrelated in the Greater London boroughs. It is therefore possible to summarize most of the variations in a single Social Conditions Index. Many techniques are available for scaling a set of variables ranging from the relatively simple addition of ranks or standard scores to the complex family of factor-analytic techniques. A comparison of these various approaches in Greater London revealed that they made relatively little difference to the overall rankings of the boroughs (Pinch, 1976), a result which must be interpreted as a reflection of the considerable differences between social conditions in areas of London. The results in Table 11.3 are derived from a principal components analysis of the correlations and reveal a 'general' dimension which accounts for almost three-quarters of the total variation, with high, albeit negative, loadings on all the variables. By deriving the scores from this component for each local authority it is possible to form a continuum of needs which are illustrated in Figure 11.2. It is clear that needs are geographically concentrated in the inner areas but especially in the 'East End' boroughs of Tower Hamlets, Newham, Hackney, and Lewisham. The nature of the index is such that it cannot be directly inferred that the older inhabitants of these areas have a greater probability of living in poor social conditions but evidence from small-scale studies of the elderly would suggest that this is not an unrealistic assumption (Department of Environment, 1977).

Table 11.3
Component loadings for social conditions variables in Greater London boroughs

Variables	Component loadings
1. Socio-economic groups 7, 10, 11, and 15	−0·89
2. Standardized mortality rate 1970−1	−0·85
3. Bronchitis mortality rate in 1971	−0·61
4. Infant mortality rate in 1971	−0·85
5. Percentage of males unemployed	−0·97
6. Percentage of households without car	−0·95
7. Percentage of households without amenities	−0·84
8. Percentage of pensioners living alone	−0·83
Percentage of variation accounted for	73·4

The Measurement of Resources

The next step is to measure the ways in which these needs may be met by local services. This task is beset with at least as many difficulties as arise in the measurement of needs and the problems are not diminished the numerous, and frequently conflicting, taxonomies which have been applied to aspects of resource allocation. Nevertheless, when reduced to essentials, it is possible to envisage resources as consisting of three inter-connected elements (see Fig. 11.3). At one extreme are the financial resources or *inputs* committed to a service by a local authority. These revenue and capital expenditures are the outcome of the local-authority decision-making process—a complex interplay between professionals, administrators, local councillors, pressure groups, and central government. These expenditures are of considerable interest in their own right, for the budget is frequently the focus for political and administrative conflict, and financial inputs may indicate the relative priority which is attached to a service. However, for various reasons expenditures may not necessarily be a good indicator of the extent of services; costs are likely to vary between areas, councils are likely to differ in the 'efficiency' with which they spend their income and the complexity

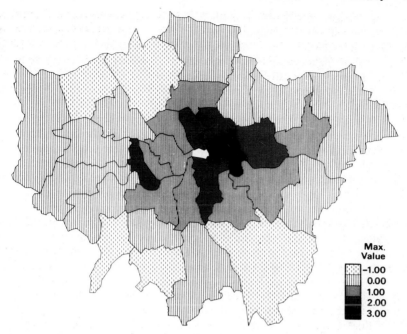

Figure 11.2 Standard scores of Social Conditions Index for Greater London Boroughs.

of many of the financial transactions makes rigorous accounting procedures, and hence strict data compatibility between authorities, difficult to achieve.

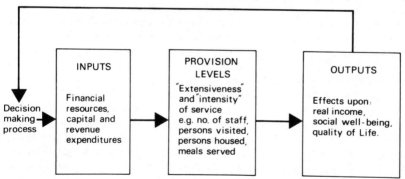

Figure 11.3 Elements of resource allocation in local social services.

It is therefore necessary to supplement financial inputs with the second element of resources shown in Figure 11.3–*physical indices* of the services procured by the expenditure. Davies (1968) uses the term 'extensiveness' of provision to indicate the proportion of a population who are in theory eligible for a service and actually receive it (e.g. the proportion of old people who receive home helps or meals-on-wheels). Other physical indices are the number of units of service (such as the number of meals-on-wheels served, the number of visits made by services to old people in their own homes, or the number of places available in residential accommodation for the elderly). These indices can, in turn, be combined with the 'extensiveness' measures to evaluate the 'intensity' of resource allocation, the average amount of monetary or physical resources provided per recipient of the service (see Davies, 1974).

Efficiency is frequently equated with the ability to provide units of service at least cost but to be useful such measures should be standardized for quality of service (Hirsch, 1968). This is sufficiently difficult, even when the units of service have reasonably well defined physical characteristics, but in the field of the local social services involving factors such as 'care' and 'advice' the problems are clearly considerable. Davies (1968) observes that in Townsend's (1962) study of residential accommodation almost half of the criteria used to evaluate the 'quality of care' were not inevitably linked with material factors or expenditures. However, the limitations of both expenditures and physical indices should not be exaggerated; not only are these factors frequently strongly related but there is also evidence to suggest that in some contexts material standards and non-material aspects of care are correlated (Davies, 1968). It is therefore hardly surprising that Hunt (1970) concluded in her study of home helps that almost all improvements would involve spending more money. However, it should be clear that detailed insights into the 'quality of care' must involve supplementing published statistics with intensive local studies.

The third component of resources in Figure 11.3 consists of *outputs*. The term 'output' is conventionally regarded in comparative studies of local governments to be synonymous with physical indices of provision. However, in this analysis it is conceptually useful to make a distinction between local provision levels and 'outputs' as defined by the effects of services upon individuals and communities. These relationships between local services and 'real income' or 'social well-being' are of crucial importance for social policy but for a variety of reasons have been neglected by social scientists. Whereas the relationships between inputs and services are largely technical, and relationships between service provisions and outputs involve consideration of the ultimate objectives of services (Davies, 1968). Not only are these objectives seldom stated explicitly (beyond the level of broad generalizations) but it is frequently extremely difficult to separate the effects of local services from other social factors which may affect the well-being of old people. Understanding these relationships is further impeded by the absence of detailed published information concerning outputs for many local services (and, in particular, those concerned with health and welfare). For these reasons the present analysis examines financial inputs and physical indices of service provision for the elderly. Nevertheless, it should be clear that consideration of the relationships between these services and outputs is an important task for future research and is an issue examined in the final section of this chapter.

The Structure of Local Social Services in London

Local social services for the elderly may be divided into two main types; residential accommodation and community-based care. The 1948 National Assistance

Act intended that residential homes should be the major service for the elderly. These homes were to include both the able-bodied and those requiring help through infirmity but without continuous medical care. However, as implemented, the service did not meet the initial aspirations. Shortages of hospital places and the tendency for the able-bodied to become progressively infirm as they grew older, meant that a larger proportion of the inhabitants of these homes became in need of medical attention than was originally anticipated. To eliminate the stigma attached to the traditions of the Poor Law workhouses it was intended that the old larger institutions should eventually be replaced by smaller purpose-built homes, but restrictions on local authority capital expenditures in the late 1940s and early 1950s meant that progress in building new homes was limited (Parker, 1965). It soon became apparent that converted accommodation was not always suitable and this factor combined with shortages of staff meant that standards of care were often low (Townsend, 1962).

These problems combined with the high costs of homes and improvements in geriatric medicine have, in recent years, led to a change in social policy for old people in favour of community-based services. One of the most important of these is the home-help service, for although initially administered to maternity cases, it has been increasingly used by the elderly. Complementary to this service are meals-on-wheels which play an important role in maintaining an adequate diet amongst old people, thereby preventing a decline in health and the need for institutional care. Voluntary organizations have in the past played an important role in the innovation of home helps and meals but local authorities are increasingly providing these services directly. Home nursing is another community-based service which has been increasingly used by the elderly and is important in keeping many sick people out of hospital. Finally, domiciliary care is provided by health visitors who give advice on general matters relating to health. These are the main services but others not considered here are purpose built accommodation supervised by wardens, chiropody, and laundry services.

Although these community-based services are largely complementary, they are to some extent substitutable, both one with another but particularly with institutional forms of care. It is therefore necessary to examine the extent of territorial justice displayed by these services when considered separately, and in combination. There may be detailed reasons why social workers choose one service in preference to another to meet needs in particular areas but it is impossible to specify such factors within aggregate social indicators.

The trend towards community-based services is illustrated in Figure 11.4. Meals-on-wheels, home helps, health visiting, and home nursing have all expanded as services for old people in the London boroughs between 1966 and 1972, but the numbers in residential accommodation have remained virtually static. This latter phenomenon is largely the result of continuing difficulties in obtaining loan sanctions for new buildings together with the need to close many of the old larger institutions (Tate, 1971).

There are a number of reasons for suspecting that the provision of these services will be correlated in a less than perfect, or even strong positive manner, with the estimated needs of the local authorities. Although the 1965 reorganization of local government in Greater London created a simplified structure in an

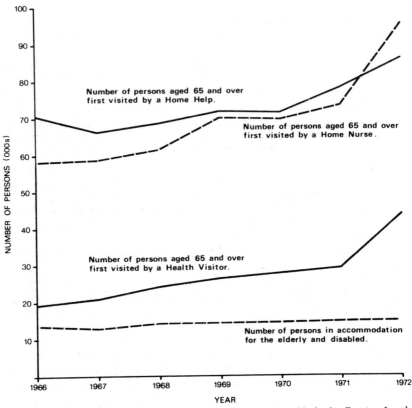

Figure 11.4 The expansion of local social services for the elderly in Greater London Boroughs between 1966 and 1972.

area which had previously been administered by a complex patchwork of various types of authorities (Rhodes, 1970), the new system has been subject to much criticism. The criticism has been principally directed at the relatively small size of the boroughs. The Royal Commission on London local government considered that the new authorities should be in the range of 100,000 to 200,000 persons in size, since this, it was argued, would enable those responsible for the social services to be in close contact with the public (Cmnd. 1164, 1962, §629). This contrasted with the view that much larger boroughs of approximately one and a half million persons were necessary in order to provide sufficient financial and manpower resources to innovate more expensive social services (Cmnd. 1164, 1962, Written Evidence, vol. 5). This recommendation anticipated the expansion of community based social services such as domestic helps and meals-on-wheels on a much larger scale than had hitherto been administered by local authorities. The Royal Commission's choice of relatively small authorities thus led to claims of excessive fragmentation of responsibility for social services and there is certainly much evidence from other parts of Great Britain to suggest that this can lead to considerable variations in local government provisions for the elderly (Parker, 1965; Tunstall, 1966; Harris, 1968; Davies, 1968; Sumner and Smith, 1969; Hunt, 1970; Karn, 1977).

Quite apart from the administrative upheaval caused by reorganization in London, the period from 1965 to 1972 was one of considerable debate and uncertainty over the future role and form of the local social services. The London boroughs were initially encouraged to establish joint health and welfare departments controlled by a Medical Officer of Health (Tate, 1971). However, during the sixties there was growing opposition to the idea of social services as merely ancillary to medical care. Indeed, it has been suggested that the home-help service would have been given much greater priority in the past had it not been administered within local health departments (Davies, 1968). These views found expression in the Seebohm Report (Cmnd. 3703, 1968) and following its recommendations the local welfare services were unified within single departments. This was largely an attempt to create a greater degree of professional autonomy within social work but also recognized that there were a large number of persons in need of social services other than those in direct contact with their general practitioner. The local health services were therefore excluded from the new departments and eventually incorporated into the Area Health authorities created by the reorganization of the National Health Service. Tate (1971) suggests that this administrative uncertainty led to some friction and lack of co-operation between local health and welfare services in Greater London and this may also have served to promote inequalities in provision levels between areas with similar levels of need.

The Relationships between Needs and Resources

Table 11.4

Correlations between Social Conditions Index and indices of provision of residential accommodation in Greater London boroughs

Residential Accommodation	Correlation with Social Conditions Index
1. Average net expenditure on residential accommodation for the elderly and disabled provided directly by London boroughs and registered voluntary and private agencies on their behalf between 1965 and 1968 (per 1,000 population)	·45
2. Number of persons (excluding staff) in residential accommodation for the elderly and disabled provided directly by London boroughs and registered voluntary and private agencies on their behalf on 31 December 1966, per 1,000 population of pensionable age in 1966	·67
3. Number of persons (excluding staff) in residential accommodation for the elderly and disabled provided directly by London boroughs and registered voluntary and private agencies in their behalf on 31 December 1971 per 1,000 population of pensionable age in 1971	·65

Sources: Welfare Statistics and Local Social Services Statistics.

The correlations between indices of needs and resources for residential accommodation are shown in Table 11.4. The first variable is the net expenditure on residential accommodation, standardized per 1,000 population. These data include expenditure on accommodation provided directly by the authority, by other local authorities under joint user arrangements, and by registered voluntary and private bodies on an agency basis, less the charges made to recipients of the service and the contributions made by other local authorities for services given to persons for whom they are financially responsible. To combat the effects of yearly fluctuations and the problems which accompanied the reorganization of London local government in 1965, a triennial average of expenditures was calculated for the period from 1965 to 1968. Table 11.4 indicates that this variable has a correlation coefficient of 0·45 associated with the Social Conditions Index and, although positive, this represents a situation far from the linear relationship prescribed by the idea of territorial justice. This point is emphasized by the scatter diagram in Figure 11.5.

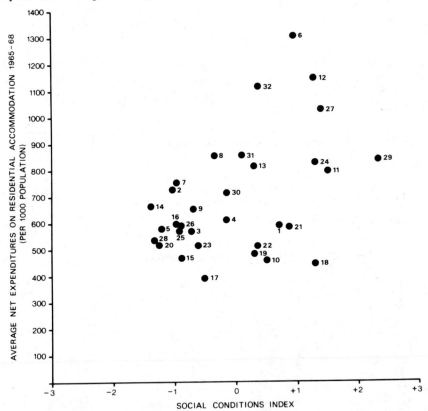

Figure 11.5 Scatter diagram of the relationship between average net expenditure on residential accommodation for the elderly and disabled provided by London Boroughs and registered voluntary and private agencies between 1965 and 1968 (per 1,000 population) and the Social Conditions Index.

The remaining variables in Table 11.4 measure the 'extensiveness' of the service. In the case of residential accommodation this is the number of persons who are accommodated in homes of all types, standardized per 1,000 population of pensionable age. It is clear that in 1966 this variable has a stronger correlation with the Social Conditions Index than the corresponding expenditure variable (0·67) and the coefficient is of similar magnitude when the same variable is measured in 1971 (0·65). This similarity of results is no doubt a reflection of the lack of expansion in this service over the period under investigation.

Table 11.5

Correlations between Social Conditions Index and indices of provision of home helps and meals-on-wheels in Greater London boroughs

Home-Helps Service	Correlation with Social Conditions Index
4. Average net expenditure by London boroughs on home helps between 1965 to 1968 per 1,000 population	·79
5. Average net expenditure by London boroughs on home helps between 1971 to 1972 per 1,000 population	·76
6. Number of home helps employed by London boroughs per 1,000 population of pensionable age in 1966	·77
7. Number of home helps employed by London boroughs per 1,000 population of pensionable age in 1971	·68
8. Number of persons aged sixty-five or over on first visit by a home-help during 1966 per 1,000 population aged sixty-five and over	·72
9. Number of persons aged sixty-five or over on first visit by a home-help during 1971 per 1,000 population aged sixty-five and over	·81
Meals-on-Wheels Service	
10. Number of persons aged sixty-five and over served with meals-on-wheels by London boroughs and voluntary agencies in a one week period in 1968 per 1,000 population aged sixty-five and over	·72
11. Number of meals-on-wheels served to persons aged sixty-five and over by London boroughs and voluntary agencies in a one-week period in 1968 per 1,000 population aged sixty-five and over	·72
12. Number of persons aged sixty-five and over served with meals-on-wheels by London boroughs and voluntary agencies in a one week period in 1970 per 1,000 population aged sixty-five and over	·67
13. Number of meals-on-wheels served to persons aged sixty-five and over by London boroughs and voluntary agencies in a one week period in 1970 per 1,000 population aged sixty-five and over	·72

Sources: Welfare Statistics and Local Social Services Statistics.

The correlations displayed by the home help service in Table 11.5 are consistently stronger than those for residential accommodation. Average net expenditures on home helps between 1965 and 1968 (variable 4) have a remarkably larger correlation of 0·79 with the Social Conditions Index and this relatively high degree of territorial justice is maintained throughout the period under investigation. There is a large correlation of 0·76 associated with average net expenditures in the financial year 1971 to 1972 (variable 5) and the numbers of home helps employed in 1966 and 1971 are also both strongly correlated with the needs index (variables 6 and 7). Strong correlations with the Social Conditions Index are also displayed by the two 'extensiveness' variables—the number of persons aged sixty-five or over first visited by a home help in 1966 and 1971 (variables 8 and 9). The relationship between the 1965 to 1968 expenditures on home helps and the Social Conditions Index is clarified by the scatter diagram in Figure 11.6. There are remarkably consistent increases in the amount of expenditures with progressive increases in the magnitude of the Social Conditions Index, but there is increased deviation from a linear relationship as needs increase.

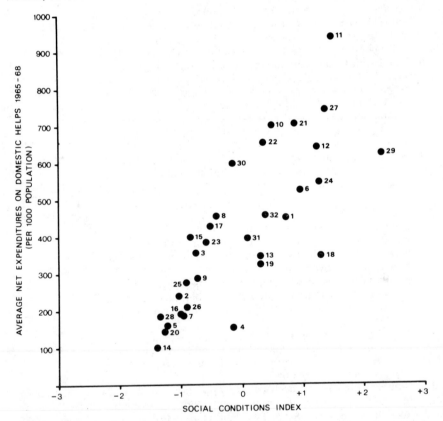

Figure 11.6 Scatter diagram of the relationship between average net expenditure on domestic helps between 1965 and 1968 (per 1,000 population) and the Social Conditions Index.

Table 11.5 also indicates the relationships between the Social Conditions Index and the meals-on-wheels services. As in the case of the home helps service, there are relatively large correlations. This applies to the number of persons aged sixty-five or over first served with meals-on-wheels in 1968 and 1970 (variables 10 and 12) and the number of meals served to persons aged sixty-five or over in these two time periods (variables 11 and 13). The relative strength of the associations with needs is emphasized by Figure 11.7 which shows the spatial distribution of the number of the elderly served with meals-on-wheels by the London boroughs in 1970. A comparison of the pattern with that for the needs index in Figure 11.2 shows the patterns to be remarkably similar.

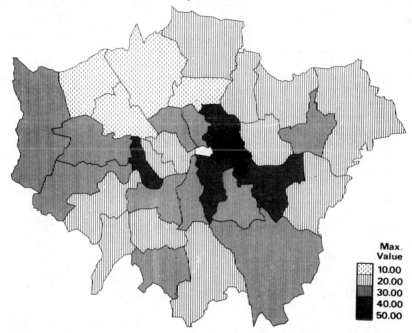

Max.
Value

10.00
20.00
30.00
40.00
50.00

Figure 11.7 The number of persons aged 65 and over served with meals-on-wheels by London Boroughs and voluntary agencies in a one-week period in 1970, per 1,000 population aged 65 and over.

The correlations between the Social Conditions Index and measures of the home nursing service are shown in Table 11.6. In contrast to the domiciliary welfare services, the variables relating to the home nursing service have either small or negative correlations with the needs index. This applies to average net expenditures between 1965 and 1968 (variable 14), the number of home nurses employed by the London boroughs in 1969 (variable 15) and the number of home-nurse cases who are elderly in 1966 and 1971 (variables 16 and 17). In the case of the health visiting service, also shown in Table 11.6, the average net expenditures between 1965 and 1968 have a relatively strong correlation of 0·55 with the needs index (variable 18). However, the 'extensiveness' variables measuring the number of persons above sixty-five first visited by a health visitor in 1966 and 1971 (variables 19 and 20) both have negative correlations with the needs index. Finally, to take account of the potential for substitution between services, Table 11.6 contains the correlation between expenditures on all services and the Social Conditions Index. The coefficient of 0·75 is in this instance relatively large.

Table 11.6
Correlations between Social Conditions Index and indices of provision of home nursing, health visiting, and all services combined in Greater London boroughs

Home Nursing	Correlation with Social Conditions Index
14. Average net expenditure on home nursing by London boroughs between 1965 and 1968 per 1,000 population	·15
15. Number of home nurses employed by London boroughs in 1969 per 1,000 population aged sixty-five and over	−·03
16. Number of persons aged sixty-five and over first visited by a home nurse during the year 1966 per 1,000 population aged sixty-five and over	·07
17. Number of persons aged sixty-five and over first visited by a home nurse during the year 1971 per 1,000 population aged sixty-five and over	−·25
Health Visiting	
18. Average net expenditure on health visiting by London boroughs between 1965 and 1968 per 1,000 population	·55
19. Number of persons aged sixty-five and over first visited by a health visitor in 1966 per 1,000 population aged sixty-five and over	−·28
20. Number of persons aged sixty-five and over first visited by a health visitor in 1971 per 1,000 population aged sixty-five and over	−·44
Combined Health and Welfare Services	
21. Average net expenditure on residential homes, home helps, home nursing, and health visiting by London boroughs between 1965 and 1968	·75

Sources: Welfare Statistics, Local Social Service Statistics, and Local Health Services Statistics.

In the light of the initial speculations, perhaps the most remarkable feature of the results presented above is the relatively high degree of association between needs and resources. Indeed, the correlations are, in general, much stronger than those observed by Davies (1968) in the old County boroughs. One possible explanation for this is that while most local authorities do not make detailed and systematic comparisons of their performance with all other local governments of their type, it is quite common for them to compare their performance with their nearest neighbours or a few authorities with similar problems. This practice may be more frequent in a set of contiguous authorities, such as in London, and may encourage a greater overall alignment with needs.

Another striking feature of the results is the way in which the variables related to the home helps and meals-on-wheels services are more strongly correlated with needs than the variables related to residential accommodation, for this is the direct converse of the situation observed by Davies for the 1950s and early 1960s. A possible reason for this is the fact that the trend towards community based care was not advanced in this earlier period. In contrast, although there were restrictions upon levels of capital expenditure on new buildings in Greater London in the late 1960s, the local authorities were able to expand their levels of revenue expenditure on manpower within the community based services, and these appear to have been most concentrated in areas of poor social conditions.

These conditions do not mean, however, that the Royal Commission's choice of relatively small boroughs should be commended unreservedly. The Greater London boroughs display much greater variation in social conditions than did the relatively homogeneous County boroughs and this may have served, through the presence of extreme values, to have 'inflated' the size of many of the correlations. It is thus apparent that within the scatter diagram in Figure 11.6 the relatively large aggregate positive correlation conceals quite considerable variation in rates of social-service provision amongst boroughs with similar social conditions. Furthermore, the community-based health services provide a major exception to the pattern for they are in general only weakly correlated with needs. This could indicate a lack of co-ordination resulting from the administrative uncertainty surrounding the service, but may also reflect the difficulty of attracting suitably qualified staff in areas of high need. Whether the integration of these local health services into the National Health Service has achieved a better co-ordination with needs is an issue for further research but some commentators have expressed reservations about a system which involves home nurses and social workers working in the same districts but responsible to different authorities (Butler and Pearson, 1970).

Implications for the Geographical Analyses of Social Policy

This brief illustration of the idea of territorial justice in practice can only display the rudiments of the approach, but a number of conclusions are possible. The concept is clearly intermediate in scale between the level of aggregate national information and knowledge of individuals. As such, it involves making a number of difficult inferences from measures of 'needs' and 'resources'. Much more knowledge is therefore required before such analyses can be used to provide firm guidelines for policies designed to achieve greater degrees of territorial justice. Of particular importance is the extent to which the social need indicators accurately reflect the conditions experienced (and perceived) by the inhabitants of areas and the extent to which those in greatest need actually receive services. (For a recent discussion of these problems see Davies, 1977.) In this context there is considerable potential for geographical analysis of the intra-authority distribution of services rather than the inter-authority patterns which have hitherto formed the major focus of research (Webster and Stewart, 1975).

Successful social policies will also need to be based upon knowledge of the processes which generate the disparities between estimated needs and resources in different areas. This raises a multitude of questions, such as:

(1) To what extent are the inequalities between areas the result of deliberately chosen policies (possibly reflecting the political character of the local council) or a consequence of financial constraints (possibly resulting from small rateable values or inadequate central government funding)?

(2) What are the effects of the complex interactions between felt needs, expressed demand and professional values upon geographical variations in resource allocations? (See Lewis, 1975.)

(3) How effective is the degree of co-ordination between services in local authorities with differing provision levels but apparently similar needs?

(4) What are the relationships between local social services and other possible forms of care (e.g. by voluntary organizations, hospitals or relatives) in areas where local authority provision is either relatively generous or restricted?

(5) What are the effects of inflation and public expenditure cuts upon the quantity and quality of services?

These issues are formidable in their complexity and it is hardly suprising that they have generated much controversy between political scientists and social administrators concerning the most appropriate research methodologies (contrast Dearlove, 1973, with Davies, 1975). Much of this controversy parallels the debate in geography over 'scale' but it should be clear from the diverse nature of these questions that a wide variety of research designs will be required.

Despite the multiplicity of these questions there remain two closely related issues which are of fundamental importance for social policy. The first is the extent to which the goals of 'territorial justice' or 'equal proportion in relation to need' can be reconciled with other criteria, in particular, with the objectives of local democracy and efficiency. The maintenance of local democracy is important because, although this concept is often used by local authorities to claim exemption from outside scrutiny or criticism, there are undoubtedly limitations to centrally formulated policies which lack sufficient flexibility to take account of local circumstances. The notion of efficiency is also important because, although the fulfilment of needs will always be the ultimate aim of the health and welfare services, they are always likely to be subject to financial constraints. The combined financial resources allocated to these services by central and local government have now reached considerable proportions and are by no means the superficial spatial reallocations often implied by critics of the welfare system. What is increasingly being appreciated, however, is that this expenditure frequently has little effect upon those in greatest need (e.g. Le Grand 1976; Field, Meacher, and Pond, 1977).

This raises the second fundamental issue, how effective are the local social services in comparison with other types of social policy? There is little doubt that in the short term even relatively simple services such as home helps and meals-on-wheels can have a dramatic impact upon the well-being of the elderly, but in many instances these services have only a marginal impact upon the overall welfare of their recipients (see Wilmott, 1976). Indeed, there would appear to be growing recognition of the fact that local social services may be substituting for deficiencies in other fields of social policy and to this extent may be envisaged as relieving the symptoms of problems while primary causes remain unchecked. Increasing old age will, of course, always bring a greater probability of illness and the need for care, but there is now considerable evidence to suggest that health needs are exacerbated by poor social conditions. In the long run, then, policies designed to reduce pollution and occupational hazards, and to improve housing conditions and living standards may have a more important effect upon the well being of the elderly—at least in future generations if not the present. It is therefore important not to exaggerate the contribution of the local social services to geographical variations in the welfare of old people. Researchers clearly have to make important choices between studying those elements of the system whose manipulation could provide benefits in the short run and analyses of other causal agents whose effects will be much longer term but possibly of much greater importance.

These patterns and processes affecting territorial justice have so far been little considered by geographers but this would seem to be the direction in which future research must proceed in order to provide insights into spatial aspects of social problems. More importantly, answers to the questions posed above are essential if social policies are to navigate successfully a course between the imposition of excessively rigid guidelines from central government and the unacceptable tolerance of inequalities in the treatment of individuals based solely upon location.

References

Alt, J. E. 1971 'Some social and political correlates for County borough expenditures', *British Journal of Political Science*, 1. 49–62.
Bassett, K., and **Hauser, D.** 1975 'Public policy and spatial structure: housing improvement in Bristol', in Peel, R., Chisholm, M., and Haggett, P., (eds.), *Processes in Physical and Human Geography: Bristol Essays,* Heinemann, London. 20–66.
Boaden, N. T. 1971 *Urban Policy making,* Cambridge University Press, Cambridge.
— — and **Alford, R. R.** 1969 'Sources of diversity in English local government decisions', *Public Administration* 47. 203–23.
Bradshaw, J. 1972 'The concept of social need', *New Society*, 496. 640–3.
Buchanan, J. M. 1968 *The Demand and Supply of Public Goods,* Rand McNally, Chicago.
Butler, J. R., and **Pearson, R. J. C.** 1970 'Face lift for the N.H.S.—a major or minor operation?' in Robson, W. A., and Crick B. (eds.), *The Future of the Social Services* Penguin, Harmondsworth.
Castle, I. M., and **Gittus, E.** 1957 'The distribution of social defects in Liverpool', *Sociological Review*, 5. 43–64.
Cmnd. 1164 1962 *Report of the Royal Commission on local government in Greater London,* The Herbert Report, H.M.S.O., London.
Cmnd. 3703 1968 *Report of the Committee on local authority and allied personal social services,* The Seebohm Report, H.M.S.O., London.
Cooper, M. H., and **Culyer, A. J.** 1972 'Equality in the national health service: intentions, performance and problems in evaluation' in Hauser, M. (ed.), *The Economics of Medical Care,* 47–57, George Allen & Unwin, London.

Cullingworth, J. B. 1973 *Problems of an Urban Society,* vol. 2, *The Social Context of Planning,* George Allen & Unwin, London.

Culyer, A. J. 1973 *Need and the National Health Service,* Martin Robertson, London.

Davies, B. P. 1968 *Social Needs and Resources in Local Services,* Michael Joseph, London.

— 1969 'Local authority size: some associations with standards of performance of services for deprived children and old people', *Public Administration* 47. 225–48.

— 1974 'Personal social services' in Maunder, W. R. (ed.), *Reviews of United Kingdom Statistical Sources* Vol. 1, Heinemann, London. 1–126.

— 1975 'Causal processes and techniques in the modelling of policy outcomes' in Young, K. (ed.), *Essays on the Study of Urban Politics,* pp. 78–105, Macmillan, London.

— 1977 'Social service studies and the explanation of policy outcomes' *Policy and Politics* 5. 41–59.

— **Barton, A.,** and **McMillan, I.** 1972 *Variations among Children's Services in British Urban Authorities,* Bell & Sons, London.

— **Barton, A.,** and **McMillan, I.** 1973 'The silting up of unadjustable resources and the planning of personal social services', *Policy and Politics* 1. 341–55.

— **Barton, A., McMillan, I.,** and **Williamson, V.** 1971 *Variations in Services for the Aged,* Bell & Sons, London.

Dearlove, J. 1973 *The Politics of Policy in Local Government,* Cambridge University Press, Cambridge.

Department of Education and Science 1967 Central Advisory Council for Education, *Children and their Primary Schools,* Plowden Report, H.M.S.O., London.

Department of Health and Social Security 1976 *Sharing Resources for Health in England,* Report of the resource allocation working party, H.M.S.O., London.

Department of the Environment 1977 *Inner Area Studies,* Consultants reports from Birmingham, Liverpool and London and summary, H.M.S.O., London.

Field, F., Meacher, M., and **Pond, C.** 1977 *To Him who Hath: A Study of Taxation and Poverty,* Penguin, Harmondsworth.

Harris, A. I. 1968 *Social Welfare for the Elderly,* H.M.S.O., London.

Harvey, D. 1973 *Social Justice and the City,* Arnold, London.

Hatch, S., and **Sherrott, R.** 1973 'Positive discrimination and the distribution of deprivations', *Policy and Politics* 1. 223–40.

Hirsch, W. Z. 1968 'The supply of urban public services' in Perloff, H. S., and Wingo L. (eds.), *Issues in Urban Economics,* John Hopkins Press, Baltimore. 477–525.

Hodge, D., and **Gatrell, A.** 1976 'Spatial constraint and the location of urban public facilities', *Environmental and Planning* A 8. 215–30.

Hunt, A. 1970 *The Home Help Service in England and Wales,* H.M.S.O., London.

Karn, V. 1977 *Retiring to the Seaside,* Routledge & Kegan Paul, London.

Le Grand, J. 1976 *The Distribution of Public Expenditure on the National Health Service,* evidence submitted to the Royal Commission on the Health Service, June 1976 (mimeo), University of Sussex.

Lewis, J. 1975 'Variations in service provision: politics at the lay professional interface' in Young, K. (ed.), *Essays on the study of urban politics* Macmillan, London. 52–79.

Massam, B. 1975 *Location and Space in Social Administration,* Arnold, London.

Morrill, R., Earickson, R. J., and Rees, P. 1970 'Factors influencing distances travelled to hospitals', *Economic Geography*, 46. 161–71.

Nicholson, R. V., and Topham, N. 1971 'The determinants of investment in housing by local authorities: an econometric approach', *Journal of the Royal Statistical Society* Series A, 134. 273–320.

—— 1973 'Investment decisions and the size of local authorities', *Policy and Politics* 1. 23–44.

Noyce, J., Snaith, A. H., and Trickey, A. J. 1974 'Regional variations in the allocation of financial resources to the community health services', *Lancet*, 1. 554–7.

Office of Population Censuses and Surveys 1973 *The General Household Survey*, H.M.S.O., London.

Oliver, F. R., and Stanyer, J. 1969 'Some aspects of the financial behaviour of county boroughs', *Public Administration*, 47. 169–84.

Packman, J. 1968 *Child Care Needs and Numbers*, George Allen & Unwin, London.

Parker, J. 1965 *Local Health and Welfare Services*, George Allen & Unwin, London.

Pinch, S. P. 1976 'The Geography of Local Authority Housing, Health and Welfare Resource Allocation in London, 1965–73', Unpub. Ph.D. thesis, University of London.

Platt, J. 1971 *Social Research in Bethnal Green*, Macmillan, London.

Rhodes, G. 1970 *The Government of London: The Struggle for Reform*, Weidenfeld & Nicholson, London.

Shanas, E., Townsend, P., Wedderburn, D., Friss, H., Milhoj, P., and Stehouwer, J. 1968 *Old People in Three Industrial Societies*, Routledge & Kegan Paul, London.

Shannon, G. W., and Dever, G. E. A. 1972 *Health Care Delivery: Spatial Perspectives*, McGraw-Hill, New York.

Smith, D. M. 1973 *The Geography of Social Well-being in the United States*, McGraw-Hill, New York.

Sumner, G., and Smith, R. 1969 *Planning Local Authority Services for the Elderly*, George Allen & Unwin, London.

Tate, B. 1971 'Personal health and welfare services' in Rhodes, G. (ed.), *The New Government of London: The First Five Years*, Weidenfeld & Nicholson, London. 84–124.

Titmus, R. M. 1968 *Commitment to Welfare*, George Allen & Unwin, London.

Townsend, P. 1962 *The Last Refuge*, Routledge & Kegan Paul, London.

Tunstall, J. 1966 *Old and Alone*, Routledge & Kegan Paul, London.

Webster, B., and Stewart, J. 1975 'The area analysis of resources', *Policy and Politics* 3. 5–16.

Williams, A. R., and Anderson, R. 1975 *Efficiency in the Social Services*, Robertson, London.

Wilmott, Peter and Young, M. 1960 *Family and Kinship in a London Suburb*, Routledge & Kegan Paul, London.

Wilmott, Phyllis 1976 'Gains and losses in health and welfare' in Wilmott, P. (ed.), *Sharing Inflation?: Poverty Report 1976* Temple Smith, London.

Young, M. and Wilmott, P. 1957 *Family and Kinship in East London*, Routledge & Kegan Paul, London.

PART THREE

THE AREAL RESPONSE TO SOCIAL PROBLEMS

We now turn to more general questions concerning the societal response to social problems. There is a strong spatial or ecological tradition, both in the attempts of government to intervene via social policy and in the explanations conventionally offered to account for the incidence of social problems. The two are clearly related: policies that focus on specific territories do so within some model of cause-and-effect (implicit or explicit), while explanations that stress the role of territories and their inhabitants encourage an area-based response.

In Chapter 12 John Eyles reviews approaches to policies designed to tackle urban social problems. The focus is on policies implemented in specific areas, as opposed to those that identify individuals in need and provide some form of income supplement or other support. Eyles finds close parallels between British and American experience. In both cases, attempts to encourage local initiatives, self-help, and the active participation of the poor have come into conflict with local power structures whose autonomy is thereby threatened. In Britain, the growing tendency to see localized poverty and 'multiple deprivation' as a response to non-local forces has somewhat blunted the area-based approach, yet government policy still remains primarily focused on specific sub-areas of cities. There is clearly a need for some area-based programmes, but the inner-city is not a place apart and local policy must take account of outside processes and forces.

The emphasis on area-based policies is given a broader perspective in Chapter 13. Chris Hamnett begins on a similar note to part of Lee's argument in Chapter 4: area-based explanations of social problems in the city are not only erroneous or incomplete but positively dangerous. They divert attention from more fundamental social processes, though it is recognized that these processes may have an important spatial component. The weakness of area-based approaches is revealed in particular in the search for explanation via the correlations among sets of data by territorial units—a problem recognized in a number of the case studies in Part Two. Hamnett explores the relationship between the role of geographical space on the one hand and of class and other elements of social structure on the other, with reference to a number of recent studies of social problems in cities. Thus space, location, and distance can be seen in the necessary broader context. This corrective to the traditional geographical perspective is shown to be especially important in explaining 'multiple deprivation' in the inner city—a matter of current concern in the public policy arena. We come full circle, back to the current 'crisis' in Britain's inner cities. How far the current (1978) research initiatives at the Department of the Environment will underline the need to broaden the present area-based policy framework remains to be seen.

12

AREA-BASED POLICIES FOR THE INNER CITY: CONTEXT, PROBLEMS, AND PROSPECTS

John Eyles

Antecedents

This chapter examines the background, nature, and difficulties of area-based policies, developed by government in the post-1945 era as a response to pressing environmental, social, and economic problems. The aftermath of the Second World War compounded the problems created by the rationalization of industry and the obsolescence of much of the housing stock. 'Regional policy' was seen as the answer to industrial change (see Hall, 1974), while the demands created by poor housing were primarily the province of urban planning. Industrial change will be discussed later, because it is only more recently that such economic considerations have been given a city dimension.

The initial post-war response to urban problems was focused on the dilapidated environments and housing of the inner districts, most of which were seen to be in need of drastic rehabilitation. Thus central government initiated comprehensive redevelopment schemes to improve housing conditions in these areas. These schemes dominated urban renewal practice for about twenty years. The programme moved slowly because of the massive costs of housing replacement. In fact, in 1963 it was estimated that 2½ million houses required repair or improvement; the replacement cost was estimated to be £5,110 m. (Bexson, 1967). It was around this time that clearance and comprehensive redevelopment began to be challenged on the grounds of cost and social impact, i.e. the destruction of established communities and social networks. Cullingworth (1960) also pointed to the fallacy that clearance was a once-and-for-all-times operation; because houses are continually ageing, there is always going to be a need for replacement and repair. Improvement became a major aspect of a housing policy known as gradual renewal, which emphasized the retention of existing stable mixed communities, the elimination of urban blight, the satisfaction of the continuing demand for low-cost housing, and the recognition that the housing problem does not have a finite end (see D.O.E., 1975). This thinking was reinforced by the Housing Condition Survey of 1967 which found that while 1·8 m. houses in England and Wales were unfit for human habitation, another 4·5 m. were in need of repair or lacked basic amenities. With the linking of the ideas of improvement and gradual renewal, there was a steady shift in policy from concentrating on individual house improvements to the improvement of streets or *areas* of poor housing and of the total environment in these areas. Thus improvement became in part area-based, a trend that was given statutory weight by the Housing Acts of 1969 and 1974.

There are, however, more explicitly social and economic antecedents of area-based policies, which stem in the main from American social reform. In the United States, private foundations as well as governmental bodies act as agents of reform. The Ford Foundation has been an important instigator of urban policy and was, during the 1950s, concerned especially with the problems of metropolitan government and urban renewal. Both initiatives sought to reintegrate inner city and suburb but both seemed to have inherent weaknesses, in the former the intransigence of suburban authorities and in the latter the aggravation of the social distress renewal was supposed to relieve (Marris and Rein, 1972). In the late 1950s the Foundation started its 'grey areas' programme aimed at the decaying residential inner city, i.e. the zone in which newcomers have always settled. The newcomers, usually blacks from the South or Puerto Ricans, lacked the necessary skills to obtain well-paid jobs in a technological society. The Foundation, therefore, sought to improve career chances, civil rights and self-respect through the school system. Being unable to fund a massive programme, they tried to demonstrate the possibilities by experiments in Oakland, New Haven, Boston, Philadelphia, Washington, and North Carolina. The Foundation also funded the New York-based Mobilisation for Youth (MFY) programme, which concentrated on the problems of juvenile delinquency. MFY adopted the idea of Cloward and Ohlin (1960) who saw delinquency as an illegitimate attempt to secure the symbols of societal status, i.e. it is caused by inequalities in economic and educational opportunity. By 1964 the Ford Foundation had committed $20 m. to support such experimental community action programmes. The other major instigator of reform, the President's Committee on Juvenile Delinquency, spent $10·7 m. over $3 m. of which went on research experiments rather than on tackling the problematic relationship between employment and delinquency. Both Foundation and Committee stressed the importance of educational and vocational opportunities and the need for reform to develop from a coherent integration of relevant institutions and from the commitment of local communities to projects. They also concentrated resources in a few projects which were seen as demonstrations and opportunities to monitor progress. The projects were not very successful, the educational ones conflicting with the objectives and values of teachers and local boards, the vocational ones producing few jobs. Public involvement was at a low level. As we shall see, these lessons were not heeded by the British policy-makers, although it should be pointed out that American experience was never directly *translated* into British policy, because of differences in the political and economic organization of the two nations. It is more accurate then to speak of parallels between them, rather than integration of American and British reform.

The Foundation and Committee-based projects were, however, overtaken by other Federal government initiatives, in particular the War on Poverty and the associated Economic Opportunity Act and Office of Economic Opportunity (OEO). OEO accepted without question the notions of previous reformers, which then became the conventional wisdom before they had been proved effective. As Marris and Rein (1972, p. 268) have said, 'The poverty programme could afford to neglect theory, since the relevance of employment, training, health and education to economic opportunity scarcely needed to be argued.' Thus the vehicle to eliminate poverty—the community-action programme—stressed the co-ordinated provision of services, the 'maximum feasible participation' of the poor in projects and the encouragement of self-help. The two latter elements created problems in that they threatened the jurisdiction of local governments by raising the issue of local control. This is perhaps one reason why OEO stressed jobs rather than participation, although both American and British programmes came to see economic opportunity as of overriding importance. During the late 1960s over 1,000 community-action programmes were started, at a total cost of around $500 m. Kasperson (1977) has argued that community action made a significant contribution to providing employment for minority groups and for the urban poor as well as helping those denied other routes of social mobility, especially young black neighbourhood leaders.

One further American scheme must be discussed—the Model Cities Programme set up in 1966 and based on the grey areas projects. Grants and technical assistance were provided to help communities to carry out 'comprehensive city demonstration programmes', i.e. locally prepared plans for rebuilding or restoring slums and blighted areas by the concentrated and co-ordinated use of federal, local and private resources. The plans were meant to suggest ways of reducing social and educational disadvantage, ill health, and under- and un-employment. In some ways the Model Cities programme was a retreat from the earlier projects. Urban renewal and blighted neighbourhoods rather than poverty *per se* were stressed. Physical and social plans were to be comprehensively co-ordinated on an area basis through recognized, established, political authority, namely city hall. Thus participation, self-help, and countervailing power became unimportant concepts in practice, though still part of policy rhetoric. The programme eventually included about 150 cities. Money (a total of $900 m.) was thus thinly spread. Resources given to any one city could not instigate massive social reform and most funds went to existing institutions. As Kasperson (1977, p. 196) commented, 'Survival paid the price of social change. Central intervention slipped from a programme of social redistribution to one of distribution.' The structure of welfare institutions, city power, and the relative economic positions of urban residents remained basically unchanged, while now self-help above all else is emphasized in the era of what Patrick Moynihan termed 'benign neglect'.

The American experience has been discussed at some length because there are important parallels in the ideas, concerns, and actions of American and British reformers. Several British government reports and inquiries have identified similar problems of delinquency, dereliction, poverty, and racial tension, particularly in inner-city areas, and have suggested similar strategies. Thus, three reports (Home Office, 1960, 1965, 1968a) highlighted the problems of juvenile delinquency, while the relationships between social stress, race, and poor housing were documented by the report on housing in Greater London (M.H.L.G., 1965). The role of education in providing disadvantaged children with the skills and outlook necessary to succeed in adult society was discussed in the Plowden report, which also developed the idea that education can serve as the way of breaking into the 'cycle of deprivation' by concentrating resources on schools in deprived areas (D.E.S. 1967, cf. 'grey area' projects).

The Seebohm report pointed to the importance of co-ordinated and integrated social services, organized on the basis of need and assisted by the stimulation of self-help (Home Office, 1968b). The report also identified *areas* of special need, particularly those with black immigrants. The plight of these newcomers was documented by Rose (1969), who pointed to the discrimination against these migrants particularly in employment and housing. Part of this problem can be explained by the newcomers' lack of involvement in the decision-making process. The need for such public participation was given wider applicability by the Skeffington report (M.H.L.G., 1969), which pointed to the need for people to be able to say what kind of community they want and how it should develop. All these reports emphasize the social and political framework for resource re-distribution. The economic perspective, that work and investment need to be redistributed, has been stated more recently by the studies of inner districts of Liverpool, Birmingham, and London (D.O.E., 1974—6), and by a recent White Paper on inner-city policies (D.O.E., 1977).

These reports and the American experience provide the bases for the area-oriented policies for British urban areas. Three main concerns underpin this appoach. First, there is a disparity between needs and tax revenue. In the British context, universal welfare benefits have not achieved a more equal society; nor are there resources available greatly to increase these benefits. Area-based policies are one of the ways of ensuring that those deemed to be in most need receive selective benefits. Secondly, newcomers have special needs that must be dealt with selectively, especially when they are black migrants from the American South or from the Caribbean and Asia. As the forces of discrimination, bigotry, and the desire for propinquity lead to the spatial concentration of such groups, an area-based strategy is seen as appropriate. Thirdly, opposition to neighbour-hood disruption is now more articulate. The needs of local democracy thus require an area-based framework, as do the integration of services and the encourage-ment of self-help that may answer the protest and enrich community life. The concerns and aims of local or community action in both countries are, therefore, geared to 'the reorganisation of local social services into an integrated plan to attack the roots of social deprivation [and physical dereliction]' (Marris and Rein, 1972, p. 10).

Policies

The targets of area policies vary from environmental improvement to social and economic development and later to the total life-structure of the resident popu-lation. As was suggested earlier, environment-oriented policies are now based on rehabilitation rather than clearance. Two such policies will be discussed initially —the general improvement area (GIA) and the housing action area (HAA).

GIAs and HAAs

GIAs were introduced by the Housing Act of 1969. Local authorities were free to declare any predominantly residential area as a GIA, the suggested size of which was between 300 and 500 houses. In fact, only about one in six GIAs fall into this category, two-thirds being smaller; this local discretion was allowed in order to avoid delays in processing applications and to permit the legislation to meet a variety of local housing conditions. Essentially, GIAs were intended to concentrate the improvement effort, but grants were available in GIAs on the same basis as everywhere else. (Preferential rates were not introduced until the 1974 Housing Act). There was no provision for compulsory improvement in GIAs, although it may be argued that the grant system itself was inflexible in its attempt to improve houses to a universally high standard by virtue of location in a GIA, with an apparent disregard of the needs and circumstances of individual owners and tenants (Duncan, 1973). The complete rehabilitation of such areas may be dysfunctional for certain groups in that the existing housing provides cheap accommodation for young families, one-parent families, and transients as well as a first-time opportunity for house purchase for several minority groups (see Mason, 1977). With rehabilitation, rents and prices are likely to rise. Indeed, GIAs are meant to apply to the private sector, although government figures indicate that 23 per cent of all GIAs have been declared on council estates. Roberts (1976) estimated that the figure was higher at 31 per cent, while McCulloch (1974) placed the pre-1973 declaration figure for the public sector at nearly 50 per cent. Local authorities have tended to avoid the less tractable problems of the private rented sector and indeed twice as many individual grants go to owner-occupiers as to private landlords.

The great rise in improvement grant uptake in England and Wales from 113,142 grants in 1969 to the peak of 360,954 in 1973 results from the success of a more general promotion of rehabilitation rather than GIA policy, with only 9 per cent of the grants approved in 1973 being in GIAs and less than 7 per cent of approvals being in GIAs and HAAs in 1976 (see Table 12.1). In 1971, though, GIAs became part of regional policy with preference being given to GIA declarations in development (now assisted) and intermediate areas. By 1973 two-thirds of all grants and areas were in such districts. The 1974 Housing Act placed such aid in a wider housing context.

Roberts (1976) has argued that the GIA is too limited a device to tackle the national housing problem but too broad to tackle areas of housing stress. It is then a selective programme aimed at an extensive problem, an attempt to improve living conditions by physical means. Housing improvements depend on voluntary uptake and grants are approved on the assumption that the house has 30 years of life left. This of course implies that the GIA has the same life, with the choice of areas being limited by the age and life-expectancy of properties. It can therefore be debated whether the life expectancy of an area is a precondition or consequence of GIA declaration.

Environmental improvement—pedestrianized streets, play areas, landscaping—is on a small scale. While the maximum grant for house improvement is £3,200 (60 per cent from public funds), the environmental budget is £200 per dwelling, making a total sum of only £100,000 available for such improvements in a 500-house GIA. Even in housing terms, the rate of improvement has been slow. In his survey of seventy-five GIAs, Roberts (1976) found that only 41 per cent of council dwellings and 18 per cent of private housing in need of improvement has been so improved. These results are similar to those achieved in housing not part of GIA declarations. As Table 12.1 shows, 1,075 GIAs have been declared up to 1976, over two-thirds of this activity being concentrated in the years

Table 12.1
Improvement Grants and Declared GIAs and HAAs 1969–1976

	No. of local authorities declaring	No. of areas declared	No. of dwellings	Improvement of dwellings		Total no. of Improvement Grants approved
				Grants Approved	Work Completed	
GIAs						
1969[1]	25	29	7,330	52	27	113,142
1970	82	108	33,982	2,511	1,119	156,557
1971	141	195	58,046	5,453	2,300	197,481
1972	161	275	89,122	18,239	7,271	319,169
1973	128	247	63,185	32,621	15,143	360,954
1974	42	67	30,152	15,799	12,968	231,918
1975	34	54	17,864	12,318	11,011	126,888
1976	70	110	27,715	5,970	6,521	125,631
HAAs						
1975[2]	49	78	26,356	782	189	
1976	54	117	40,699	2,413	1,143	

Notes. [1] In 1969, GIA policy operated from August to December only.
[2] Includes one HAA declared in December 1974.
Later figures subject to D.O.E. revision.

Sources: Housing and Construction Statistics No. 8 (1973), No. 21 (1977).

1971–3. These 1,075 declarations involve around 327,000 dwellings but only some 93,000 grants have been approved and 56,000 dwellings renovated. Because of this apparent failure, recognized by the Government, the 1974 Housing Act introduced several changes. GIAs were given a revised role and would now consist of fundamentally sound houses capable of providing good living conditions for many years and would be unlikely to be affected by existing redevelopment proposals. The areas should offer scope for creating a better environment and contain stable communities largely free from housing stress. Districts with predominantly private rented accommodation were considered unsuitable for GIA treatment as it relies mainly on voluntary action on the part of owners (see D.O.E. circular 13/75).

Housing stress would be dealt with by a new device—the HAA. These could be declared in areas with the following characteristics: large dwellings but small households, i.e. with problems of multioccupation and shared amenities; where low incomes or high unemployment prevail, i.e. problem of housing disrepair; where physical conditions justify clearance but where there is no 'decanting' space, i.e. to avoid social disruption; where private rented accommodation predominates, i.e. where private developments might be to the detriment of the occupier; and of low demand, unattractive surroundings, and abandoned houses (see D.O.E. circular 14/75). In other words, HAAs were part of the strategy of gradual renewal and were to apply to areas where bad physical and social conditions interact. The emphasis on social stress, measured by overcrowding, numbers of one-parent families and ethnic minorities, levels of eviction and harassment, etc., was an addition to the usual environmental criteria and links HAA with the area experiments described below. Physical criteria have, however, predominated in any declaration submission. A D.O.E. (1976) survey of the first eighty-one HAAs declared found that 77 per cent of the areas were blighted by the delays of public planning, that the average percentage of households in the private rented sector was 53 per cent in HAAs compared with a national average of 16 per cent, that the average percentage of households lacking one basic amenity was 66 per cent and that all but two of the HAAs were at least as bad as the worst 15 per cent of enumeration districts (EDs) nationally for car ownership (i.e. more than 70·6 per cent of households without a car). The housing in HAAs is mainly terraced, much of it built in the 1870–1910 period with considerable disrepair stemming from the undermaintenance which affects most properties in the areas and justifies, according to D.O.E., an area approach.

Although the suggested size of an HAA is 300 to 400 dwellings, the range was found to be 14 to 1,258, the larger ones (over 500) being concentrated in London and the West Midlands, the smaller (under 200) in the north and north-west. As Table 12.1 shows, up to the end of 1976, 195 HAAs had been declared containing 67,000 dwellings. It has been estimated that 600,000 dwellings ought to be in HAAs; given the size guidelines this represents 2,000 HAAs, 200 of which would be in London. But many individual properties outside HAAs require attention. There are 383,000 unfit or inadequate dwellings in London, only 100,000 of which are concentrated in suitable HAAs. If resources are concentrated on these, the power to act elsewhere is greatly diminished.

Although local authorities have compulsory purchase powers in HAAs, voluntary improvement and persuasion are first priorities. The take-up of grants is likely to be affected by inflation: Paris (1977) has calculated that with the grant static at £3,200 and government contribution at 75 per cent (90 per cent in hardship cases), the real contribution of the owner has increased from £800 in 1974 to £2,390 in 1976. This may make landlords even less willing to improve their properties. The general lack of resources has meant that the HAA programme has had a slow, patchy start. Only a few cities have ambitious programmes. Of the 133 HAAs declared as at 30 September 1976, twenty-five were in London (Islington most with five), twenty-one in Liverpool, ten in both Birmingham and Manchester, and seven in Newcastle (see D.O.E., 1976). Paris has argued though that if HAAs are to provide any source of remedy, there must be comprehensive declaration linked to other policies such as municipalisation, redevelopment and improved housing management. But it is likely that social stress is only partly caused by housing conditions and that other social and economic forces are at work. It is, therefore, necessary to consider other area approaches, the briefs of which have been wider than housing change.

Educational Priority Areas

The concern of government with the specifically social problems of small areas was first given concrete expression by the recommendations of the Plowden report, which examined social conditions using such measures as socio-economic status of parents, the lack of home amenities, proportion of children both with language difficulties and receiving welfare benefits. They reported a coexistence of deprivation and considered education to be one of the keys to the alleviation of such deprivation, recommending a national policy of positive discrimination to make *schools* in the most *deprived area* as good as the best in the country. This policy was also meant to devise new ways of overcoming the disadvantages of children from poor neighbourhoods and pioneer innovation by experiment. The method of achieving these aims was the educational priority area (EPA) in which were introduced community schools, in-service training, and special payments for teachers, attached social work, and expanded nursery education. Thus the main concerns were the interaction of home and school and the cultural barriers between teacher and pupil. A total of 150 schools in fifty-one local educational authorities shared a £16 m. grant, an amount hardly likely to alter the pattern of deprivation. In fact, the concept EPA became diluted to one of educational-priority *school*, with resources being given to educational institutions alone. Leaving aside the relationship between education and poverty (see Jencks, 1972), it is questionable whether EPA school resources are being concentrated on the right schools and children. Barnes (1975) has shown that resources going to EPA schools in inner London reach 13·6 per cent of *all* children, but only 20·2 per cent of the most disadvantaged children in the I.L.E.A. area. It has also been found that for every immigrant child in an EPA school, there are three who are not. There are also five times as many children from large families, five times as many unskilled workers' children, three and a half times as many children receiving free school meals and four and a half times as many children with low verbal reasoning outside EPA schools as there are in them. The area-based approach to educational policy seems, then, to be problematic.

234   Social Problems and the City

The Urban Aid Programme

The areas of special need identified by Seebohm, and the concern over the problems of juvenile delinquency and racial tension in the inner city, led to further government initiatives. The Urban Aid Programme was set up in 1968 as an adjunct to the major programmes of social provision. These were positive discrimination projects aimed at selected groups and areas, particularly at localized districts which bear the marks of 'multiple' deprivation. The funds come from the rate support grant (RSG), being taken from the general allocation and placed in the special grant category. Local authorities and some voluntary agencies are invited by the Home Office to bid for funds. Batley and Edwards (1974) have pointed out that there had been some 2300 projects worth around £32 m. (cf. community-action programmes) in 216 English and Welsh local authorities up to 1973. The majority of the projects are on a small scale: holiday schemes, day nurseries, play groups, housing aid centres, community worker provision, and general information and advice centres. It was found that funding was generally low, the only large projects being two management-oriented neighbourhood schemes in Liverpool and Teesside costing a total of £300,000 (see Batley, 1975), and that there was a time-lag between grant application and project commencement averaging twenty months for capital projects and thirteen months for non-capital ones. According to the recent White Paper (D.O.E. 1977), the present annual sum available is £30 m., although it is unclear exactly what is included. Urban aid has been the most expensive and extensive of the government's poverty initiatives, although there have been about five times more applications made than those granted. Under its new inner-city strategy, the government intends to increase the annual budget to £125 m. in 1978–9 and certain authorities—those pursuing comprehensive community programmes and partnership schemes (see below)—will be given preferential treatment in the allocation of these funds.

Community Development Projects

The urban programme is but one of the Home Office's community-action strategies. Close parallels with American thought and practice can be seen in another of their initiatives, the community-development projects (C.D.P.s). Established in 1969, these were not so much area policies as experiments concentrating on small pockets of deprivation, the co-ordination of services, and the encouragement of participation (C.D.P., 1974). C.D.P. was then to demonstrate the advantages of a unified or total approach to the problems of deprivation. A Home Office press release stated that C.D.P. 'will be a neighbourhood-based experiment aimed at finding new ways of meeting the needs of people living in areas of high social deprivation, by bringing together the work of all the social services under the leadership of a special project team and also tapping the resources of self-help and mutual help which may exist among people in neighbourhoods' (quoted in C.D.P., 1977a, p. 12). The aim of C.D.P. was to be evolutionary change to overcome the sense of disintegration and depersonalization felt by residents of deprived areas. Twelve C.D.P.s were set up, in Hillfields (Coventry), Vauxhall (Liverpool), Newington (Southwark), Glyncorrwg (Glamorgan), Benwell (Newcastle), Canning Town (Newham), Batley (West Yorkshire), Ferguslie Park (Paisley), Cleaton Moor (Cumbria), Saltley (Birmingham),

Percy and Trinity (Tynemouth), and Clarksfield (Oldham). They had life-spans of five years and a total budget of £5 million.

Thus, the original conception of C.D.P. was based implicitly on the assumption that deprivation results from the particular qualities and attributes of local residents, i.e. from individual 'pathologies', and that these could be resolved by co-ordinating services and mobilizing self-help (see C.D.P., 1974). In their initial work the projects adopted these views and identified five major issues: employment (the devising of retraining schemes and programmes to create new job opportunities), income and income maintenance (the ensuring of maximum take-up of welfare benefit, lobbying the Department of Health and Social Security, the establishment of advice centres), housing (the setting up of a more sensitive and co-ordinated approach to housing management), education (setting up nurseries, playgroups, and adult education projects), and local bureaucratic management (focusing attention on the receptive servicing of needs of such groups as teenagers and the elderly). But as the projects progressed, there was a change in emphasis, with poverty becoming to be seen by the C.D.P. teams as resulting from fundamental inequalities in the capitalist politico-economic system. Improved welfare services would only have a marginal effect on such inequalities, while the influencing of policy must not be divorced from the development of working-class action (see C.D.P., 1975a). Fundamental changes, therefore, are required in the distribution of wealth and power. Experiments like C.D.P. simply become political-education programmes, useful in raising the consciousness of the disadvantaged. Such a perspective is illustrated by the final report of the Hillfields project (C.D.P., 1975b), which argued that the post-war boom in the car and engineering industries brought prosperity to some parts of Coventry, but has only been maintained at the expense of the older areas. The report asserted that large companies benefit from keeping such areas in a state of limbo, although this may soon be the fate of all of Coventry, given the multi-national horizons of the car firms. Hillfields, then, has cushioned the city's economy by being a buffer against labour, land, and housing market fluctuations, i.e. it provides an expendable reservoir of local, unskilled labour, a pool of fluid land near the city centre, and a stop–go valve for local authority finances. Compensatory services and administrative tinkering are not real solutions and areas like Hillfields will be a constant drain on welfare resources. The report suggested the basic structure of inequality in economic opportunity must be challenged. While advice centres, city-created jobs, and local trade-union pressure will help, central-government action is necessary. Several members of Coventry C.D.P. did, however, dissent from elements of the report, questioning the link made between the car industry and Hillfields, arguing that this connection owed more to an *a priori* commitment by most of the team to a neo-Marxian perspective than anything else.

From the example of Coventry, it can be seen that an area-based experiment ended by pointing to the need for structural changes in the British economy and polity. The C.D.P.s also clashed with their parent local authorities, mobilizing self-help into conflicts between residents and agencies. Many councillors saw C.D.P. workers as political agitators. At the same time, the developing structural analysis brought conflict with the Home Office which suggested that local authorities should themselves decide whether they could continue to afford to support the projects given financial stringency. Whether for economic or political reasons, these experiments are coming to an end. But this does not mean that the Government has rejected the area-based approach.

Comprehensive Community Programmes

In 1974 the Home Office Urban Deprivation Unit developed the idea of comprehensive community programmes (C.C.P.s). It was thought that there were about ninety areas in Britain that qualify as districts of 'intense urban deprivation'. C.C.P. concerns areas of highly concentrated urban problems which represent a sharp imbalance of need in local authority and other services and which merit concentrated effort and financial aid to redress the balance. To be effective this effort must be comprehensive in scope and involve a co-ordinated approach on the part of all agencies, while a study of the area's problems should lead to a sensitive identification of needs and appropriate action. Thus it is intended to identify a whole range of economic, social, and physical problems in each area and draw up a comprehensive set of policies (see Black, 1977). As the Home Secretary said: 'It is not a question of providing extra money on top of the existing programmes. The real question is to find within existing programmes the right order of priority so that money is spent in urban areas of acute need rather than in other areas' (quoted in C.D.P., 1977a, p. 15). The feasibility of C.C.P. is being tested in a series of experiments, as at Motherwell, Gateshead, Bradford, and Wandsworth. Essentially, C.C.P. is management-oriented in that the statutory agencies have the responsibility of drawing up a corporate plan and then of informing central government of the state of and solutions for deprivation (cf. model cities). Budgetary requirements are important elements and attempts to create area budgets will focus on comparability with the R.S.G. formula.

Partnerships

C.C.P. has not yet progressed far, the first one being set up in Motherwell in the summer of 1976. Their unified, corporate approach has, however, been given wider significance by the recent White Paper on the inner city (D.O.E., 1977). This document, too, stresses the need for combining economic, social and environmental policies to tackle the multiple deprivation of the inner city districts. The government intends to set up special partnerships with a limited number of local authorities to regenerate the inner city. In the first instance, these were Liverpool, Birmingham, Manchester-Salford, Lambeth, and the Docklands authorities in London, the initial list pointed to the influence of recent government-sponsored inquiries (D.O.E., 1974-6; Travers Morgan 1973; D.J.C., 1976). Central government involvement is intended to underline its commitment to inner areas, to bring national experience to bear and to unify central and local government action. The initial task of these partnerships is to draw up an inner-area programme which will receive priority in terms of both the R.S.G. and the expanded urban programme. (C.C.P.s are the second priority with respect to financial support). No partnership is yet (1977) underway. There have, however, been critical comments concerning their corporate, experimental, low-funded nature and a questioning of the likely economic impact of such schemes.

Key Elements and Assumptions

So far in this chapter, the area framework of policy has been accepted uncritically. It is now necessary to examine the difficulties of such a framework, but firstly some of the key elements and assumptions implicit in the policy statements will be discussed. Government attention has been directed at those elements which would produce immediate results, i.e. the accomplishment first of those programmes which came easiest. Thus by far the larger proportion of resources has been directed at environmental and housing projects and the urban aid programme. Even so, the amounts spent have been small. Urban policy is dominated by parsimony. The total urban aid programme budget stands at some £60 m. and its annual expenditure up to 1975 was around £3 m. to £4 m. While the 1969–72 budget of the programme totalled £22 m. (half of which had been spent on nursery education and day nurseries, with the largest recipient, Birmingham, obtaining £670,000), the social-services budget for 1972–3 was over £11 billion (Hudson, 1974). Put another way, the urban programme constitutes a quarter of 1 per cent of the R.S.G. The allocation of E.P.A. schools was less than half of 1 per cent of total educational expenditure during the 1970s (Townsend, 1976). This low level of funding compares with such massive private property investments (mainly in central city offices) as the insurance companies' £450 m. invested in land and property in 1976 (15 per cent of their total net investment) and the private pensions funds' £226 m. (18 per cent of their total net investment). It can also be compared with the $900 million that the United States spent on its community action and model cities programmes.

These relatively low levels of policy funding may stem in part from the fact that the British view inequality and poverty as primarily *regional* phenomena while Americans see them as primarily racial and therefore urban. Such an explanation is reinforced by the change in GIA policy in 1971 to favour the assisted and intermediate regions. This argument does not suggest that Britain recognizes no urban problems or the U.S. no regional ones, but the scarcity of resources for the city in Britain determines in part the experimental nature of so many of these programmes. It should perhaps be added that British regional policy and the expanded and new town programmes may have taken resources away from certain inner city areas, thus worsening their relative poverty. It is true to say, however, that such policies and programmes were instigated to tackle important problems in their own right.

The low level of funding may be associated with another policy assumption, namely that poverty, deprivation, and dereliction affect only small groups and marginal areas. As the Home Office commented: 'CDP is based on the recognition that although the Social Services cater reasonably well for the majority, they are less effective for a minority who are caught up in a chain reaction of related social problems' (quoted in C.D.P., 1977a, 53). Much depends on the definitions of deprivation and poverty adopted, although as early as the 1950s Townsend (1954) was suggesting that poverty must be seen in relative terms, relative to the material wealth, expectations, and goals of the society in question. The idea of marginality fitted well with the optimistic, technocratic growth-oriented values of the 1960s. 'Backward' groups and territories simply required greater resources so that they could take their rightful place in the general prosperity fostered by economic growth (see below). Their eventual success was even more likely, given the prevailing explanations of poverty. It has already been stated that the initial assumption of C.D.P. was that deprivation had its origins in the pathologies of individuals, i.e. that there were defects that could be put right by caring policy initiatives. Poverty was seen, therefore, as the result of defective socialisation. Certain families have inadequate child-rearing methods and do not provide their children with the skills necessary to benefit from educational and job opportunities. There is a need, therefore, to compensate these individuals, especially in education. We can see grey areas, E.P.A.s, and the urban programme as exemplifying such an approach.

Connected with this explanation of deprivation are the notions of the poverty cycle and transmitted deprivation. Poverty is seen as self-perpetuating. Children start school at a disadvantage and as they receive little support from parents they may drop out of school. In any event, they become marginally employable. If they cannot obtain a decent wage, they may not be able to sustain marriage and may also enter crime. They pass on to their children the inheritance of ignorance, broken homes, and violence. The circularity of this argument means that it is possible to intervene at any and every point, but intervention often occurs at the most malleable age-groups—children and adolescents with educational, vocational, and compensatory programmes and the elderly with domiciliary services, day centres, etc.—while others are ignored. There is, however, a general attempt to reduce apathy and dependency and increase self-reliance. Hence self-help after the style of the community action programme and C.D.P. is a crucial element in many schemes. It has the practical advantage of reducing the demand for state-provided welfare services. In fact, the encouragement of self-help may be seen as the state off-loading many of its statutory responsibilities. The eradication of transmitted deprivation may also be a major implicit reason for environmental policies (GIAs, HAAs) which aim at providing a suitable ambience for social development. GIAs and HAAs can be said then to tackle the visible signs of deprivation, but not necessarily the causes.

A slightly different explanation of poverty—suggested in certain strategies (C.D.P., C.C.P., partnerships)—calls into question the functioning of institutions which may have objectives, methods, and delivery systems that fail to meet the needs of the poor and may even reinforce their condition. This explanation has two consequences: there is a need to improve the access and knowledge of the poor about services and there is a need to sensitise and co-ordinate services themselves. Thus participation of the poor, and the attempt to create centres of countervailing power among them, should be key elements in many area-based programmes. Participation can become problematic, however, especially if it is seen to threaten established political authority. Kasperson (1977) has pointed to the dilution of participation and its transformation into self-help in the American programmes. The blandness and paternalism of participation in British urban planning have been documented by Jones and Eyles (1977). Pranger (1968) has distinguished between the *participant* as a passive citizen attached to a programme, and the *participator* as an active citizen involved in decision-making. While most of the poor remain apathetic or participants, established political authorities demonstrate great flexibility by co-opting many participators into their ranks.

The co-ordination of services was stressed in many policies. It is an integral element of the total approach advocated in C.D.P., C.C.P., and the partnership schemes and of the effort to escape the fragmented central government activity in the early programmes. Co-ordination is seen as the way of improving administrative practice and as a means of involving all statutory bodies in corporate plan-making. In fact, area management trials have been instigated in Dudley and Haringey in order to co-ordinate policy and act as information points for the local population. This corporatism does, however, suggest that participation of the active kind is now a low priority. Indeed the ordering of priorities in a time of financial stringency is now a major feature of government policy (see D.O.E., 1977). Thus, the key features of area-based policies are experimentation and low funding, participation and self-help, co-ordination and corporatism, and an emphasis on the easily assailable and outward manifestations of deprivation. There is evidence, though, that there is a shift in stance on the causes of deprivation.

Problems and Prospects

In September 1976 the Secretary of State for the Environment said that the decline of the inner cities had its causes '. . . primarily in their relative economic decline, in a major migration of people often the most skilled and in a massive reduction in the number of jobs which are left . . . Many facilities in our inner urban areas need qualitative improvement and some need total and often expensive improvement' (quoted in C.D.P., 1977a, p. 57). There is a recognition of the dominance of economic forces in effecting the inner area decline and in causing their relative deprivation. This view is a pale reflection of the argument forcibly presented by the C.D.P.s. In their view, poverty is caused by fundamental inequalities that arise from the nature of the capitalist system. The existence of areas of industrial and economic decline is a symptom of the uneven development of capitalism. 'The empty shipyards on the Tyne, the derelict mills of Batley, the redeveloped sites of Vickers (Benwell) and British Leyland (Saltley) and the empty berths along the Thames all date from the time when these places were the industrial heartland of the country' (C.D.P., 1977b, p. 58). But new activities and technologies have replaced these industries, often demanding different, more spacious locations. There is, then, a migration of industry, jobs, and prosperity, leaving the early-developed areas in a state of continuing decline, unattractive to the young as homes and to industrial capital as places for investment. There is a certain inevitability about these processes of growth and decay and it is an open question whether government activity can do more than militate against their worst effects. C.D.P. (1977b, p. 96) may demand 'measures to control the activities of capital' but, given the international nature of the economy, too stringent controls may force investment elsewhere. The revitalization of areas like London's Docklands requires massive public expenditure (c. £1 billion) and a long time-scale (c. 20 years). The Community Land Act will do little to cheapen or speed the process (see Land Campaign Working Party, n.d.). In the meantime, such cramped environments with poor infrastructures attract mainly marginal employers such as warehousing and sweat-shops. Given the virtual impossibility of one national government tackling the economic root-causes of group and territorial inequality, reform seems likely to be slow and piecemeal.

But must its reformist policies be area-based? Such an approach is said to have many advantages, concentrating effort and resources, being relatively in-expensive and easily monitored. There are, however, significant problems. Area policies are based on the drawing of boundaries, including some people and excluding other, perhaps similar, individuals. Such policies may therefore encourage a certain parochialism among professionals and public. They may also divide sections of the population who may achieve more if they were united. Indeed much working-class action depends on a broad class-base rather than a narrow residential one; the latter may well reduce the likelihood of achieving objectives. It must be remembered, though, that political pressures generated within small local communities are most effective in vetoing action, but to obtain desired changes such groups must gain the support of larger populations and higher levels of government, for '. . . a major and sustained redistribution [of resources] cannot be achieved *without* using the powers and resources of govern-ment—the law, the courts, taxation and the social services—[while] initiatives which are confined to voluntary institutions and never win the support of the bureaucracy cannot [succeed]' (Donnison, 1973, p. 390). Thus the importance of the main programmes and agencies of government must not be under-emphasized.

The drawing of boundaries raises other problems that must be briefly men-tioned. These mainly relate to the ecological trap of assuming that the majority if not all individuals in a sub-area conform to the pattern of characteristics derived from aggregate data—an error clearly illustrated by E.P.A. policy. In fact, there has been much recent investigation on the relationship between deprivation and area. Holtermann (1975, p. 39), in her analysis of the 1971 census material, said that 'the degree of spatial concentration of individual aspects of deprivation is really quite low'. There were EDs in the worst 15 per cent on three factors (male unemployment, over-crowding, and lack of all basic amenities), but they only accounted for one-fifth of these 15 per cent. In London Berthoud (1976) has shown that most variation in household income has nothing to do with area. At ward level, only 9·4 per cent of income inequality is attributable to variations between wards. EDs only account for a total of 13·2 per cent of inequality between households. Berthoud did construct a low-income inner ring, skewed towards the East End, but he found that only half of London's poor were in it. Finally, mention can be made of Hatch and Sherrott's (1973) analysis of deprivation in Newham and Southwark. They concluded that it is more realistic to conceive of deprivation as multi- rather than uni-dimensional, and of deprived areas as being of different kinds containing different combinations of depriva-tions.

Such findings have led many to doubt the effectiveness of the areal-policy approach even for environmental improvements. Townsend (1976) has argued that positive discrimination based on ecology will miss out more of the poor or deprived than it will include (see Chapter 2). Deprivation can be seen as household- and group-based, while its extent is determined in the national system of resource allocation—nationally determined wage structures and taxation systems, national social security, national housing, and commercial market conditions. There is therefore a need for national action to remedy poverty (income policy, tax reform, higher and new welfare benefits and allowances).

Others are less sure. Hatch and Sherrott (1973) have commented that small areas may still be of strategic importance for reformist intervention but only if such projects are seen as experimental and the lessons learnt from them applied more widely. Deakin (1977) has argued that the criticism of area-based action is really directed against such action masquerading as a total programme. He thought that *area-biased* approaches would be useful as relatively inexpensive demonstrations of the feasibility of action, and that the neighbourhood is still an important social entity and a useful basis of reform, especially if that means the provision of much needed facilities in poorer environments (see also Donnison, 1974).

It is also pertinent to ask whether our view of the relationship between deprivation and area (as an aggregate of households) has been affected by the nature of available data. There has been much debate on the relevant geographical scale but little on the data used to define deprivation. Virtually every study has relied on the Census, which is strongly biased towards housing conditions (see Chapter 2). Yet Britain is one of the best-housed nations in Europe and it is not surprising that the remaining housing inadequacies are scattered among many local authority areas. If we defined deprivation differently, would it appear more spatially concentrated? The evidence is ambiguous. E.P.A. material shows a dispersed pattern but the Community Relations Commission (1977) has found that 70 per cent of the ethnic population is concentrated in 10 per cent of EDs, in which they constitute one-fifth of the total population. These EDs compare unfavourably with others in terms of housing conditions; levels of unemployment (especially among youth), wages, and skills; numbers of single-parent families and children in care; and the level of educational qualifications. It would seem therefore that racial disadvantage and associated deprivation may have an areal bias. Are there other social and economic phenomena which present similar pictures? Rutter and Madge (1976) have pointed to the geographical concentration and stability of certain psychological and social problems and have argued for intensive longitudinal locally based studies. Until we definitely know, it would be foolhardy to abandon area-based policies which may simply require refining. In the meantime they are useful as experiments, as ways of dealing with certain aspects of racial disadvantage and as methods of implementing certain environmental strategies. But such policies must be undertaken in association with the government's main programmes. Small areas and the inner city are not places apart, but are integral parts of society being affected by outside processes and forces. It is this combination which is necessary for tackling the widespread nature of identified deprivation and for militating against some of the effects of industrial and financial capital.

References

Barnes, J. A. 1975 *Educational Priority*, Vol. 3, *Curriculum Innovation in London's EPAs*, H.M.S.O., London.

Batley, R. 1975 'The neighbourhood scheme: cases of central government intervention in local deprivation', Research Paper 19, Centre for Environmental Studies, London.
— and Edwards, J. 1974 'The urban programme: a report on some programme funded projects', *British Journal of Social Work*, 4. 305–31.
Berthoud, R. 1976 'Where are London's poor?', *Greater London Intelligence Quarterly*, 36. 5–12.
Bexson, P. J. 1967 'Twilight areas: problems and solutions', *Chartered Surveyor*, 100. 308–11.
Black, D. 1977 'Comprehensive community budgets', *Public Finance and Accountancy*, 4. 124–7.
Cloward, R., and L. Ohlin 1960 *Delinquency and Opportunity*, Free Press, Glencoe, Ill.
Community Development Project 1974 *Inter-project Report*, C.D.P. Information Unit, London.
— 1975a *Forward Plan 1975–6*, C.D.P. Information Unit, London.
— 1975b *Coventry and Hillfields: Prosperity and the Persistence of Inequality*, 2 vols., C.D.P., Coventry.
— 1977a *Gilding the Ghetto*, C.D.P. Inter-Project Team, London.
— 1977b *The Costs of Industrial Change*, C.D.P. Inter-Project Team, London.
Community Relations Commission 1977 *Urban Deprivation, Racial Inequality and Social Policy*, H.M.S.O., London.
Cullingworth, J. B. 1960 *Housing Needs and Planning Policy*, Routledge & Kegan Paul, London.
Deakin, N. 1977 'Inner area problems: positive discrimination revisited', *Greater London Intelligence Journal*, 37. 4–8.
Department of Education and Science 1967 *Children and their Primary Schools*, Plowden Report, 2 vols., H.M.S.O., London.
Department of the Environment 1974–6 *Inner Area Studies: Reports*, H.M.S.O., London.
— 1975 'Gradual renewal', *Area Improvement Occasional Paper*, 2–75.
— 1976 'Housing action areas: a detailed examination of declaration reports', *Improvement Research Note* 2–76.
— 1977 *Policy for the Inner Cities*, Cmnd. 6845, H.M.S.O., London.
Docklands Joint Committee 1976 *London Docklands: A Strategic Plan*, D.J.C., London.
Donnison, D. 1973 'Micro-politics of the city' in Donnison, D., and Eversley, D. (eds.), *London: Urban Patterns, Problems and Policies*, Heinemann, London. 383–404.
— 1974 'Policies for priority areas', *Journal of Social Policy*, 3. 127–35.
Duncan, T. L. C. 1973 *Housing Improvement Policies in England and Wales*, Centre for Urban and Regional Studies, Birmingham.
Hall, P. 1974 *Urban and Regional Planning*, Pelican, Harmondsworth.
Hatch, S., and Sherrott, R. 1973 'Positive discrimination and the distribution of deprivations', *Policy and Politics* 1. 223–40.
Holtermann, S. 1975 'Areas of urban deprivation in Great Britain: an analysis of 1971 census data', *Social Trends*, 6. 33–47.
Home Office 1960 *Report of the Committee on Children and Young Persons*, Ingleby Report, Cmnd. 1191, H.M.S.O., London.
— 1965 *The Child, the Family and the Young Offender*, Cmnd. 2742, H.M.S.O., London.

—— 1968a *Children in Trouble*, Cmnd. 3601, H.M.S.O., London.

—— 1968b *Report of the Committee on Local Authority and Allied Personal Social Services*, Seebohm Report, Cmnd. 3703, H.M.S.O., London.

Hudson, B. 1974 'A finger in the dyke', *Municipal Journal*, 82. 1255–7.

Jencks, C. 1972 *Inequality*, Harper & Row, New York.

Jones, E., and Eyles, J. 1977 *An Introduction to Social Geography*, Oxford University Press, Oxford.

Kasperson, R. E. 1977 'Participation through centrally planned social change: lessons from the American experience on the urban scene', in Sewell, W. R. D., and Coppock, J. T., (eds.), *Public Participation in Planning*, Wiley, London. 173–190.

Land Campaign Working Party (n.d.) *Lie of the Land: Community Land Act; Land Nationalisation Betrayed*, L.C.W.P., London.

Marris, P., and Rein, M. 1972 *Dilemmas of Social Reform*, Penguin, Harmondsworth.

Mason, T. 1977 'Intention and implication in housing policy', *Journal of Social Policy*, 6. 17–30.

McCulloch, D. C. 1974 'General improvement areas: housing function and their relation to the local housing market', *Environmental Health*, 82. 48–50.

Ministry of Housing and Local Government 1965 *Report of the Committee on Housing in Greater London*, Milner Holland Report, Cmnd. 2605, H.M.S.O., London.

—— 1969 'People and planning', Skeffington Report, H.M.S.O., London.

Paris, C. 1977 'Housing action areas', *Roof*, 2. 9–14.

Pranger, R. 1968 *The Eclipse of Citizenship*, Holt, Rinehart, & Winston, New York.

Robert, J. T. 1976 *General Improvement Areas*, Saxon House, Farnborough.

Rose, E. J. B. 1969 *Colour and Citizenship*, Oxford University Press, London.

Rutter, M., and Madge, N. 1976 *Cycles of Deprivation*, Heinemann, London.

Townsend, P. 1954 'Measuring poverty', *British Journal of Sociology*, 5. 130–7.

—— 1976 'The difficulties of policies based on the concept of area deprivation', *Queen Mary College, Department of Economics, Barnett Shine Foundation Lecture*.

Travers Morgan 1973 *Docklands: Redevelopment Proposals for East London*, Dockland Study Team, London.

13

AREA-BASED EXPLANATIONS:
A CRITICAL APPRAISAL

Chris Hamnett

Introduction

Area-based explanations in geography have a long history—almost as long as geography has endeavoured to be an explanatory science. Given the focus of the discipline on space and area and their independent determining influence on phenomena, such a tendency is understandable if dangerous—not least where the explanation of social problems in the city is concerned. The term 'dangerous' is deliberate, the contention of this essay being that by virtue of the stress given by geographers to the *spatial distribution* of phemonema *in vacuo*, largely abstracted from their wider socio-economic contexts, they have unwittingly moved into an explanatory *cul-de-sac* productive of little more than often erroneous, spatially grounded, causal inferences, which simultaneously divert attention away from underlying social causes. It should be stressed here that my comments are directed towards explanation and not prediction.

Although the distribution of some phenomena over space undoubtedly exercises influence on the distribution of other phenomena over space, it is suggested that the frequent attempts by geographers to explain spatial phenomena largely, or even exclusively, by reference to the distribution of other spatial phenomena, is a manifestation of what Anderson (1973, p. 3) has referred to as the 'fetishism of space' whereby, at least in a human geographical context, 'relations between social groups or classes are presented as relations between areas.'

Notwithstanding the pioneering work of Snow in tracing the origins of the 1855 cholera epidemic in the Soho district of London to a polluted well through mapping the distribution of the place of residence of those who died of cholera and finding that they decreased with distance from the well (Howe, 1972, p. 178), the causes of geographical phenomena can hardly ever be ascribed to spatial factors (Sack, 1972). Only rarely can they be successfully analysed in purely spatial terms, even though Castle and Gittus (1957, p. 44) suggest the methods used to discover the causes of infectious diseases may be profitably transferred to the study of social 'defects'. Their causation, if not their manifestation, is instead a product of other factors in the social structure or the physical environment, and spatial analysis can often conceal as much, if not more, than it reveals. Yet, by focusing initially on spatial distribution geographers are frequently drawn to look for either distance *per se* or co-varying phenomena as possible causes. Although there are notable exceptions where *both* distance *and* social structure have been considered as possible causes (see Bradley *et al.*, 1976), the tendency has frequently been to look for causes in space or area rather than within the social structure, thereby often diverting attention away from what are possibly the fundamental causes towards surface manifestations or appearances (see Anderson, 1973, p. 3; Gray, 1976, p. 38). As Peet (1977, p. 251) has put it: 'geographers try to find "causes" of the problems they observe in what is the spatial distribution of the *results* of far deeper causes.'

This is not to say that space is unimportant, quite the contrary. Pahl (1968) has stressed the interrelationships between spatial and social structures and as Sayer (1978) has pointed out: 'Almost invariably the form of spatial organization makes a difference to processes, and hence the latter cannot be fully understood without reference to the former.' So too, Peet (1977, p. 254) comments that

geographic variations give a strong spatial weight to social process, so much so that we can speak of *spatial* processes. These are originally social processes whose spatial manifestations have become so strong that they are highly significant, even co-dominant, features of the process.

Space clearly plays an important role in social processes (cf. the role of diffusion in ghetto expansion or the existence of the spatial segregation of different social groups (Harvey, 1975)). The criticisms presented here relate rather to the analysis of phenomena in dominantly spatial terms, thereby treating them in isolation and divorcing them from the totality of phenomena. Just as much classical economics erred in treating the economy as a spaceless, dimensionless point, so too much recent human geography has erred in neglecting the social, economic, and political aspects of its objects of study. As Castells (in Pickvance, 1976, p. 30) points out: 'Society cannot be "reflected" in space since it is not external to space. What is necessary, rather, is to show how space and other material elements of social organization are articulated within a coherent theoretical or conceptual whole.'

To summarize, it is suggested that to abstract spatial phenomena as things in themselves, and to treat space in isolation is to abstract from the totality of phenomena and thereby to limit severely the possible explanations that can be offered, frequently mystifying and obscuring more fundamental causes in the process (Gregory, 1978). We turn now to the explanatory problems posed by the concentration of many social problems in cities.

Area-Based Explanations of Urban Social Problems

Where urban social problems are concerned, the very fact of the concentration of many such problems superficially points to some kind of specifically urban or area-based explanation, such as that formulated by Wirth (1938) in his seminal paper 'Urbanism as a way of life'. Although reviewed from time to time, by Fischer (1972) and Guterman (1969) amongst others, only Gans (1962) subjected the hypothesis to critical examination, suggesting that class and life-cycle stage were of more explanatory importance than size, density, and heterogeneity. More recently, Wirth's formulation has been challenged by Castells (in Pickvance, 1976) on the grounds that spatial form or settlement type is only an intervening variable which, in common with the characteristics of urbanism, is a direct consequence of industrialism and the capitalist mode of production. It is not my intention to pursue this argument here, as Pickvance (1974) has examined in some detail the extent to which the contemporary western city as a spatial form can be said to be determined or relatively autonomous. Lee also addresses related issues in Chapter 4 of the present volume. My concern is more with the general dangers of inferring spatial causation from spatial concentrations or manifestations.

Harloe (1977) has commented on the assumption that because problems occur within cities, they are necessarily 'urban problems' and Sayer (1978) refers to 'the very fact that planning operates on an areal basis produces a tendency to treat social problems which are *manifested* in spatial concentrations as problems of *areas as such*.' Herbert and Johnston (1976, p. 1) specifically distinguished problems *in* the city such as poverty 'which appear to be urban simply because of the population concentration' with problems *of* the city which are 'created by the pattern of population concentration'. They instance two examples of the latter, the first being those that are a function of size and high population densities, some of which have been examined or reviewed by Gad (1973), Dye (1975), Galle *et al.*, (1972), amongst others. As a second type they suggest those that are said to be brought about 'by the internal spatial structure of the urban place'. Referring to spatial segregation they state (p. 3) that 'to many people this spatial separation of population groups is a cause of, or at least exacerbates, a a number of social problems. Certain districts housing a particular type of family, for example, might be seen as "breeding places" for crime and delinquency . . .' The distinction between causation and exacerbation is a significant one which we shall have cause to return to, the position taken here being that area-based exacerbation of social problems is much more likely than area-based causation. Although the differentiation of problems *in* and *of* the city is to be welcomed, it may bring with it the tendency for geographers to concentrate their explanatory efforts on problems *of* the city where area effects are more likely to be distinguished than on problems *in* the city such as poverty which, it is contended, are the most important ones.

This aside, the growing realization that 'urban' or 'areal' problems are not necessarily urban or areal in origin is not new, despite the recent statements quoted above. Twenty years ago, Castle and Gittus (1957, p. 43) observed that 'the mere demonstration . . . that an accumulation of problems coexist within a particular area cannot be held to prove that they have arisen as a result of a connected process of cause and effect.' More generally, the dangers of inferring causation from spatial correlations at the aggregate level were pointed out by Robinson (1950) and Lander (1954) amongst others. Such warnings appear to have gone unheeded in some cases however, as several subsequent area-based studies and 'explanations' testify. Indeed, Castle and Gittus themselves suggest in relation to the aetiology of social 'pathologies', that in the absence of any significant 'drift' factor (i.e. the selective migration into an area of persons exhibiting such 'pathologies') 'causation factors might be found to exist within the areas themselves.' In their efforts to derive some kind of spatial causation from a spatial correlation, frequently by virtue of the specifically *spatial* focus of such studies, such 'explanations' are perpetuated at the expense of more fundamental social explanations which, though sometimes recognized, are ignored or set aside.

At the simplest level there are studies such as that by Wallis and Maliphant (1967) which are almost exclusively descriptive and which make little or no attempt at explanation, though often leaving a series of question marks over significant correlations which point the reader in certain directions. They introduce their paper with the words that its purpose 'is to relate the distribution of delinquency in the London County Council area to a variety of ecological factors, and thus attempt to define the attributes that distinguish "delinquent areas" '. After doing this at some length and stating, amongst other things, that (p. 281) 'over forty years of considerable change a number of the economic, educational and class related factors that tended to define delinquent areas in London in the early twenties still appear to do so almost to the same extent in the early sixties', they conclude that

a description of the environment to be found in high delinquent areas may highlight certain features that would appear, from previous theoretical considerations, to be criminogenic in influence . . . [although] . . . a problem still remains as to how the types of urban environment customarily found in delinquent areas predispose their residents towards crime.

This seems to obfuscate rather than clarify the underlying problems concerning the differential incidence of delinquency by social class.

Turning to explanatory studies, Giggs (1973, p. 71) in an attempt to explain the concentration of schizophrenics in and around the city centre of Nottingham concludes that his findings reveal

that the rates of schizophrenia are closely correlated with those for a whole set of unfavourable life circumstances, notably low social status, high unemployment and low social cohesion (indexed by high rates of spatial mobility and social isolation—minority groups status, family disruption and single-person households).

In itself such a statement is unexceptional as is the subsequent statement that 'Importantly, those unfavourable social and economic traits collectively assume their greatest intensity in the inner slum areas of the city.' The difficulties begin with the statement (ibid.) that 'here, as in other large cities, there are pathogenic areas which seem to destroy mental health . . . Some social and urban environmental settings *may* create schizophrenia.' Although Giggs qualifies his conclusions (see also Chapter 6 for an elaboration of his position), the underlying line of thought is clear as are the policy implications that 'The identification of highly localized pathogenic areas could be used as a basis for preventive policies, possibly by means of renewal.'

The essential futility of such a policy of renewal if the rates of schizophrenia are highly correlated with a 'set of unfavourable life circumstances' of an essentially *social* nature are all too obvious and correspond to the belief of early town planners and social reformers in the efficacy of social improvement through physical reconstruction or what Niebuhr has termed 'Salvation through bricks' (see Cherry, 1970; Steadman-Jones, 1971).

This aside, Gudgin (1975, pp. 148–9) observes that Giggs's analysis appears to ignore an intuitively more plausible reason why schizophrenia should be much more prevalent in the central areas of cities. It is possible that sufferers from schizophrenia move into areas of poor quality housing, and may thus *not* be a product of that environment in any meaningful sense . . . An understanding of process always requires long-profile information and often no amount of manipulation of aggregate cross-sectional data will differentiate between critical hypotheses.

When processes are understood ecological analyses present no danger. Johnston (1976) has outlined a method based on Blau's (1960) work on 'structural effects' for partially circumventing the deficiencies of such 'areal' approaches. Basically, it attempts to determine whether the clustering of certain behaviours in congenial environments occurs to a greater extent than it would without neighbourhood influences.

Although they manage to avoid the pitfall of inferring causation from ecological correlation, a number of other studies illustrate the dubious relevance of attempts to analyse spatially and explain what are essentially social rather than spatial problems. Thus Griffiths (1971), in a study of the intra-urban variations in mortality in Exeter, sought to explain significant differences between ward mortality rates in terms of variations in the physical and social environment, utilizing altitude as a summary variable for physical topography and social class as a summary variable for the social environment. Not surprisingly, in the light of subsequent work by Preston (1974) on the clear class differences in standardized mortality rates, Griffiths identified the overriding role of social class as a determinant of mortality differences, the only exception being deaths from bronchitis among males which were independently correlated with altitude. Griffiths concluded that mere improvements in housing conditions would be insufficient to reduce mortality but the question must be asked why the study was undertaken at all given the well-known class-related basis of mortality. What could the spatial basis of the analysis be expected to add apart from the fact that bronchitis is more frequent in damper, lower-lying areas. To argue that such analyses *may* highlight the causal role of spatial factors may prove diversionary. I say 'may', because it is also well known (Learmonth, 1972) that variations in rock-type and soil and water conditions along with other geographical factors can have a significant causal effect on the distribution of certain diseases and other medical conditions. My argument is not directed against this kind of work (except where important causal factors related to the social and economic structure of the population are overlooked) but against those aspects of medical geography where the dominant effect of social class on mortality or morbidity is neglected or ignored in the search for more directly spatial causes.

Much the same question can be asked of Bagley's (1965) study of juvenile delinquency in Exeter which, although clearly pointing to the social-class-related nature of delinquency, still undertook a spatial approach. He also appears initially to state the problem wrongly, his opening words being: 'Crime is principally an urban problem. It has frequently been studied in an urban setting, especially in relation to urban living conditions and the social relations and networks which arise in an urban setting.'

Like Griffiths's work, all Bagley's analysis does is to reconfirm a relationship between certain types of crime and delinquency and class which is already well known from other, non-ecological, sources. (See, e.g. Morris (1957, p. 167 n. 9) who states that: 'legally defined delinquency is a social characteristic of the working class in general and of the family of the unskilled worker in particular.') Indeed, Bagley quotes Mays' (1963) statement that

It is almost inevitable that, in a society which is largely concerned with the acquisition and retention of property, goods and money, some people and certain disadvantaged classes will feel themselves debarred from enjoying their share of the rewards of industrial productivity. As a result, feelings of frustration and subsequent resentment may arise which may, in certain circumstances, result in aggression against a wider society and instruments of the legal codes.

Peet (1975) takes a similar view in his radical critique of much existing work on the geography of crime. Apart from its tendency to ignore middle-class or white-collar crime, Peet states that nearly all the literature on the geography of lower-class crime deals with the measurement of its spatial occurrence and various correlates of this. It largely ignores what, in his view, constitutes the major underlying cause of lower-class crime—namely the existence of marked social inequalities –in favour of the management of its symptoms.

Notwithstanding this, Bagley concludes by suggesting a multi-causal hypothesis for delinquency involving low social class (and its associated variables), low expenditure on youth services, and (on the basis of a marked concentration of delinquents in one ward, most of whom have Social Class V parents) the existence of a well-established delinquent subculture. Although he admits that nothing is known about the genesis of the subculture he goes on to assert that 'it has a continuing existence'. This is precisely what requires to be proved.

It is not my intention to assert that there are no such things as 'area-effects' nor that all urban social problems both *in* and *of* the city are exclusively class related. Such a suggestion would be misplaced, especially in the light of Lander's (1954) ecological study of delinquency in Baltimore where he found that 'socio-economic variables were *not* fundamentally related to the prediction and/or understanding of juvenile delinquency.' Social disorganization and lack of social stability were found to be more important. This is why, in the introduction to this chapter, the term 'social structure' rather than 'social class' was used; while class is a crucial explanatory variable it is not all-embracing, whereas the term 'social structure' implies the existence of other important factors apart from class. Lander did find however, that when other variables were held constant there was no correlation between overcrowding and substandard housing on the one hand and delinquency on the other, and he therefore lent no support to what he described as 'the assumption that seems to be more or less tacit in the work of some ecologists that physical space or locale *per se* is an independent or causal factor in the prediction or understanding of delinquency.'

Lander (1954) none the less suggested that 'The analysis of delinquency in terms of its spatial distribution may . . . still be a valuable heuristic device in terms of Quinn's (1950) recommendation that "In such studies the spatial distribution affords only a beginning clue that suggests critical problems of a non-spatial nature" '.

It is precisely this recommendation that is questioned here, on the grounds that rather than suggesting 'critical problems of a non-spatial nature', such an approach can often divert attention away from them and towards putative causes of a specifically spatial or area-based nature.

Lander dismisses the role of physical space or locale *per se* as an independent causal factor, but clearly this does not exclude the possibility of area-effects generated not by locale *per se* but by the cumulative or continuing influence exercised directly or indirectly by some groups or individuals upon others as a result of spatial proximity. This is presumably what Bagley had in mind when suggesting the role of an area-based delinquent subculture and it would seem to be supported by the work of Carter, Jephcott, and Sprott (1954) on Radby where within delinquent areas, some streets were found to manifest heavy and continuing concentrations of delinquency whilst others were largely free of it. In so far as the distinction was basically between streets of 'rough' and 'respectable' working class, the area effect could still be argued to be class based, however, as Morris (1957) points out. This raises the question as to whether an area based delinquent subculture, or any other area-effect for that matter, is wholly independent of class or other elements of the social structure, or whether it compounds such existing factors.

In his examination of the sociological effects of urban areal differentiation, Robson (1969) took parental attitudes towards education as his dependent variable, arguing that although social class is of major importance, the role of parental encouragement in affecting the progress of a child through its education is indisputable even when class is held constant. Robson (p. 199) suggested that 'The neighbourhood, or immediate physical and social environment in which people live, is an important source of some of [the] common forces which influence the development of attitudes towards education', a conclusion which would seem to be supported by Harvey (1975, p. 216). He also makes the valid point that the many studies of education which take class or the class structure as their starting-point 'tend to abstract the individual from the social setting in which his attitudes are largely formed', and in his study he examined both areal variations in attitude and 'the forces which could operate through the sub-area of a town to influence the development of attitudes towards education', finding that neighbourhood effects played a role over and above that of social class.

Robson's study is a good example of how such neighbourhood effects can be identified without losing sight of the fundamental underlying influence of class. Similarly, Herbert (1976) in his study of delinquency areas in Cardiff, argued (p. 477) that whilst delinquency is undoubtedly class-based, class does not provide the entire explanation, the intensified incidence rate characteristic of certain districts pointing to the existence of a neighbourhood effect. However, despite his efforts to link aggregate and individual scales through the use of individual information and ED data, and his statement (p. 473) that 'delinquency areas exist and invite a spatial perspective', he admits (p. 489) that 'the preoccupation with area differences has effectively limited analysis to the aggregate scale with some of its inherent restrictions'. Herbert concludes (p. 490) by suggesting that although his findings strongly support the existence of a neighbourhood effect, additional strategies are necessary before its definite existence can be asserted.

To summarize, it is suggested on the basis of the studies examined above that whilst locale, area, or physical characteristics of an *area* may exercise significant effects where certain classes of problem, particularly some of a medical nature, are concerned, this is unlikely to prove the case with respect to most social problems in the city, and the search for such effects could well prove unproductive or, even, counter productive. The term *area* is stressed because it is accepted that certain types of housing (such as high-rise blocks) can give rise to distinct social, psychological, and physical health problems. With the exception of the problems generated by the relative isolation and distance from the city centre of some peripheral council estates where personal mobility is low and public transport costly, which can be attributed in part to specifically geographical causes, the problems generated by specific housing types are not considered here as falling within the ambit of area problems. Area-effects on the other hand may, through the spatial concentration and proximity of certain social groups, exert a not inconsiderable influence over and above, though not perhaps entirely independently of, the social structure. It has also been suggested that studies which focus largely or exclusively on area-effects or, worse, on straightforward aggregate spatial correlations, are likely to prove of little value, merely reproducing in a spatial context what are already well-known social relationships or diverting attention from such social factors to secondary influences.

Area-Based Explanations of Multiple Deprivation in the Inner City

We have looked at the contribution of area-based explanations of individual social problems—both *in* and *of* the city—including delinquency, differential mortality rates, and parental attitudes towards education—but what of the situation where combinations of such problems exist on an area basis such as in the deprived inner areas of many of our larger towns and cities? Such areas have recently come to the forefront of government attention with the establishment of the Urban Programme in 1968, the Community Development Projects in 1969, and the three inner area studies of Liverpool, Birmingham, and the London borough of Lambeth (see Chapter 12), the findings of which were published in 1977 along with the government White Paper 'Policy for the Inner City' (D.O.E., 1977).

Given the fact that concentrations of deprivation are found in such areas, there exists a strong temptation for spatial causation to be inferred from spatial manifestations. Although the existence of area-effects is by no means ruled out, any tendency to view inner area problems as largely, if not solely, the result of area-effects should be rejected, given, amongst other things, the quite widespread nature of deprivation. Sheppard (1975) and Donnison (1974) have both referred to the fact that educational deprivation is by no means exclusively concentrated in the inner city. Holtermann (1974), in her national study of a number of different indicators of deprivation on an enumeration district basis, found that

The degree of spatial concentration of individual deprivation is really quite low. Even with severe overcrowding which is the direct indicator showing one of the highest levels of concentration, you would have to give priority treatment to 15 per cent of E.Ds in order to bring within the net as many as 61 per cent of households with this type of deprivation. If only 1 per cent of E.Ds were given priority area treatment, only 10·6 per cent of all severely overcrowded households could be given help. (1974, p. 10)

We saw something of the situation in London in Chapter 2.

As its name implies, multiple deprivation is seen as a series of correlated, cross-cutting deprivations which often compound one another on an individual if not an area basis. Cullingworth (1972, vol. 2, p. 77) speaks of an 'interlocking series of cycles of deprivation', Coates and Silburn (1970) suggest that 'different types of deprivation mesh into one another, to create, for those who must endure them, a total situation shot through and through by one level of deprivation after another', and Edwards (1975, p. 5) argues that disadvantage in one sphere will often determine disadvantage in others much as the SNAP circle of poverty diagram (see Fig. 13.1) suggests.

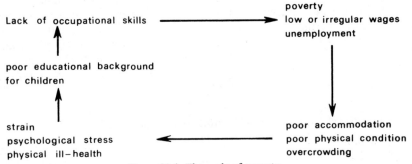

Figure 13.1 The cycle of poverty.

But 'to what extent do areas with a high proportion of people with one kind of deprivation tend to contain people with other sorts of deprivation?' (Holtermann, 1974). By taking the worst 15 per cent, 10 per cent, 5 per cent and the worst 1 per cent of wards on each of three indicators, the percentages of households living at more than 1·5 persons per room, the percentage of households lacking exclusive use of basic amenities, and the percentages of unemployed males seeking work or sick, Holtermann analysed the degree of overlap at an ED (not an individual) level. She found that whilst there was a considerable degree of coincidence in the spatial distribution of the three types of deprivation it was still under 20 per cent of the maximum possible overlap even on the worst 15 per cent of EDs. It should be added however, that when she examined the position of the worst 10 per cent and the worst 5 per cent of EDs on these indicators *vis-à-vis* a number of other indicators such an educational qualification, tenure, New Commonwealth origin, and the like, her findings led her to suggest that 'the extent of multiple deprivation is greater than is apparent from the use of only three indicators in these overlap tests.'

Finally, in Hatch and Sherrott's (1973) study of multiple deprivation at a ward level in the predominantly working-class Inner London boroughs of Newham and Southwark, they found that (p. 237):

Deprivations seem to be widely though unevenly distributed . . . and areas suffering from multiple deprivation do not seem to form a quite separate category easily distinguished from other less deprived areas. It is more realistic to think of deprivation as multi—rather than uni-dimensional, and of deprived areas as being of different kinds containing different combinations of deprivations. *This implies . . . that picking on a small number of areas is not a short-cut method for tackling a large proportion of the deprivations that exist in society* [my emphasis].

This conclusion should be compared with that of Donnison (1974) who argued that programmes based on the 'Social structure' and 'life time cycle of income' explanations of deprivation had repeatedly failed to reach the most deprived, and that 'the problems of multiply-deprived people in multiply-deprived areas are so complex that they are often impervious to the efforts of conventional services', (p. 132). Donnison clearly comes down on the side of area-based policies (which he sees as reflecting a new explanation of social problems) on the grounds that although by no means all the deprived live in deprived areas, those that live there do tend to suffer from the interrelationships and multiple incidence of deprivations, the overall effect of which is to compound individual deprivations such that the whole is greater than the sum of its parts: there is an 'area-effect'.

That this a central, if not the central, aspect of current government thinking is clearly shown by the following statement from 'Policy for the Inner Cities' (D.O.E., 1977, p. 4, §17)

The Inner Area Studies have shown that there is a collective deprivation in some inner areas which affects all the residents, even though individually the majority of people may have satisfactory homes and worthwhile jobs. It arises from a pervasive sense of decay and neglect which affects the whole area . . . . This collective deprivation amounts to *more than the sum* of all the individual disadvantages with which people have to contend. It is an important argument for tackling inner city deprivation on an area basis.

Whilst it may be true that area-based policies constitute a valuable weapon where deprivation is areally concentrated and, to a certain limited extent, areally caused, it is most unlikely that such policies *in isolation* can significantly reduce or ameliorate the extent and incidence of multiple deprivation given that they are only partly attributable to areal causation.

This question of causation is, of course, the crucial one and Donnison's distinction between multiply deprived individuals and multiply deprived areas is important here. Although areas are commonly referred to as being 'multiply deprived' it is not really the area that is so deprived (except perhaps environmentally or in terms of facility provision), it is the individuals within it. To use this label is a convenient shorthand, but one that may lead to erroneous inference about causation. If there is an 'area' or 'neighbourhood effect' then the spatial concentration, the area itself, becomes part of the problem. If not, it is merely the context or setting for a number of (multiply) deprived individuals who happen to reside there, and whose deprivations are solely the result of non-areal causes.

To argue that there are no area effects whatsoever seems as misplaced as to argue that multiple deprivation is solely a result of area effects operating on an initially undisadvantaged section of the population. The danger of concentrating on area effects is, however, that the internal psycho-dynamics of such areas are emphasized at the expense of social processes which are essentially autonomous with regards to area (C.D.P., 1974, 1975). I refer, of course, to the effect of market processes under capitalism (Stewart, 1973), and viewed from this perspective the existence and concentration of deprivations in certain areas are no more than one would expect given the age and condition of the housing stock in such areas, a markedly unequal distribution of incomes, and the filtering effect of many market and institutional processes (Pahl, 1971). The Coventry C.D.P. (1975) argued that the Hillfields area of Coventry fulfilled the role of a reserve labour tank for the outer industries, thereby enabling local firms to adjust to market fluctuations in the economy. As Gans (1973, p. 320) has put it: 'poverty exists because it has so many positive functions for the affluent society'. Along with Coates and Silburn (1970), Gans firmly rejects the idea of an area-based 'culture of poverty' (though see Banfield, 1974, for a contrary view).

The role of individual pathologies versus the operation of market processes is fundamental where the explanation of concentrations of multiple deprivation is concerned. The C.D.P. Inter-Project Report (1974, p. 1) commented that 'action teams backed by research teams were set up with the aim of the better field co-ordination of personal social services, combined with the realization of self-help and mutual aid in the community. . . . It was assumed that the problems of urban deprivation had their origins in the characteristics of local population—in individual pathologies'. The C.D.P. however, rejected this Home Office model of deprivation with all its associated implications, stating (1974, p. 8) that:

The problems of multiple deprivation have to be re-defined . . . in terms of structural constraints rather than psychological motivation, external rather than internal factors. The project teams are increasingly clear that the symptoms of disadvantage in their twelve areas cannot be explained adequately by any abnormal preponderance of individuals or families whose behaviour could be defined as 'pathological'.

In response to a consistent pattern of declining local job opportunities and mutual shifts in production systems such as the closure of manufacturing plants and the like, the Coventry C.D.P. (1975) produced a typology of explanations of urban problems (see Table 13.1). Most of the C.D.P. teams were eventually converted to, or persuaded by, the explanation offered by the final model, on the grounds that the other models either failed satisfactorily to explain the problems experienced by the C.D.P. areas or failed to offer any fundamental solutions. This was the major cause of the C.D.P. being run down from 1975 onwards. As the C.D.P. Inter-Project report (1974, p. 52) concluded: 'The twelve CDP areas are not . . . isolated pockets suffering an unfortunate combination of circumstances. They are a central part of the dynamics of the urban system and as such represent those who have lost out in the competititon for jobs, housing and educational opportunity.'

＊   As a result of the C.D.P. analysis (developed in other reports—C.D.P., 1976, 1977a, 1977b.) Carney and Taylor (1974, p. 231) were led to ask:

The basic question is simply how long will it take before a national state initiated

Table 13.1
Differing Explanations of Urban Problems

Theoretical Model of Problem	Explanation of the Problem	Location of the Problem	Key Concept	Type of Change Aimed for	Method of Change
Culture of poverty	Problems arising from the internal pathology of deviant groups	In the internal dynamics of deviant groups	Poverty	Better adjusted and less deviant people	Social education and social work treatment of groups
Cycle of deprivation	Problems arising from individual psychological handicaps and inadequacies transmitted from one generation to the next	In the relationships between individuals families and groups	Deprivation	More integrated self-supporting families	Compensatory social work, support, and self-help
Institutional mal-functioning	Problems arising from failures of planning, management or administration	In the relationship between the 'disadvantaged' and the bureaucracy	Disadvantage	More total and co-ordinated approaches by the bureaucracy	Rational social planning
Maldistribution of resources and opportunities	Problems arising from an inequitable distribution of resources	Relationship between the underprivileged and the political machine	Underprivilege	Reallocation of resources	Positive discrimination policies
Structural class conflict	Problems arising from the divisions necessary to maintain an economic system based on private profit	Relationship between the working class and the political and economic structure	Inequality	Redistribution of power and control	Changes in political consciousness and organization

Source: Community Development Project Final Report, Part One (1975).

programme to abolish poverty and inequality is established in Britain. . . . This is the key question to ask of the CDP programme and of all other forms of area-based positive discrimination. Where are such programmes leading? If they are not leading towards the abolition of poverty then, sadly, they must be regarded at best as minor palliatives, at worst as experiments in regulating the poor.

The Inner City—Its Role and Location

Taking up the point made above regarding the central role of the C.D.P.s and other similar areas in the dynamics of the urban system as a whole it is important to stress that there is nothing magical about the location of the *inner* city as a locus of deprivations. Apart from the age and condition of many houses in inner-city areas at this point in time, seventy to a hundred years after they were built, the cramped and out-of-date factories, the congested and often out-moded transport networks, the generally high densities and lack of environmental provisions, and the consequent outward movement of those people and jobs able and willing to move, it is intrinsically no more prone to concentrations of deprivation than any other area, as the growth of deprived peripheral council estates testifies. The only specifically *spatial* factor, and even this is a result of other factors, is the growing separation of residence and workplace caused by the increasing suburbanization of industry and intensified by the development of 'outside-in' transportation systems to the neglect of 'inside-out' systems. This is particularly marked in the United States, as the work of Meyer, Kain and Wohl (1965), Meyer (1968), Ornati (1969), Wheeler (1969), Davies and Albaum (1972), and Harvey (1973) shows.

That multiple deprivations are frequently concentrated in the inner city is a reflection of the particular conjunction of one set of economic and social forces operating in advanced western capitalist societies. If these forces changed such that parts of the inner city once again became attractive to industry, for speculative office developments (Ambrose and Colenutt, 1975) or residentially for the more affluent, then the deprived would be likely to find themselves concentrated in some other undesirable area which, in many developing countries, is the peripheral shanty town. As Harvey (1973, p. 135) has put it:

Since the shape of the bid-rent curve of the rich is really a function of their preferences for space relative to transportation costs . . . the spatial structure of the city will change if the preferences of the rich group change . . . the rich group can always enforce its preferences over a poor group because it has more resources to apply either to transport costs or to obtaining land in whatever location it chooses.

This point has been reinforced by Herbert and Johnston (1976, p. 8). They argue in relation to the competition for urban externalities that

the competitors do not begin on an equal footing. Those with wealth and power are better able to manipulate the socio-economic and political systems which distribute—sometimes unintentionally—the externalities . . . As a consequence of this unequal competition, those with the most wealth and power are able to dictate the form of the urban residential mosaic . . .

I would argue from this that the problem of multiple deprivation *in the inner city* is not spatially fixed and immutable for all time, as area-based explanations perhaps give the impression. Multiple deprivation could and has been, concentrated in alternative areas of cities. It is not, therefore, a problem connected to the inner city *per se*. It reflects rather the relationship between the changing physical and locational characteristics of the city and disadvantaged market position, possibly compounded by area or neighbourhood effects. Thus, although socio-economic clustering can be generally viewed as 'a function of prior clustering of housing of specific characteristics' (Elgie, 1970, p. 41), this does not necessarily imply a rigid relationship between poverty and deprivation and the inner city, but a potentially changeable relationship which depends both on the preferences of those with greater market power and changes in the perceived or actual profitability of such areas where capital is concerned. To a limited extent this changeable relationship is illustrated by the gentrification of some older inner-city working-class areas in London (see Hamnett, 1973) and other cities. The important point is that the poor and multiply deprived are likely to be concentrated in the least desirable areas, wherever they may happen to be. As Sharrad has put it:

the slum is the catch-all for the losers, and in the competitive struggle for the city's goods, the slum areas are also the losers in terms of schools, jobs, garbage collection, street lighting, libraries, social services, and whatever else is communally available but always in short supply.

Conclusion

A concentration on area-based explanations of deprivation is likely to obscure the fundamentally structural rather than spatial or pathological origins of deprivation. Attention is likely to be diverted away from the existence of a socially structured opportunity set which entails that given the existence of poor jobs, poor housing, poor schools, and the like, some people are going to be filling those jobs, living in those houses, and attending those schools wherever they may be. Area effects may intensify or compound such deprivations but they should not blind us to their origins. As Gad (1973, p. 386) has commented in relation to the crowding/pathology question

One might be tempted to explain the pre-occupation with the physical housing environment in general and the crowding issue in particular as an evasion of the political and humanitarian sphere. Instead of resolving class conflicts and abolishing unjust economic systems we have focused on housing codes and minimum room dimensions. Instead of social reform we resort to the less controversial 'physical planning' and urban design and the pouring of concrete.

More generally, Lee (1976, p. 43) has pointed out that:

an emphasis on spatial reformism transforms *allocational structures* into *distributional* problems and so suggests *distributional solutions* to *structural conditions*. But allocational causes are not area based and cannot be cured by spatial reformism. Indeed the superficial (distributional) inequalities between *areas* obscure, in an area-based approach to reform, fundamental (allocational) *class* divisions.

Acknowledgement

I would like to acknowledge the extremely valuable critical comments made by Philip Sarre at the Open University.

References

Ambrose, P., and Colenutt, R. 1975 *The Property Machine*, Penguin, Harmondsworth.

Anderson, J. 1973 'Ideology in geography: an introduction', *Antipode*, 5. 3. 1—6.

Bagley, C. 1965 'Juvenile delinquency in Exeter: an ecological and comparative study', *Urban Studies*, 2. 1. 33—50.

Banfield, E. C. 1974 *The Unheavenly City Revisited*, Little, Brown, & Co., Boston.

Blau, P. M. 1960 'Structural effects', *American Sociological Review*, 25. 178—93.

Bradley, J. E., Kirby, A. M., and Taylor, P. J. 1976 *Distance Decay and Dental Decay*, University of Newcastle upon Tyne, Department of Geography, Seminars Paper No. 31.

Carney, J. G., and Taylor, C. 1974 'Community development projects: review and comment', *Area*, 6. 3. 226—31.

Carter, M. P., Jephcott, A., and Sprott, W. J. H. 1954 'The Social Background of Delinquency', University of Nottingham: Rockfeller Research Foundation, unpublished study.

Castle, I. M., and Gittus, E. 1957 'The distribution of social defects in Liverpool', *Sociological Review*, 5. 43—64.

Cherry, G. E. 1970 *Town Planning in its Social Context*, Leonard Hill, London.

Coates, K., and Silburn, R. 1970 *Poverty: The Forgotten Englishman*, Penguin, Harmondsworth.

Community Development Project 1974 *Inter-Project Report, 1973*, C.D.P. Information and Intelligence Unit, February 1974, H.M.S.O.

— — Coventry 1975 Final Report Part 1, *Coventry and Hillfields: Prosperity and the Persistence of Inequality.*

— — 1976 *Profits versus Housing* (available from the Home Office Urban Deprivation Unit).

— — Inter-Project Editorial Team 1977a *The Costs of Industrial Change* (available from the Home Office Urban Deprivation Unit, London.

— — Inter-Project Editorial Team 1977b. *Gilding the Ghetto* (available from the Home Office, Urban Deprivation Unit).

Cullingworth, J. B. 1972 *Problems of an Urban Society*, Vol. II *The Social Content of Planning*, George Allen & Unwin, London.

Davies, S., and Albaum, M. 1972 'Mobility problems of the poor in Indianapolis', *Antipode*, Monographs in Social Geography, No. 1.

Department of the Environment 1977 *Policy for the Inner Cities*, Cmnd. 6845, H.M.S.O., London.

Donnison, D. 1974 'Policies for priority areas', *Journal of Social Policy*, 3. 2. 127—35.

Dye, T. R. 1975 'Population density and social pathology', *Urban Affairs Quarterly*, 11. 2. 265—75.

Edwards, J. 1975 'Social indicators, urban deprivation and positive discrimination', *Journal of Social Policy*, 4. 275—87.

Elgie, R. 1970 'Rural immigration, urban ghettoization, and their consequences', *Antipode*, 2. 2, Special issue on 'Geography of American Poverty'.

Fischer, C. S. 1972 'Urbanism as a way of life: a review and an agenda', *Sociological Methods and Research*, 1. 2. 187–242.

Gad, G. 1973 ' "Crowding" and "Pathologies": some critical remarks', *Canadian Geographer*, 17. 4. 373–90.

Galle, O. R. *et al.* 1972 'Population density and pathology: what are the relations for man?', *Science*, 176 (April), 23–30.

Gans, H. 1962 'Urbanism and suburbanism as ways of life', reprinted in Pahl, R. (ed.) (1968), *Readings in Urban Sociology*, Pergamon, Oxford, 95–118.

— — 1973 'Culture and class in the study of poverty,' chapter 15 of *People and Plans*, Penguin, Harmondsworth.

Giggs, J. A. 1973 'The distribution of schizophrenics in Nottingham', *Transactions of the IBG*, 59. 55–76.

Gray, F. 1976 'Radical geography and the study of education', *Antipode*, 8. 1. 38–44.

Gregory, D. 1978 *Ideology, Science and Human Geography*, Hutchinson, London.

Griffiths, M. 1971 'A geographical study of mortality in an urban area', *Urban Studies*, 8. 2. 111–20.

Gudgin, G. 1975 'The distribution of schizophrenics in Nottingham: a comment', *Transactions of the IBG*, 64. 148–9.

Guterman, S. S. 1969 'In defense of Wirth's urbanism as a way of life', *American Journal of Sociology*, 74. 492–9.

Hamnett, C. 1973 'Improvement grants as an indicator of gentrification in Inner London', *Area*, 5. 3. 252–61.

Harloe, M. 1977 (ed.) *Captive Cities: Studies in the Political Economy of Cities and Regions*, John Wiley & Sons, London.

Harvey, D. 1973 *Social Justice and the City*, Edward Arnold, London.

— — 1975 'Class structure in a capitalist society and the theory of residential differentiation', in Chisholm, M. (ed.), *Processes in Physical and Human Geography: Bristol Essays*; Heinemann Educational, London.

Hatch, S., and Sherrott, R. 1973 'Positive discrimination and distributions of deprivations', *Policy and Politics*, 1. 3. 223–40.

Herbert, D. T. 1976 'The study of delinquency areas: a social geographical approach', *Transactions of the IBG*, N.S. 1. 4. 472–92.

— — and Johnston, R. J. (eds.) 1976 *Spatial Processes and Form*, Volume 1 of *Social Areas in Cities*, John Wiley & Sons, London.

Holtermann, S. 1974 *Census Indicators of Urban Deprivation*, Department of the Environment, ECUR Divison, working note No. 6.

Howe, G. M. 1972 *Man, Environment and Disease in Britain*, Barnes & Noble, New York.

Johnston, R. J. 1976 'Areal studies, ecological studies, and social patterns in cities', *Transactions of the IBG*, N.S. 1. 1. 118–22.

Kain, J. F. 1968 'Housing segregation, negro employment and metropolitan decentralization', *Quarterly Journal of Economics*, 82 (May) 195–7.

Lander, B. 1954 *Towards an Understanding of Juvenile Delinquency*, Columbia University Press, New York.

Learmonth, A. T. A. L. 1972 'Medicine and Medical Geography' in McGlashan, N. D. (ed.), *Medical Geography Techniques and Field Studies*, Methuen & Co., London.

Lee, R. 1976 'Public finance and urban economy: some comments on spatial reformism', *Antipode*, 8. 1. 43–50.

Mays, J. B. 1963 'Delinquency areas—a re-assessment', *British Journal of Criminology*, 3. 216–30.

Meyer, J. R. 1968 'Urban Transportation' in Wilson, J. Q. (ed.), *The Metropolitan Enigma*, Cambridge, Mass.
— — Kain, J. F., and Wohl, M. 1965 *The Urban Transportation Problem*, Harvard University Press, Cambridge, Mass.
Morris, T. 1957 *The Criminal Area*, Routledge & Kegan Paul, London.
Ornati, O. A. 1969 *Transportation Needs of the Poor*, Praeger, New York.
Pahl, R. 1968 'Spatial structure and social structure', *Centre for Environmental Studies*, Working Paper Series No. 10.
— — 1971 'Poverty and the urban system', in Chisholm, M. and Manners, G. (eds.), *Spatial Policy Problems of the British Economy*, Cambridge University Press, Cambridge.
Peet, R. 1975 'The geography of crime: a political critique', *Professional Geographer*, 27. 3.
— — 1977 'The development of radical geography in the United States', *Progress in Human Geography*, 1. 2. 240—63.
Pickvance, C. G. 1974 'On a materialist critique of urban sociology', *Sociological Review*, 22. 2. 203—20.
— — 1976 *Urban Sociology: Critical Essays*, Tavistock Publications, London.
Preston, B. 1974 'Statistics of inequality', *Sociological Review*, 22. 1, 103—18.
Quinn, J. A. 1950 *Human Ecology*, Prentice Hall, New Jersey.
Robinson, W. S. 1950 'Ecological correlations and the behaviour of individuals', *Amer. Soc. Rev.* 15. 351—57.
Robson, B. T. 1969 *Urban Analysis: A Study of City Structure*, Cambridge University Press, London.
Sack, R. D. 1972 'Geography, geometry and explanation', *Annals of the Association of American Geographers*, 62. 1. 61—78.
Sayer, A. 1978 'Official statistics in geography and urban and regional planning', in J. Evans and J. Irvine (eds.), *Demystifying Social Statistics* J. Pluto Press, (forthcoming).
Sheppard, J. 1975 'Urban Structure and the Characteristics of Primary Schools: Some Macro- and Micro- Aspects of Urban Social Indicators', paper presented at the IBG annual conference, University of Oxford, January.
Steadman-Jones, G. 1971 *Outcast London*, Clarendon Press, Oxford.
Stewart, M. 1973 'Markets, choice and urban planning', *Town Planning Review*, 44. 3. 203—20.
Wallis, C. P., and Maliphant 1967 'Delinquent areas in the county of London: ecological factors', *British Journal of Criminology*, 7. 250—84.
Wheeler, J. 1969 'Transportation problems in negro ghettoes', *Sociology and Social Research*, 53. 71—9.
Wirth, L. 1938 'Urbanism as a way of life', *American Journal of Sociology*, 44. 1—24.

14

CONCLUSION

David M. Smith

In previous chapters we have presented some geographical perspectives on a variety of conditions which might be viewed as social problems in cities. These perspectives vary from pattern identification and mapping, in the well-established tradition of descriptive geographical research, to the more controversial proposition that the 'fetishism of space' is in some fundamental sense misguided. The range of approaches between these extremes reveals something of the richness and diversity of contemporary geography. While by no means rejecting the traditional empirical focus, social geographers are becoming much more process-oriented in their approach to urban problems, more inclined to cross conventional disciplinary boundaries, and more circumspect about the value of an exclusively spatial perspective. In these respects, urban social geography reflects trends in human geography as a whole.

The individual contributions in this book are clear enough in their findings not to require repetition or summary here. All that will be attempted in rounding off the collection is to highlight some of the main points. Certain familiar approaches and arguments can be found, linking a number of the papers. Elsewhere, new ideas emerge to provoke speculation as to the future role of the geographer, or to question whether there really is a role for exclusively spatial analysis. Our concluding observations attempt to balance these views, in an overall assessment of 'geographical perspectives'.

The Introduction (Chapter 1) and the background chapters in Part One identified three main strands of research, which are explicitly explored in Brian Robson's discussion of housing in Chapter 5. First came the social-ecological approach stressing the identification of areal distribution patterns, with 'explanation' confined to a description of the evolution of the patterns or to interpretation of association among patterns. Then came a more direct attempt to explain social problems as the outcome of a process of resource allocation, in which certain individuals (managers or 'gatekeepers') exert a major influence in some process of competitive bargaining through which the conflict generated by scarcity is resolved. Finally comes the contemporary political-economy perspective, which is much influenced by Marxian analysis and especially that of the contemporary French school of urban studies led by Castells.

Not surprisingly perhaps, most of what we have found in our case studies can be fairly closely identified with the tradition of ecological inquiry. Major reservations and caveats are made, almost as a matter of routine, but the description of patterns of spatial incidence are often a necessary starting point nevertheless. Chapter 2 recognizes that urban problems are perceived by policy makers (and by the public) very much in terms of spatial manifestation, the concentration of adverse life conditions in 'problem areas' of the inner city being an obvious case in point. The chapters on health, crime, and violence stress the continuing importance of pattern identification in geographical research. But it is in the discussion of race that the issue of geographical concentration comes out most strongly, for this concentration is itself a feature that makes what some sections of society perceive to be a problem more visible—quite literally.

The dangers of purely descriptive research on pattern identification have been mentioned often enough in previous chapters to require no repetition here. So have the deficiencies of seeking explanation via ecological association. In addition to Hamnett's full critique we have evidence from the cases themselves, nowhere more bluntly expressed than in Murray and Boal's statement that areal studies have been of relatively little value in understanding violent behaviour and their doubts whether the traditional areal or ecological approach can make *any* important contribution. Those familiar with the disciplinary chauvinism so characteristic of professional geography may indeed be puzzled at the extent to which we now question what was for generations *the* spatial perspective.

It is important to recognize the role of the so-called quantitative revolution in the perpetuation of the tradition of largely descriptive ecological inquiry in urban geography. The discovery of factor analysis at the beginning of the 1960s enabled geographers greatly to extend the social-area analysis popularized in sociology in the 1950s. But such analyses had very little to say about the problems of the city, so clearly evident in the actual life of the ghetto in the 1960s. Factorial ecology actually retarded the development of a problem focus, and the indiscriminate replication of this form of speculative empiricism may, in retrospect, be viewed with great concern. What is more, factorial ecology strengthened the impression that the reasons for the spatial structure of the city can be found within the matrix of small-area data from which the patterns themselves were distilled. Attention was diverted from broader institutional considerations such as the markets for labour and housing. There is still a place for factor analysis and other sophisticated numerical methods, as some of our case studies have demonstrated, but they are now used with more discrimination.

One change reflected in our case studies is a more careful evaluation of the role of spatial organization, location, distance effects, and so on, within a broader behavioural or structural context. An example is the notion of the vulnerable environment. At its crudest, this goes little beyond ecological correlation and the discovery that the incidence of high crime rate (for example) tends to correspond with a poor social and physical environment at a local-area level. It begins to take on more subtlety and interest with the realization that, given the broader societal structure that places certain groups in poor environments, aspects of the built form of the city may be instrumental in promoting or encouraging 'deviant' or pathological behaviour. The impact of residential density on mental health is an example, recognized in sociological literature for a quarter of a century. Another is the notion of the 'offence-prone' environment, where the existence of such physical features as dark corners, badly lit stairways, or narrow alleys makes such crimes as robbery with violence or rape easier to commit with impunity. Many city shopkeepers in Britain know to their cost that a location near a football stadium carries some risk of property damage. At a more extreme level, threats of domestic violence in the American ghetto are still perceived to be such that property insurance may be impossible to obtain.

Another aspect of this argument is that the physical propinquity of people can exacerbate problems. Infectious illness is the most obvious example, and a current topic of some interest is how epidemics spread across geographical space. Clearly, human networks of contact have a spatial expression, though the fact that the epidemic could arise in the first place reflects (non-spatial) aspects of societal structure—including the level of resources allocated to urban sanitation and preventive medicine. The inclination to commit crime such as burglary and to indulge in hooliganism may also be transferred from one individual to another, a learning experience which, again, is vividly illustrated by the behaviour of some of the occupants of the terraces at football grounds. As Herbert points out in Chapter 7, criminals are highly prone to spatial clustering. But this type of analysis can degenerate into the self-fulfilling prophesy of the 'problem estate' argument, whereby high crime or delinquency is attributed to some autonomous deviant sub-culture which thus qualifies for the greater police scrutiny that guarantees a higher *recorded* rate of crime.

While on the subject of crime it might be worth asking whether some features of the contemporary urban environment might be regarded as perhaps 'inviting' crime. The jeweller's shop window has long been a temptation to passers-by, who see a fortune within reach facilitated by a deftly thrown brick. The open shelves of supermarkets and other shops make theft a simple and even routine matter—so much so that some retailers apparently measure the immediate attraction of new lines by the volume of shoplifting that they stimulate. The urban-planning consultant, Leslie Ginsberg, recently described shoplifting as one of the few adventures left to children in the modern city. Parked cars amply stocked with stereos and radios offer easy opportunities for theft, in societies where people are primed to desire such goods but not guaranteed the wherewithal to acquire them in a 'legitimate' manner. How far such crime is really a social problem rather than a necessary informal method of wealth redistribution could be usefully interpreted in the context of the analysis in Chapter 4. It might be regarded as functional, defusing frustrated acquisitive desire which might otherwise be much more threatening to social order.

The clearest local-environmental effects can probably be found in health. That particular environments pose hazards to health has been recognized for a long time, 'tropical' diseases being an obvious case in point. Such physical conditions as polluted air and water also have a direct bearing on the incidence of particular diseases. Poor housing operates in a similar manner via the effects of rodents, damp, and the cold. The impact of particular physical structures such as tower blocks on mental health is less clearly identifiable, as is the 'new town blues' publicized a few years ago. And, of course, there is no denying the fact that in any city, capitalist or socialist, some people will be closer to social services and other sources of care or need satisfaction than others, and some closer to sources of nuisance, by virtue of the discrete spatial occurrence of facilities.

As we shift our scale of analysis from the local mini-environment to wider aspects of spatial organization the role of space and distance becomes more complex. It is clear, however, that the spatial arrangement of the city—its physical fabric in the form of residential areas, means of transport, schools, hospitals, and so on—has the capacity differentially to bestow advantages and disadvantages on people according to where they live. This realization was a major feature of the 'relevance' movement in the early 1970s. We saw something of this in the chapter on education. Education is a 'good' of critical importance in relation to employment opportunity and social mobility. Who gets what quality of education where is clearly capable of manipulation: there is a spatially structured system of educational inequality articulated via local authority organ-ization (including territorial jurisdiction), level of resource allocation, and the cut and thrust of local politics. Similar if less obvious struggles exist over access to and control of other public resources in the city—a major point of David Harvey's work in the early 1970s.

It is at this level that the role of the 'urban managers' identified by Pahl in Chapter 3 becomes important. Who has political power, and where, is critical in urban resource allocation. The spatial structure of political jurisdictions also enters the analysis here. The practice of gerrymandering in the interests of the political advantage of certain groups in society is well known in electoral geography (an aspect of the context of urban-social inequality that we have not been able to touch on earlier in this volume). Political jurisdiction in geographical space has an extreme manifestation in the fragmentation of the American metropolis, which enables many wealthy suburban areas to avoid contribution to the city tax base. Some of the problems of the inner city are exacerbated by the inability of city government to obtain the money to pay for effective garbage collection, police forces, education, and so on. The impact of the local politics of territorial control on resource allocation within British cities would bear closer geographical investigation. In the field of education, for example, choice of residence in relation to school catchment areas may have an important bearing on quality of education available; there is differentiation among schools within individual local-authority areas reflecting the socio-economic status (and political power) of the local population.

Turning to the political-economy perspective, realization of the importance of the broader social structure has been in the background of most of the chapters of this book. In some it has been rather muted, in others it has been the domin-ant theme. Perhaps the most interesting aspect of contemporary human geog-raphy is the emerging dialectic between the role of social structure and the role of space, so clearly examplified by Hamnett in the last chapter.

At its extreme, the more radical political-economy perspective seems to leave the geographer and the spatial viewpoint with no role at all. Indeed, the only progressive role for anyone is as a revolutionary. The argument that social reproduction is the imperative of economic activity and its attendant social relationships can easily leave no room for improvement of the present situation, if it is asserted that all social change and social policy is inevitably in the interests of some monolithic capitalist class whose sole aim is to wring the last ounce of surplus value from downtrodden workers. To the geographer not fully steeped in contemporary Marxism there is a certain difficulty in reconciling this (deliber-ately exaggerated) position with the proposition that working-class solidarity and the power of organized labour can exert pressure on the ruling class which can result in a desirable redistribution of income or wealth from capital to labour. How can we in fact judge whether a particular event, such as an innovation in social policy, is ultimately in the interests of the ruling class or a real and worthwhile concession to labour? One answer, of course, is that it can be both. But to understand truly the nature and significance of such events is clearly beyond the scope of any geographical perspective that can be meaningfully labelled as such. It requires an understanding of the process of historical development of the entire system of production and social relationships, as Roger Lee so persuasively argues in Chapter 4. This is the strength of the historical-materialist approach that Lee advocates. It is increasingly within this framework of analysis that understanding of urban social problems will be found, though the remedies may remain elusive.

Something of the impotence of what may be thought of as the extreme structuralist or Marxist position is hinted at by Williamson and Byrne in their chapter on education. Whilst they clearly see the historical-materialist focus on the mode of production and the process of social reproduction as vital to the analysis of educational deprivation in the city, they provide this important warning: that the logical outcome of believing that inequality and social problems are the inevitable consequences of capitalism is to do nothing (except, of course, work for the revolution). This they aptly categorize as 'the structural trap of informed inactivity'. But just what to do when we reach this state of enlightenment is still a serious question, of course. To some, the answer is informed activity, in the role of advocates working with the deprived groups, to inform them better and enable them more effectively to fight the local school board, 'City Hall', or whatever is the immediate source of their distress. With so many people living seriously deprived lives in our cities, it is difficult to persuade them simply to wait for the revolution—especially when radical social change hardly seems imminent under any realistic scenario of contemporary political development in Britain. Thus, we firmly reject the proposition that it is futile to attempt to work for such 'incremental' changes as improved education and medical care in the inner city. We are, however, rather sceptical about the capacity of British society and institutions, as currently structured, to solve the so-called inner-city crisis and eliminate 'multiple deprivation'. We see the area-based policies still favoured by government as largely impotent, in the face of the general forces of capitalist development to which the British economy and its cities inevitably responds, to a significant extent beyond British government control.

These comments bring us back, finally, to the geographical or areal perspectives that this book has set out to explore. However much a reflection of underlying non-spatial forces, the incidence of poverty, illness, ignorance, and violence among people *in particular places* is part of the reality of human experience. It is part of the perception of the world that stimulates concern, analysis, and policy—for good or ill. As Murray and Boal suggest, the local incidence of a condition such as violence may be the equivalent of a community cry for help, rather like an individual's suicide attempt. Perhaps we need more such means of immediate sensing of symptoms of social distress, manifest in particular places. As long as our response takes us to the root of the problem, the recognition of such a geographically specific condition serves a useful purpose.

Recent years have seen a growing awareness of the equity implications of spatial inequality or the local incidence of poverty and social deprivation. The notion of territorial justice has been aired. There is clearly some merit to the idea that location or place of residence may be just as much a source of discriminatory treatment as race, colour, creed, or sex. But the territorial analysis of social justice is replete with both ethical and technical difficulties. These arise largely from the problem of geographical scale and the distinction between individual and aggregate conditions. For example, Pinch (Chapter 11) shows a high degree of association between need and resources available, with respect to social services for the elderly by London boroughs. In other words, something close to territorial justice in the sense proposed by Bleddyn Davies exists. But individual pensioners will suffer disproportionately from poverty and loneliness. How can we reconcile the fact that many thousands of old people cannot afford to keep warm in winter with any abstract conception of social justice, not to mention basic human decency? Territorial concepts are necessarily aggregate and lose the individual human being. And ultimately, of course, the plight of pensioners must be related to the wider processes of resource allocation that give us Concorde, an electronic calculator in every pocket, and elaborate systems for mutual atomic annihilation, while old people in Britain's 'welfare state' are afraid to turn on the electric fire because of the cost of electricity.

The significance of this point with respect to the role of the geographer must not be lost. Within the existing institutional framework, careful spatial analysis can no doubt contribute to changes in social policy that can benefit the poor or deprived. But such improvements are likely to be merely a drop in the ocean compared with what could be achieved by basic shifts in resource allocation. These could take the form of reallocation from the sphere of private consumption (e.g. of the trappings of the affluent society) to collective consumption via social services. They could also take the form of reallocation in the public sector, for example from defence and prestige aeronautical technology to health care or education. But such developments require changes in attitudes and values, in the forces that mould them, and in the political response. And this brings us back to the structure of society—to questions of political economy.

The road ahead must involve a continuing dialectic between the notions of social process and spatial process. This, above all, is the message that this book has attempted to convey. While recognizing that there is no such thing as an autonomous spatial process, space certainly takes a leading role in some social processes—a fact clearly recognized by such people as Peet and Harvey writing from a Marxian perspective. There is still a role for the geographer as analyst of spatial pattern and process, but only within the broader, multi-disciplinary perspective of contemporary political economy.

GENERAL INDEX

PLACE INDEX